YAMATONADESHIKO SHICHIHENGE

19

Tomoko Hayakawa

**Translated and adapted by
David Ury**

**Lettered by
North Market Street Graphics**

DEL
REY

Ballantine Books · New York

A Del Rey Manga/Kodansha Trade Paperback Original

The Wallflower volume 19 copyright © 2007 by Tomoko Hayakawa
English translation copyright © 2008 by Tomoko Hayakawa

Published in the United States by Del Rey Books, an imprint of The Random House Publishing Group, a division of Random House, Inc., New York.

DEL REY is a registered trademark and the Del Rey colophon is a trademark of Random House, Inc.

Publication rights arranged through Kodansha Ltd.

First published in Japan in 2007 by Kodansha Ltd., Tokyo, as *Yamatonadeshiko Shichihenge*

ISBN 978-0-345-50661-0

Printed in the United States of America

www.delreymanga.com

9 8 7 6 5 4 3 2 1

Translator/Adapter—David Ury
Lettering—North Market Street Graphics

Contents

A Note from the Author

♥ I WENT TO THE WRAP PARTY FOR THE WALLFLOWER ANIME. YOU CAN READ ALL ABOUT IT IN THE "BEHIND THE SCENES" SECTION. IT WAS REALLY FUN, BUT IT WAS SAD KNOWING THAT IT WAS ALL OVER. I COULD REALLY TELL THAT EVERYBODY PUT A LOT OF LOVE INTO THEIR WORK, AND IT MADE ME SO HAPPY. THANK YOU ALL SO MUCH. ♥ AND THANK YOU FOR YOUR SUPPORT. ♥

—Tomoko Hayakawa

Honorifics Explained

Throughout the Del Rey Manga books, you will find Japanese honorifics left intact in the translations. For those not familiar with how the Japanese use honorifics and, more important, how they differ from American honorifics, we present this brief overview.

Politeness has always been a critical facet of Japanese culture. Ever since the feudal era, when Japan was a highly stratified society, use of honorifics—which can be defined as polite speech that indicates relationship or status—has played an essential role in the Japanese language. When addressing someone in Japanese, an honorific usually takes the form of a suffix attached to one's name (example: "Asuna-san"), is used as a title at the end of one's name, or appears in place of the name itself (example: "Negi-sensei," or simply "Sensei!").

Honorifics can be expressions of respect or endearment. In the context of manga and anime, honorifics give insight into the nature of the relationship between characters. Many English translations leave out these important honorifics and therefore distort the feel of the original Japanese. Because Japanese honorifics contain nuances that English honorifics lack, it is our policy at Del Rey not to translate them. Here, instead, is a guide to some of the honorifics you may encounter in Del Rey Manga.

-san: This is the most common honorific and is equivalent to Mr., Miss, Ms., or Mrs. It is the all-purpose honorific and can be used in any situation where politeness is required.

-sama: This is one level higher than "-san" and is used to confer great respect.

-dono: This comes from the word "tono," which means "lord." It is an even higher level than "-sama" and confers utmost respect.

-kun: This suffix is used at the end of boys' names to express familiarity or endearment. It is also sometimes used by men among friends, or when addressing someone younger or of a lower station.

-chan: This is used to express endearment, mostly toward girls. It is also used for little boys, pets, and even among lovers. It gives a sense of childish cuteness.

Bozu: This is an informal way to refer to a boy, similar to the English terms "kid" and "squirt."

Sempai/
Senpai: This title suggests that the addressee is one's senior in a group or organization. It is most often used in a school setting, where underclassmen refer to their upperclassmen as "sempai." It can also be used in the workplace, such as when a newer employee addresses an employee who has seniority in the company.

Kohai: This is the opposite of "sempai" and is used toward underclassmen in school or newcomers in the workplace. It connotes that the addressee is of a lower station.

Sensei: Literally meaning "one who has come before," this title is used for teachers, doctors, or masters of any profession or art.

-[blank]: This is usually forgotten in these lists, but it is perhaps the most significant difference between Japanese and English. The lack of honorific means that the speaker has permission to address the person in a very intimate way. Usually, only family, spouses, or very close friends have this kind of permission. Known as *yobisute*, it can be gratifying when someone who has earned the intimacy starts to call one by one's name without an honorific. But when that intimacy hasn't been earned, it can be very insulting.

THE wallflower

YAMATONADESHIKO SHICHIHENGE

ヤマトナデシコ七変化♡

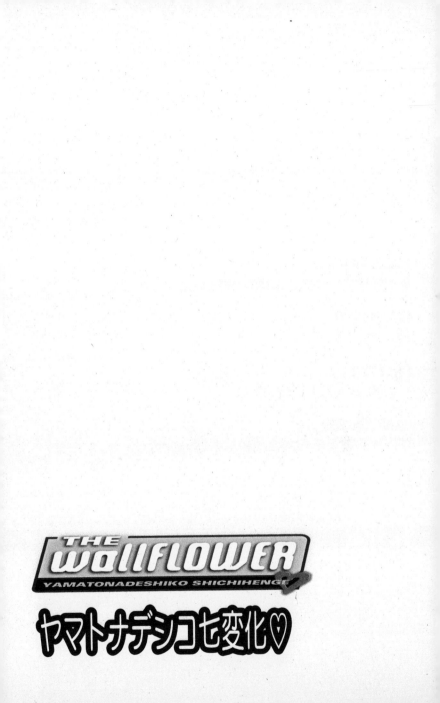

CONTENTS

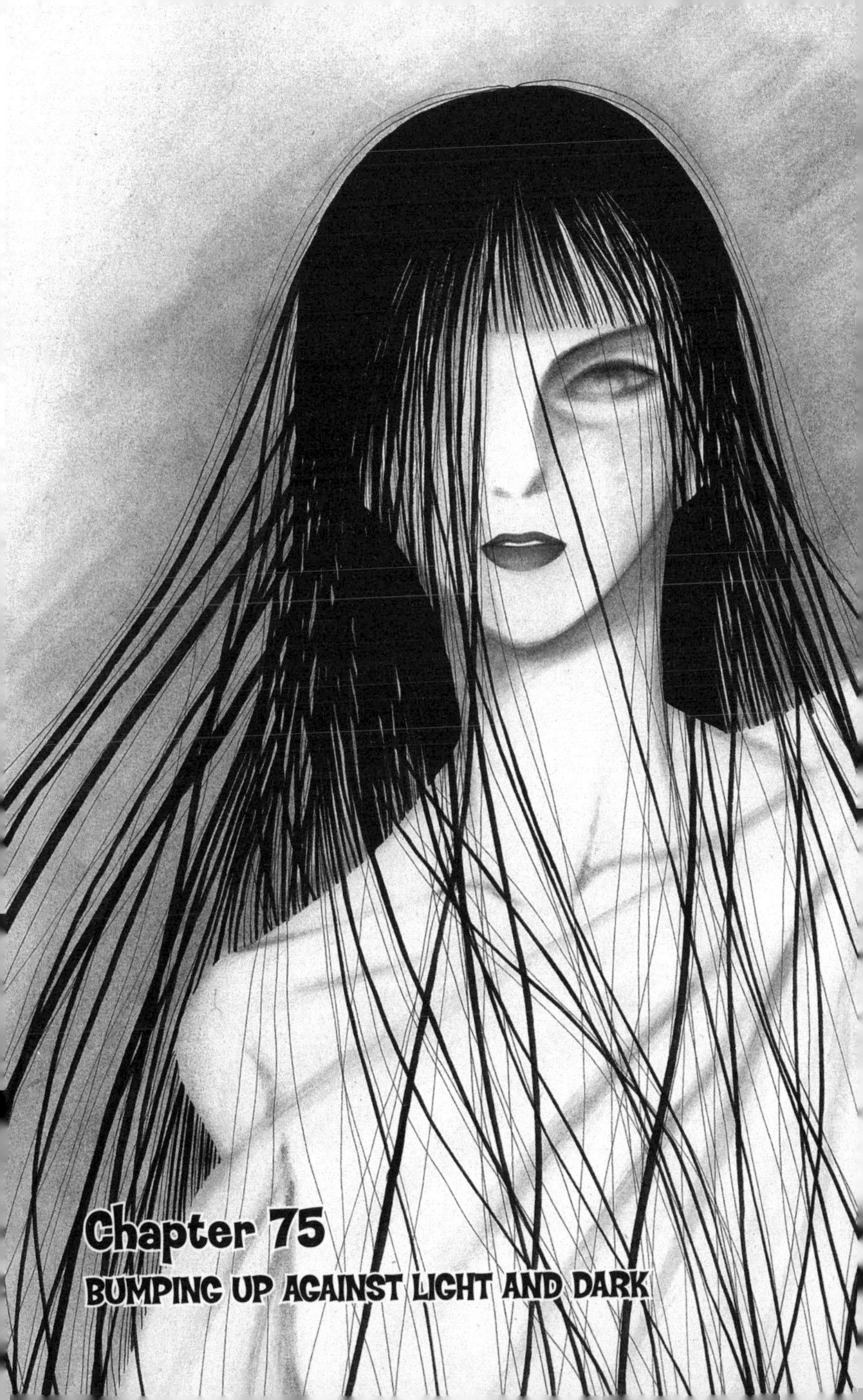
Chapter 75
BUMPING UP AGAINST LIGHT AND DARK

WALLFLOWER'S BEAUTIFUL CAST OF CHARACTERS (?)

SUNAKO IS A DARK LONER WHO LOVES HORROR MOVIES. WHEN HER AUNT, THE LANDLADY OF A BOARDINGHOUSE, LEAVES TOWN WITH HER BOYFRIEND, SUNAKO IS FORCED TO LIVE WITH FOUR HANDSOME GUYS. SUNAKO'S AUNT MAKES A DEAL WITH THE BOYS, WHICH CAUSES NOTHING BUT HEADACHES FOR SUNAKO. "MAKE SUNAKO INTO A LADY, AND YOU CAN LIVE RENT FREE FOR THREE YEARS. TO MAKE MATTERS WORSE, NOI KEEPS TRYING TO SET SUNAKO UP WITH KYOHEI. WHEN KYOHEI SUDDENLY FEELS THE URGE TO KISS HER, SUNAKO IS LEFT LYING IN A POOL OF HER OWN BLOOD.

KYOHEI TAKANO—
A STRONG FIGHTER,
"I'M THE KING"

TAKENAGA ODA—
A CARING FEMINIST

RANMARU MORII—
A TRUE LADY'S MAN

YUKINOJO TOYAMA—
A GENTLE, CHEERFUL, AND
VERY EMOTIONAL GUY

SUNAKO NAKAHARA

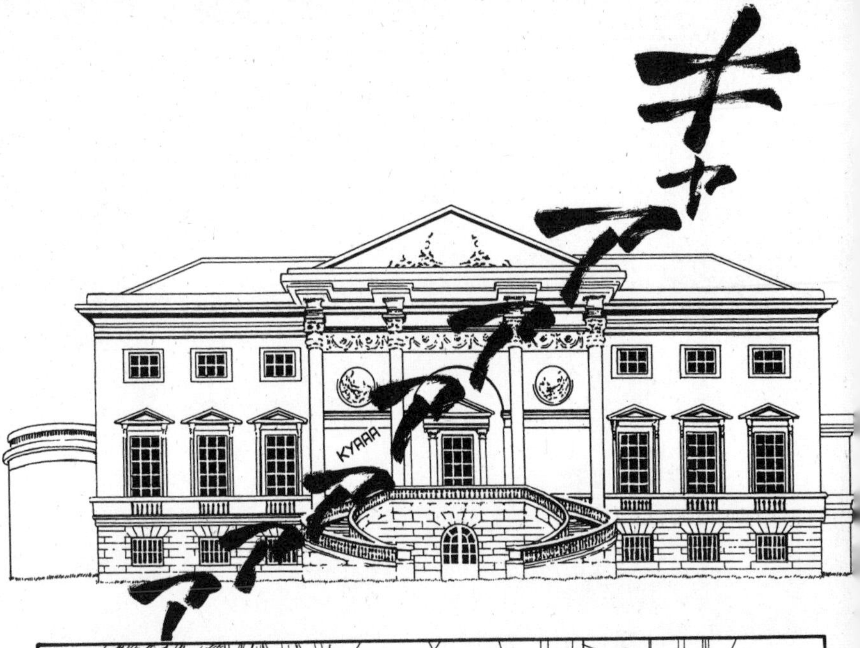
KYAAA

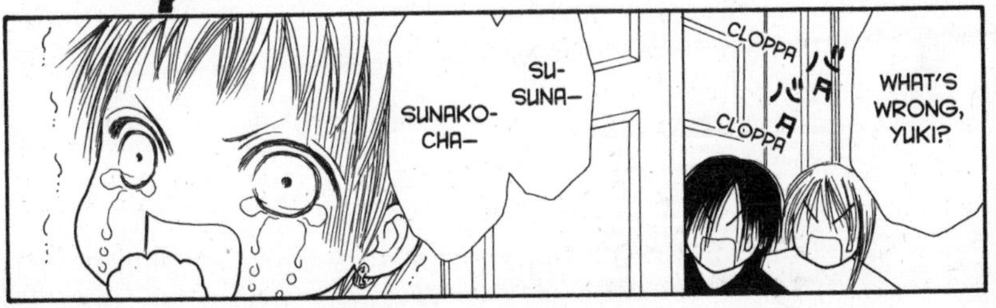
WHAT'S WRONG, YUKI?
CLOPPA
CLOPPA
SU- SUNA-
SUNAKO-CHA-

BEHIND THE SCENES

THANK YOU FOR BUYING DEL REY MANGA. ♥

BECAUSE OF THE WAY VOLUME 18 ENDED, TONS OF PEOPLE HAVE BEEN ASKING "ARE SUNAKO AND KYOHEI GONNA GET TOGETHER?"

WHAT WILL HAPPEN TO THOSE TWO? I HOPE YOU'LL KEEP READING A LITTLE LONGER SO THAT YOU CAN FIND OUT.

I HAD A HARD TIME WITH MY DEADLINE AGAIN FOR THIS STORY. RIGHT BEFORE MY DEADLINE, I ALWAYS HOPE THAT I'LL BE ABLE TO FINISH WITHOUT CAUSING TOO MUCH TROUBLE... AND THAT I'LL BE ABLE TO GET SOME SLEEP. I HOPE I CAN ACTUALLY ACHIEVE THOSE GOALS SOMEDAY. NO, SCRATCH THAT, I *MUST* ACHIEVE THEM.

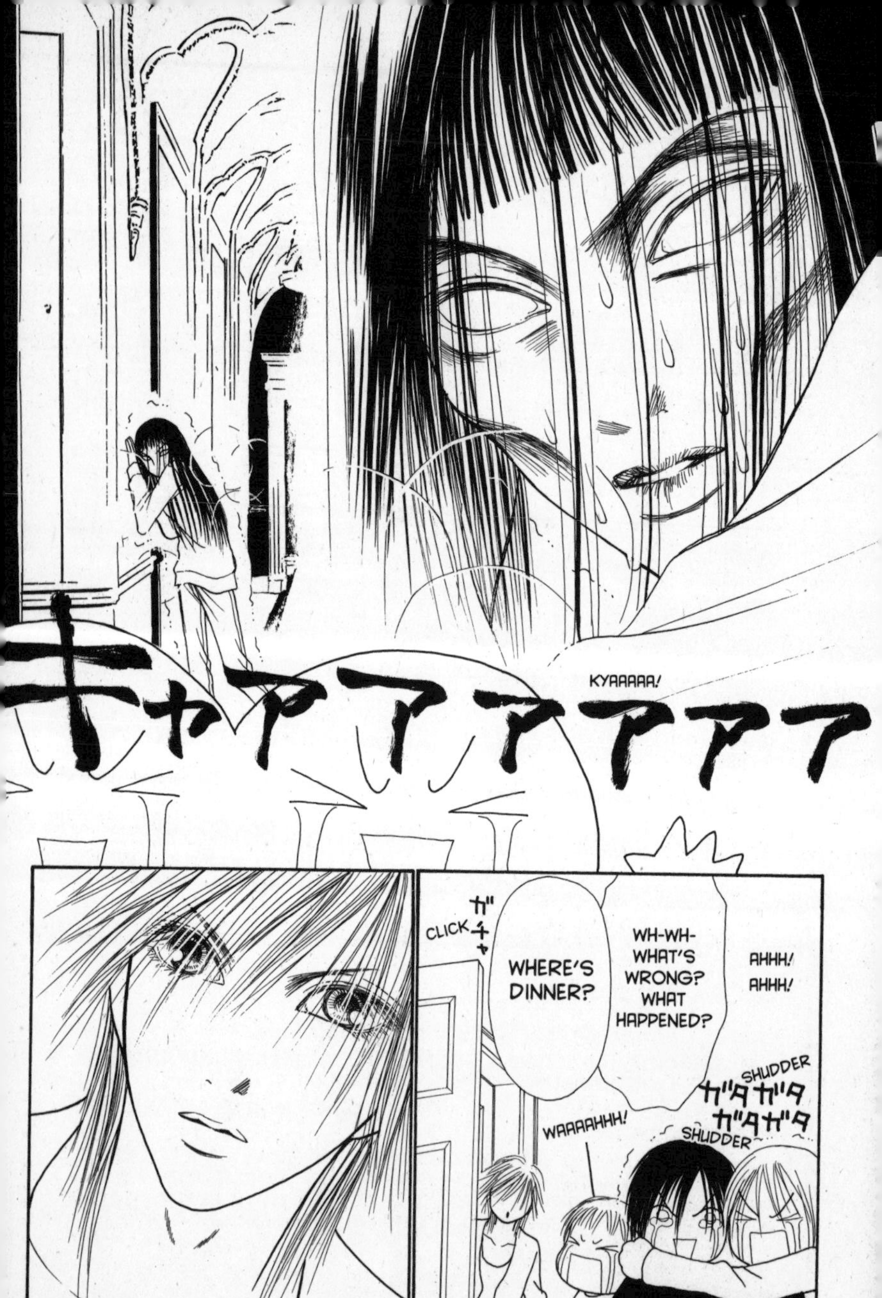
キャアアアアアア
KYAAAAA!
AHHH!
AHHH!
WH-WH-WHAT'S WRONG? WHAT HAPPENED?
WHERE'S DINNER?
ガチャ
CLICK
SHUDDER
ガタガタ
ガタガタ
SHUDDER
WAAAAHHH!

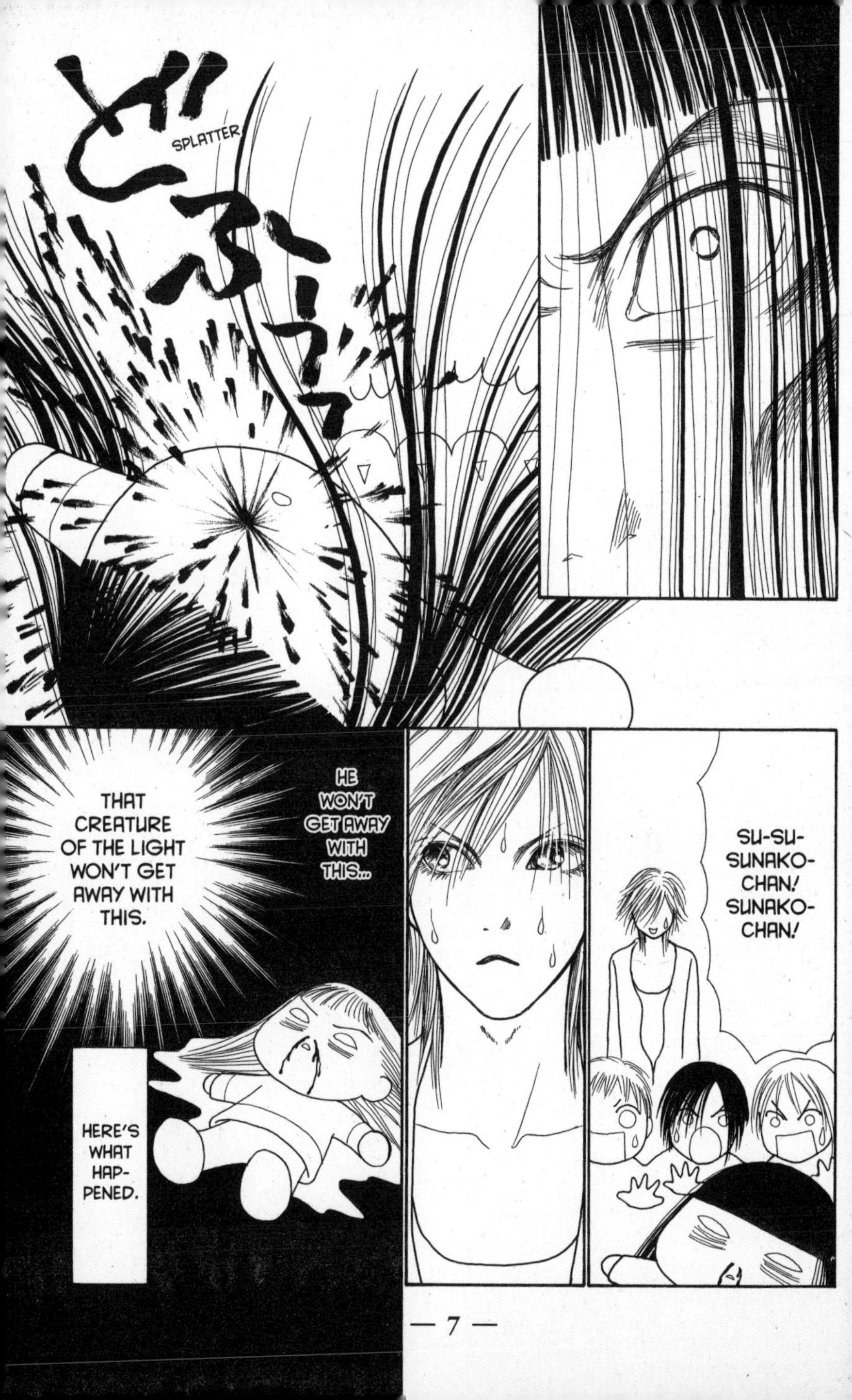
SPLATTER
SU-SU-SUNAKO-CHAN! SUNAKO-CHAN!
HE WON'T GET AWAY WITH THIS...
THAT CREATURE OF THE LIGHT WON'T GET AWAY WITH THIS.
HERE'S WHAT HAP-PENED.

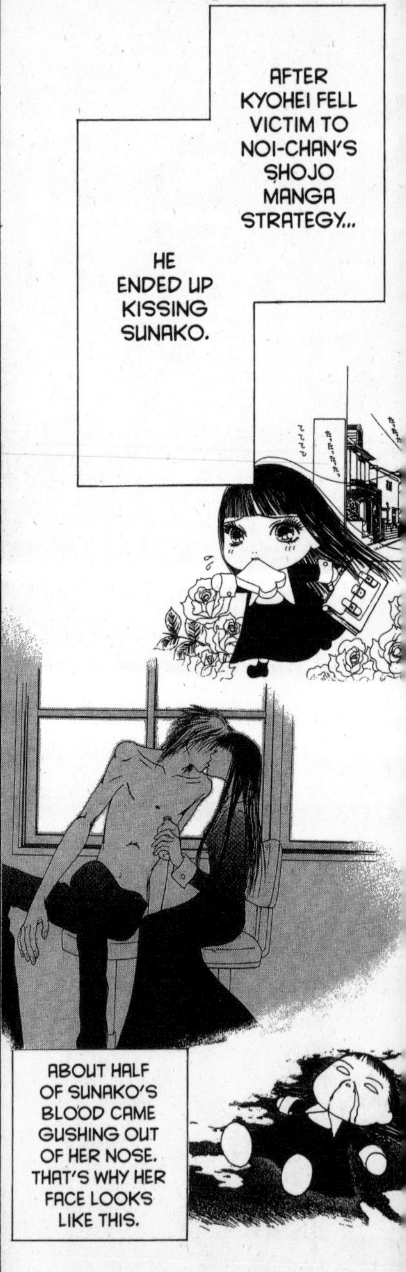
AFTER KYOHEI FELL VICTIM TO NOI-CHAN'S SHOJO MANGA STRATEGY...
HE ENDED UP KISSING SUNAKO.
ABOUT HALF OF SUNAKO'S BLOOD CAME GUSHING OUT OF HER NOSE. THAT'S WHY HER FACE LOOKS LIKE THIS.

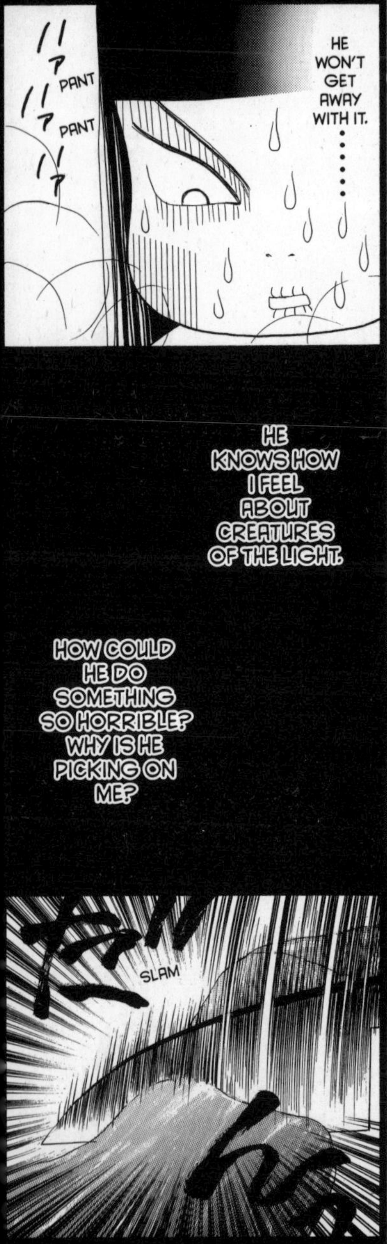
HE WON'T GET AWAY WITH IT. ......
PANT
PANT
HE KNOWS HOW I FEEL ABOUT CREATURES OF THE LIGHT.
HOW COULD HE DO SOMETHING SO HORRIBLE? WHY IS HE PICKING ON ME?
SLAM

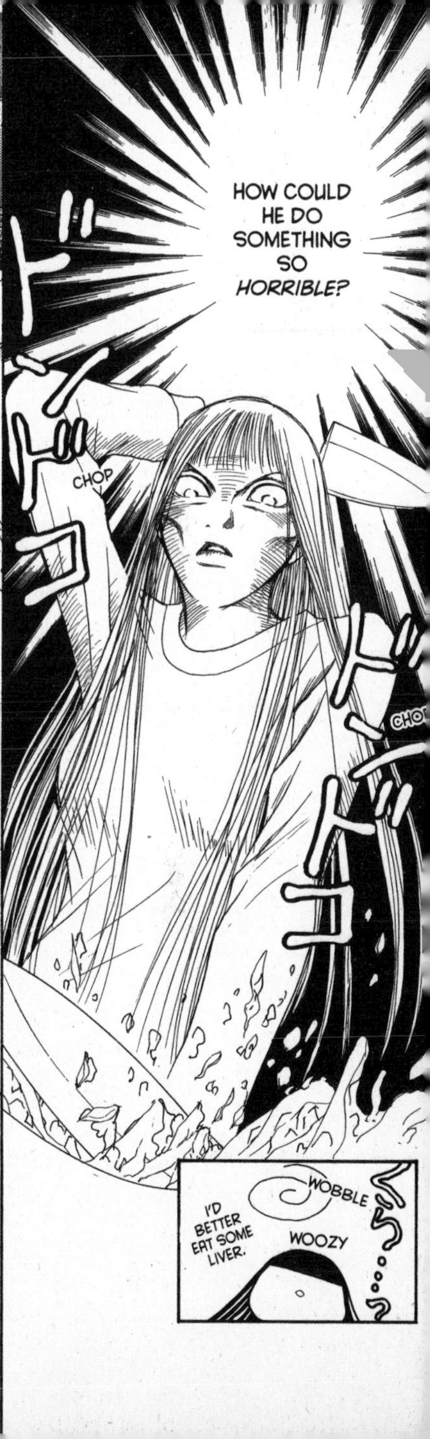
HOW COULD HE DO SOMETHING SO *HORRIBLE?*
CHOP
CHOP
I'D BETTER EAT SOME LIVER.
WOBBLE
WOOZY
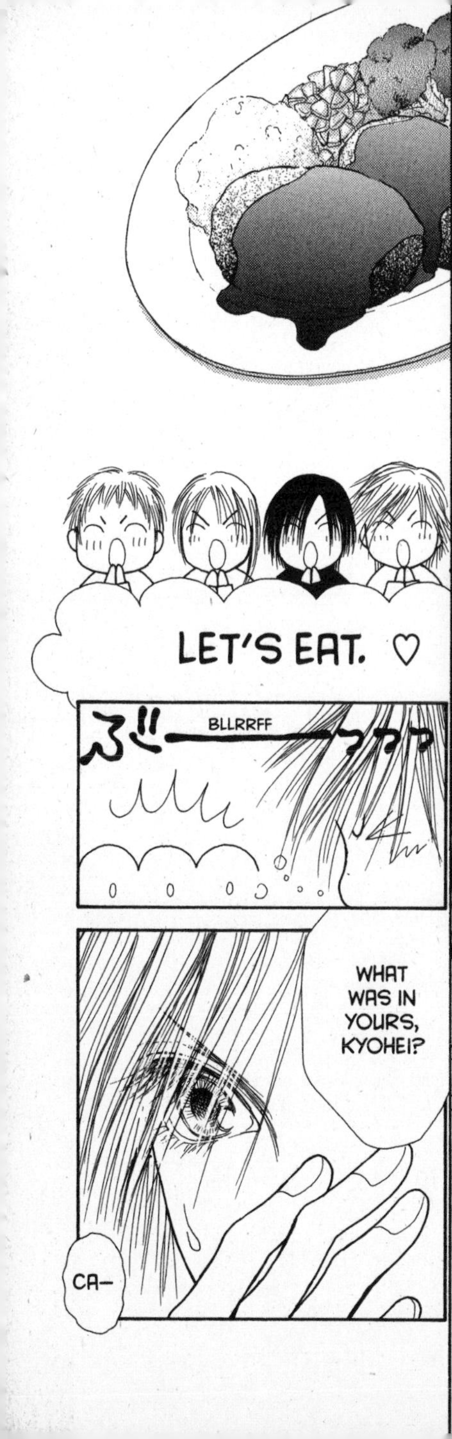
LET'S EAT. ♡
BLLRRFF
WHAT WAS IN YOURS, KYOHEI?
CA—

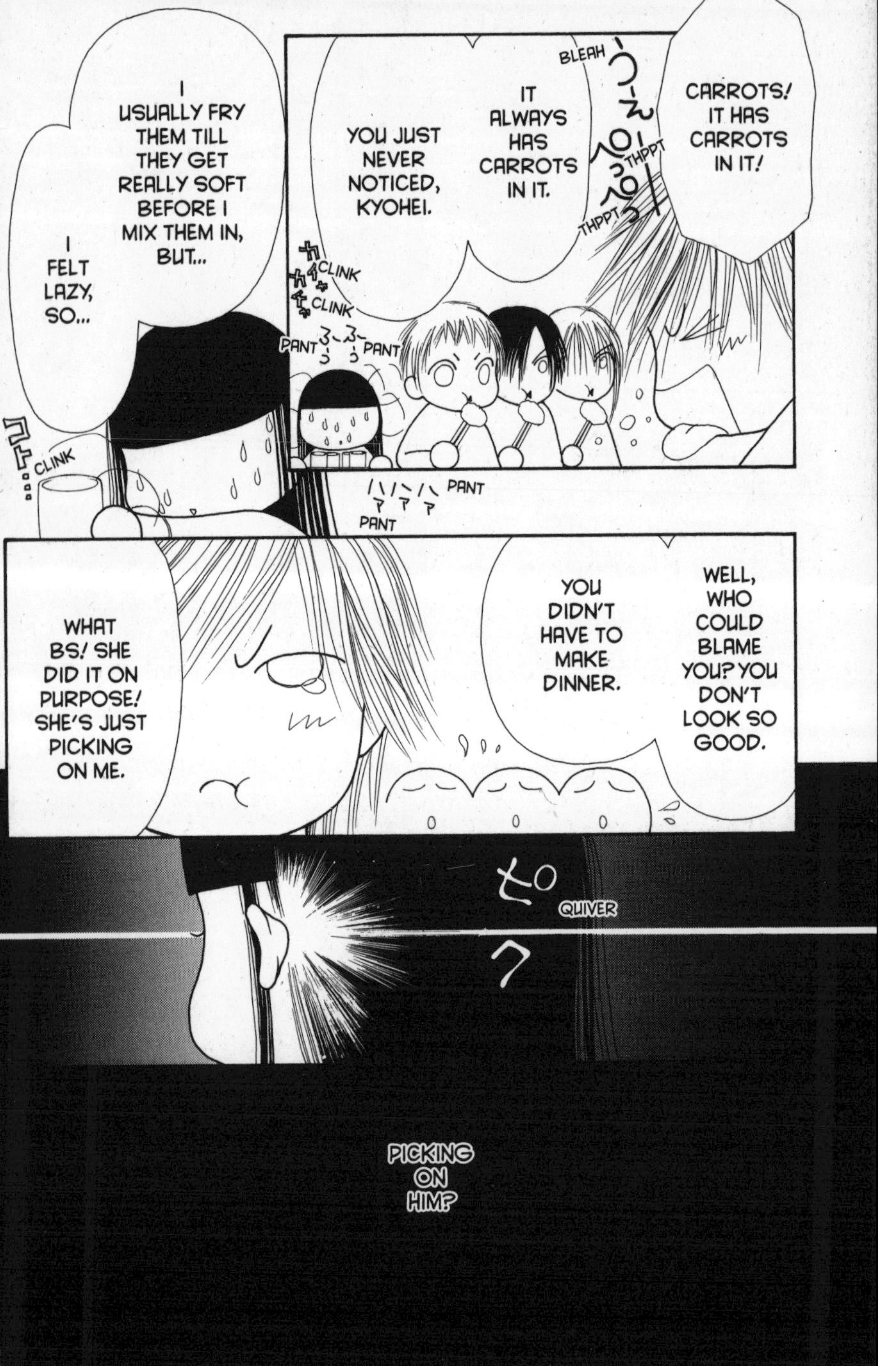
CARROTS! IT HAS CARROTS IN IT!
BLEAH
THPPT
THPPT
IT ALWAYS HAS CARROTS IN IT.
YOU JUST NEVER NOTICED, KYOHEI.
CLINK
CLINK
PANT
PANT
I USUALLY FRY THEM TILL THEY GET REALLY SOFT BEFORE I MIX THEM IN, BUT...
I FELT LAZY, SO...
CLINK
PANT
PANT
WELL, WHO COULD BLAME YOU? YOU DON'T LOOK SO GOOD.
YOU DIDN'T HAVE TO MAKE DINNER.
WHAT BS! SHE DID IT ON PURPOSE! SHE'S JUST PICKING ON ME.
QUIVER
PICKING ON HIM?

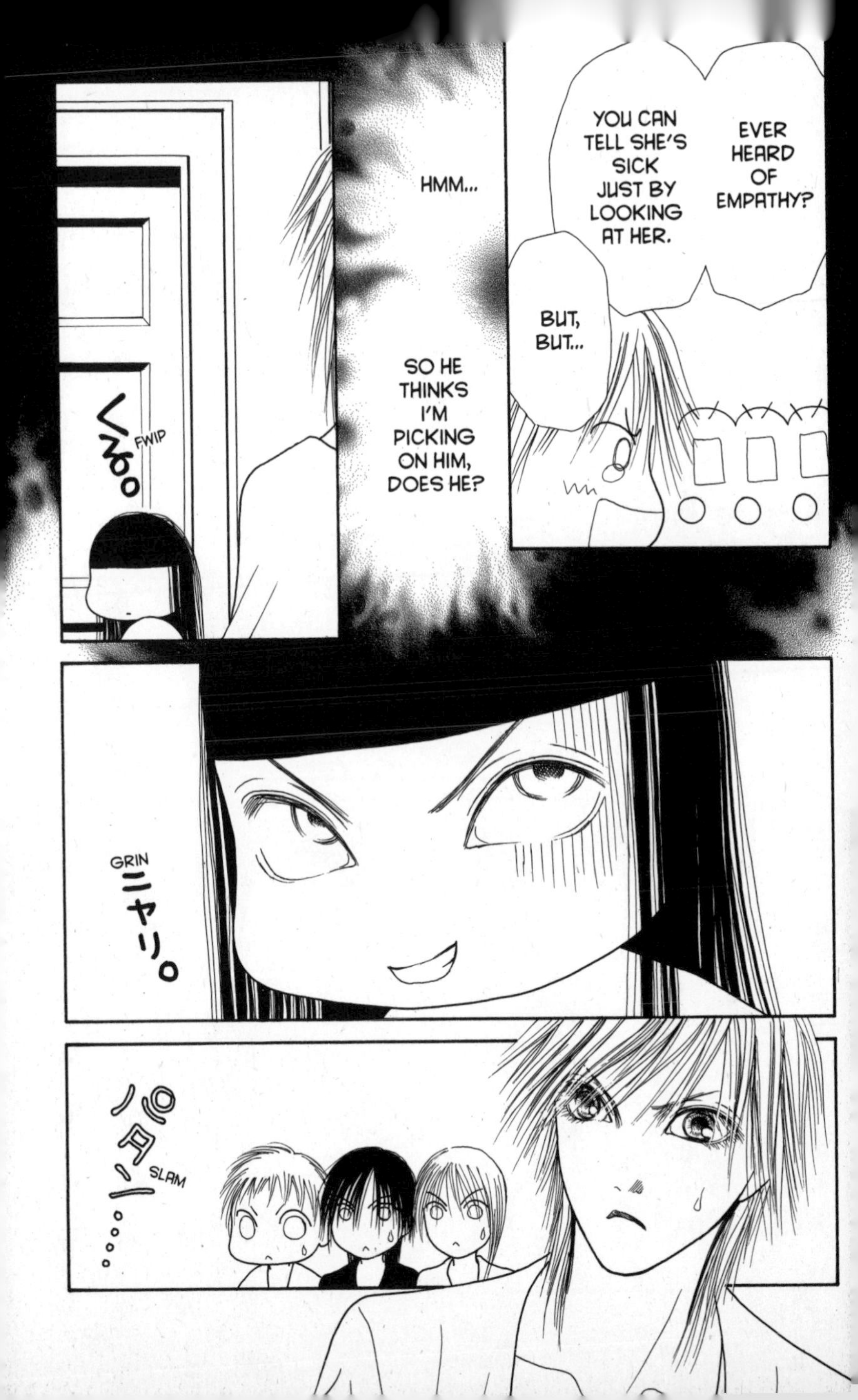
EVER HEARD OF EMPATHY?
YOU CAN TELL SHE'S SICK JUST BY LOOKING AT HER.
BUT, BUT...
HMM...
SO HE THINKS I'M PICKING ON HIM, DOES HE?
くるっ
FWIP
GRIN
ニヤリ。
パタン……
SLAM

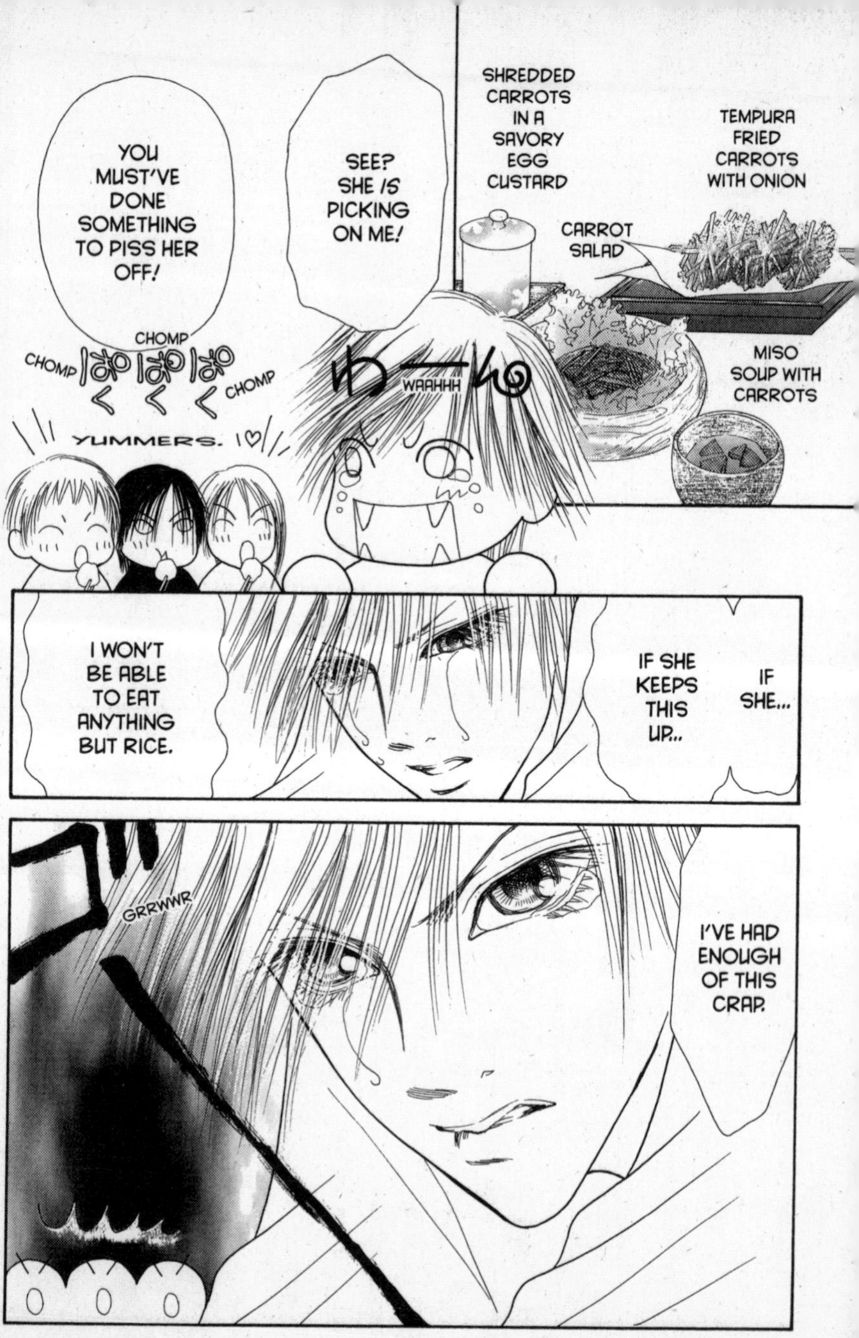
SHREDDED CARROTS IN A SAVORY EGG CUSTARD
TEMPURA FRIED CARROTS WITH ONION
CARROT SALAD
MISO SOUP WITH CARROTS
SEE? SHE IS PICKING ON ME!
YOU MUST'VE DONE SOMETHING TO PISS HER OFF!
WAAHHH
CHOMP
CHOMP
CHOMP
YUMMERS. ♡
IF SHE...
IF SHE KEEPS THIS UP...
I WON'T BE ABLE TO EAT ANYTHING BUT RICE.
I'VE HAD ENOUGH OF THIS CRAP.
GRRWWR

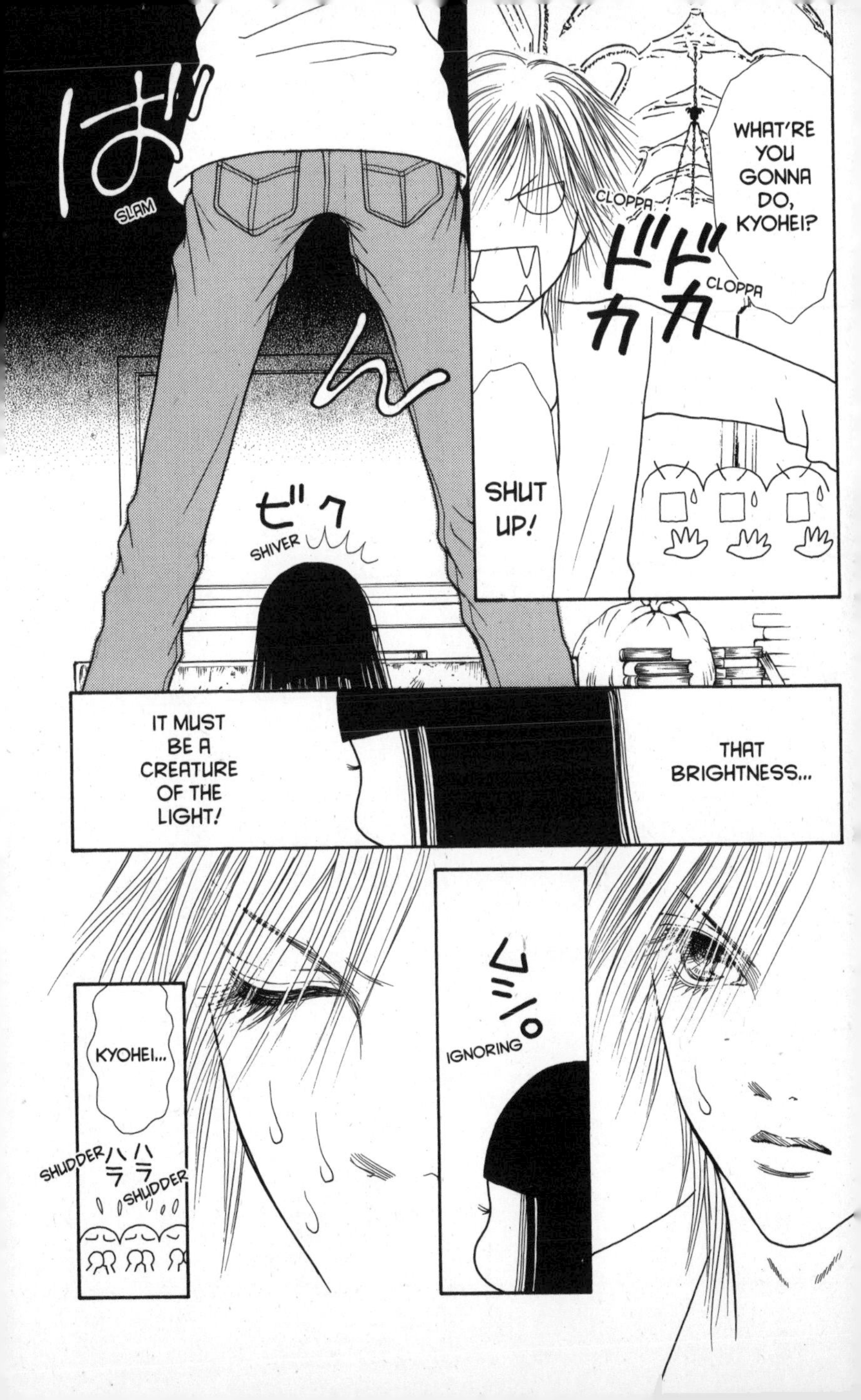

WHAT'RE YOU GONNA DO, KYOHEI?
CLOPPA
ドドカカ
CLOPPA
SHUT UP!
ばん
SLAM
ビク
SHIVER
THAT BRIGHTNESS...
IT MUST BE A CREATURE OF THE LIGHT!
ムシ
IGNORING
KYOHEI...
ハラハラ
SHUDDER
SHUDDER

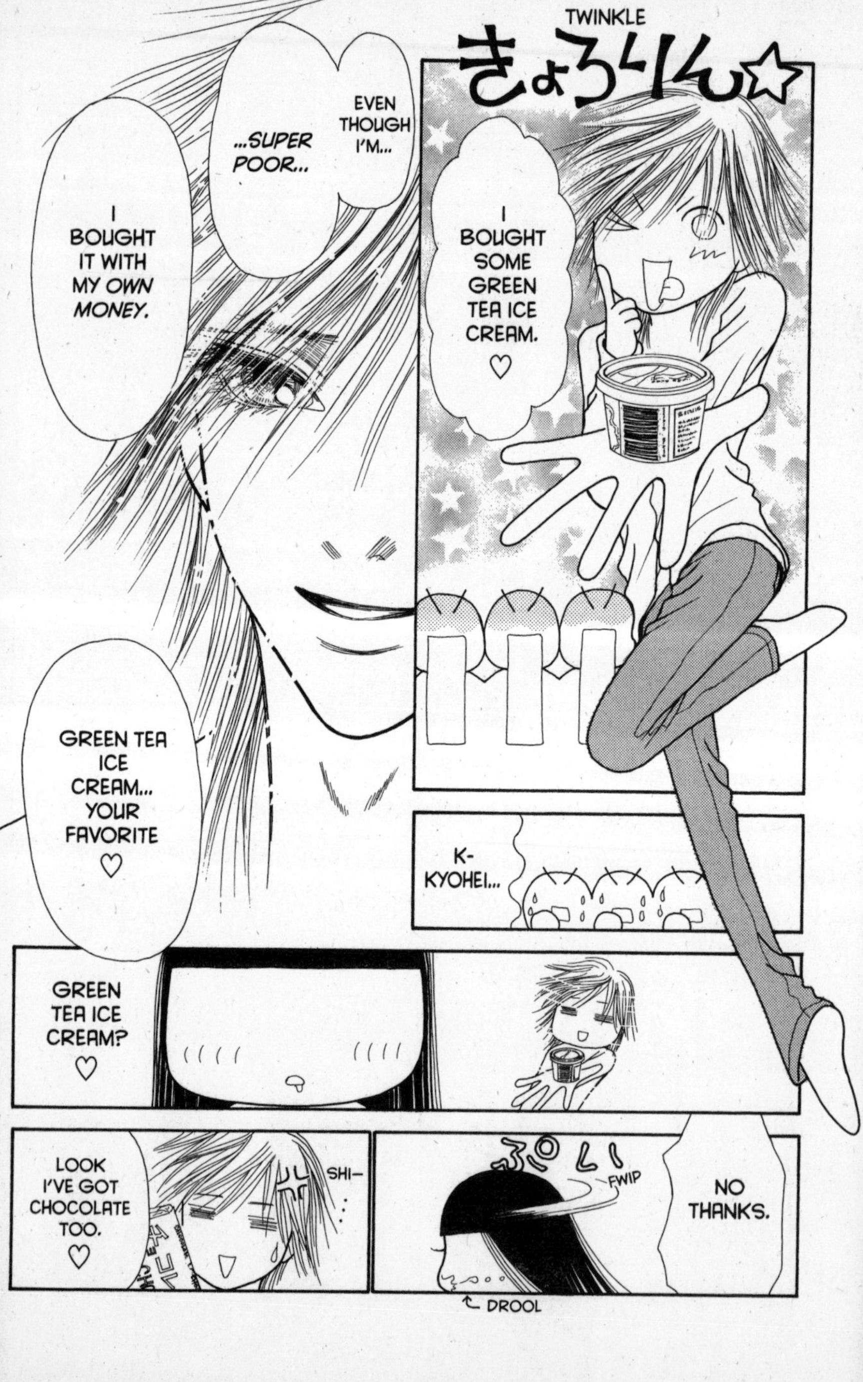
TWINKLE
きょろりん☆
I BOUGHT SOME GREEN TEA ICE CREAM. ♡
K-KYOHEI...
EVEN THOUGH I'M...
...SUPER POOR...
I BOUGHT IT WITH MY OWN MONEY.
GREEN TEA ICE CREAM... YOUR FAVORITE ♡
GREEN TEA ICE CREAM? ♡
NO THANKS.
ぷい
FWIP
DROOL
SHI—
LOOK I'VE GOT CHOCOLATE TOO. ♡

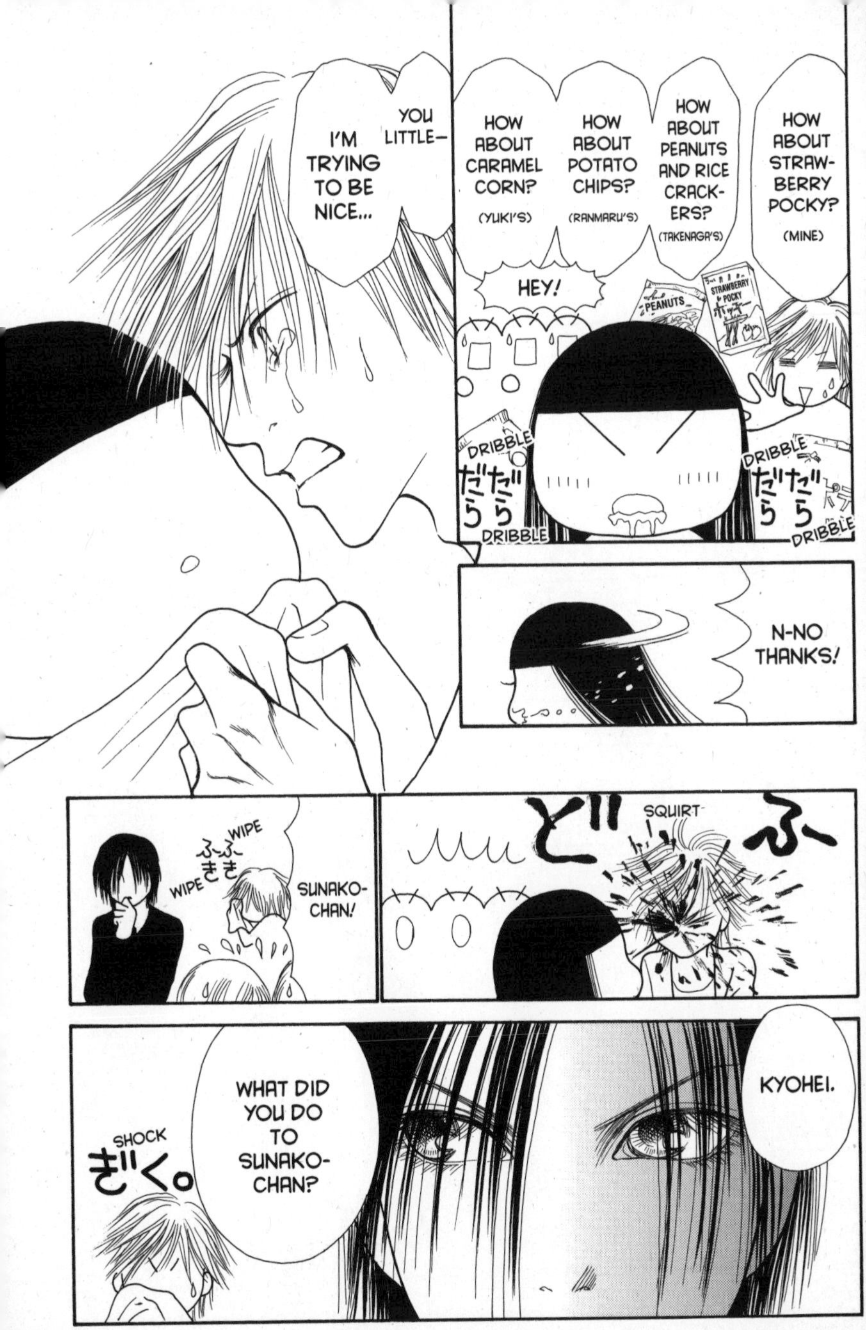
HOW ABOUT STRAWBERRY POCKY?
(MINE)
HOW ABOUT PEANUTS AND RICE CRACK-ERS?
(TAKENAGA'S)
HOW ABOUT POTATO CHIPS?
(RANMARU'S)
HOW ABOUT CARAMEL CORN?
(YUKI'S)
HEY!
STRAWBERRY POCKY
PEANUTS
DRIBBLE だらだら DRIBBLE
DRIBBLE だらだら DRIBBLE
N-NO THANKS!
YOU LITTLE—
I'M TRYING TO BE NICE...
ふ
ど
SQUIRT
WIPE ふきふき WIPE
SUNAKO-CHAN!
KYOHEI.
WHAT DID YOU DO TO SUNAKO-CHAN?
SHOCK ぎく。

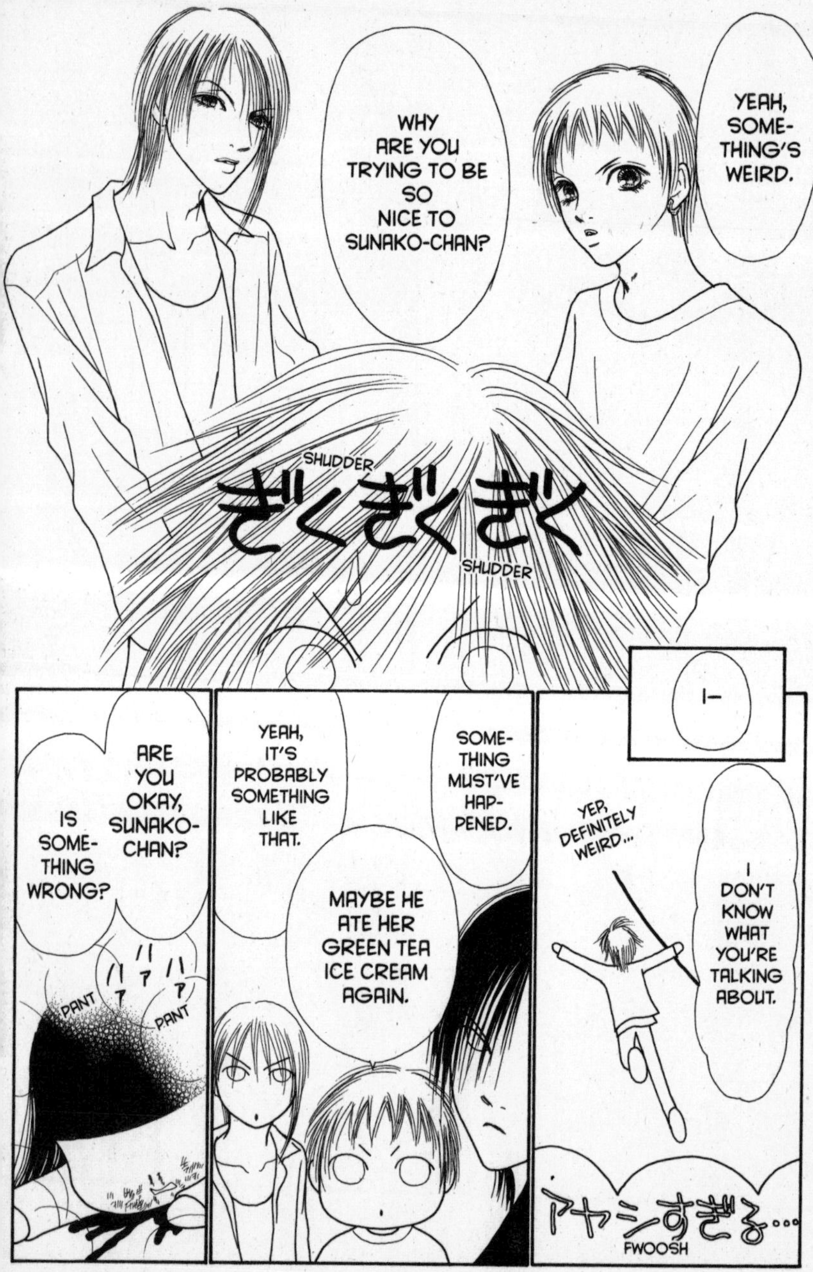
YEAH, SOMETHING'S WEIRD.
WHY ARE YOU TRYING TO BE SO NICE TO SUNAKO-CHAN?
ぎくぎくぎく
SHUDDER SHUDDER
I—
I DON'T KNOW WHAT YOU'RE TALKING ABOUT.
YEP, DEFINITELY WEIRD...
アヤシすぎる…
FWOOSH
SOMETHING MUST'VE HAPPENED.
YEAH, IT'S PROBABLY SOMETHING LIKE THAT.
MAYBE HE ATE HER GREEN TEA ICE CREAM AGAIN.
ARE YOU OKAY, SUNAKO-CHAN?
IS SOMETHING WRONG?
ハァハァ
PANT PANT

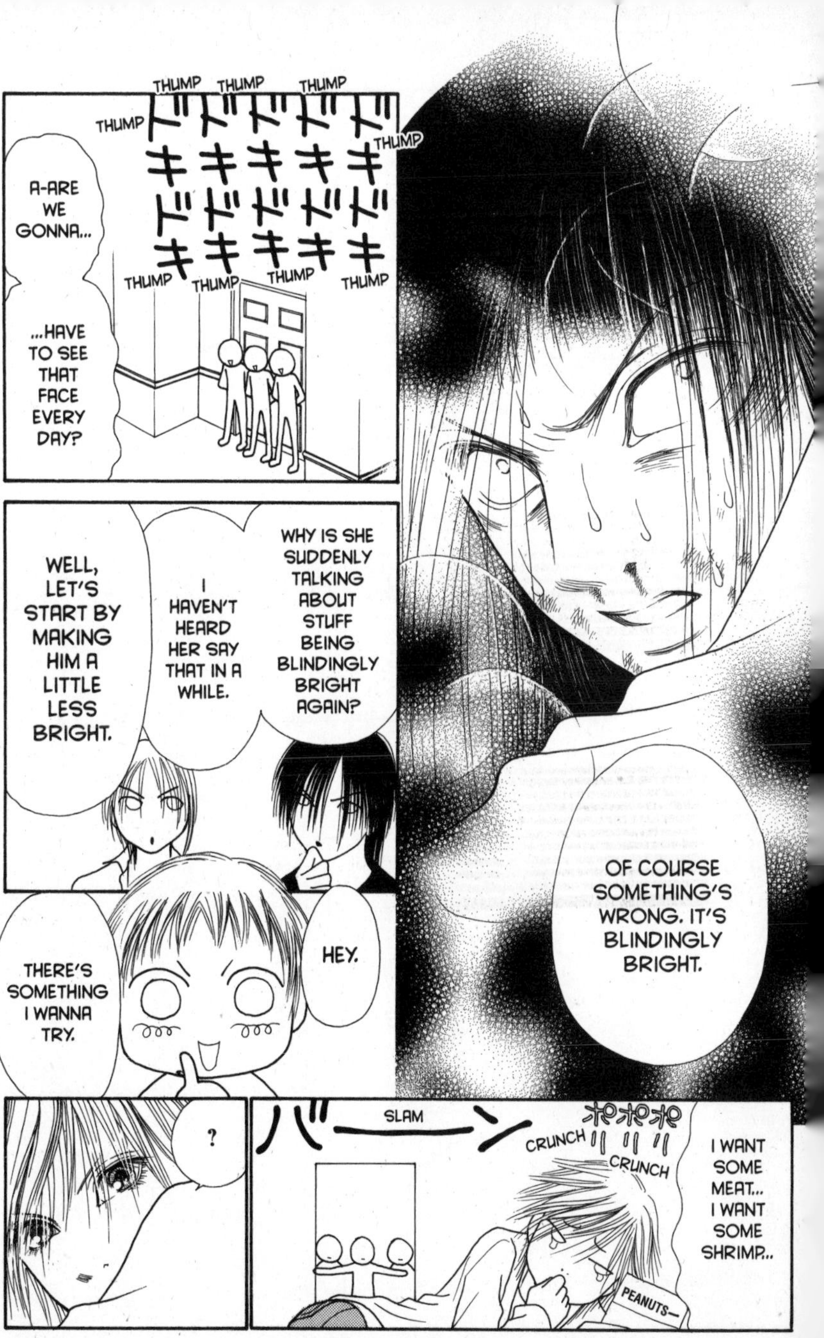
OF COURSE SOMETHING'S WRONG. IT'S BLINDINGLY BRIGHT.
THUMP THUMP THUMP THUMP THUMP
ドキドキ
THUMP THUMP THUMP THUMP
A-ARE WE GONNA...
...HAVE TO SEE THAT FACE EVERY DAY?
WHY IS SHE SUDDENLY TALKING ABOUT STUFF BEING BLINDINGLY BRIGHT AGAIN?
I HAVEN'T HEARD HER SAY THAT IN A WHILE.
WELL, LET'S START BY MAKING HIM A LITTLE LESS BRIGHT.
HEY.
THERE'S SOMETHING I WANNA TRY.
バーン
SLAM
ポリポリ
CRUNCH
CRUNCH
I WANT SOME MEAT... I WANT SOME SHRIMP...
PEANUTS—
?

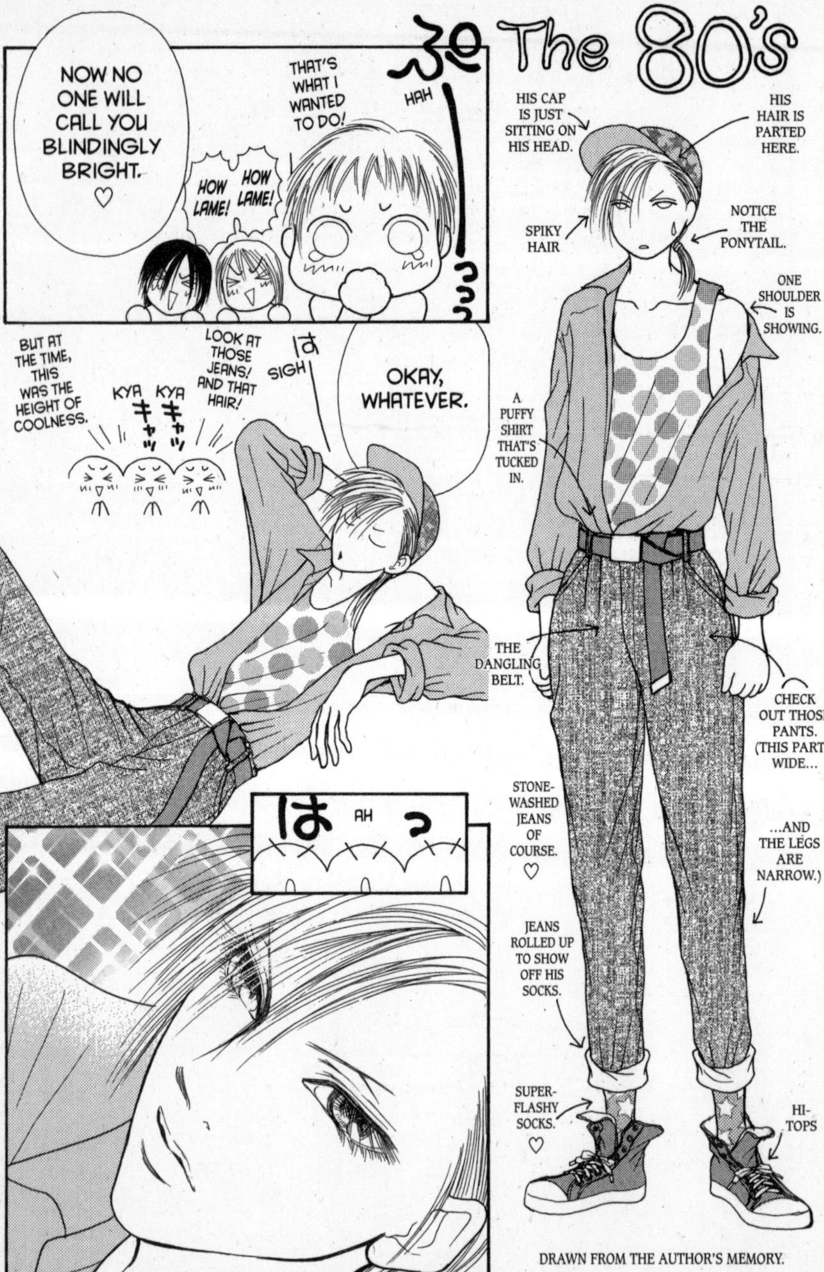
The 80's
HIS HAIR IS PARTED HERE.
HIS CAP IS JUST SITTING ON HIS HEAD.
NOTICE THE PONYTAIL.
SPIKY HAIR
ONE SHOULDER IS SHOWING.
A PUFFY SHIRT THAT'S TUCKED IN.
THE DANGLING BELT.
CHECK OUT THOSE PANTS. (THIS PART'S WIDE...
...AND THE LEGS ARE NARROW.)
STONE-WASHED JEANS OF COURSE. ♡
JEANS ROLLED UP TO SHOW OFF HIS SOCKS.
HI-TOPS
SUPER-FLASHY SOCKS. ♡
DRAWN FROM THE AUTHOR'S MEMORY.
HAH
THAT'S WHAT I WANTED TO DO!
HOW LAME!
HOW LAME!
NOW NO ONE WILL CALL YOU BLINDINGLY BRIGHT. ♡
OKAY, WHATEVER.
は SIGH
LOOK AT THOSE JEANS! AND THAT HAIR!
KYA キャッ
KYA キャッ
BUT AT THE TIME, THIS WAS THE HEIGHT OF COOLNESS.
はっ AH

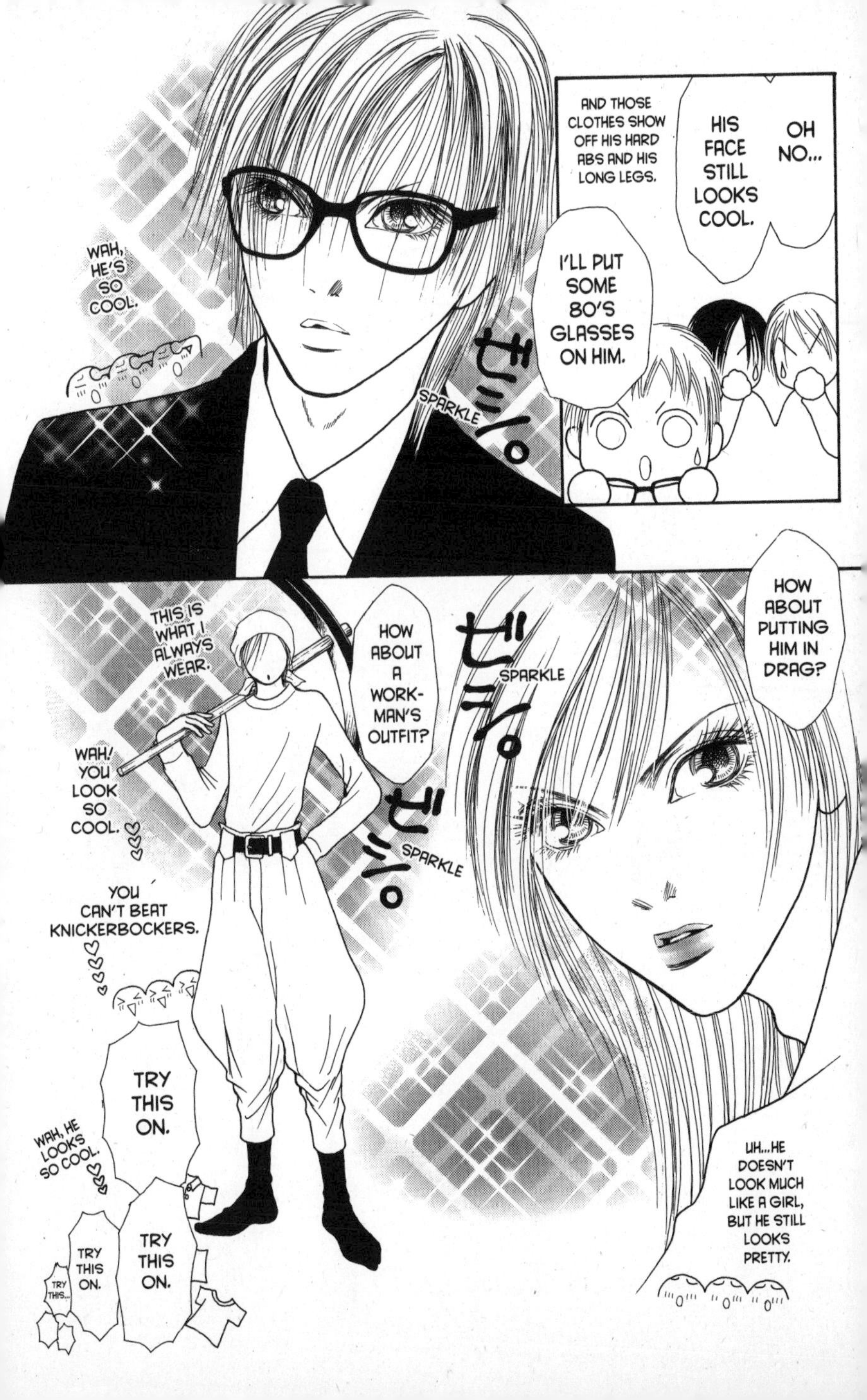
OH NO...
HIS FACE STILL LOOKS COOL.
AND THOSE CLOTHES SHOW OFF HIS HARD ABS AND HIS LONG LEGS.
I'LL PUT SOME 80'S GLASSES ON HIM.
SPARKLE
WAH, HE'S SO COOL.
HOW ABOUT PUTTING HIM IN DRAG?
SPARKLE
UH...HE DOESN'T LOOK MUCH LIKE A GIRL, BUT HE STILL LOOKS PRETTY.
HOW ABOUT A WORK-MAN'S OUTFIT?
SPARKLE
THIS IS WHAT I ALWAYS WEAR.
WAH! YOU LOOK SO COOL.
YOU CAN'T BEAT KNICKERBOCKERS.
TRY THIS ON.
WAH, HE LOOKS SO COOL.
TRY THIS ON.
TRY THIS ON.
TRY THIS...

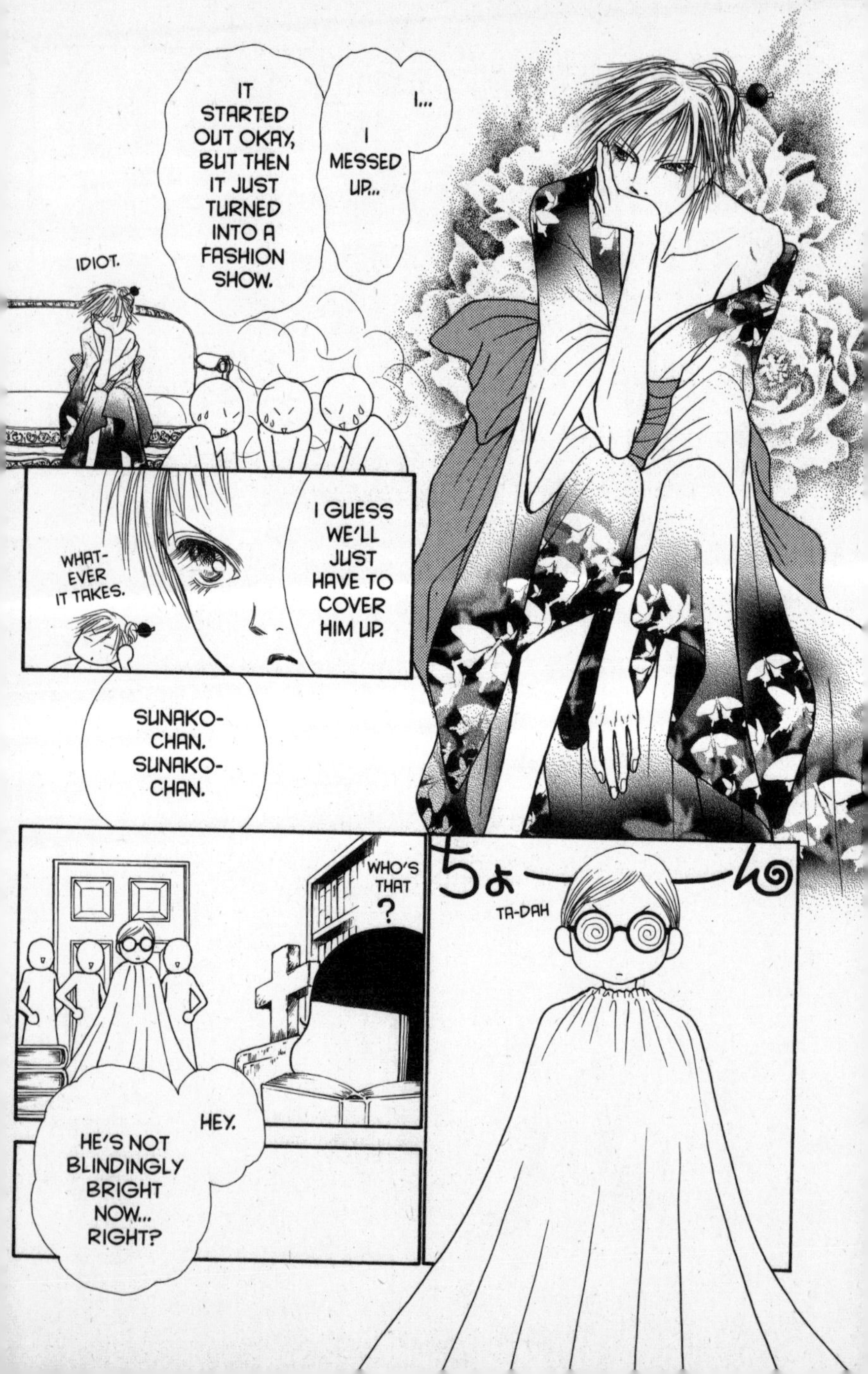
I...
I MESSED UP...
IT STARTED OUT OKAY, BUT THEN IT JUST TURNED INTO A FASHION SHOW.
IDIOT.
I GUESS WE'LL JUST HAVE TO COVER HIM UP.
WHATEVER IT TAKES.
SUNAKO-CHAN. SUNAKO-CHAN.
ちょーーん
TA-DAH
WHO'S THAT ?
HEY.
HE'S NOT BLINDINGLY BRIGHT NOW... RIGHT?

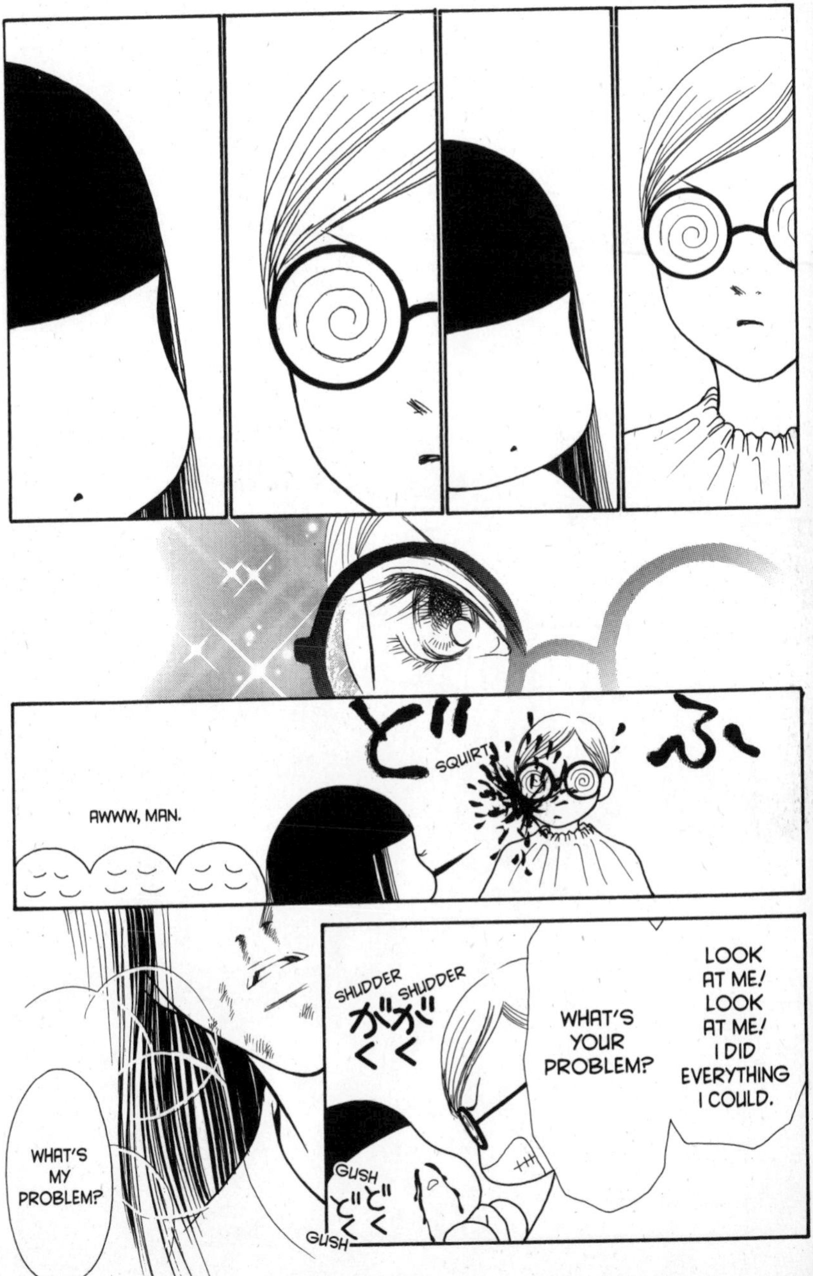
どふ
SQUIRT
AWWW, MAN.
LOOK AT ME! LOOK AT ME! I DID EVERYTHING I COULD.
WHAT'S YOUR PROBLEM?
SHUDDER SHUDDER
がくがく
GUSH GUSH
どくどく
WHAT'S MY PROBLEM?

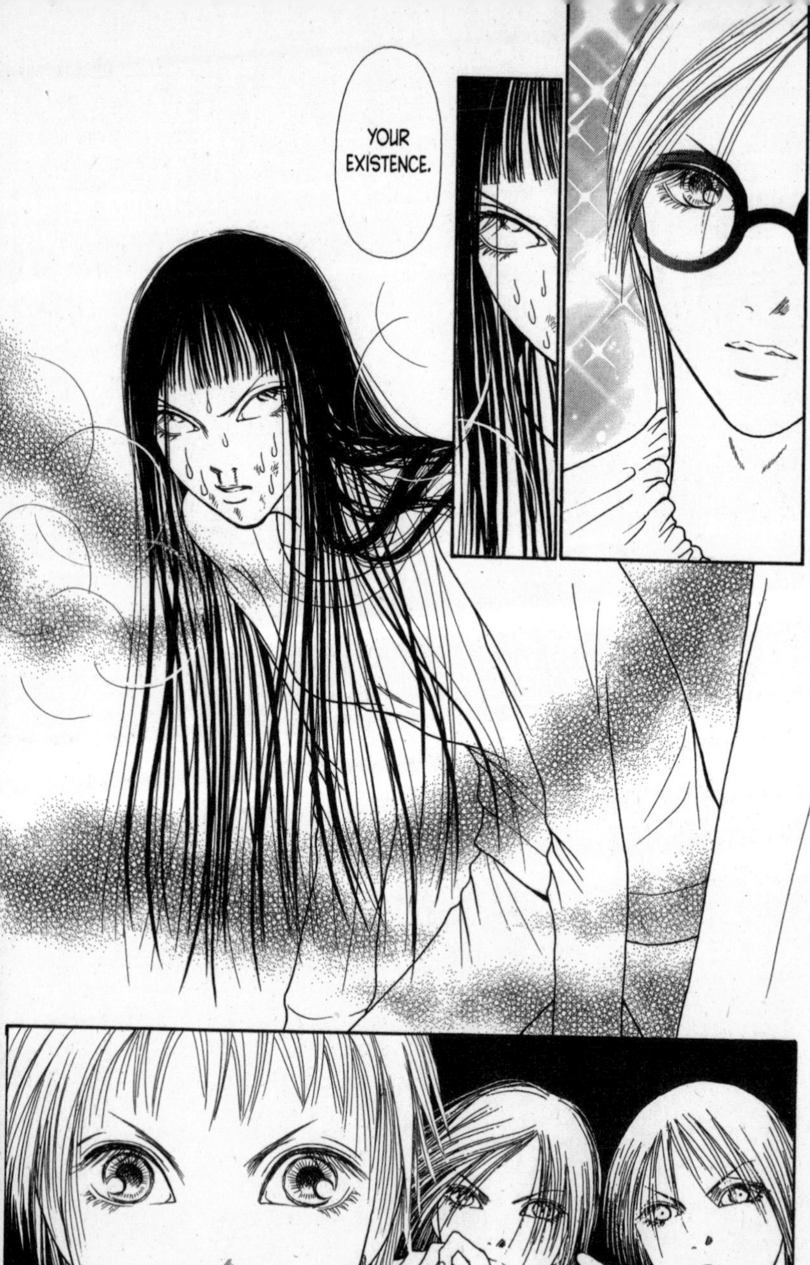
YOUR EXISTENCE.

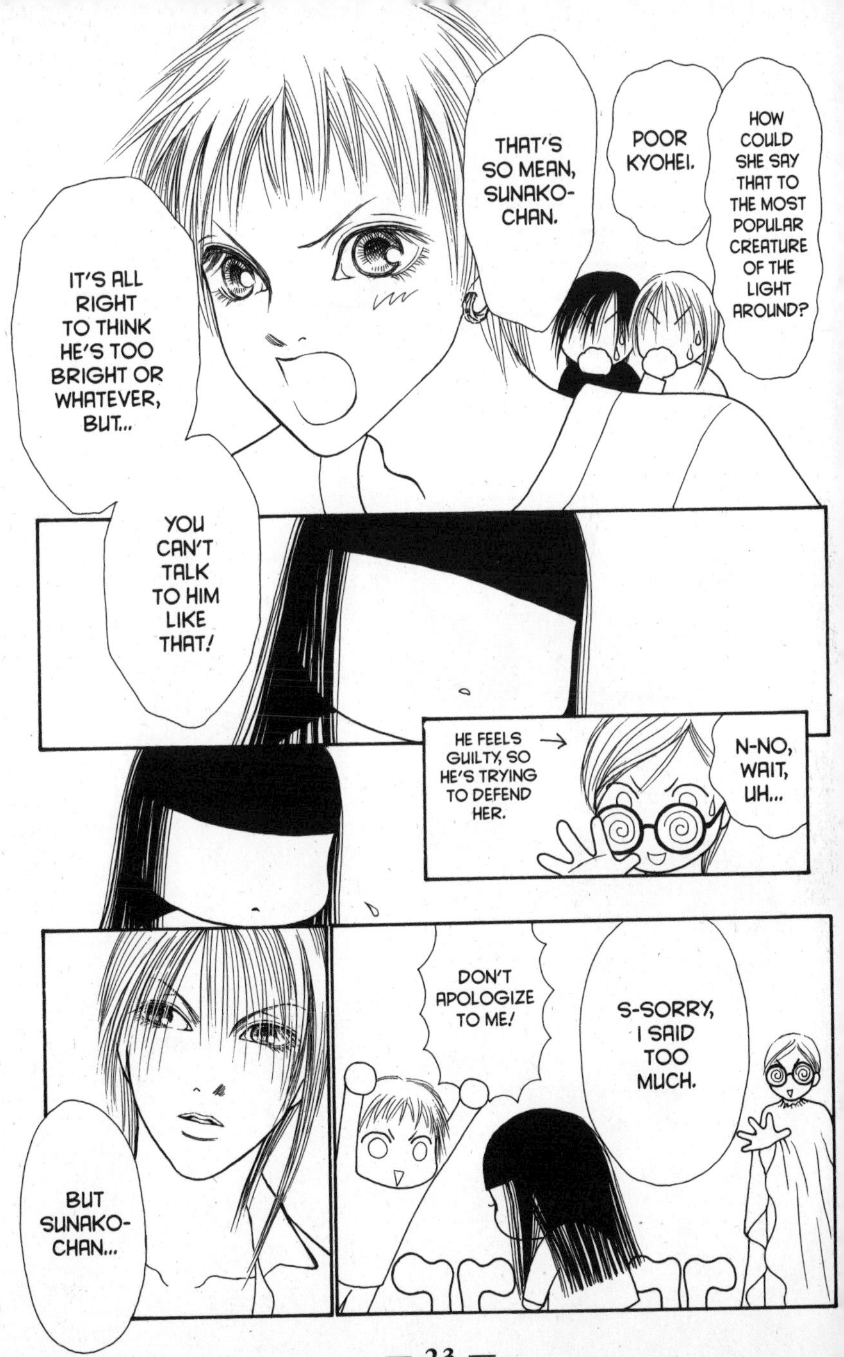
HOW COULD SHE SAY THAT TO THE MOST POPULAR CREATURE OF THE LIGHT AROUND?
POOR KYOHEI.
THAT'S SO MEAN, SUNAKO-CHAN.
IT'S ALL RIGHT TO THINK HE'S TOO BRIGHT OR WHATEVER, BUT...
YOU CAN'T TALK TO HIM LIKE THAT!
N-NO, WAIT, UH...
HE FEELS GUILTY, SO HE'S TRYING TO DEFEND HER.
S-SORRY, I SAID TOO MUCH.
DON'T APOLOGIZE TO ME!
BUT SUNAKO-CHAN...

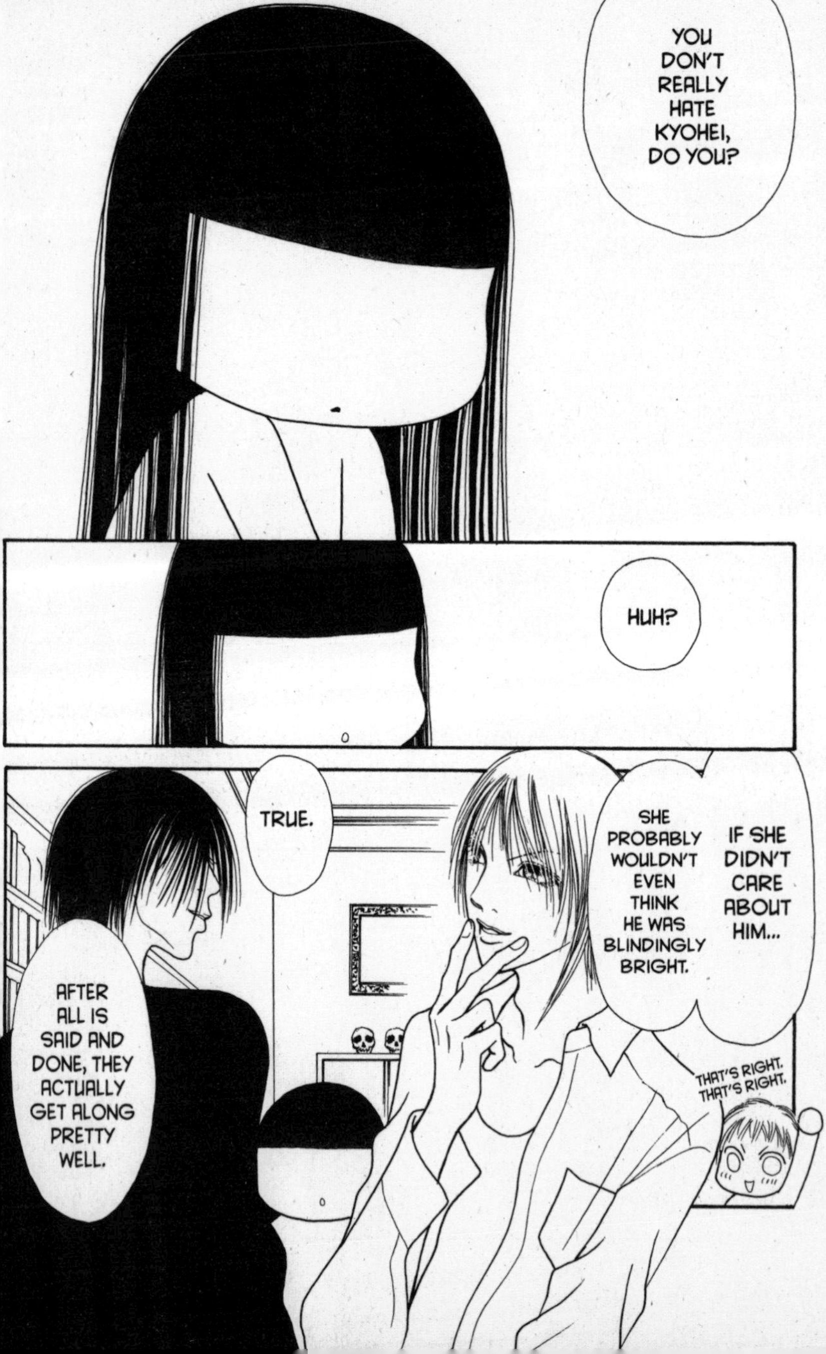
YOU DON'T REALLY HATE KYOHEI, DO YOU?
HUH?
IF SHE DIDN'T CARE ABOUT HIM...
SHE PROBABLY WOULDN'T EVEN THINK HE WAS BLINDINGLY BRIGHT.
TRUE.
THAT'S RIGHT. THAT'S RIGHT.
AFTER ALL IS SAID AND DONE, THEY ACTUALLY GET ALONG PRETTY WELL.

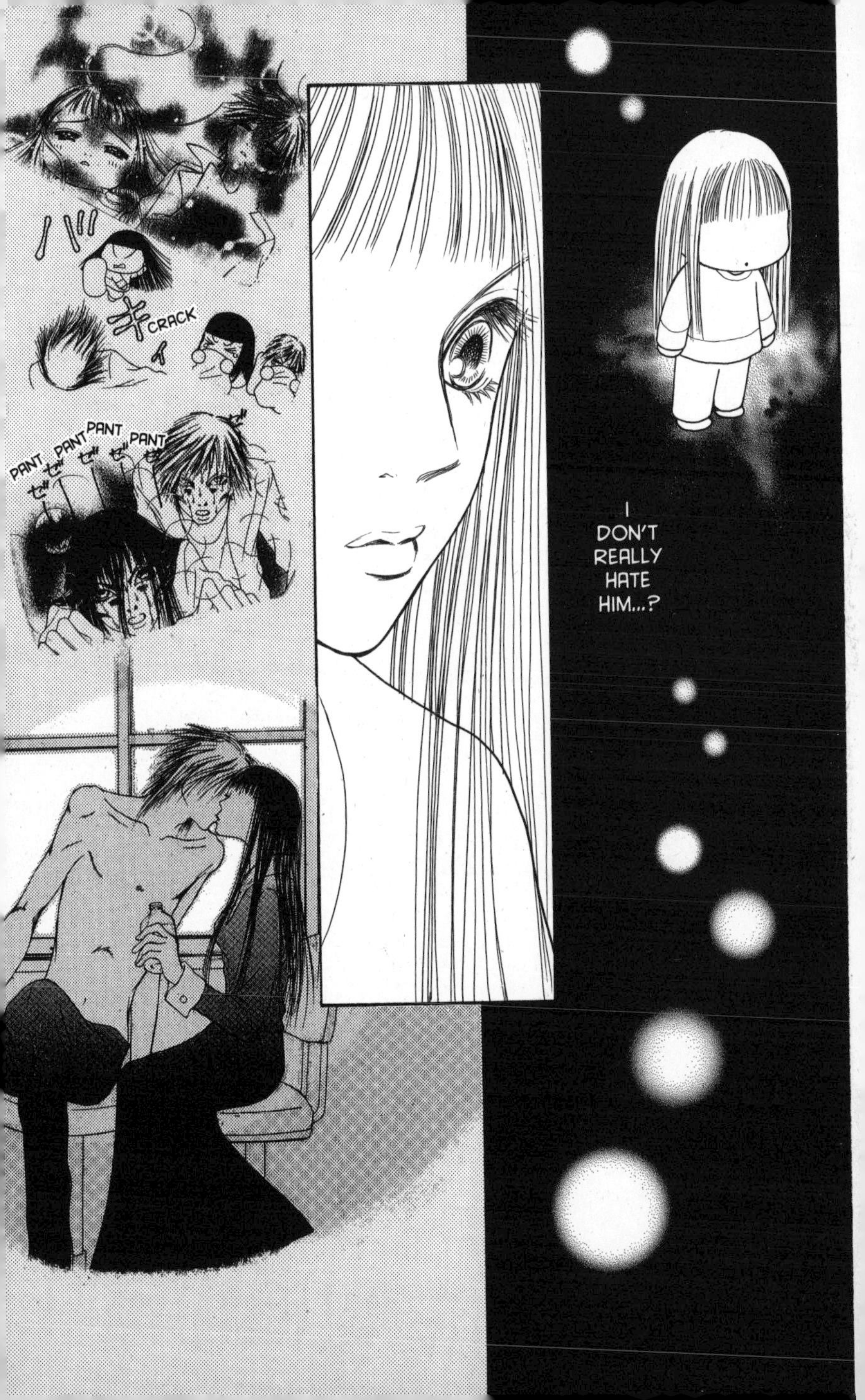
I DON'T REALLY HATE HIM...?
CRACK
PANT
PANT
PANT
PANT

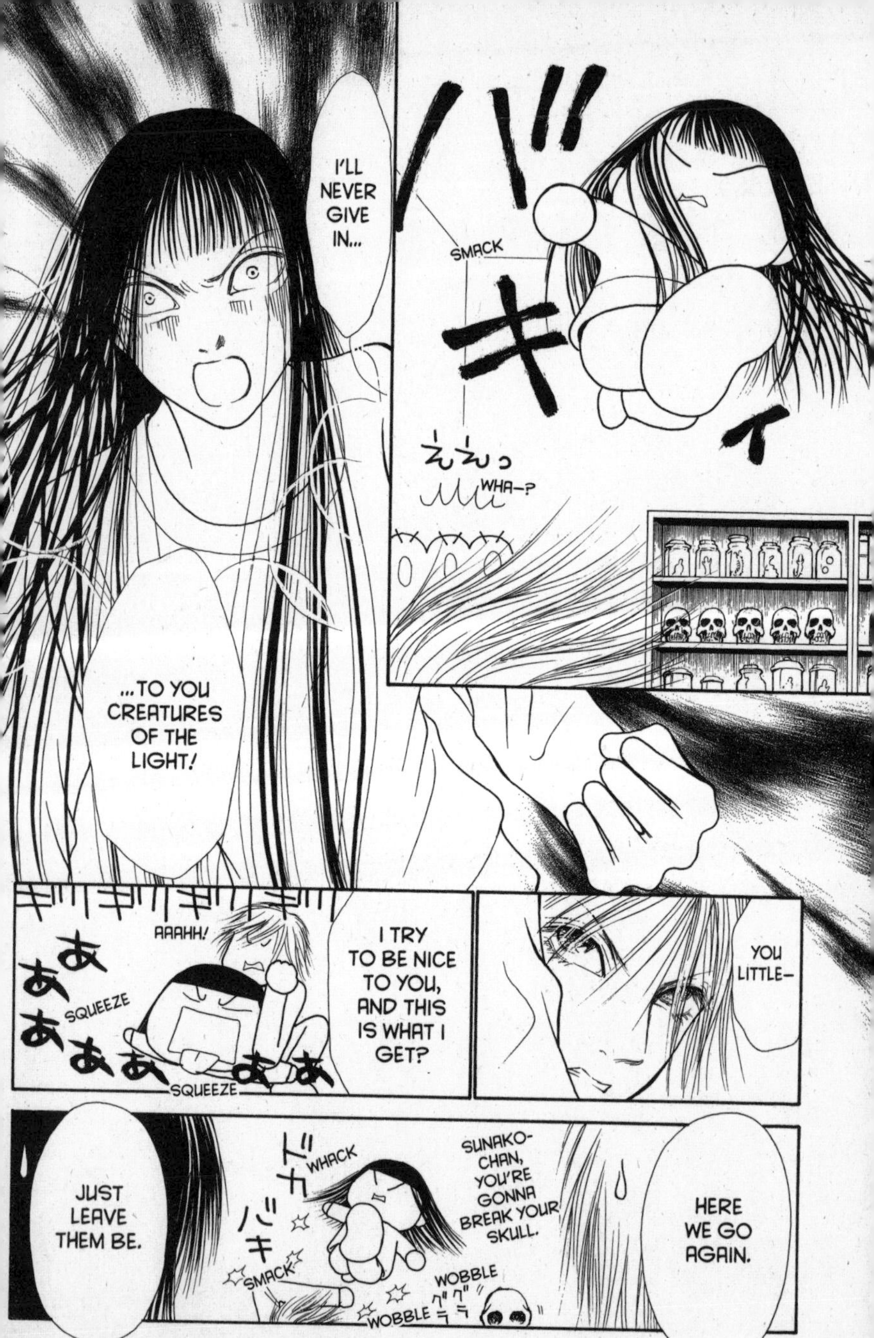
バキィ
SMACK
ええっ
WHA—?
I'LL NEVER GIVE IN...
...TO YOU CREATURES OF THE LIGHT!
YOU LITTLE—
I TRY TO BE NICE TO YOU, AND THIS IS WHAT I GET?
AAAHH!
SQUEEZE
SQUEEZE
HERE WE GO AGAIN.
SUNAKO-CHAN, YOU'RE GONNA BREAK YOUR SKULL.
WHACK
SMACK
WOBBLE
WOBBLE
JUST LEAVE THEM BE.

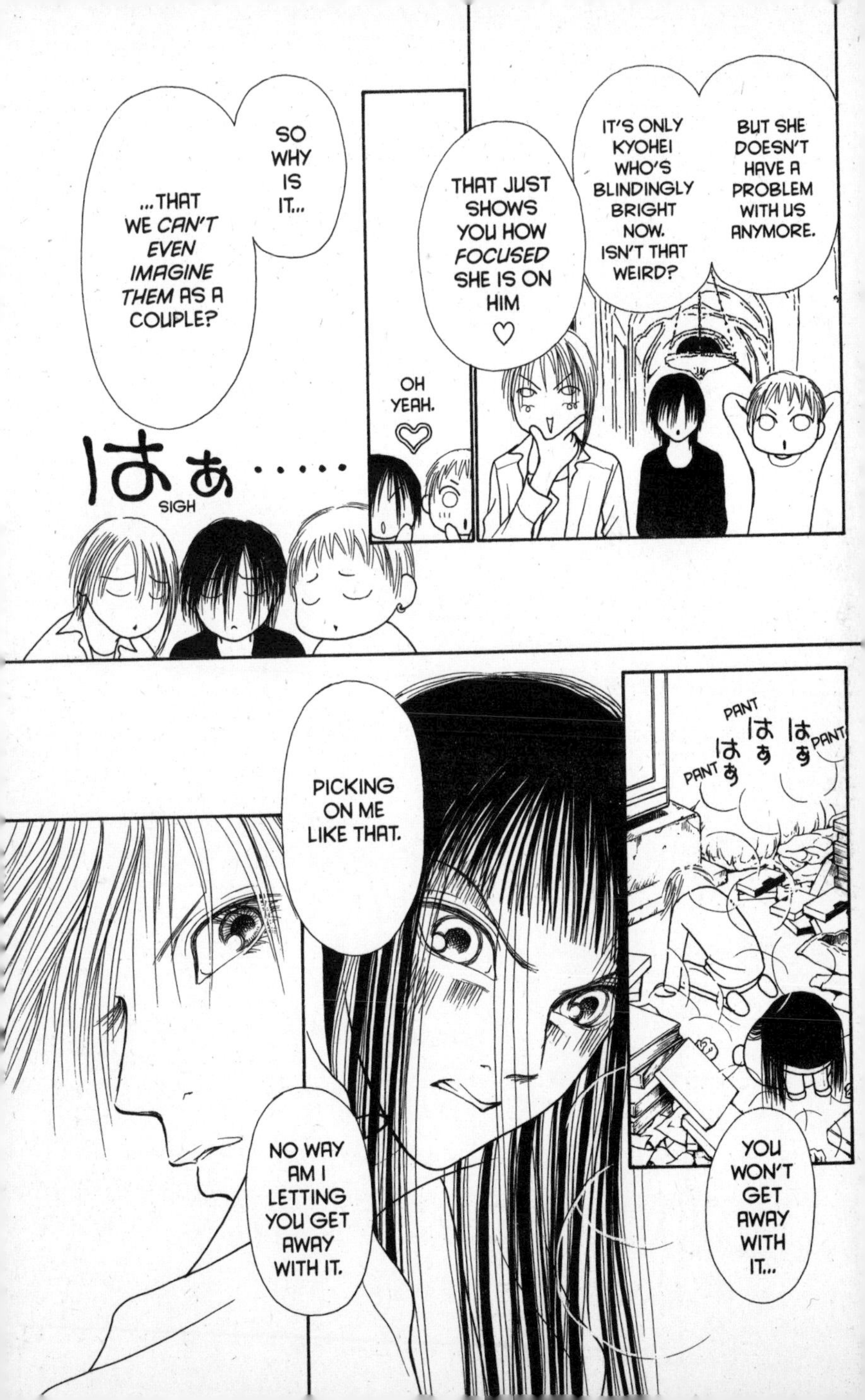

BUT SHE DOESN'T HAVE A PROBLEM WITH US ANYMORE.
IT'S ONLY KYOHEI WHO'S BLINDINGLY BRIGHT NOW. ISN'T THAT WEIRD?
THAT JUST SHOWS YOU HOW *FOCUSED* SHE IS ON HIM ♡
OH YEAH. ♡
SO WHY IS IT...
...THAT WE *CAN'T EVEN IMAGINE THEM* AS A COUPLE?
はぁ・・・・・
SIGH
はぁ はぁ はぁ
PANT PANT PANT
YOU WON'T GET AWAY WITH IT...
PICKING ON ME LIKE THAT.
NO WAY AM I LETTING YOU GET AWAY WITH IT.

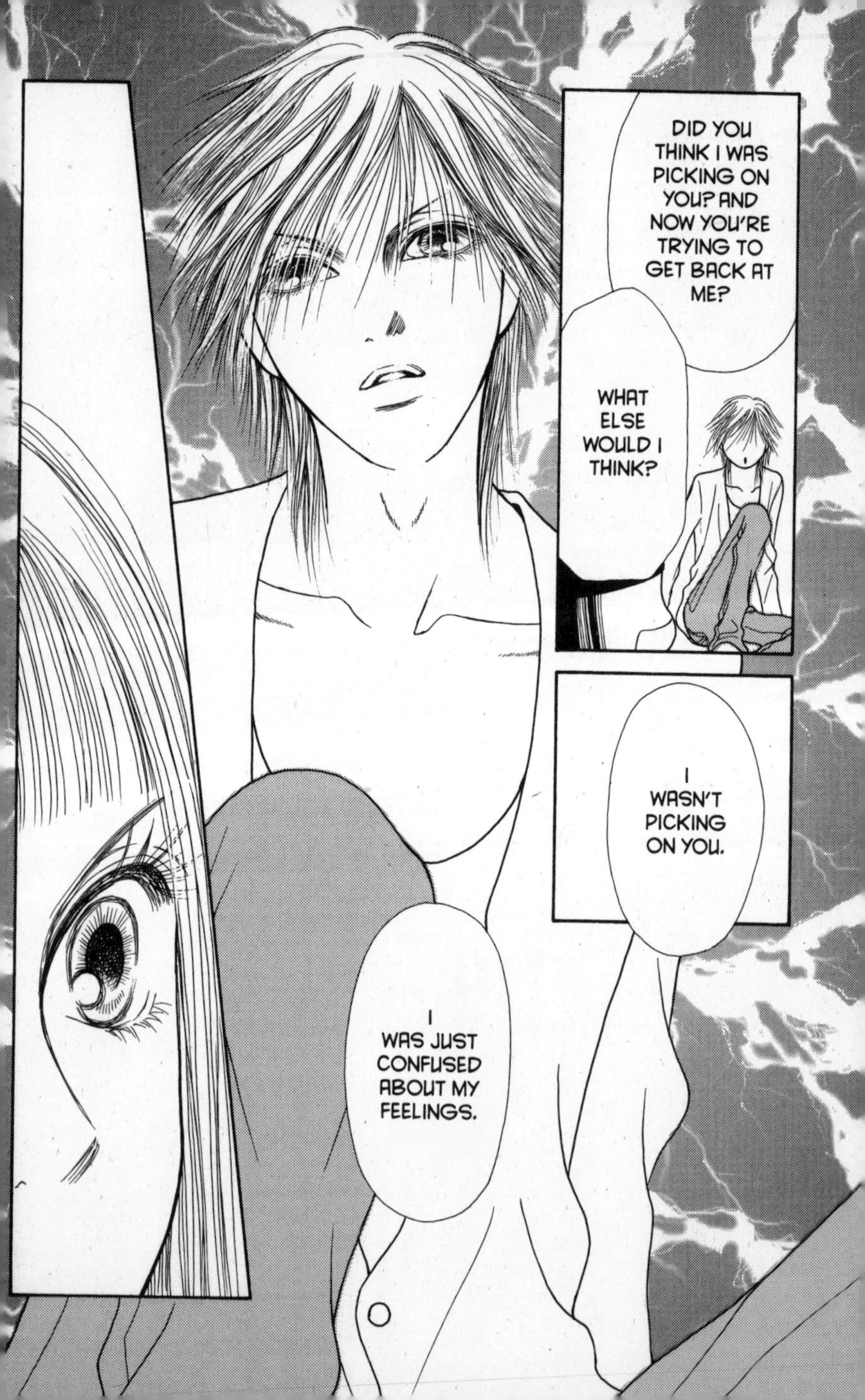
DID YOU THINK I WAS PICKING ON YOU? AND NOW YOU'RE TRYING TO GET BACK AT ME?
WHAT ELSE WOULD I THINK?
I WASN'T PICKING ON YOU.
I WAS JUST CONFUSED ABOUT MY FEELINGS.

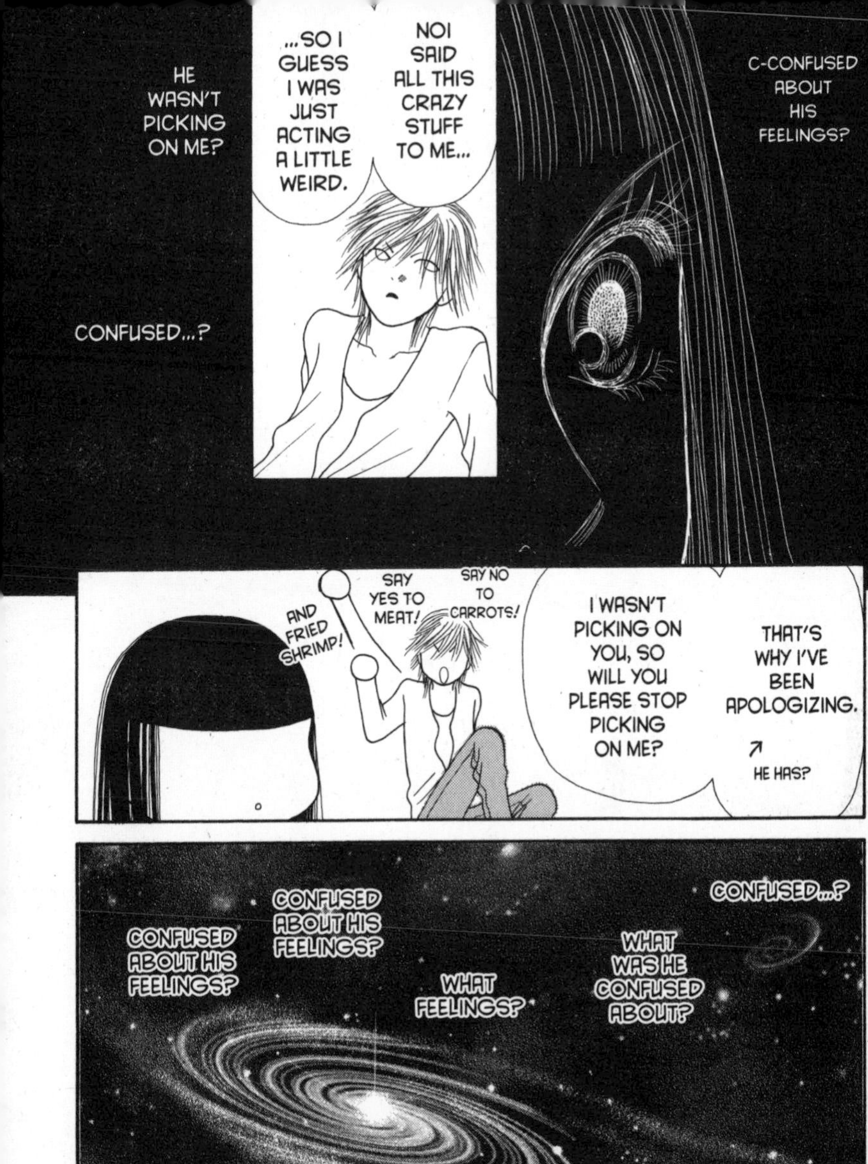
C-CONFUSED ABOUT HIS FEELINGS?
NOI SAID ALL THIS CRAZY STUFF TO ME...
...SO I GUESS I WAS JUST ACTING A LITTLE WEIRD.
HE WASN'T PICKING ON ME?
CONFUSED...?
I WASN'T PICKING ON YOU, SO WILL YOU PLEASE STOP PICKING ON ME?
THAT'S WHY I'VE BEEN APOLOGIZING.
HE HAS?
SAY NO TO CARROTS!
SAY YES TO MEAT!
AND FRIED SHRIMP!
CONFUSED...?
WHAT WAS HE CONFUSED ABOUT?
WHAT FEELINGS?
CONFUSED ABOUT HIS FEELINGS?
CONFUSED ABOUT HIS FEELINGS?

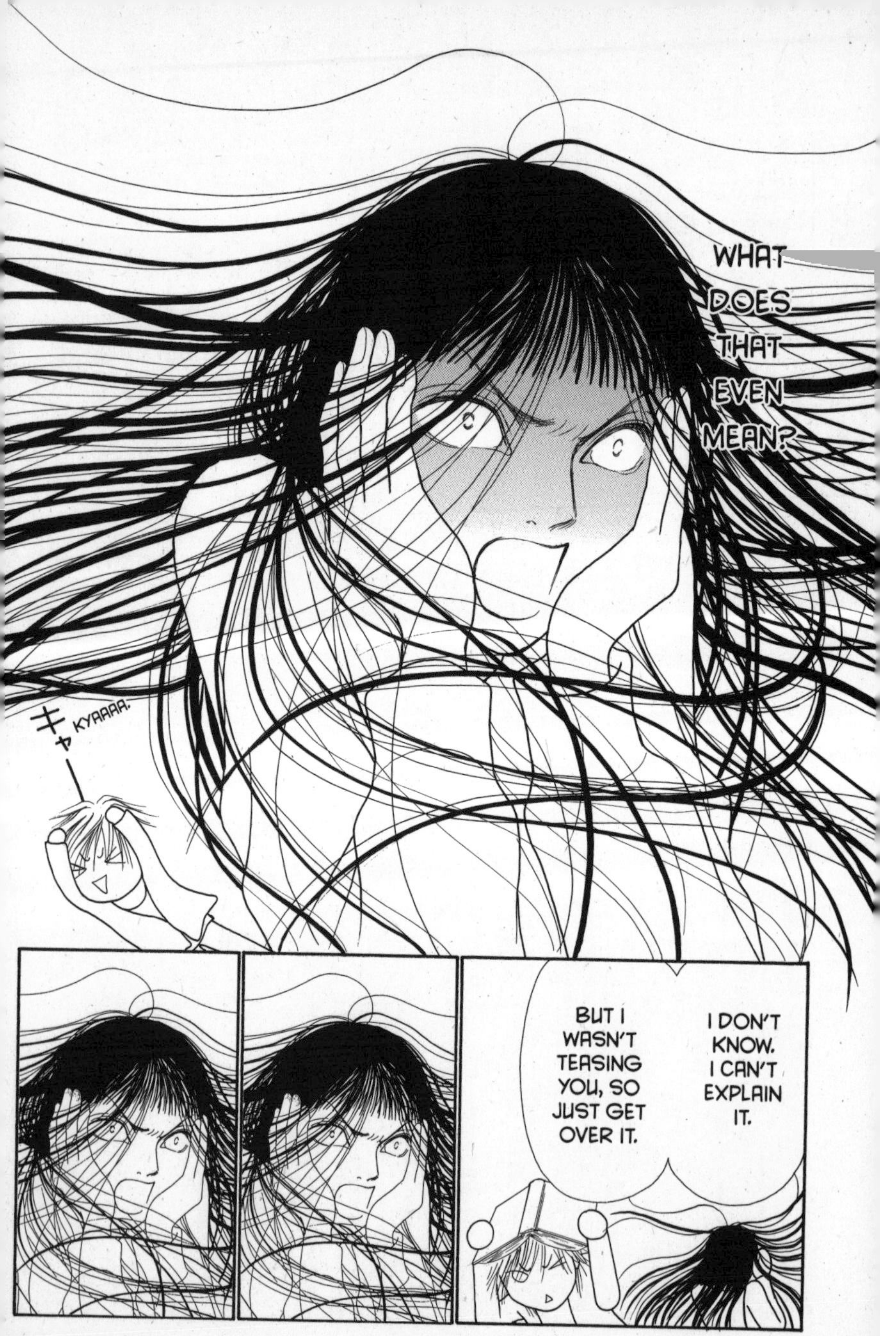
WHAT DOES THAT EVEN MEAN?
キャー KYAAAA.
I DON'T KNOW. I CAN'T EXPLAIN IT.
BUT I WASN'T TEASING YOU, SO JUST GET OVER IT.

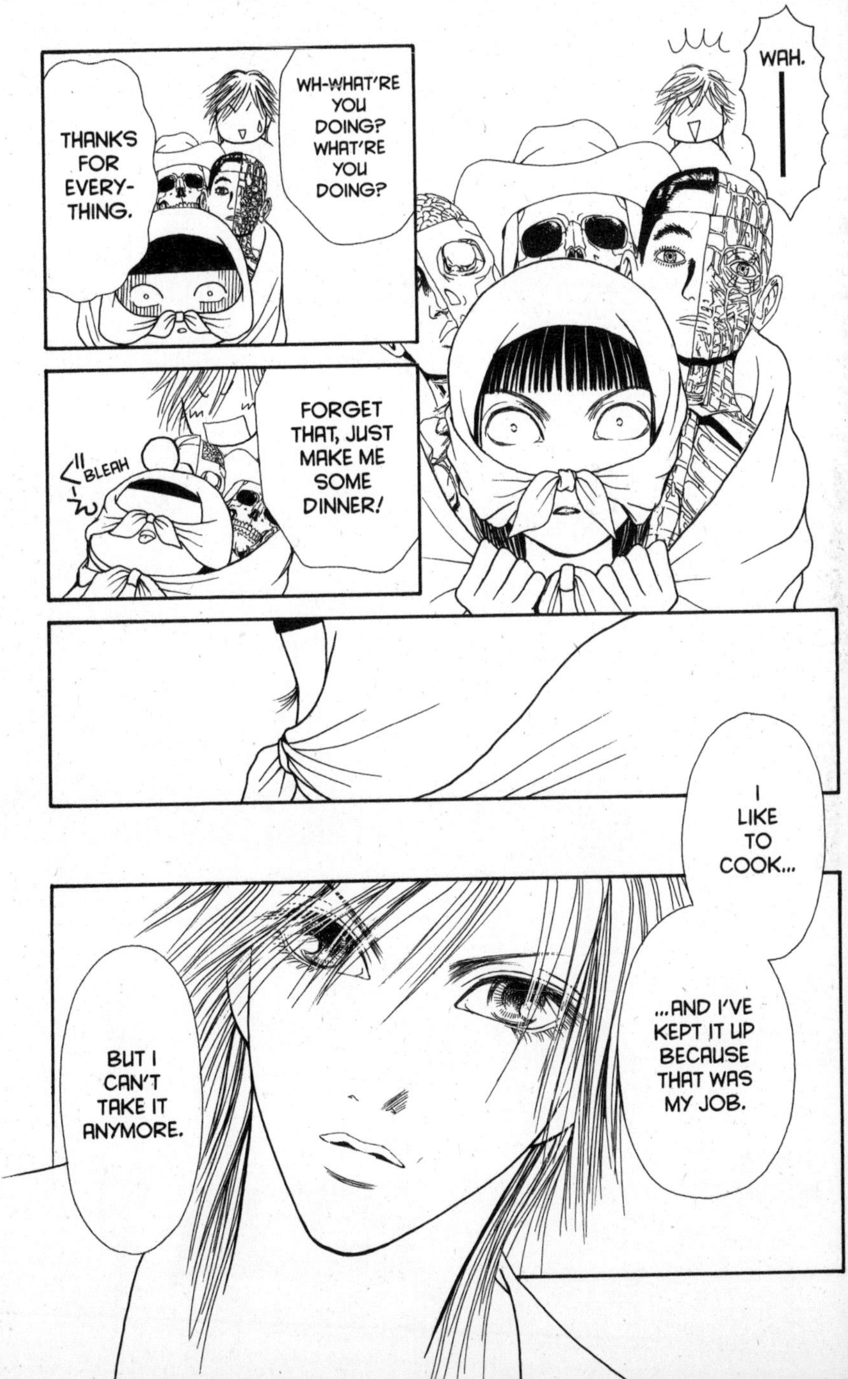
WAH.
WH-WHAT'RE YOU DOING? WHAT'RE YOU DOING?
THANKS FOR EVERY-THING.
FORGET THAT, JUST MAKE ME SOME DINNER!
BLEAH
I LIKE TO COOK...
...AND I'VE KEPT IT UP BECAUSE THAT WAS MY JOB.
BUT I CAN'T TAKE IT ANYMORE.

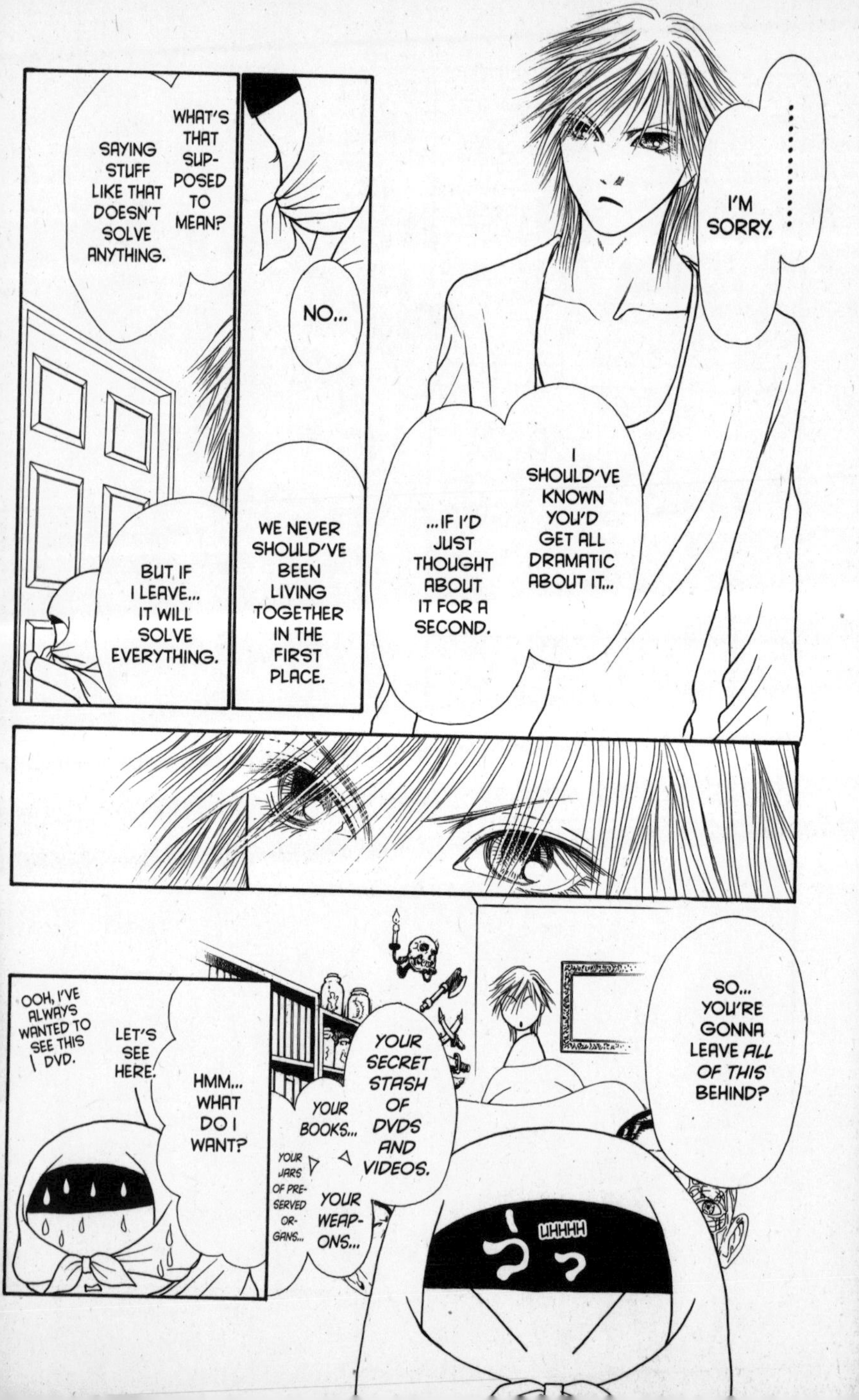
......
I'M SORRY.
I SHOULD'VE KNOWN YOU'D GET ALL DRAMATIC ABOUT IT...
...IF I'D JUST THOUGHT ABOUT IT FOR A SECOND.
NO...
WE NEVER SHOULD'VE BEEN LIVING TOGETHER IN THE FIRST PLACE.
WHAT'S THAT SUP-POSED TO MEAN?
SAYING STUFF LIKE THAT DOESN'T SOLVE ANYTHING.
BUT IF I LEAVE... IT WILL SOLVE EVERYTHING.
SO... YOU'RE GONNA LEAVE *ALL OF THIS* BEHIND?
YOUR SECRET STASH OF DVDS AND VIDEOS.
YOUR BOOKS...
YOUR WEAP-ONS...
YOUR JARS OF PRE-SERVED OR-GANS...
UHHHH
HMM... WHAT DO I WANT?
LET'S SEE HERE.
OOH, I'VE ALWAYS WANTED TO SEE THIS DVD.

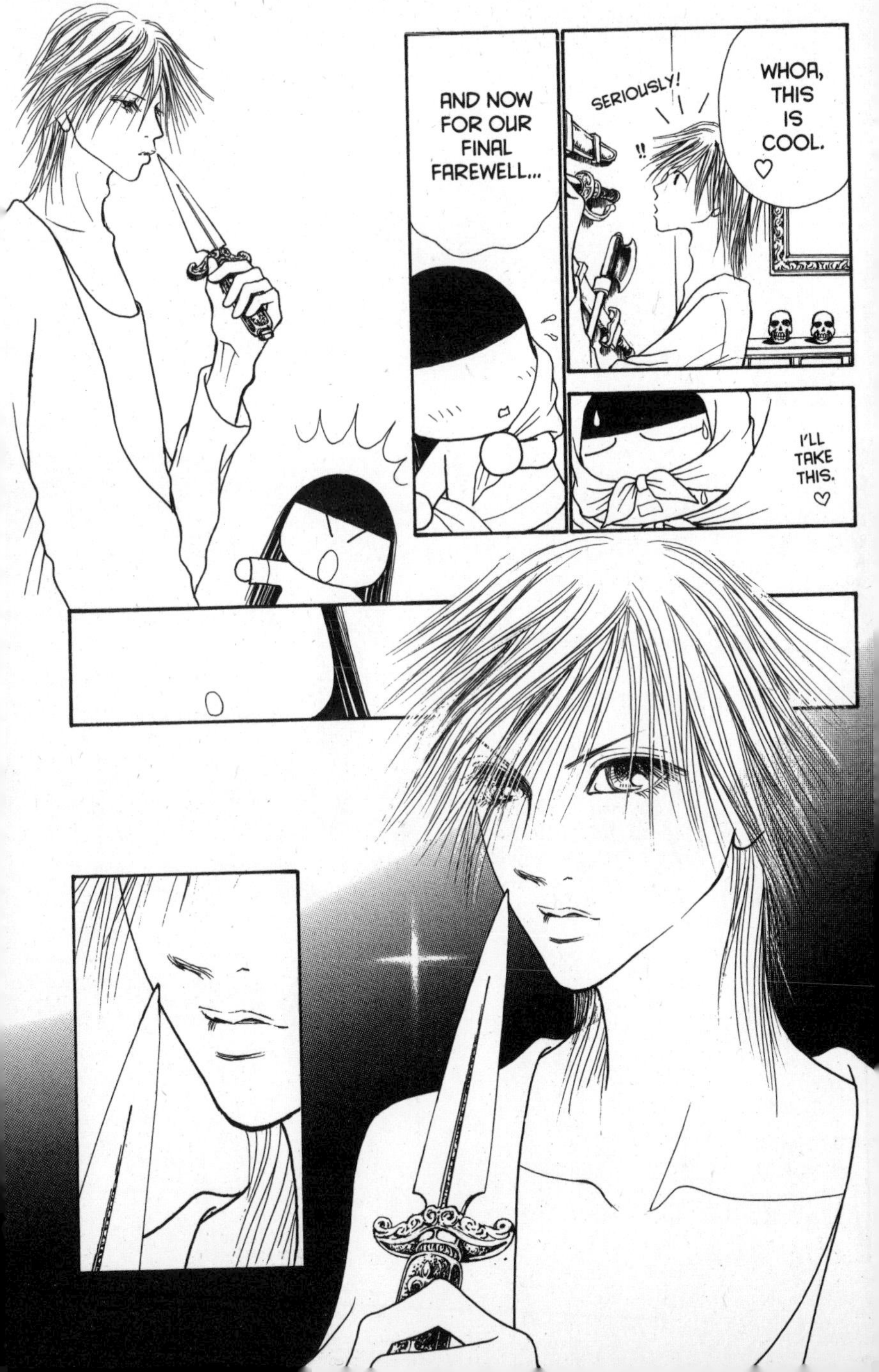
WHOA, THIS IS COOL. ♡
SERIOUSLY!
!!
AND NOW FOR OUR FINAL FAREWELL...
I'LL TAKE THIS. ♡

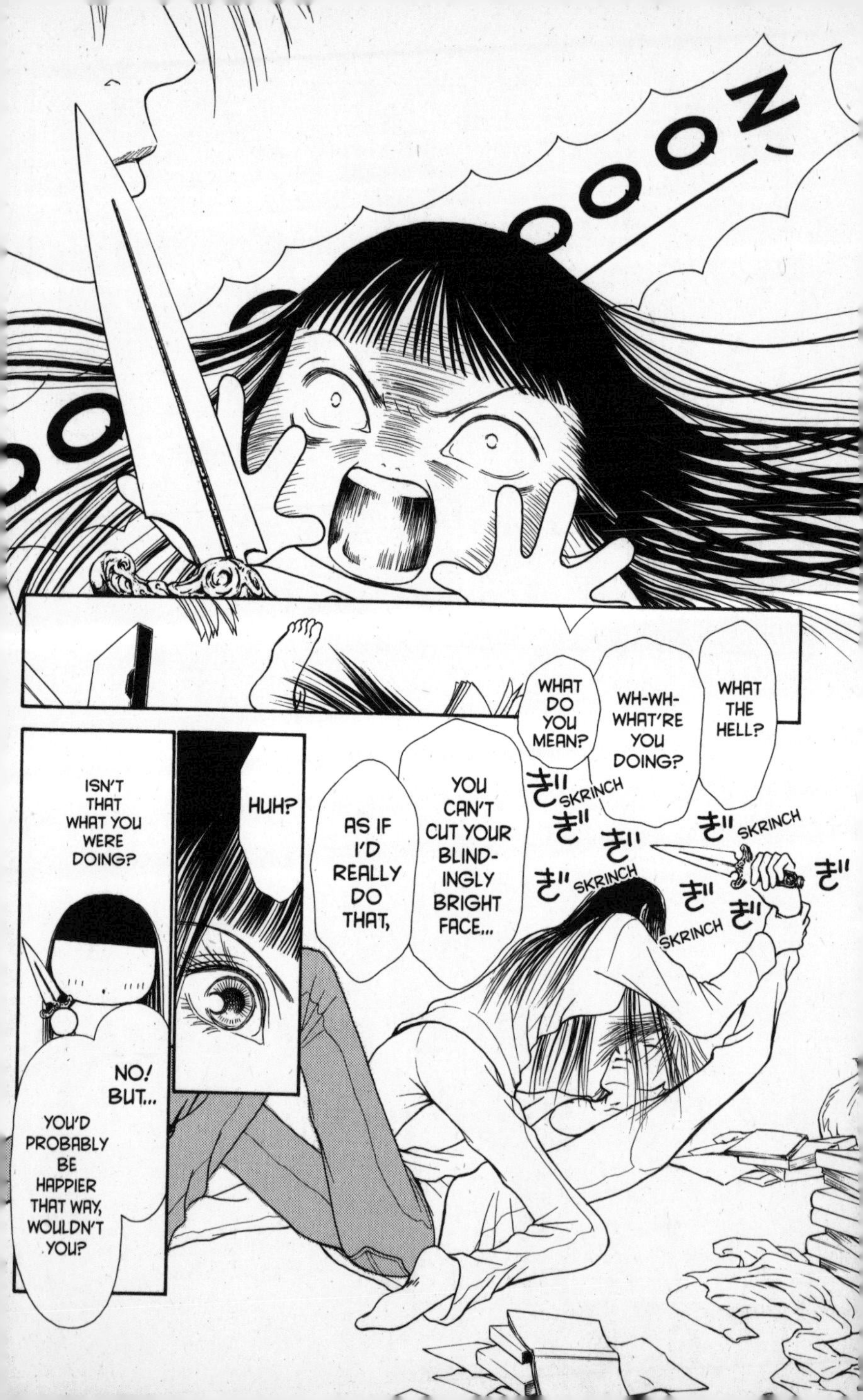
DOOOOOON
WHAT THE HELL?
WH-WH-WHAT'RE YOU DOING?
WHAT DO YOU MEAN?
ぎぎ SKRINCH
ぎぎ SKRINCH
ぎぎ SKRINCH
ぎぎ SKRINCH
YOU CAN'T CUT YOUR BLIND-INGLY BRIGHT FACE...
AS IF I'D REALLY DO THAT,
HUH?
ISN'T THAT WHAT YOU WERE DOING?
NO! BUT...
YOU'D PROBABLY BE HAPPIER THAT WAY, WOULDN'T YOU?

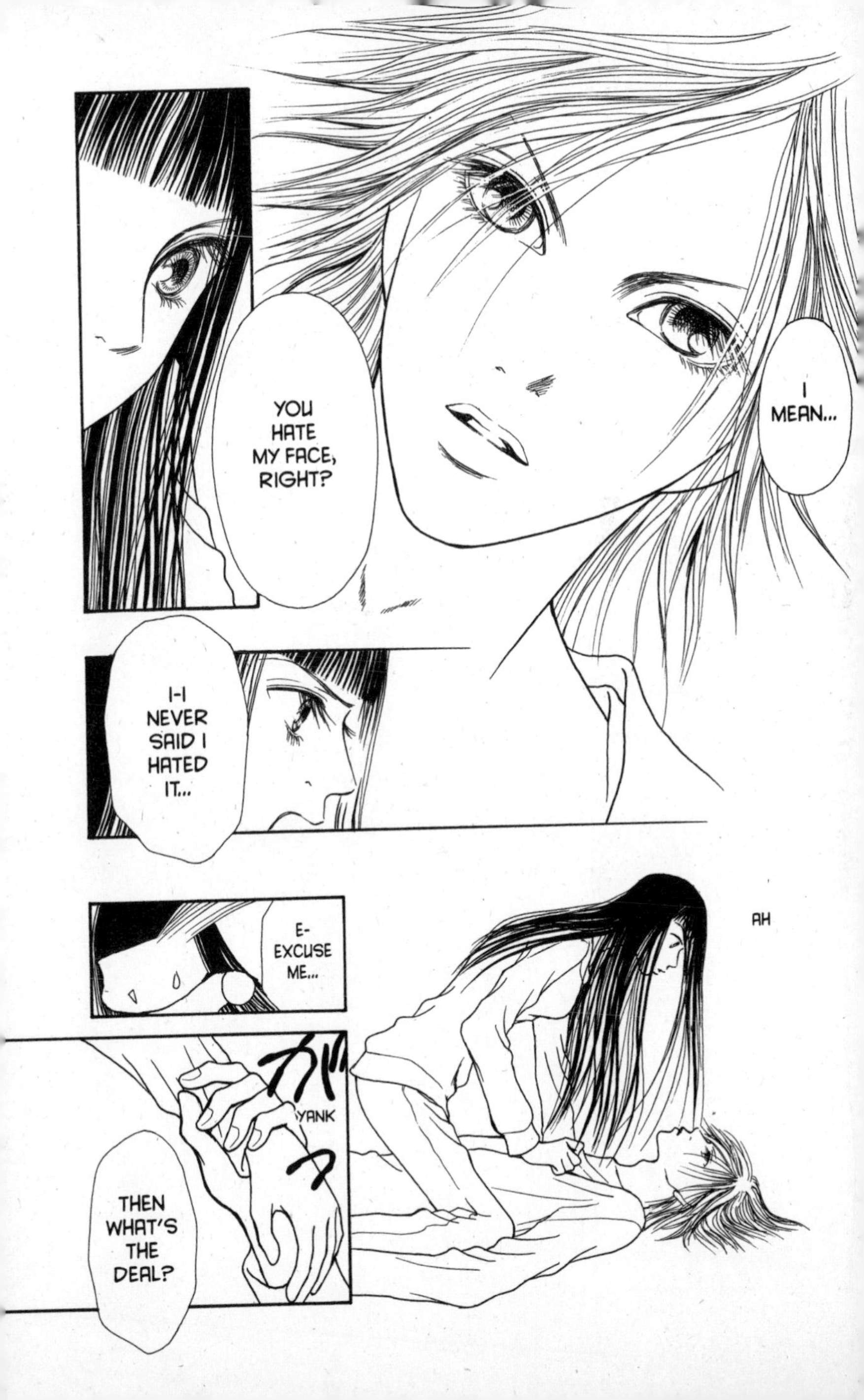

I MEAN...
YOU HATE MY FACE, RIGHT?
I-I NEVER SAID I HATED IT...
AH
E-EXCUSE ME...
YANK
THEN WHAT'S THE DEAL?

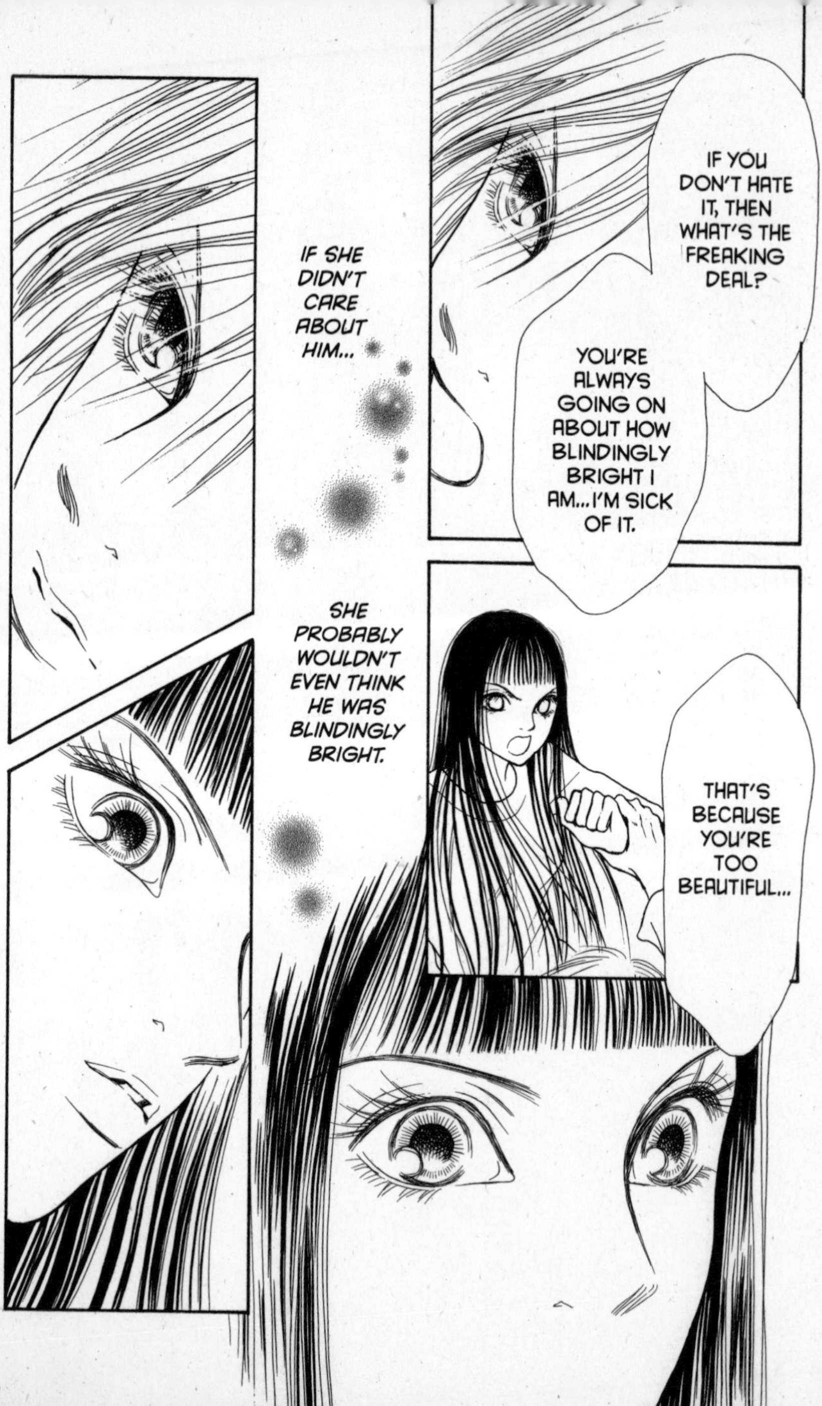
IF YOU DON'T HATE IT, THEN WHAT'S THE FREAKING DEAL?
YOU'RE ALWAYS GOING ON ABOUT HOW BLINDINGLY BRIGHT I AM...I'M SICK OF IT.
IF SHE DIDN'T CARE ABOUT HIM...
SHE PROBABLY WOULDN'T EVEN THINK HE WAS BLINDINGLY BRIGHT.
THAT'S BECAUSE YOU'RE TOO BEAUTIFUL...

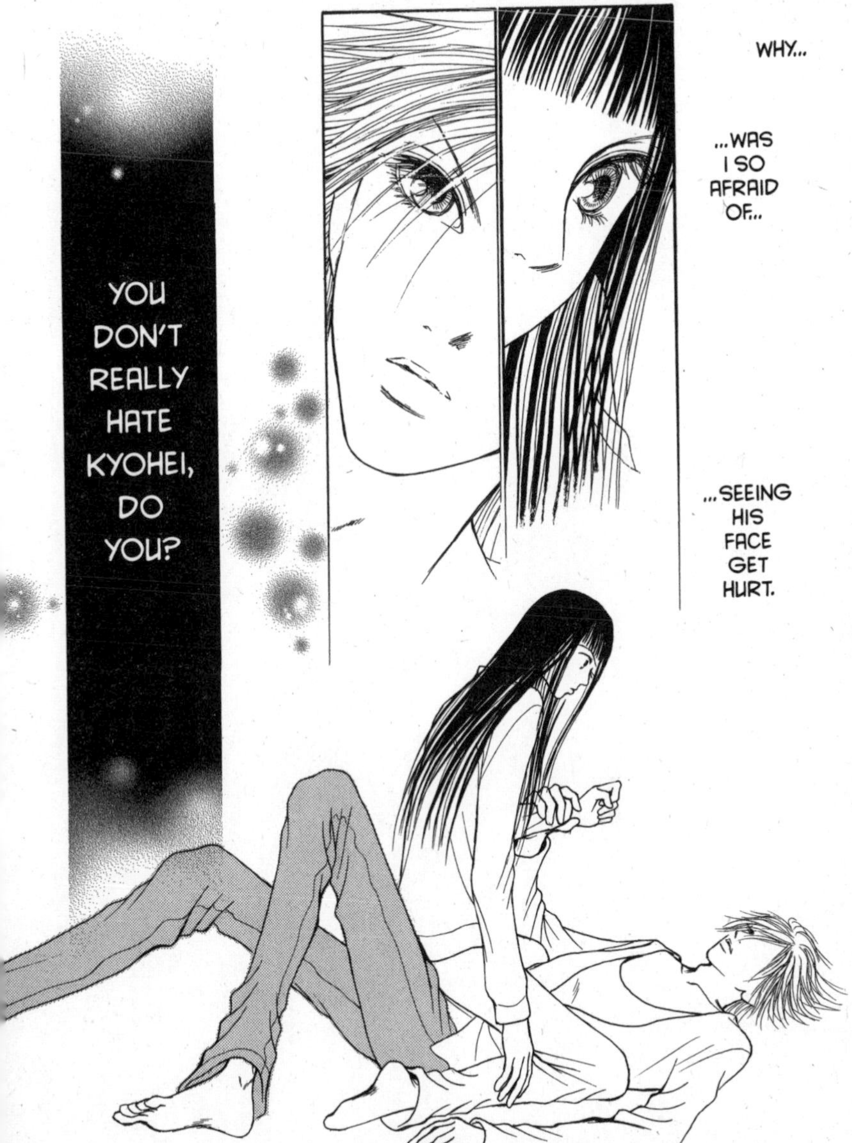
WHY...
...WAS I SO AFRAID OF...
...SEEING HIS FACE GET HURT.
YOU DON'T REALLY HATE KYOHEI, DO YOU?

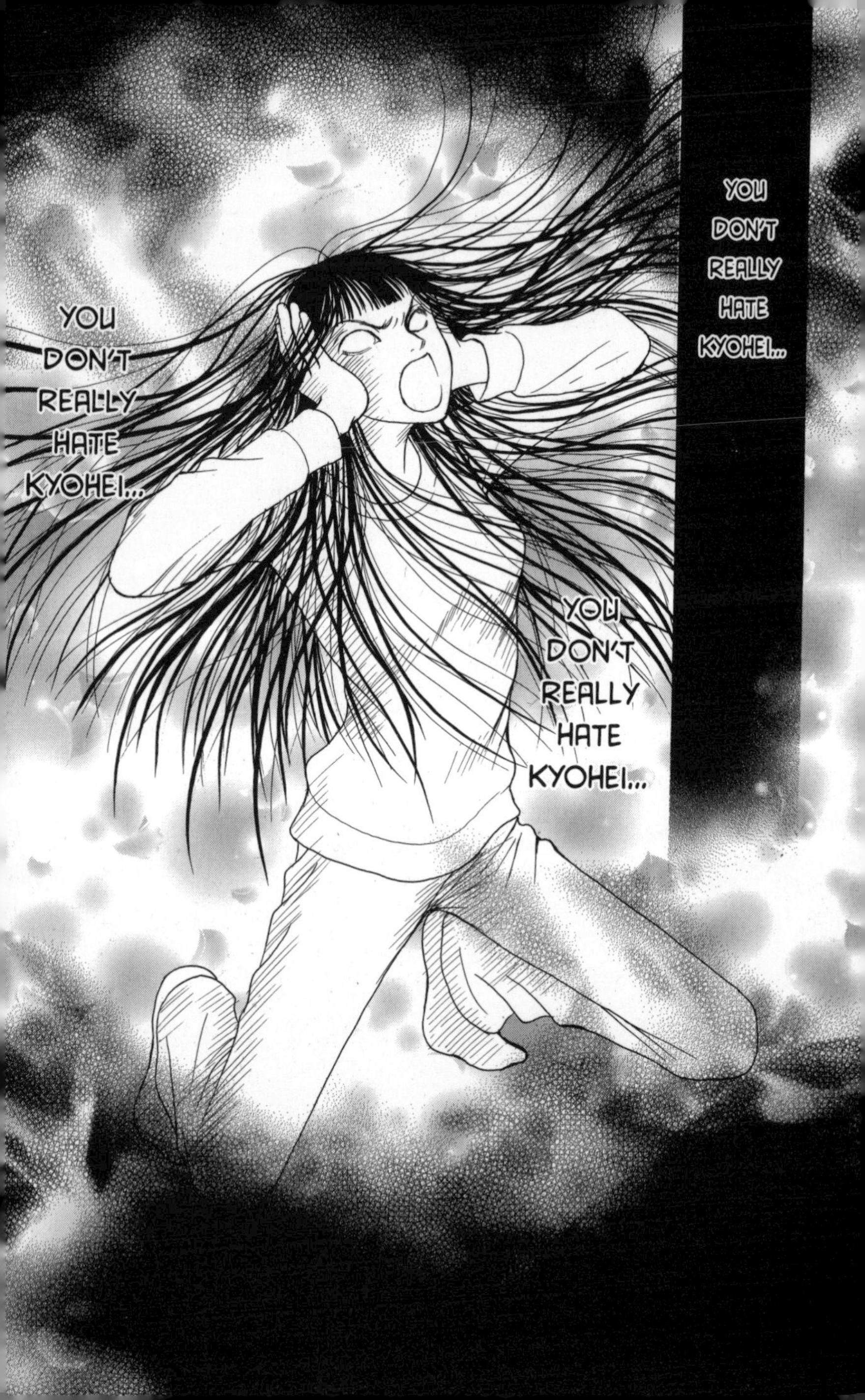
YOU DON'T REALLY HATE KYOHEI...
YOU DON'T REALLY HATE KYOHEI...
YOU DON'T REALLY HATE KYOHEI...

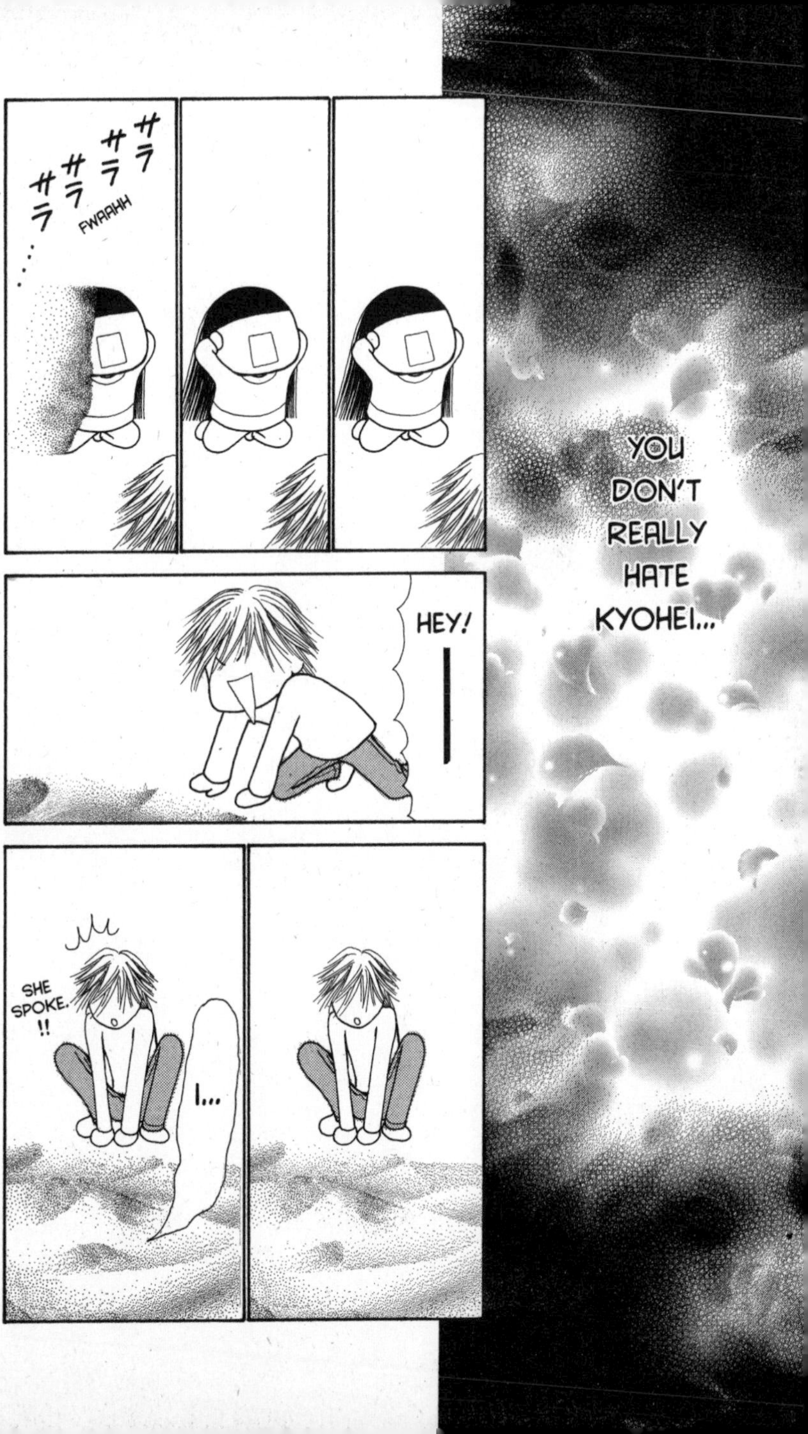
YOU DON'T REALLY HATE KYOHEI...
サラサラサラ
FWAAHH
...
HEY!
SHE SPOKE.!!
I...

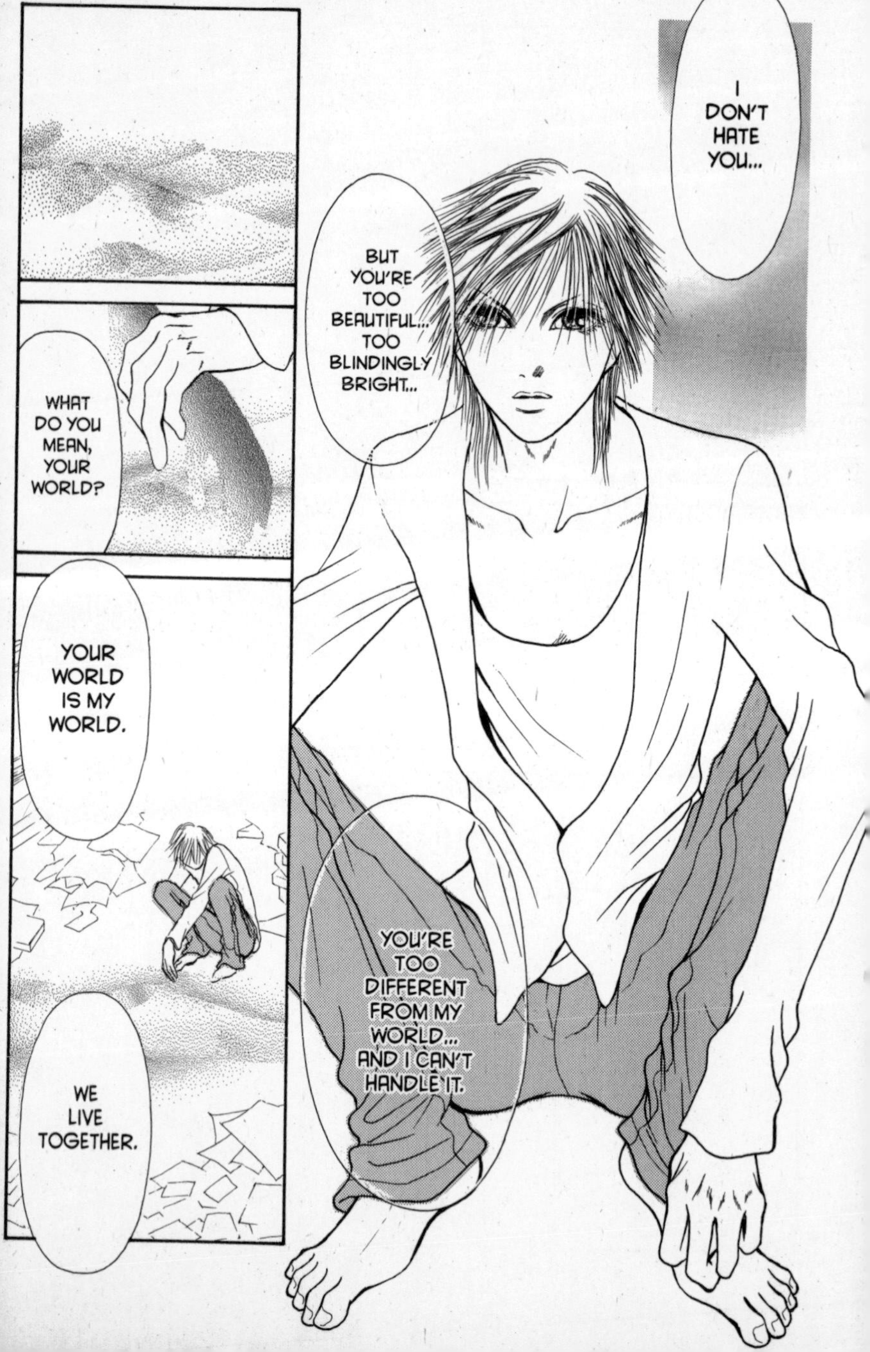
I DON'T HATE YOU...
BUT YOU'RE TOO BEAUTIFUL... TOO BLINDINGLY BRIGHT...
YOU'RE TOO DIFFERENT FROM MY WORLD... AND I CAN'T HANDLE IT.
WHAT DO YOU MEAN, YOUR WORLD?
YOUR WORLD IS MY WORLD.
WE LIVE TOGETHER.

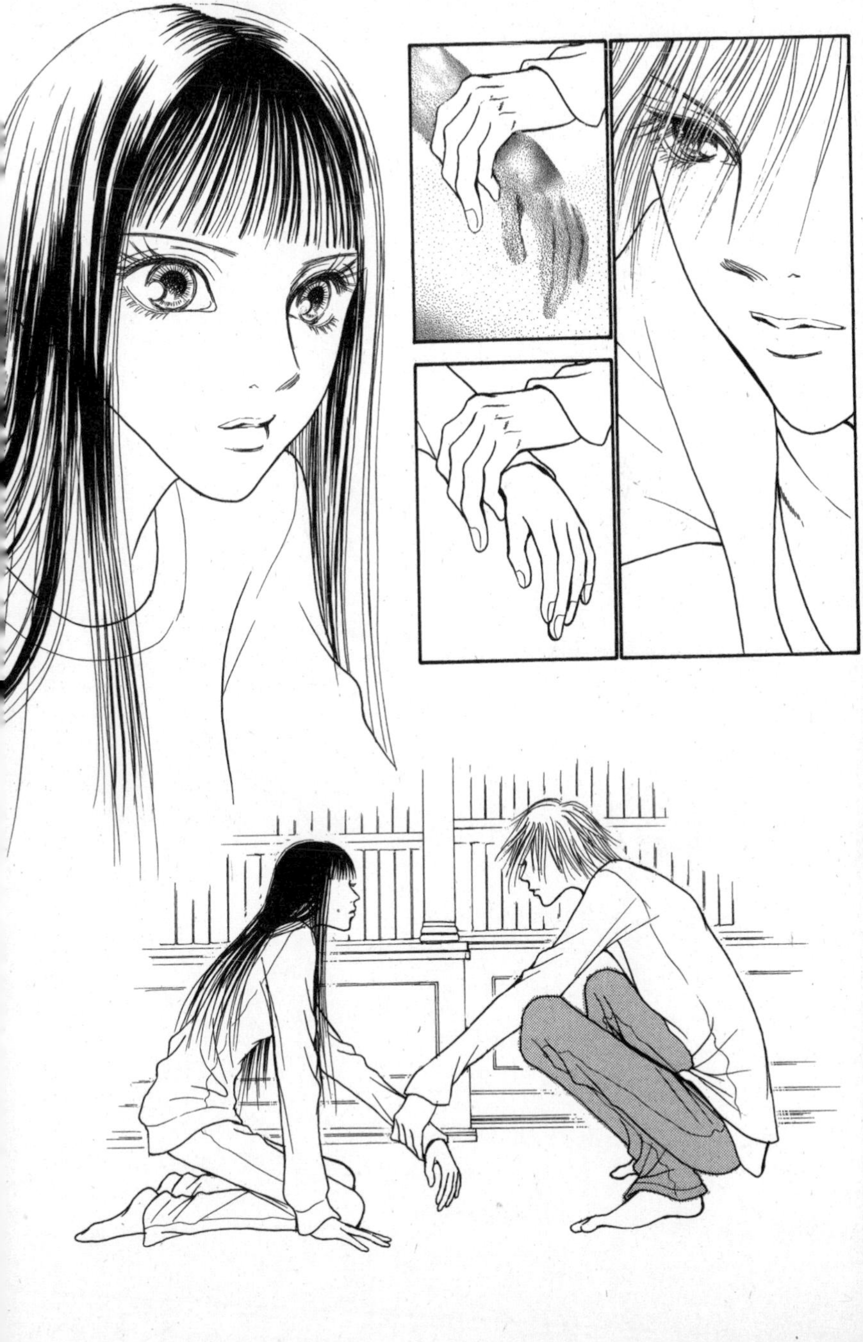

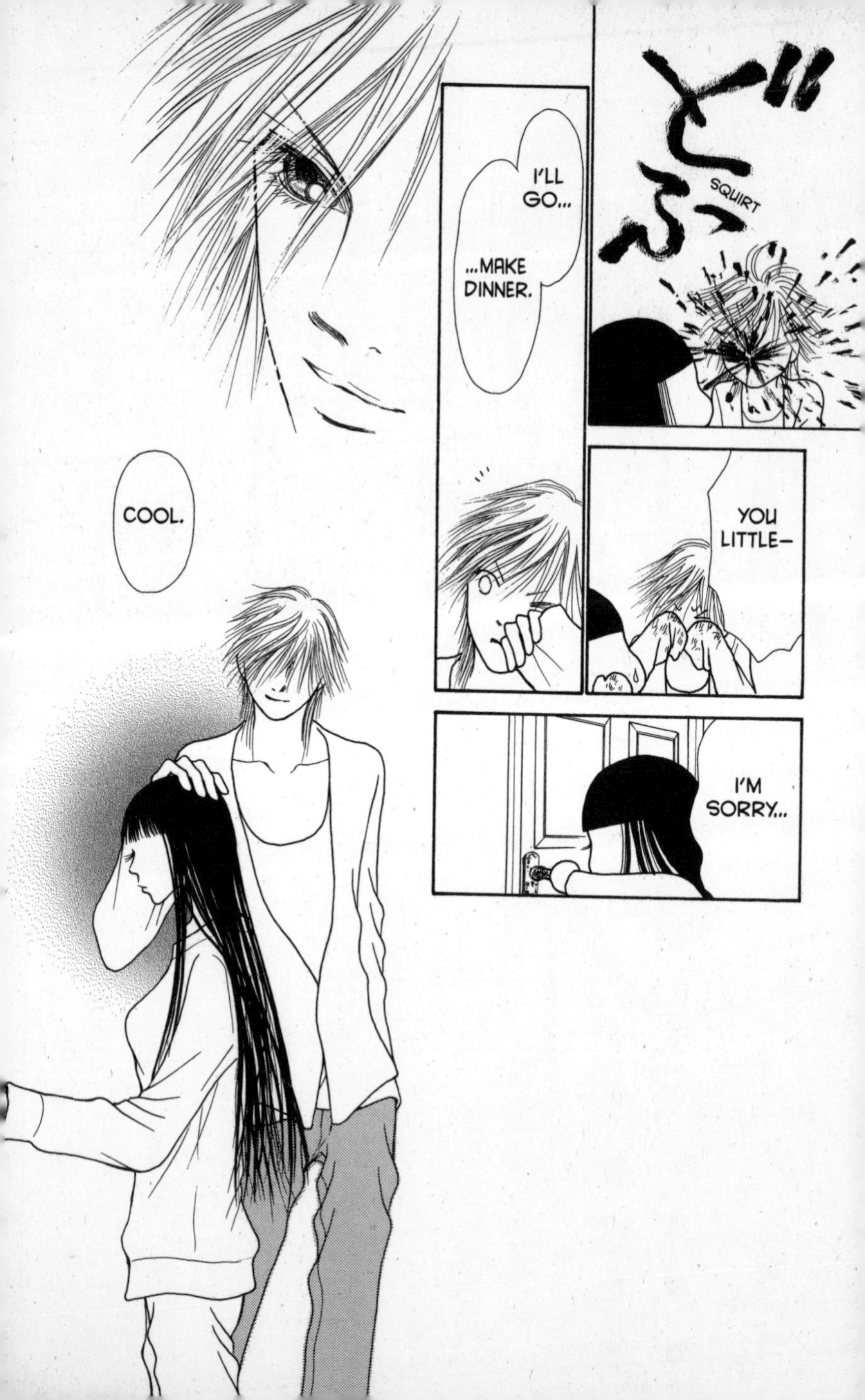
SQUIRT
YOU LITTLE—
I'LL GO...
...MAKE DINNER.
I'M SORRY...
COOL.

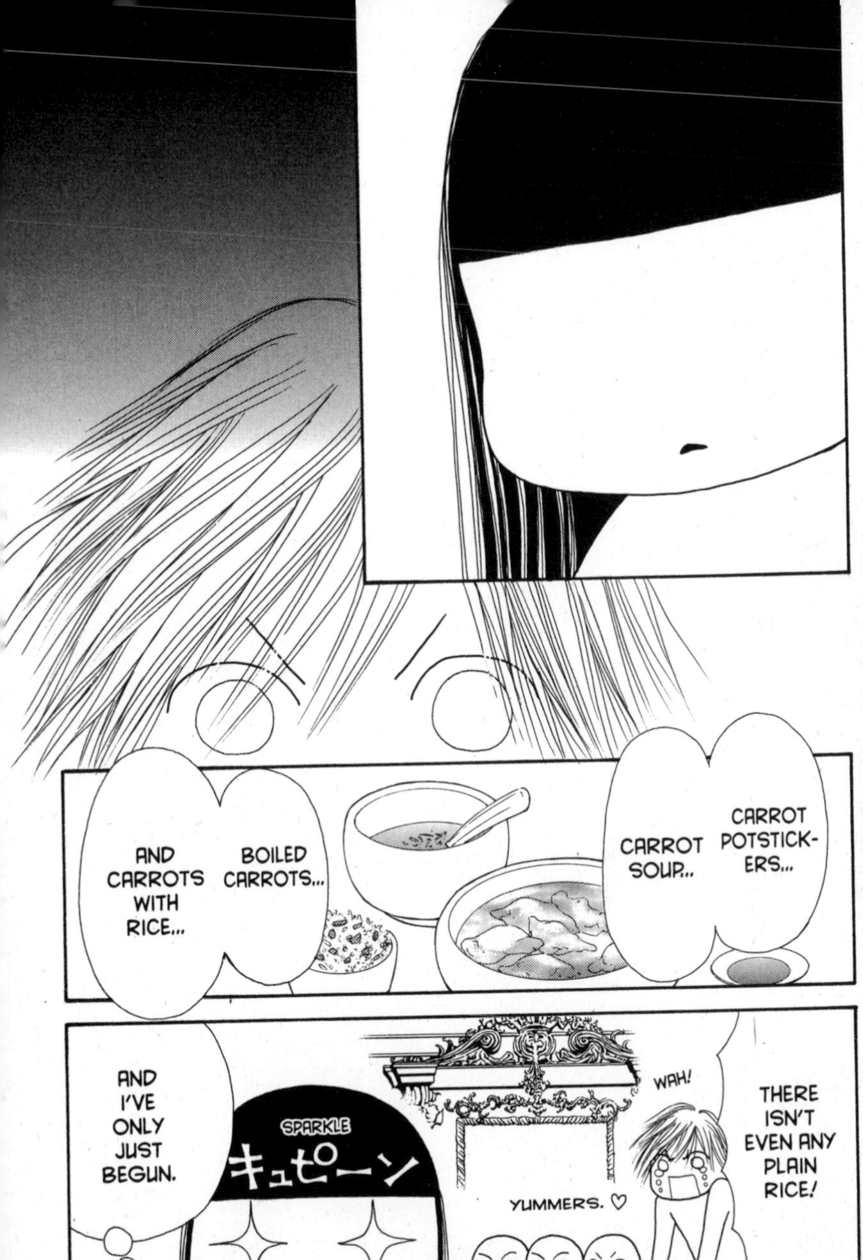
CARROT POTSTICKERS... CARROT SOUP...
BOILED CARROTS... AND CARROTS WITH RICE...
THERE ISN'T EVEN ANY PLAIN RICE!
WAH!
YUMMERS. ♡
SPARKLE
キュピーン
AND I'VE ONLY JUST BEGUN.

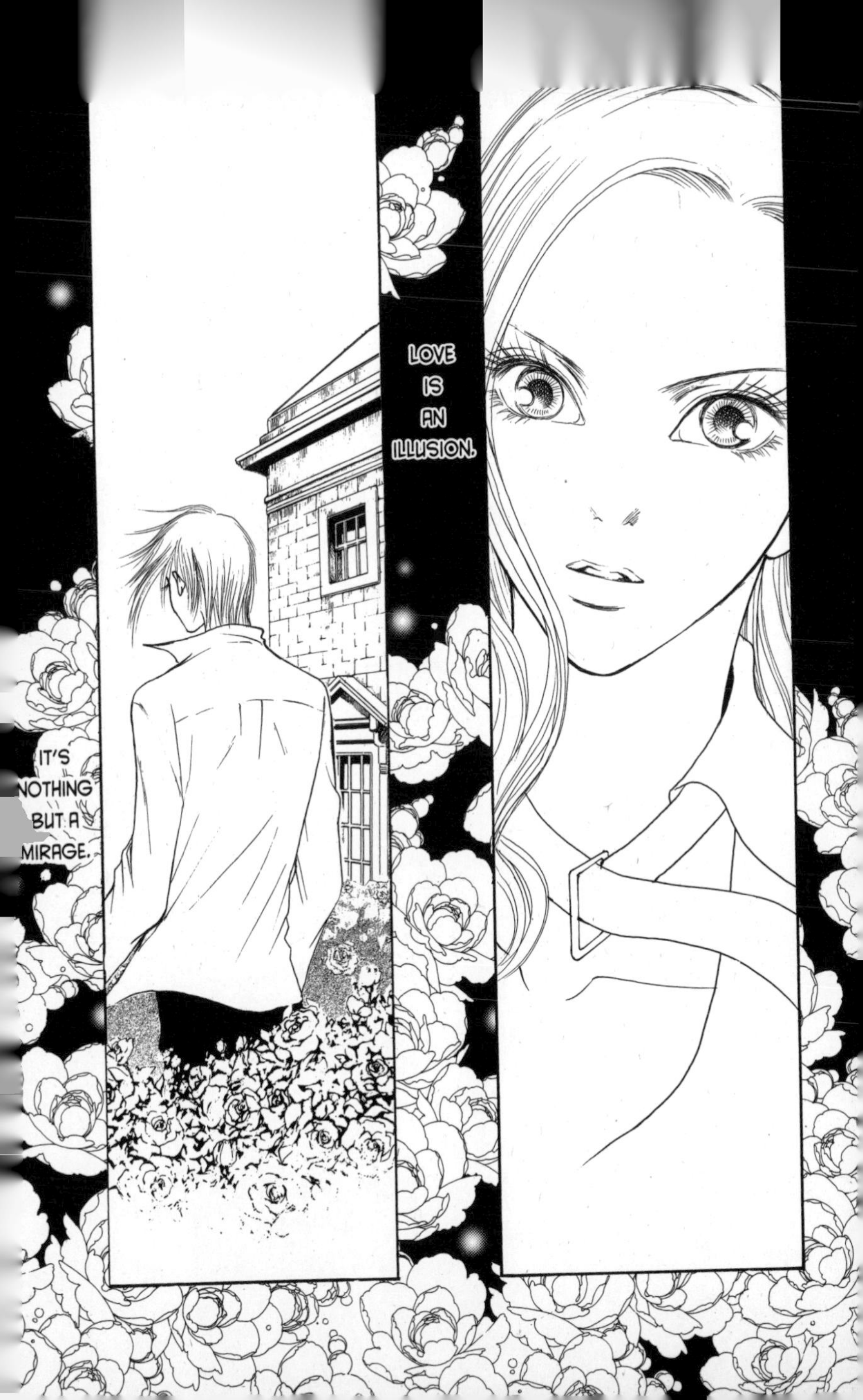
LOVE IS AN ILLUSION.
IT'S NOTHING BUT A MIRAGE.

Chapter 76

LOVE IS A MIRAGE

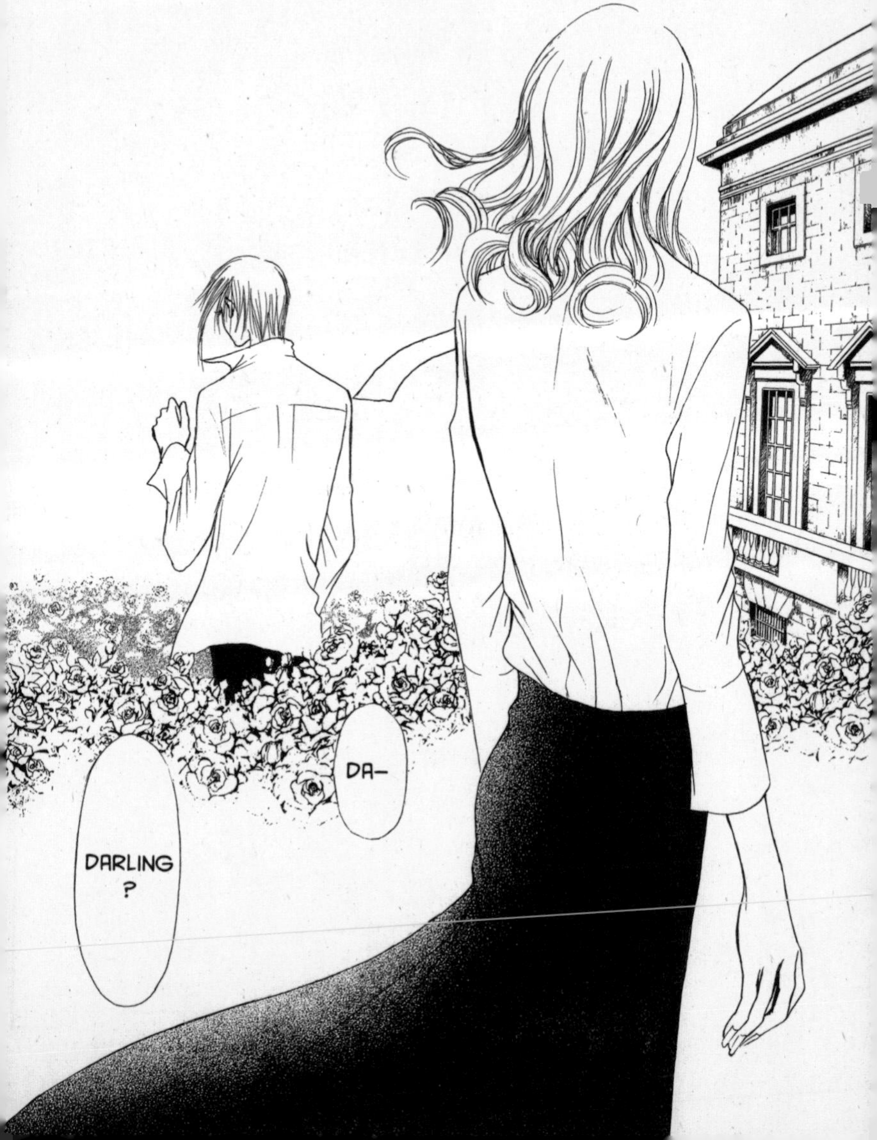
DA-
DARLING ?

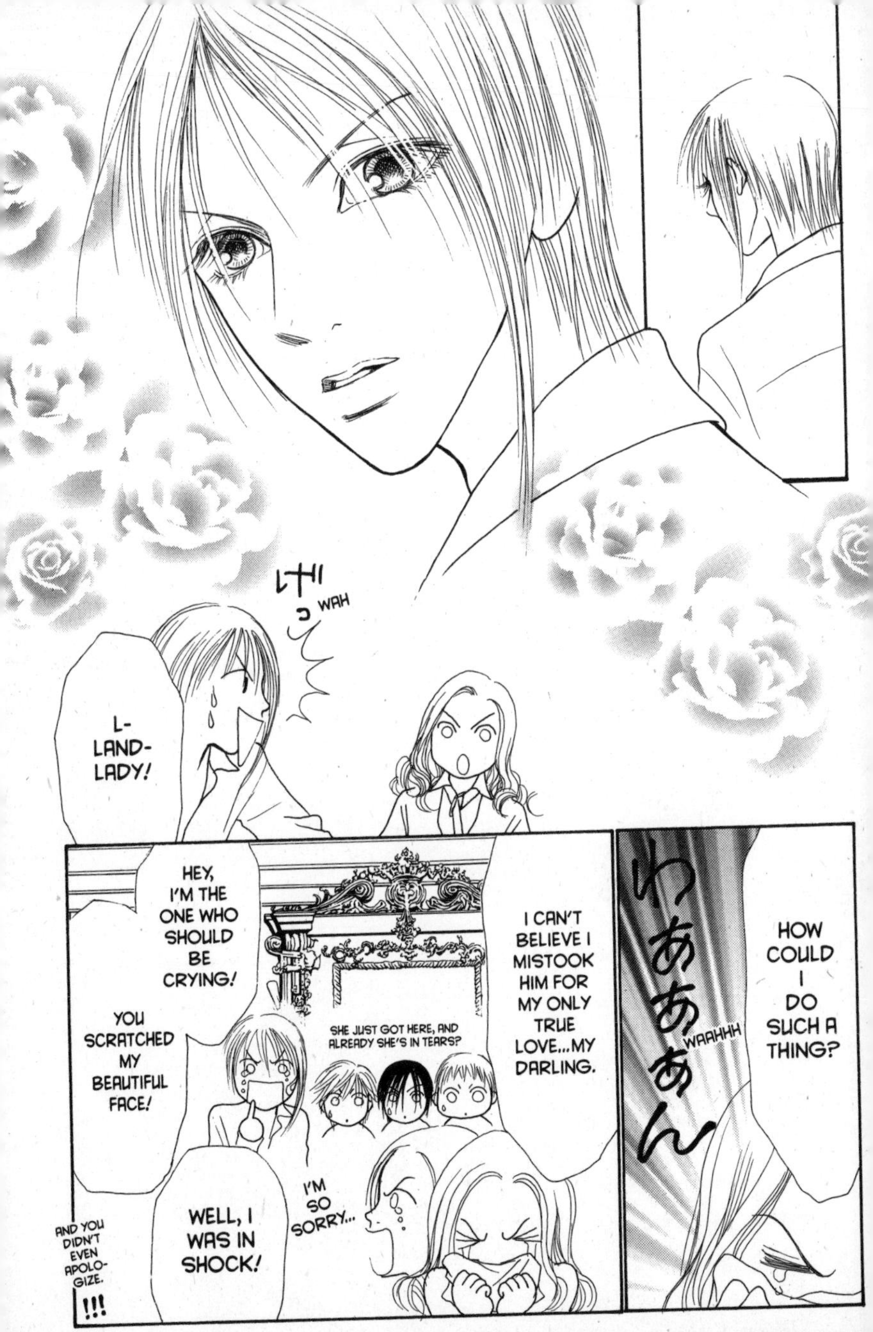

げっ
WAH
L-LANDLADY!
わあああん
WAAHHH
HOW COULD I DO SUCH A THING?
I CAN'T BELIEVE I MISTOOK HIM FOR MY ONLY TRUE LOVE...MY DARLING.
HEY, I'M THE ONE WHO SHOULD BE CRYING!
YOU SCRATCHED MY BEAUTIFUL FACE!
SHE JUST GOT HERE, AND ALREADY SHE'S IN TEARS?
I'M SO SORRY...
WELL, I WAS IN SHOCK!
AND YOU DIDN'T EVEN APOLOGIZE.
!!!

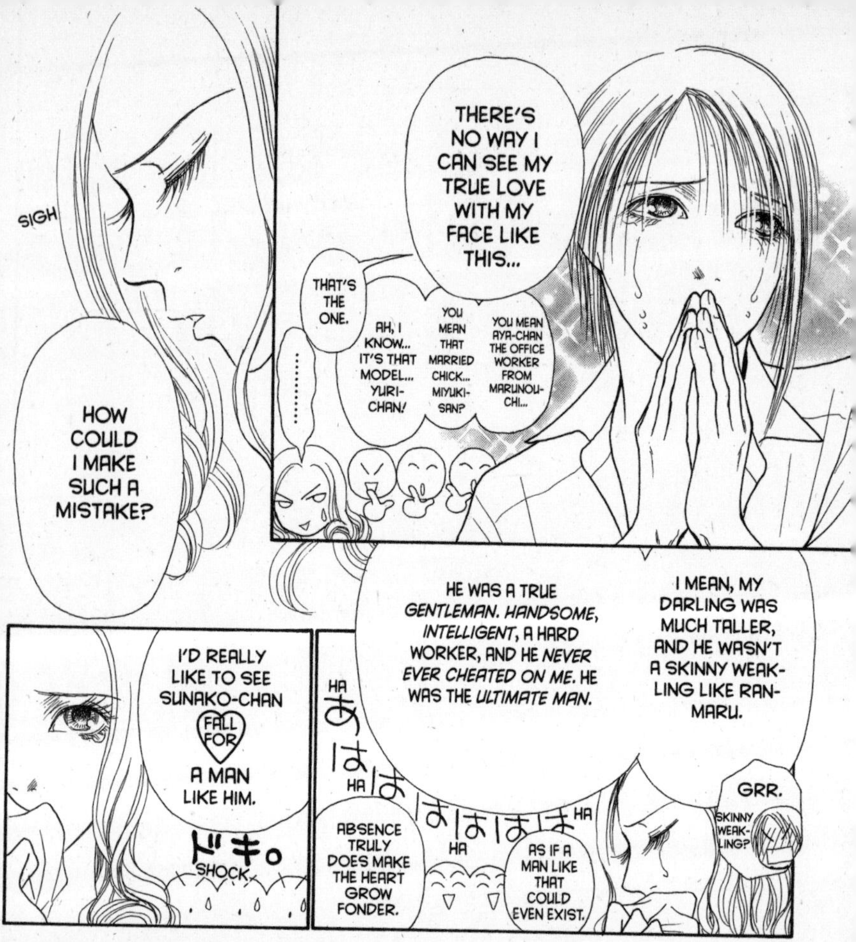
THERE'S NO WAY I CAN SEE MY TRUE LOVE WITH MY FACE LIKE THIS...
YOU MEAN AYA-CHAN THE OFFICE WORKER FROM MARUNOUCHI...
YOU MEAN THAT MARRIED CHICK... MIYUKI-SAN?
AH, I KNOW... IT'S THAT MODEL... YURI-CHAN!
THAT'S THE ONE.
....
SIGH
HOW COULD I MAKE SUCH A MISTAKE?
I MEAN, MY DARLING WAS MUCH TALLER, AND HE WASN'T A SKINNY WEAKLING LIKE RANMARU.
HE WAS A TRUE *GENTLEMAN. HANDSOME, INTELLIGENT*, A HARD WORKER, AND HE *NEVER EVER CHEATED ON ME*. HE WAS THE *ULTIMATE MAN*.
GRR.
SKINNY WEAKLING?
あははははは
HA HA HA HA
AS IF A MAN LIKE THAT COULD EVEN EXIST.
ABSENCE TRULY DOES MAKE THE HEART GROW FONDER.
I'D REALLY LIKE TO SEE SUNAKO-CHAN FALL FOR A MAN LIKE HIM.
ドキ。
SHOCK

BEHIND THE SCENES

BETWEEN THIS EPISODE AND THE PREVIOUS ONE, WE HAD A BIG WRAP PARTY FOR THE ANIME. IT WAS REALLY AMAZING TO SEE EVERYBODY INVOLVED WITH THE PROJECT IN ONE ROOM. EVERYBODY WAS REALLY NICE TO ME EVEN THOUGH I ONLY WENT TO ONE VOICE-OVER SESSION. ♡ ALL OF THE ACTORS WERE SO KIND. ♡ THE GIRLS WHO PLAYED THE MAIN CHARACTERS WERE SUPER-CUTE. ♡ THEY WERE SMILING THE WHOLE TIME. THE GUYS WERE REALLY COOL TOO... AND FUNNY. THEY'RE HILARIOUS, AND THEY HAVE GREAT VOICES. THEY'RE SO LUCKY. ♡ EVERYONE REALLY WAS SUPER-COOL. MORIKUBO-SAN WHO PLAYS KYOHEI WAS REALLY CARING, AND HE TOTALLY HELPED ME OUT. THANKS FOR ALWAYS BEING THERE TO BACK ME UP. YOU'RE SUCH A COOL-GUY. ♡ MY ASSISTANT CHOBI-SAN IS A HUGE FAN OF MORIKUBO-SAN'S. SHE WAS GIDDY ALL DAY LONG. TO BE CONTINUED.

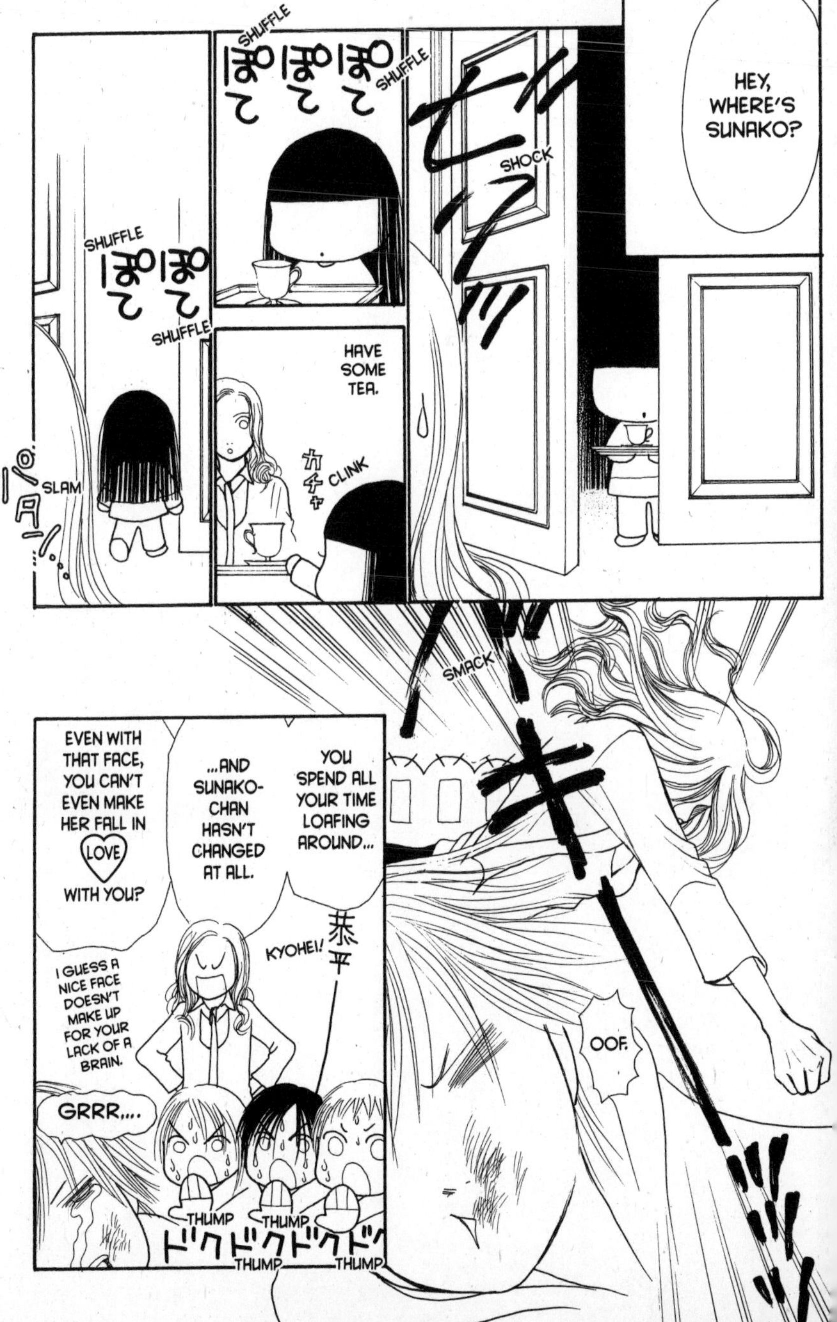
HEY, WHERE'S SUNAKO?
SHOCK
ぽぽぽ てててSHUFFLE SHUFFLE
HAVE SOME TEA.
カチャ CLINK
ぽぽ てて SHUFFLE SHUFFLE
SLAM
SMACK
OOF.
YOU SPEND ALL YOUR TIME LOAFING AROUND...
...AND SUNAKO-CHAN HASN'T CHANGED AT ALL.
EVEN WITH THAT FACE, YOU CAN'T EVEN MAKE HER FALL IN LOVE WITH YOU?
恭平 KYOHEI!
I GUESS A NICE FACE DOESN'T MAKE UP FOR YOUR LACK OF A BRAIN.
GRRR,...
ドクドクドクドク THUMP THUMP THUMP THUMP

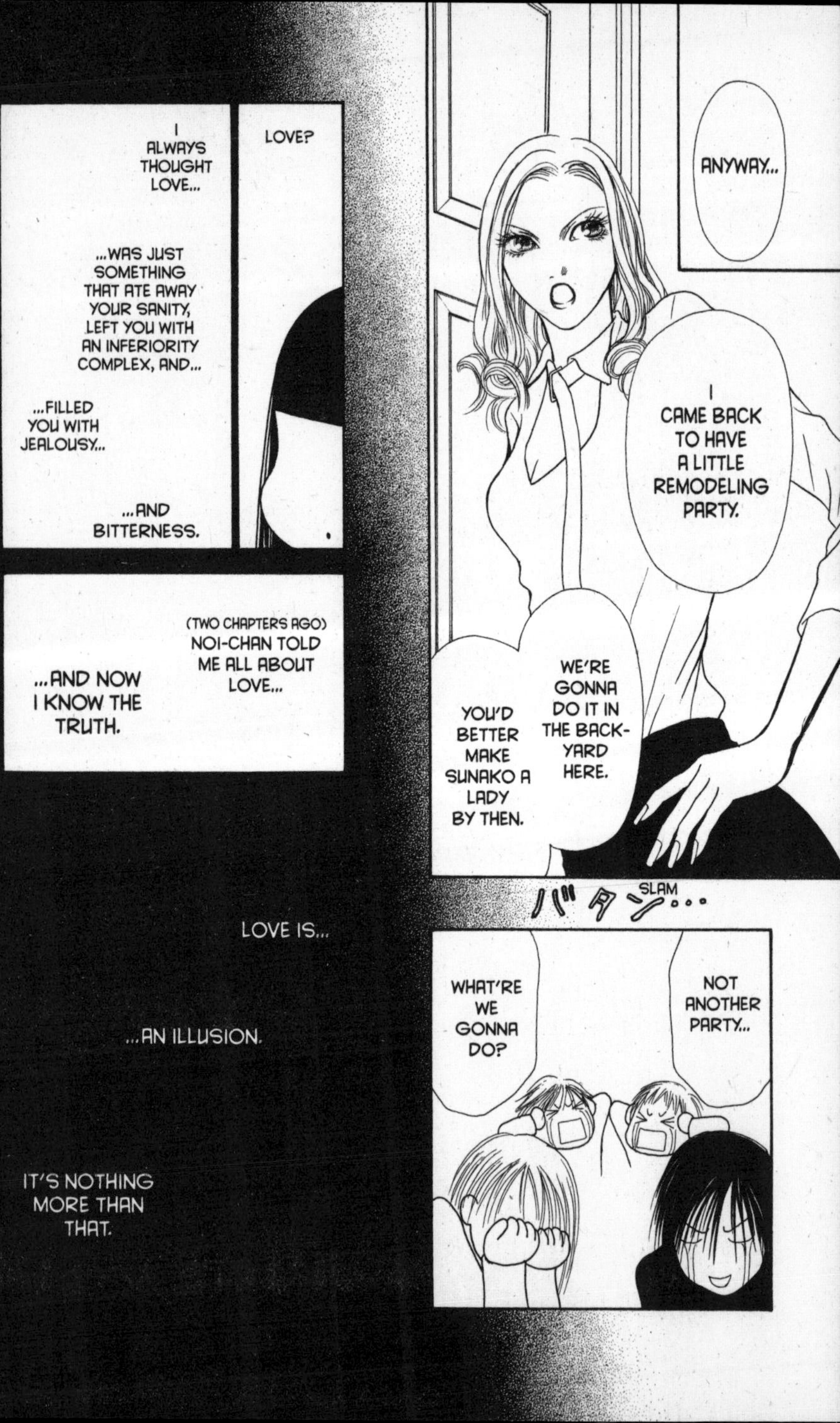
ANYWAY...
I CAME BACK TO HAVE A LITTLE REMODELING PARTY.
WE'RE GONNA DO IT IN THE BACK-YARD HERE.
YOU'D BETTER MAKE SUNAKO A LADY BY THEN.
バタン SLAM
NOT ANOTHER PARTY...
WHAT'RE WE GONNA DO?
LOVE?
I ALWAYS THOUGHT LOVE...
...WAS JUST SOMETHING THAT ATE AWAY YOUR SANITY, LEFT YOU WITH AN INFERIORITY COMPLEX, AND...
...FILLED YOU WITH JEALOUSY...
...AND BITTERNESS.
(TWO CHAPTERS AGO) NOI-CHAN TOLD ME ALL ABOUT LOVE...
...AND NOW I KNOW THE TRUTH.
LOVE IS...
...AN ILLUSION.
IT'S NOTHING MORE THAN THAT.

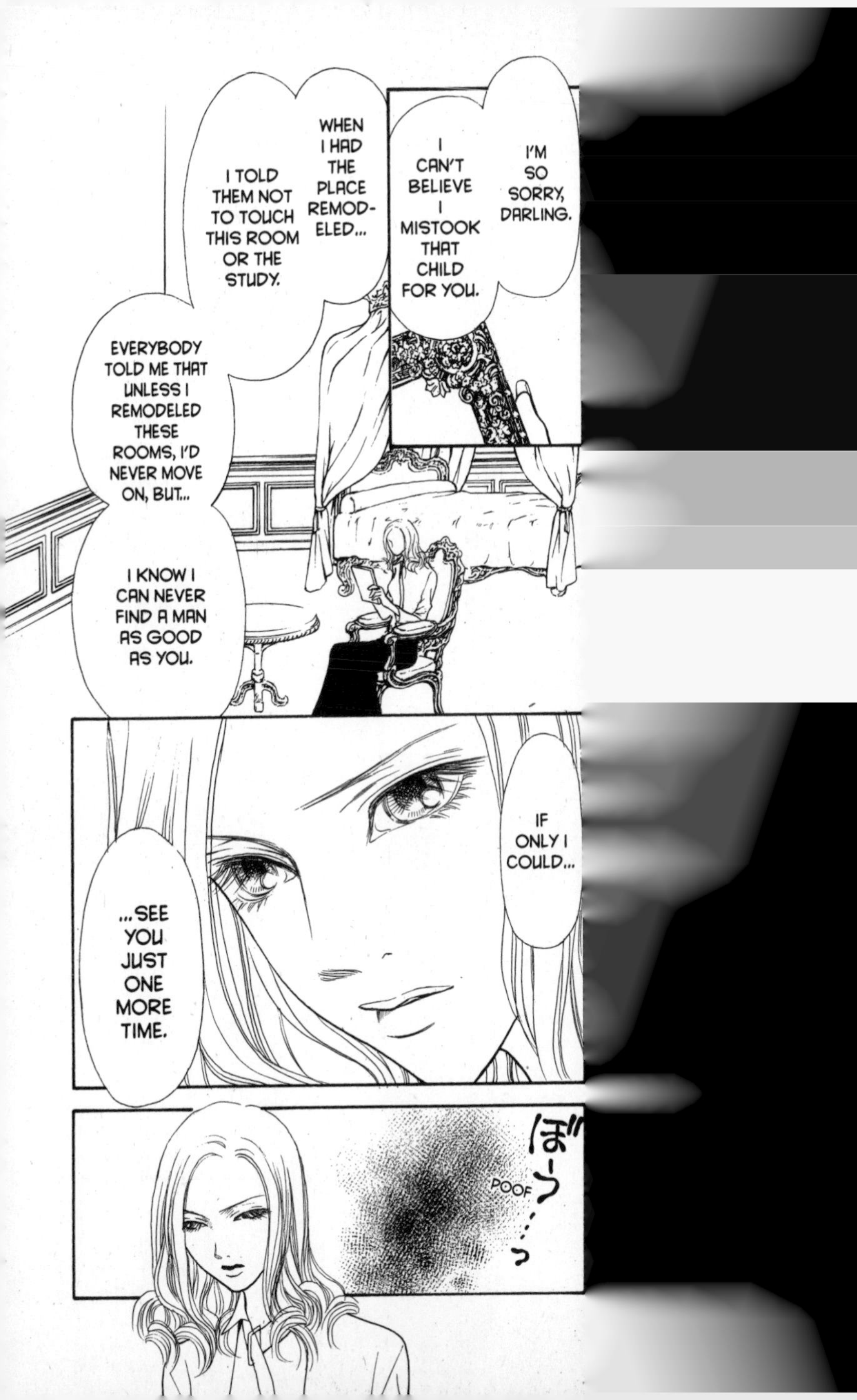
I'M SO SORRY, DARLING.
I CAN'T BELIEVE I MISTOOK THAT CHILD FOR YOU.
WHEN I HAD THE PLACE REMODELED...
I TOLD THEM NOT TO TOUCH THIS ROOM OR THE STUDY.
EVERYBODY TOLD ME THAT UNLESS I REMODELED THESE ROOMS, I'D NEVER MOVE ON, BUT...
I KNOW I CAN NEVER FIND A MAN AS GOOD AS YOU.
IF ONLY I COULD...
...SEE YOU JUST ONE MORE TIME.
ぼうっ
POOF

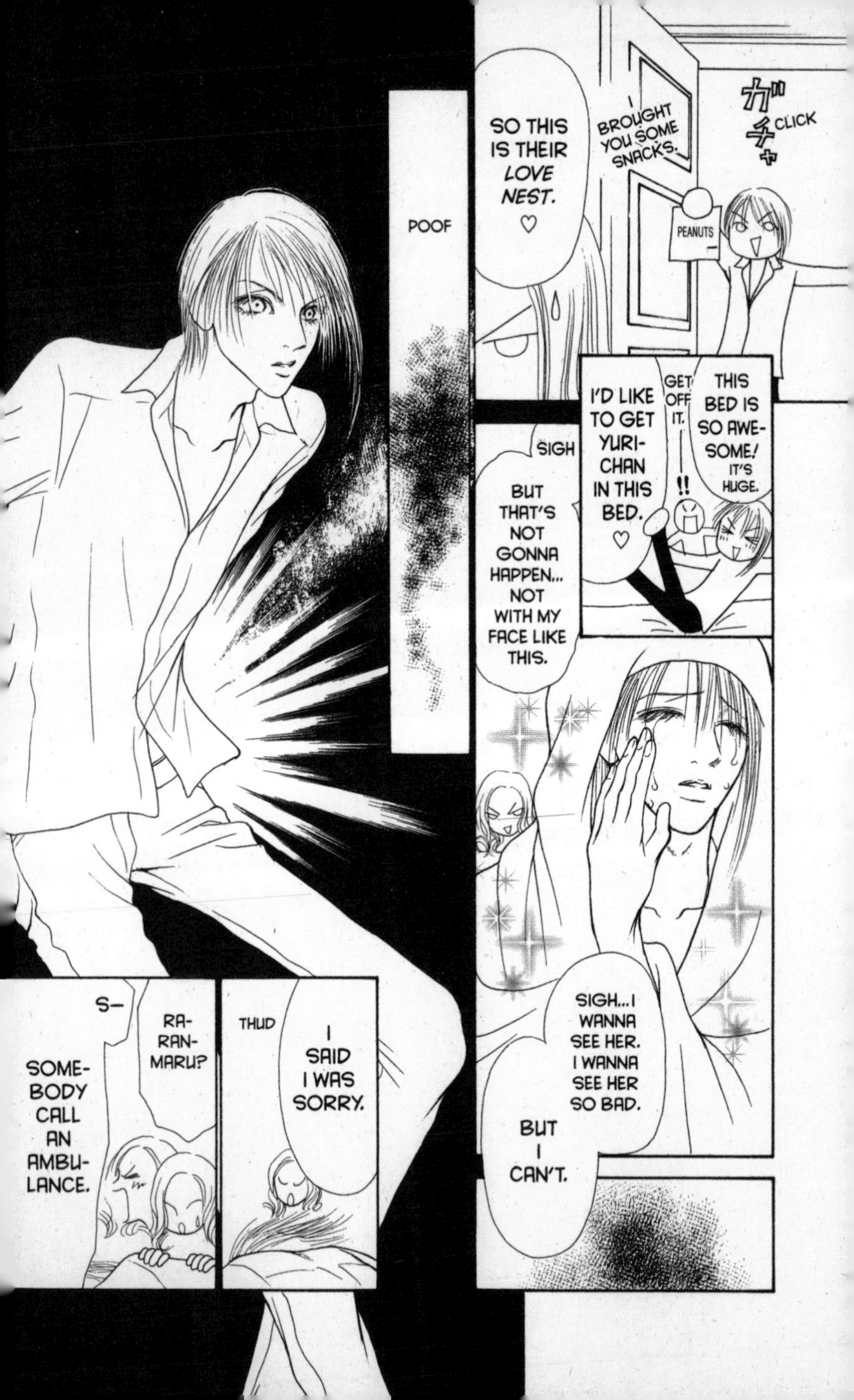
ガチャ CLICK
I BROUGHT YOU SOME SNACKS.
PEANUTS
SO THIS IS THEIR LOVE NEST. ♡
THIS BED IS SO AWESOME! IT'S HUGE.
GET OFF IT.
!!
I'D LIKE TO GET YURI-CHAN IN THIS BED. ♡
SIGH
BUT THAT'S NOT GONNA HAPPEN... NOT WITH MY FACE LIKE THIS.
SIGH...I WANNA SEE HER. I WANNA SEE HER SO BAD.
BUT I CAN'T.
POOF
THUD
I SAID I WAS SORRY.
RA-RANMARU?
S—
SOMEBODY CALL AN AMBULANCE.

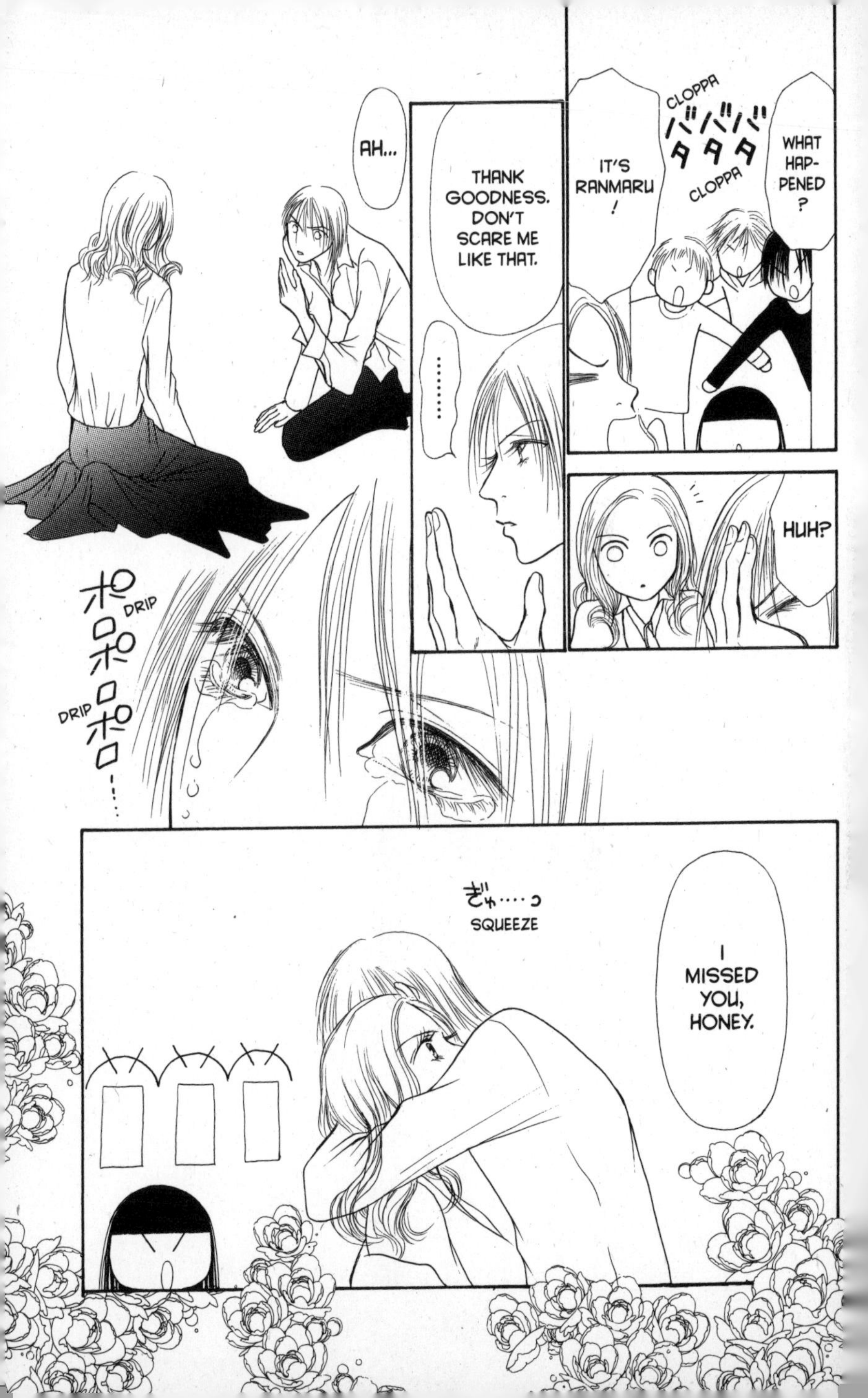
WHAT HAP-PENED?
CLOPPA
バタバタバタ
CLOPPA
IT'S RANMARU!
HUH?
THANK GOODNESS. DON'T SCARE ME LIKE THAT.
....
AH...
ポロポロポロポロ・・・
DRIP
DRIP
ぎゅ‥‥っ
SQUEEZE
I MISSED YOU, HONEY.

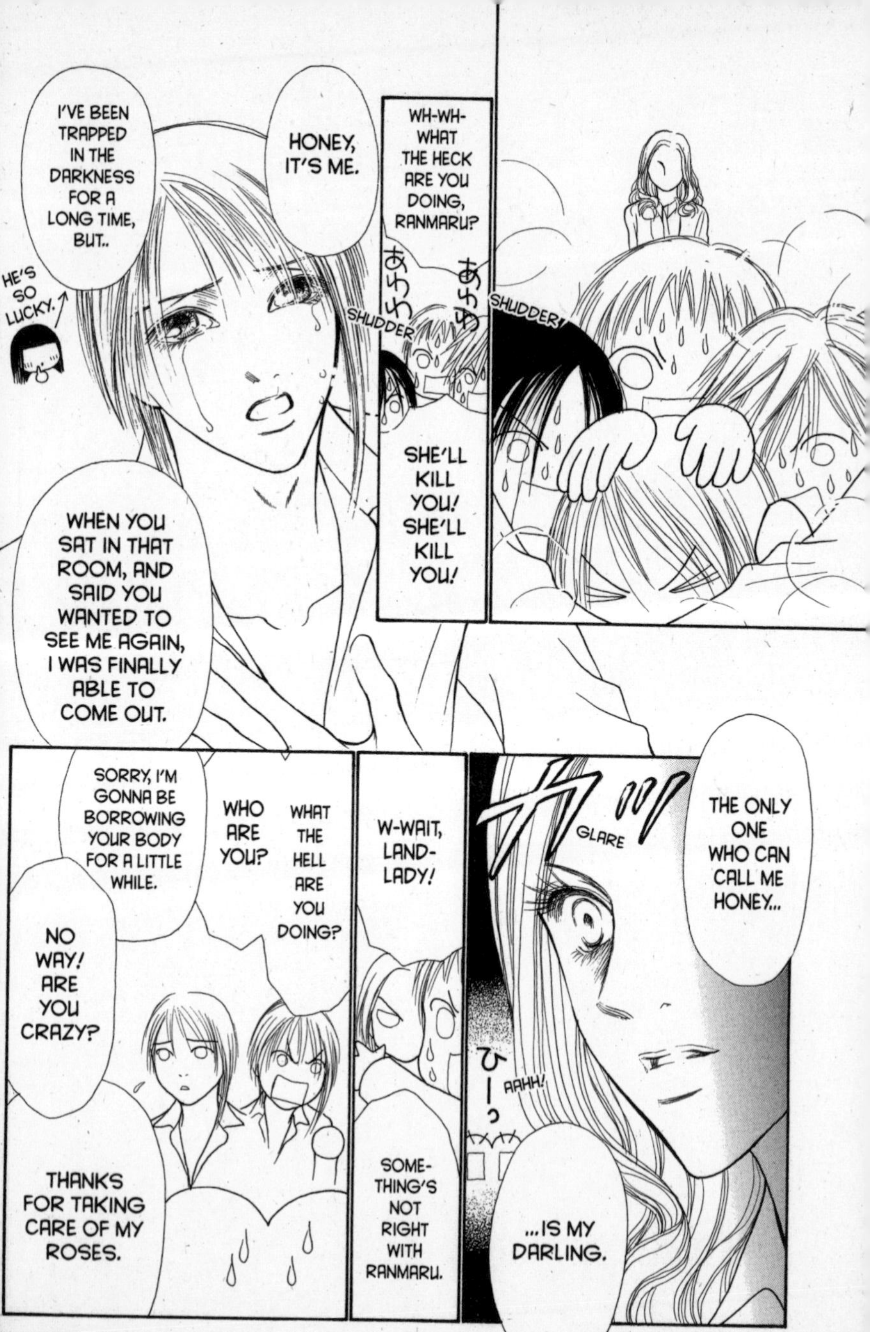
SHUDDER!
WH-WH-WHAT THE HECK ARE YOU DOING, RANMARU?
SHUDDER
SHE'LL KILL YOU! SHE'LL KILL YOU!
HONEY, IT'S ME.
I'VE BEEN TRAPPED IN THE DARKNESS FOR A LONG TIME, BUT..
HE'S SO LUCKY.
WHEN YOU SAT IN THAT ROOM, AND SAID YOU WANTED TO SEE ME AGAIN, I WAS FINALLY ABLE TO COME OUT.
GLARE
THE ONLY ONE WHO CAN CALL ME HONEY...
ひーっ
AAHH!
...IS MY DARLING.
W-WAIT, LANDLADY!
SOMETHING'S NOT RIGHT WITH RANMARU.
WHAT THE HELL ARE YOU DOING?
WHO ARE YOU?
SORRY, I'M GONNA BE BORROWING YOUR BODY FOR A LITTLE WHILE.
NO WAY! ARE YOU CRAZY?
THANKS FOR TAKING CARE OF MY ROSES.

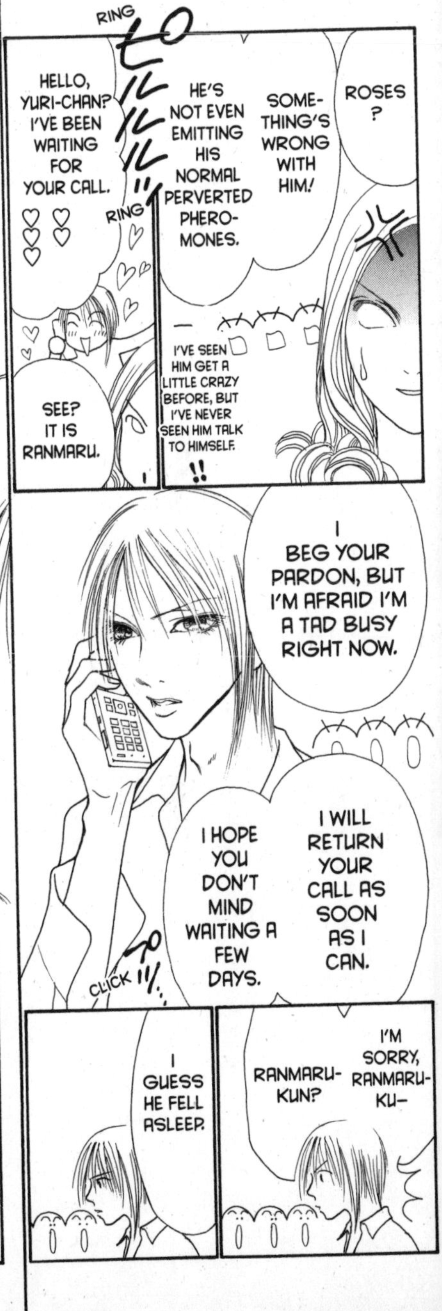
RING
ROSES?
SOMETHING'S WRONG WITH HIM!
HE'S NOT EVEN EMITTING HIS NORMAL PERVERTED PHEROMONES.
I'VE SEEN HIM GET A LITTLE CRAZY BEFORE, BUT I'VE NEVER SEEN HIM TALK TO HIMSELF.
!!
RING
HELLO, YURI-CHAN? I'VE BEEN WAITING FOR YOUR CALL.
SEE? IT IS RANMARU.
I BEG YOUR PARDON, BUT I'M AFRAID I'M A TAD BUSY RIGHT NOW.
I WILL RETURN YOUR CALL AS SOON AS I CAN.
I HOPE YOU DON'T MIND WAITING A FEW DAYS.
CLICK
I'M SORRY, RANMARU-KU-
RANMARU-KUN?
I GUESS HE FELL ASLEEP.
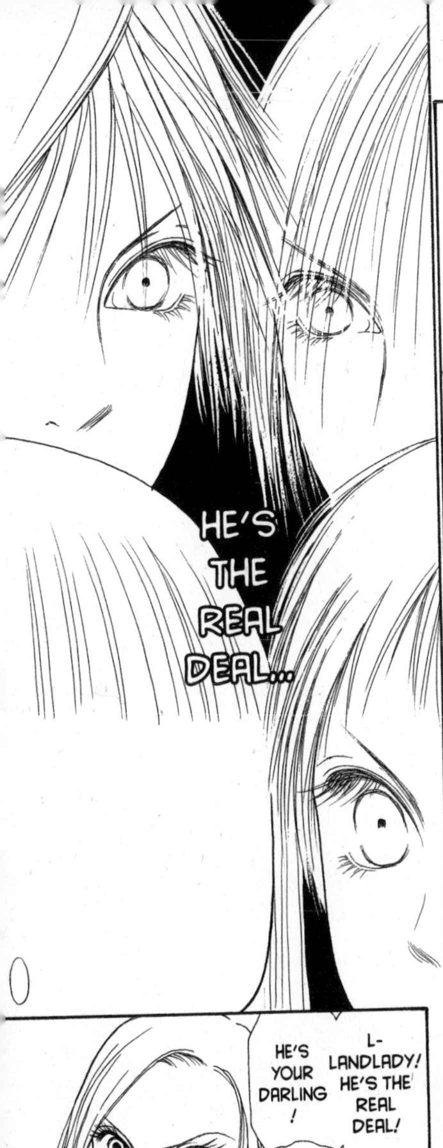
HE'S THE REAL DEAL...
L-LANDLADY! HE'S THE REAL DEAL!
HE'S YOUR DARLING!
I-IT'S NOT RANMARU...?

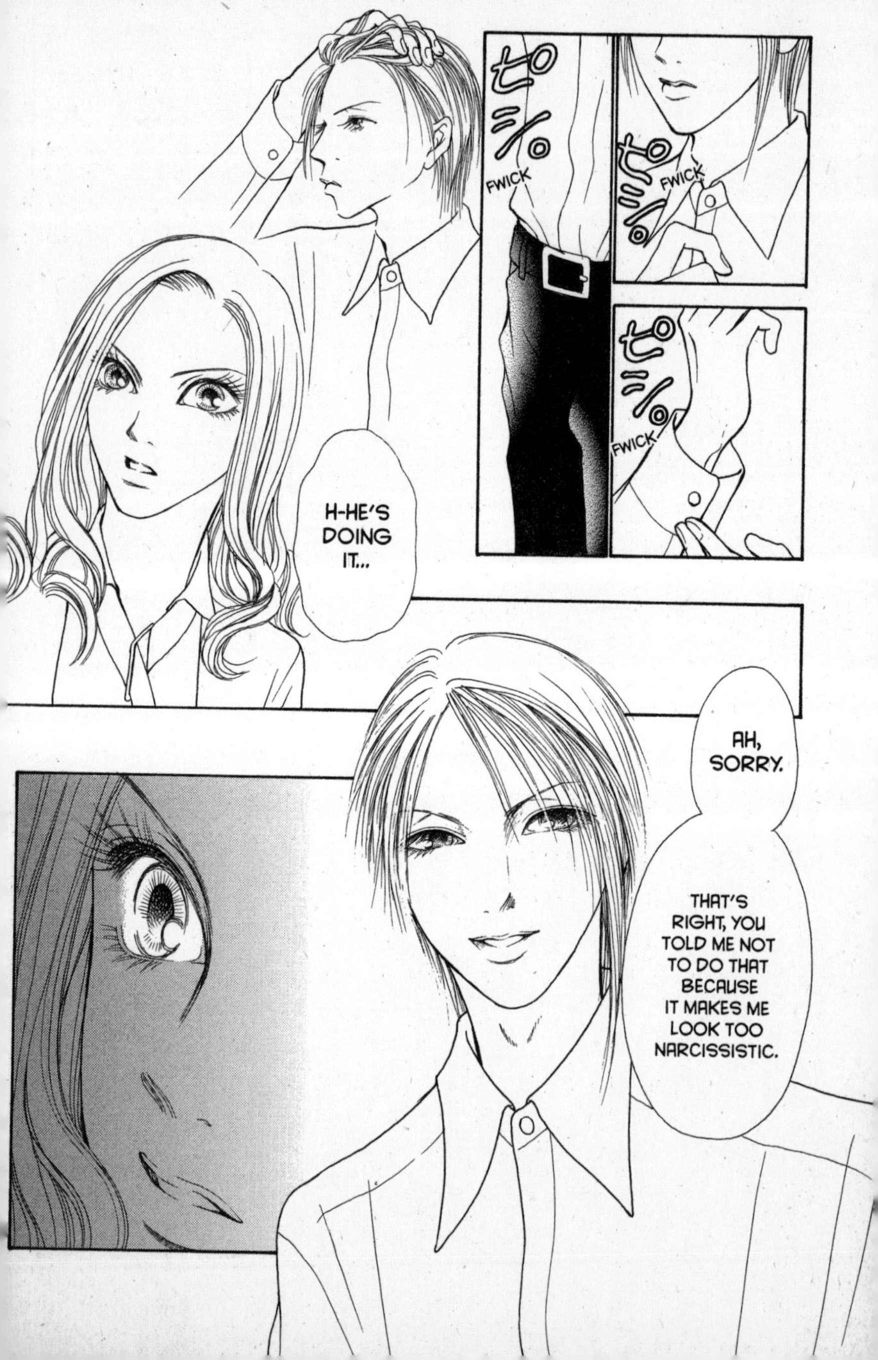
FWICK
FWICK
FWICK
H-HE'S DOING IT...
AH, SORRY.
THAT'S RIGHT, YOU TOLD ME NOT TO DO THAT BECAUSE IT MAKES ME LOOK TOO NARCISSISTIC.

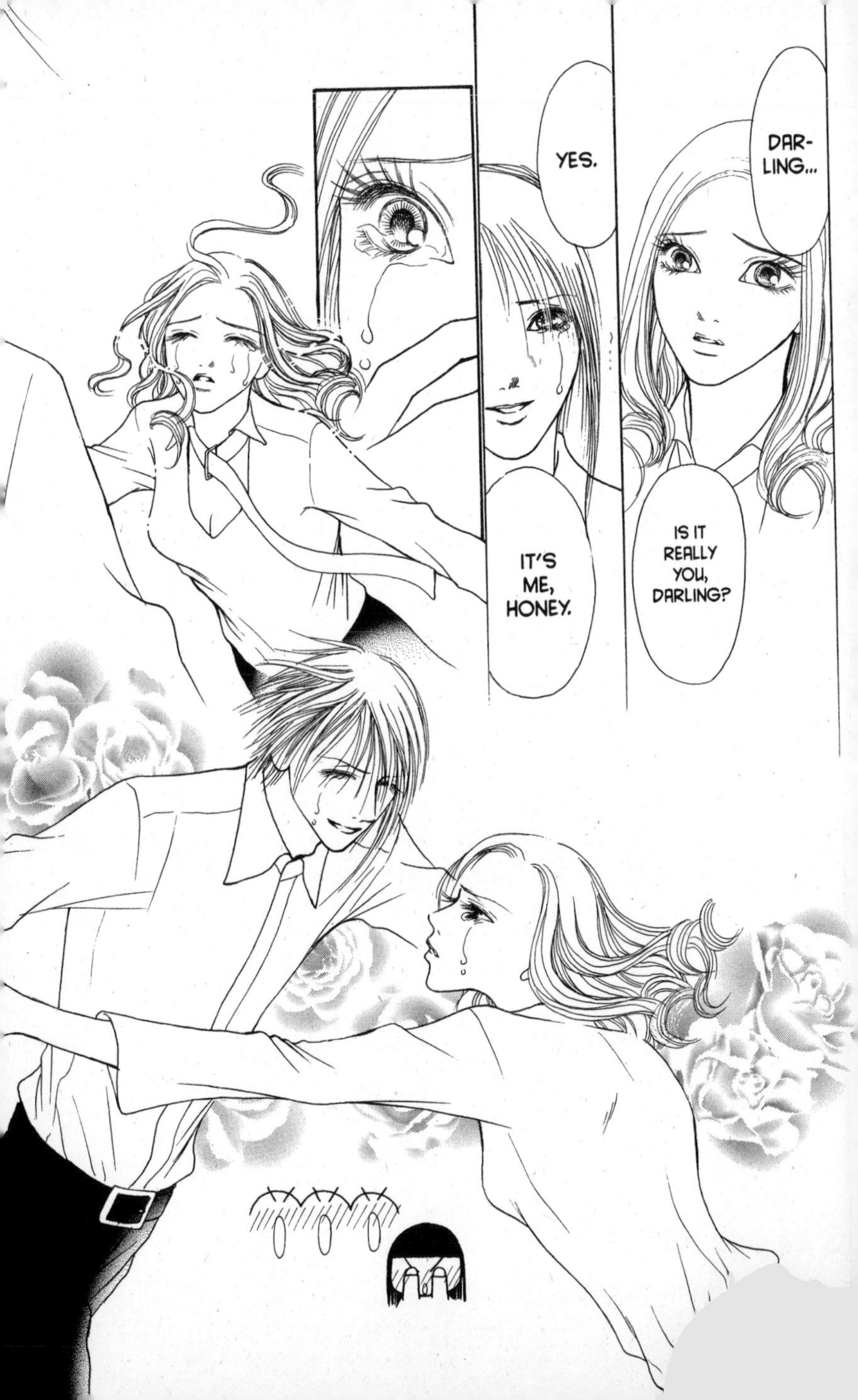
DAR-LING...
IS IT REALLY YOU, DARLING?
YES.
IT'S ME, HONEY.

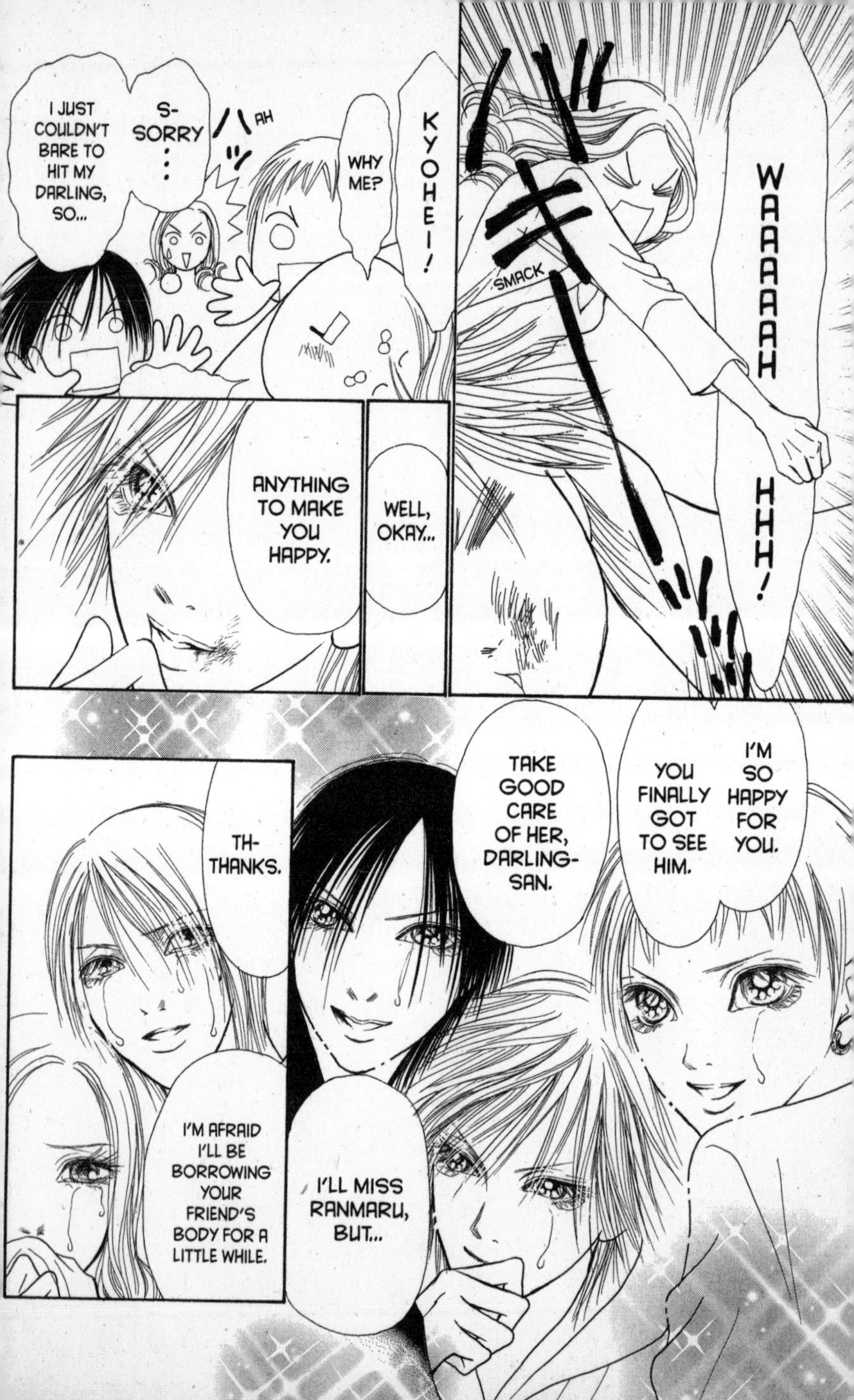
WAAAAAAHHHH!
バキーッ!!
SMACK
KYOHEI!
WHY ME?
ハッ AH
S-SORRY...
I JUST COULDN'T BARE TO HIT MY DARLING, SO...
WELL, OKAY...
ANYTHING TO MAKE YOU HAPPY.
I'M SO HAPPY FOR YOU.
YOU FINALLY GOT TO SEE HIM.
TAKE GOOD CARE OF HER, DARLING-SAN.
TH-THANKS.
I'LL MISS RANMARU, BUT...
I'M AFRAID I'LL BE BORROWING YOUR FRIEND'S BODY FOR A LITTLE WHILE.

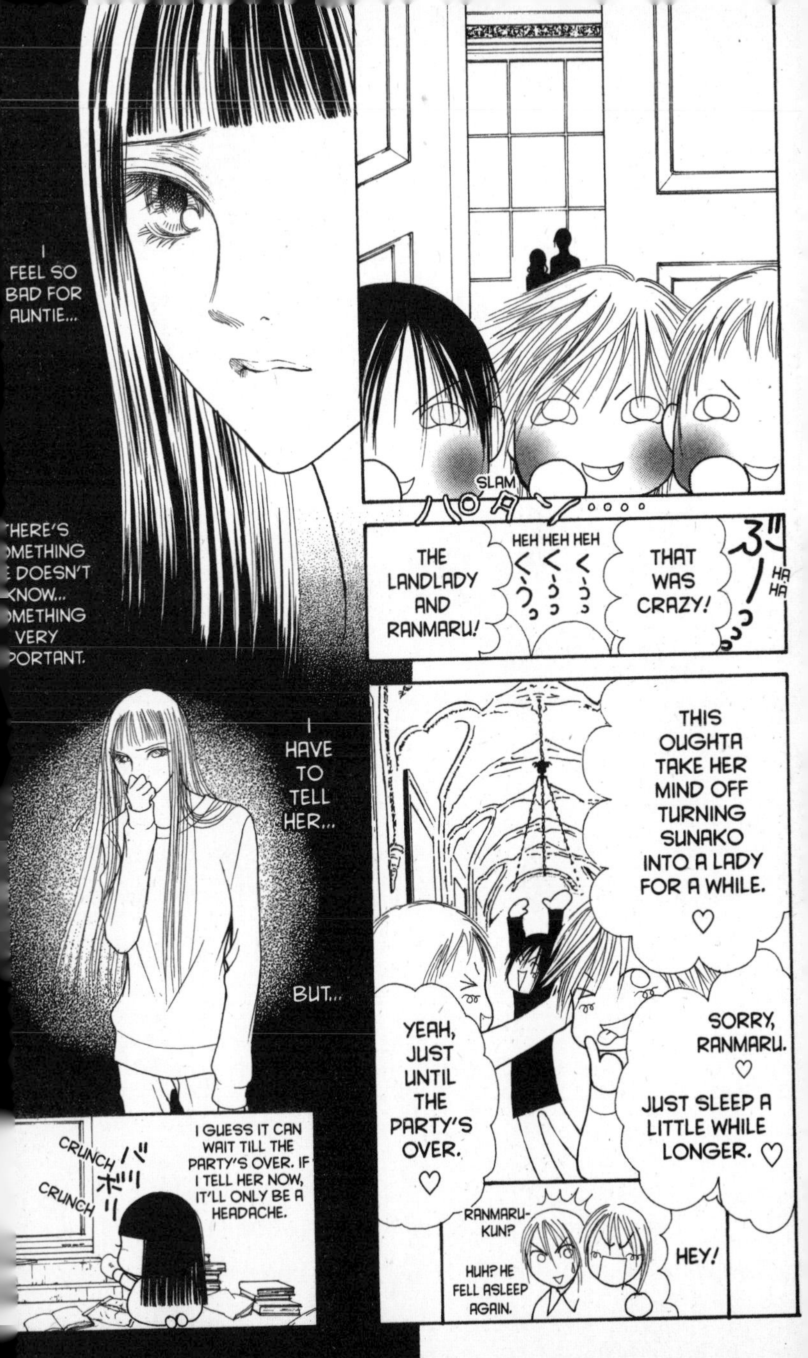
SLAM
HEH HEH HEH
THAT WAS CRAZY!
HA HA
THE LANDLADY AND RANMARU!
THIS OUGHTA TAKE HER MIND OFF TURNING SUNAKO INTO A LADY FOR A WHILE. ♡
SORRY, RANMARU. ♡
JUST SLEEP A LITTLE WHILE LONGER. ♡
YEAH, JUST UNTIL THE PARTY'S OVER. ♡
HEY!
RANMARU-KUN?
HUH? HE FELL ASLEEP AGAIN.
I FEEL SO BAD FOR AUNTIE...
THERE'S OMETHING E DOESN'T KNOW... OMETHING VERY PORTANT.
I HAVE TO TELL HER...
BUT...
I GUESS IT CAN WAIT TILL THE PARTY'S OVER. IF I TELL HER NOW, IT'LL ONLY BE A HEADACHE.
CRUNCH
CRUNCH

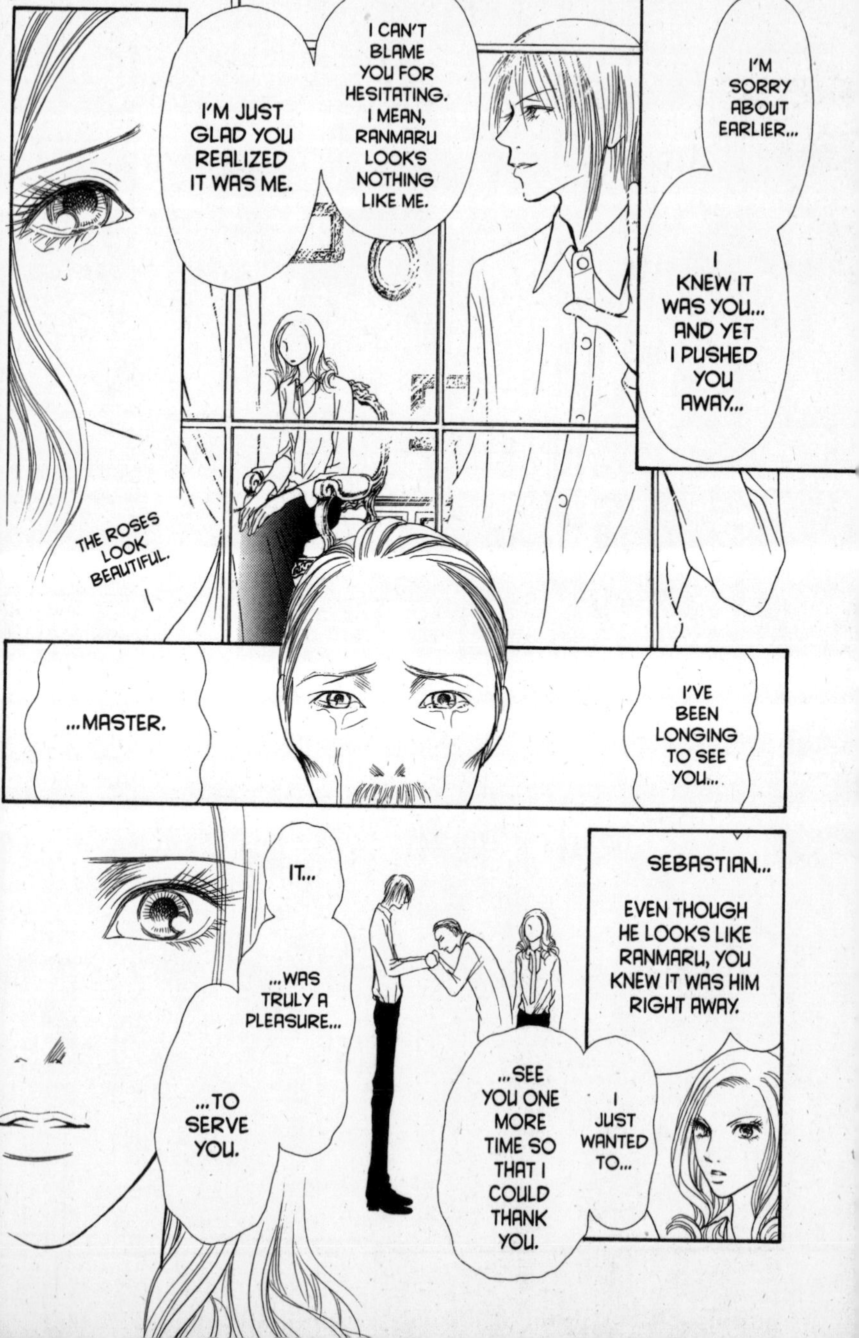
I'M SORRY ABOUT EARLIER...
I KNEW IT WAS YOU... AND YET I PUSHED YOU AWAY...
I CAN'T BLAME YOU FOR HESITATING. I MEAN, RANMARU LOOKS NOTHING LIKE ME.
I'M JUST GLAD YOU REALIZED IT WAS ME.
THE ROSES LOOK BEAUTIFUL.
I'VE BEEN LONGING TO SEE YOU...
...MASTER.
SEBASTIAN...
EVEN THOUGH HE LOOKS LIKE RANMARU, YOU KNEW IT WAS HIM RIGHT AWAY.
I JUST WANTED TO...
...SEE YOU ONE MORE TIME SO THAT I COULD THANK YOU.
IT...
...WAS TRULY A PLEASURE...
...TO SERVE YOU.

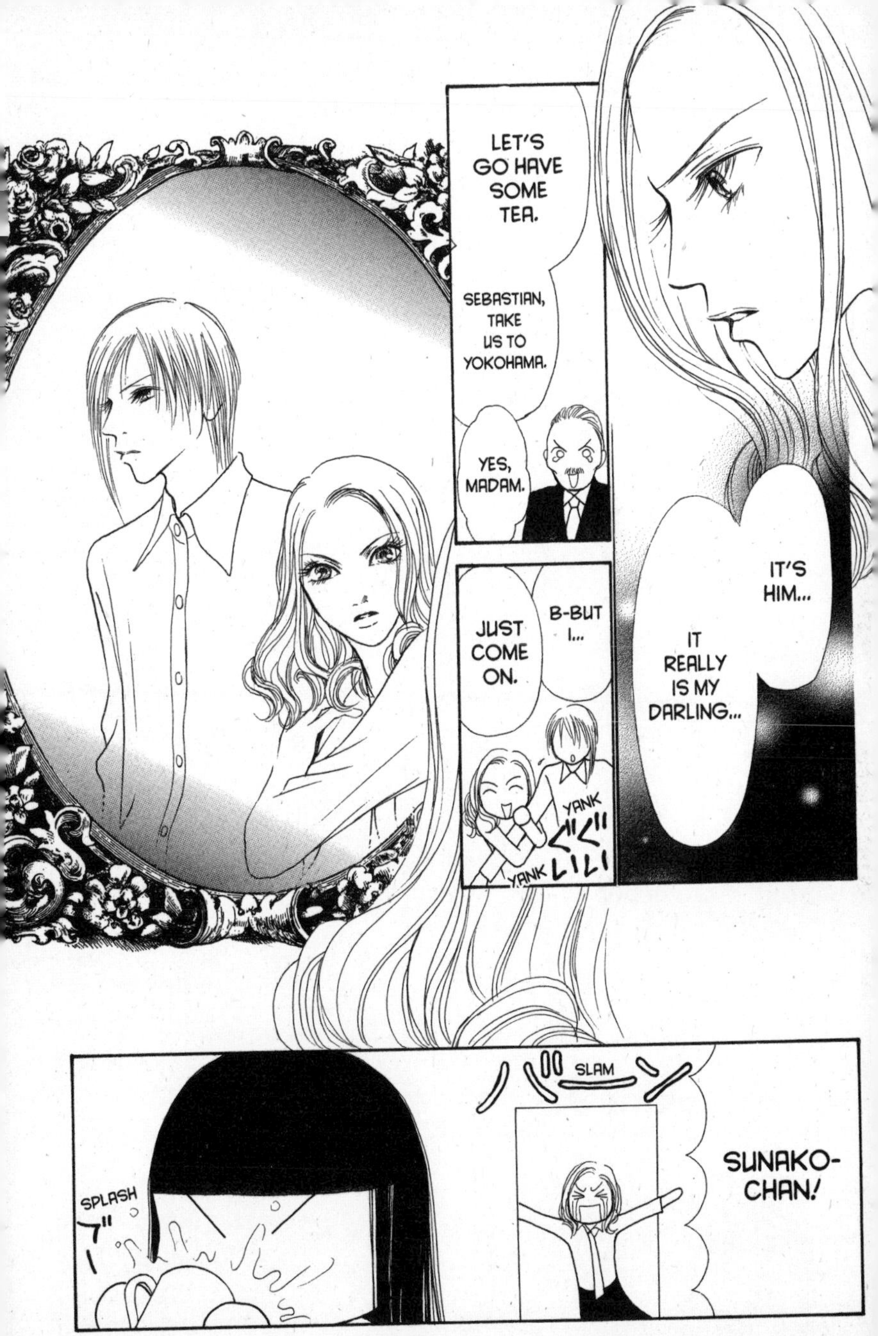
IT'S HIM...
IT REALLY IS MY DARLING...
LET'S GO HAVE SOME TEA.
SEBASTIAN, TAKE US TO YOKOHAMA.
YES, MADAM.
B-BUT I...
JUST COME ON.
YANK
YANK
SLAM
SUNAKO-CHAN!
SPLASH

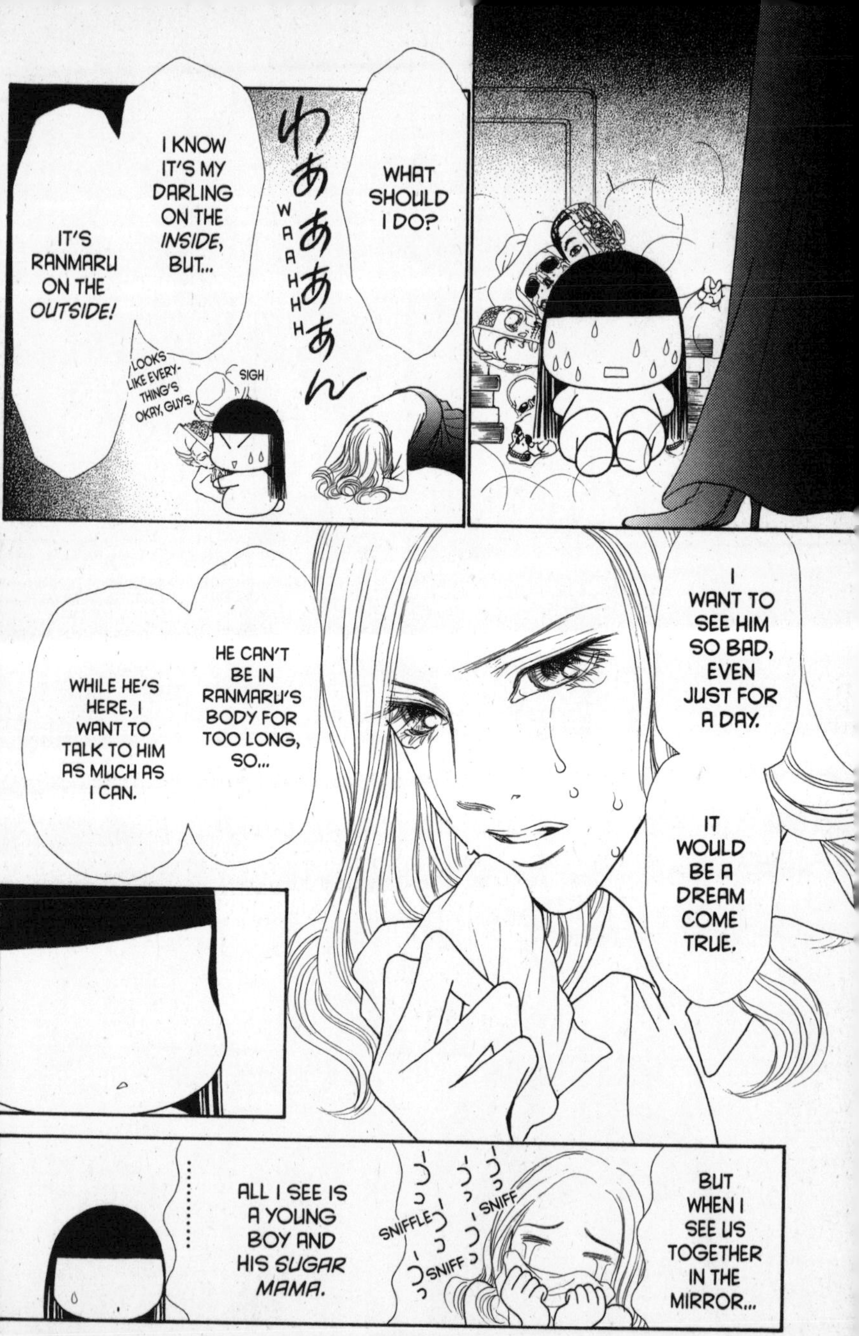
WHAT SHOULD I DO?
わあああん
WAAAHHH
I KNOW IT'S MY DARLING ON THE *INSIDE*, BUT...
IT'S RANMARU ON THE *OUTSIDE!*
SIGH
LOOKS LIKE EVERY-THING'S OKAY, GUYS.
I WANT TO SEE HIM SO BAD, EVEN JUST FOR A DAY.
IT WOULD BE A DREAM COME TRUE.
HE CAN'T BE IN RANMARU'S BODY FOR TOO LONG, SO...
WHILE HE'S HERE, I WANT TO TALK TO HIM AS MUCH AS I CAN.
BUT WHEN I SEE US TOGETHER IN THE MIRROR...
SNIFF
SNIFFLE
SNIFF
ALL I SEE IS A YOUNG BOY AND HIS *SUGAR MAMA.*
......

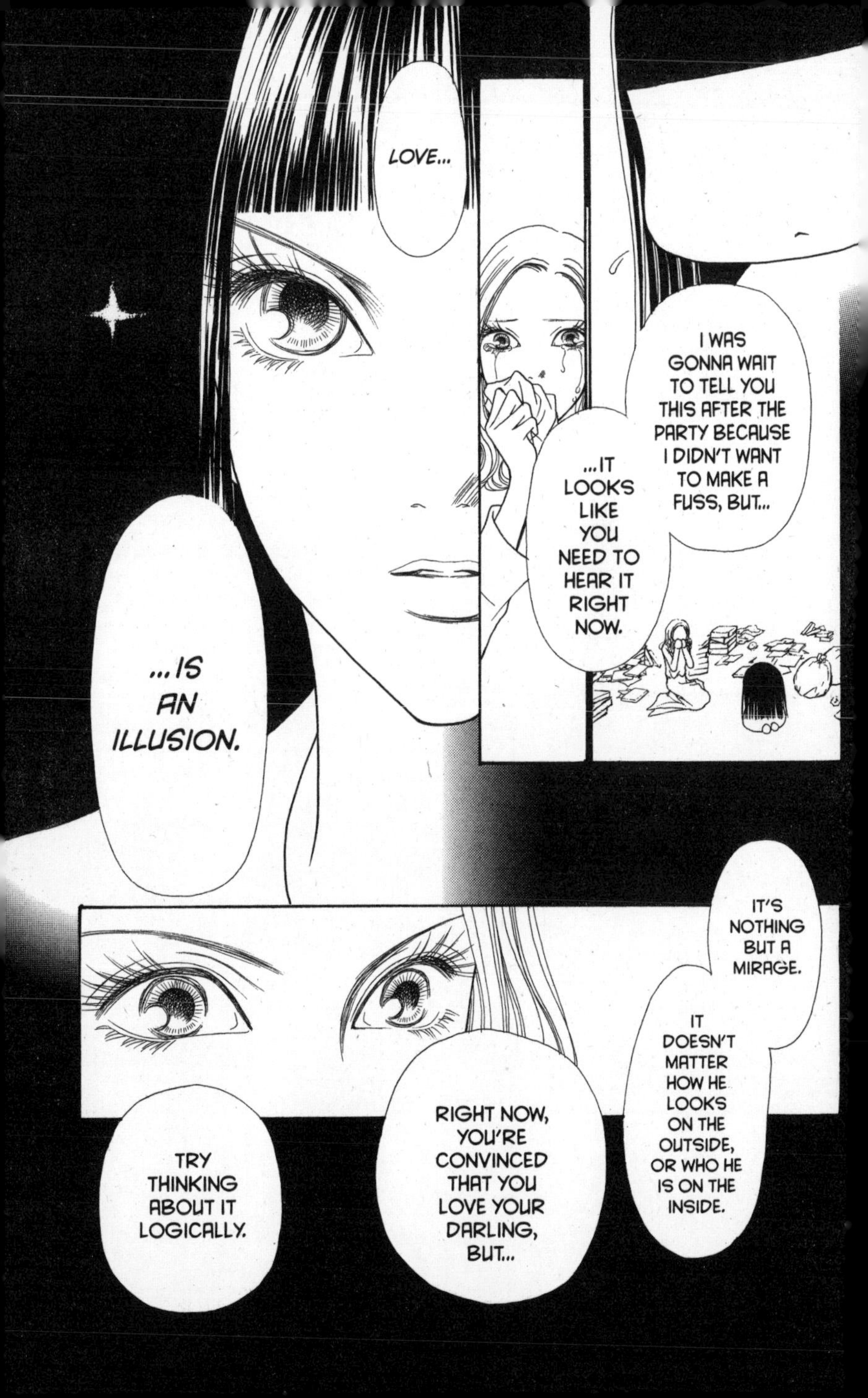
I WAS GONNA WAIT TO TELL YOU THIS AFTER THE PARTY BECAUSE I DIDN'T WANT TO MAKE A FUSS, BUT...
...IT LOOKS LIKE YOU NEED TO HEAR IT RIGHT NOW.
LOVE...
...IS AN ILLUSION.
IT'S NOTHING BUT A MIRAGE.
IT DOESN'T MATTER HOW HE LOOKS ON THE OUTSIDE, OR WHO HE IS ON THE INSIDE.
RIGHT NOW, YOU'RE CONVINCED THAT YOU LOVE YOUR DARLING, BUT...
TRY THINKING ABOUT IT LOGICALLY.

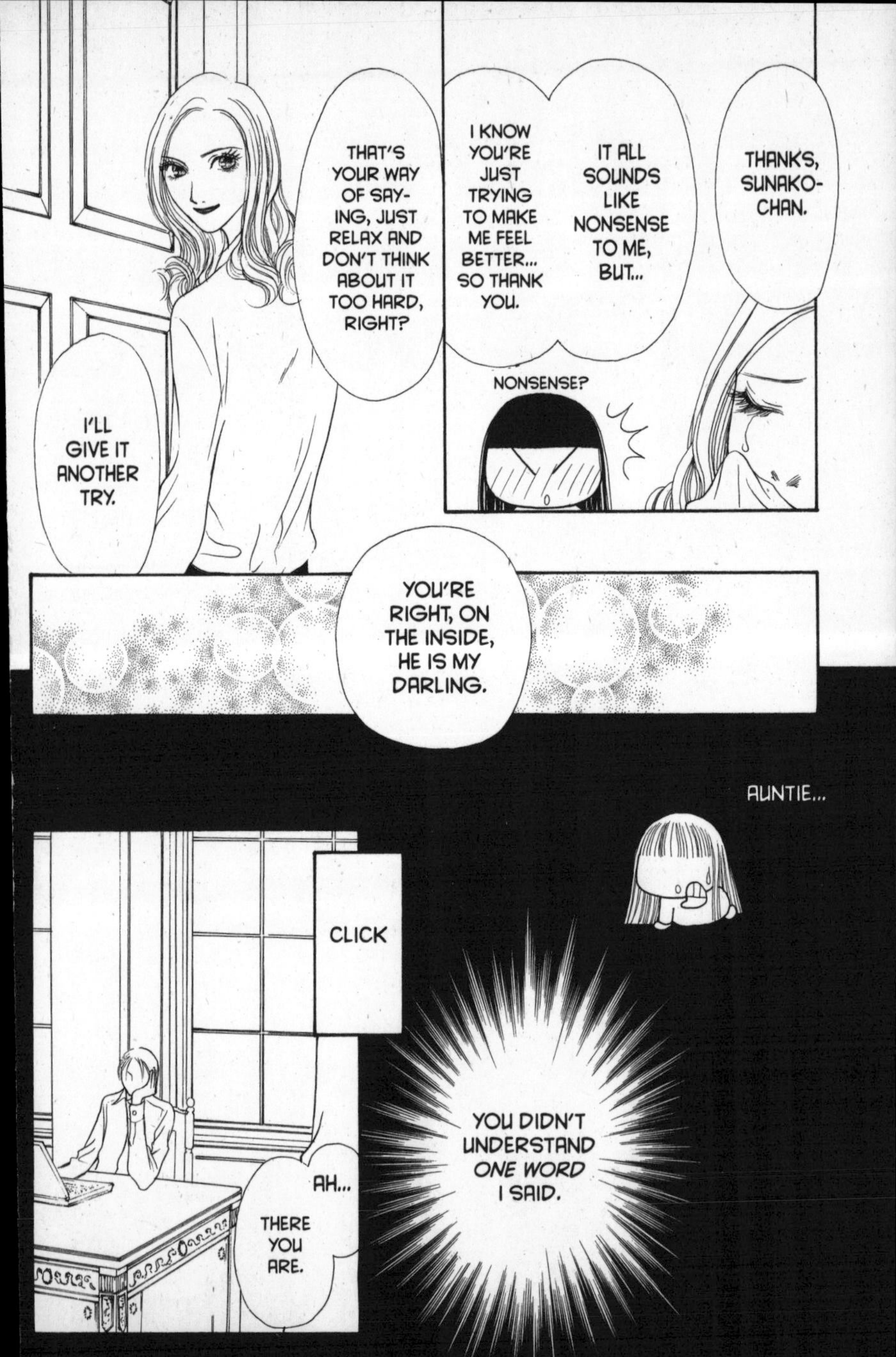
THANKS, SUNAKO-CHAN.
IT ALL SOUNDS LIKE NONSENSE TO ME, BUT...
I KNOW YOU'RE JUST TRYING TO MAKE ME FEEL BETTER... SO THANK YOU.
NONSENSE?
THAT'S YOUR WAY OF SAY-ING, JUST RELAX AND DON'T THINK ABOUT IT TOO HARD, RIGHT?
I'LL GIVE IT ANOTHER TRY.
YOU'RE RIGHT, ON THE INSIDE, HE IS MY DARLING.
AUNTIE...
YOU DIDN'T UNDERSTAND *ONE WORD* I SAID.
CLICK
AH...
THERE YOU ARE.

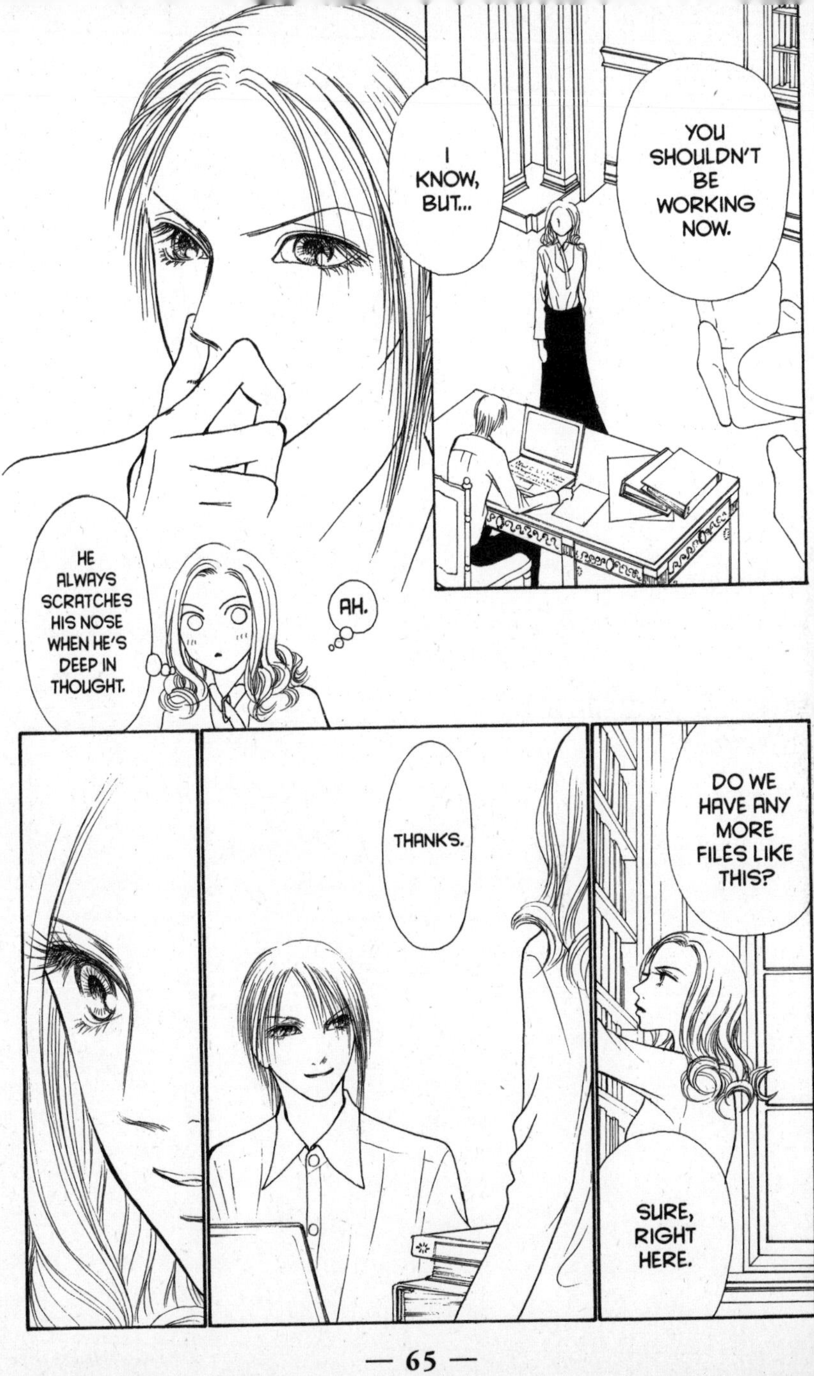
YOU SHOULDN'T BE WORKING NOW.
I KNOW, BUT...
AH.
HE ALWAYS SCRATCHES HIS NOSE WHEN HE'S DEEP IN THOUGHT.
DO WE HAVE ANY MORE FILES LIKE THIS?
SURE, RIGHT HERE.
THANKS.

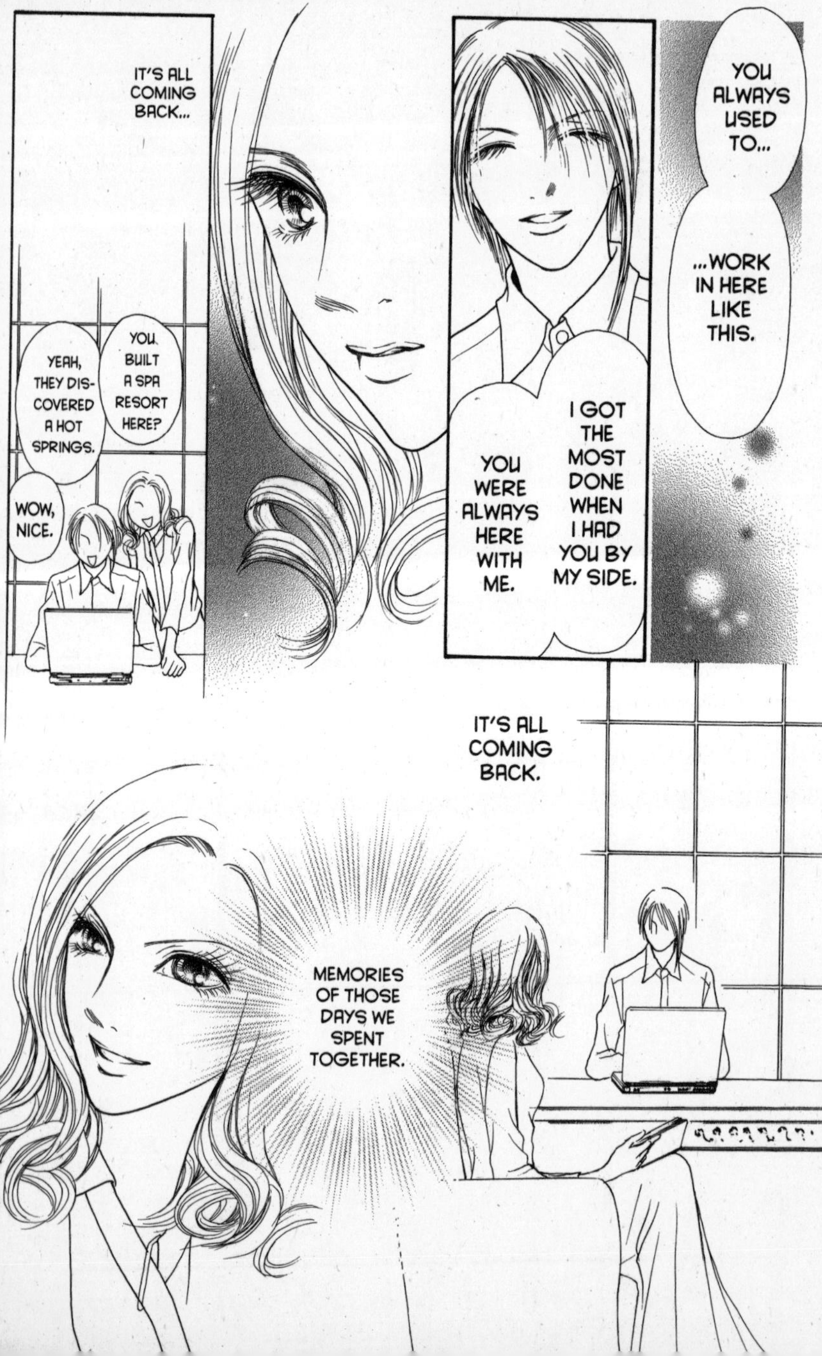
YOU ALWAYS USED TO...
...WORK IN HERE LIKE THIS.
I GOT THE MOST DONE WHEN I HAD YOU BY MY SIDE.
YOU WERE ALWAYS HERE WITH ME.
IT'S ALL COMING BACK...
YOU BUILT A SPA RESORT HERE?
YEAH, THEY DIS-COVERED A HOT SPRINGS.
WOW, NICE.
IT'S ALL COMING BACK.
MEMORIES OF THOSE DAYS WE SPENT TOGETHER.

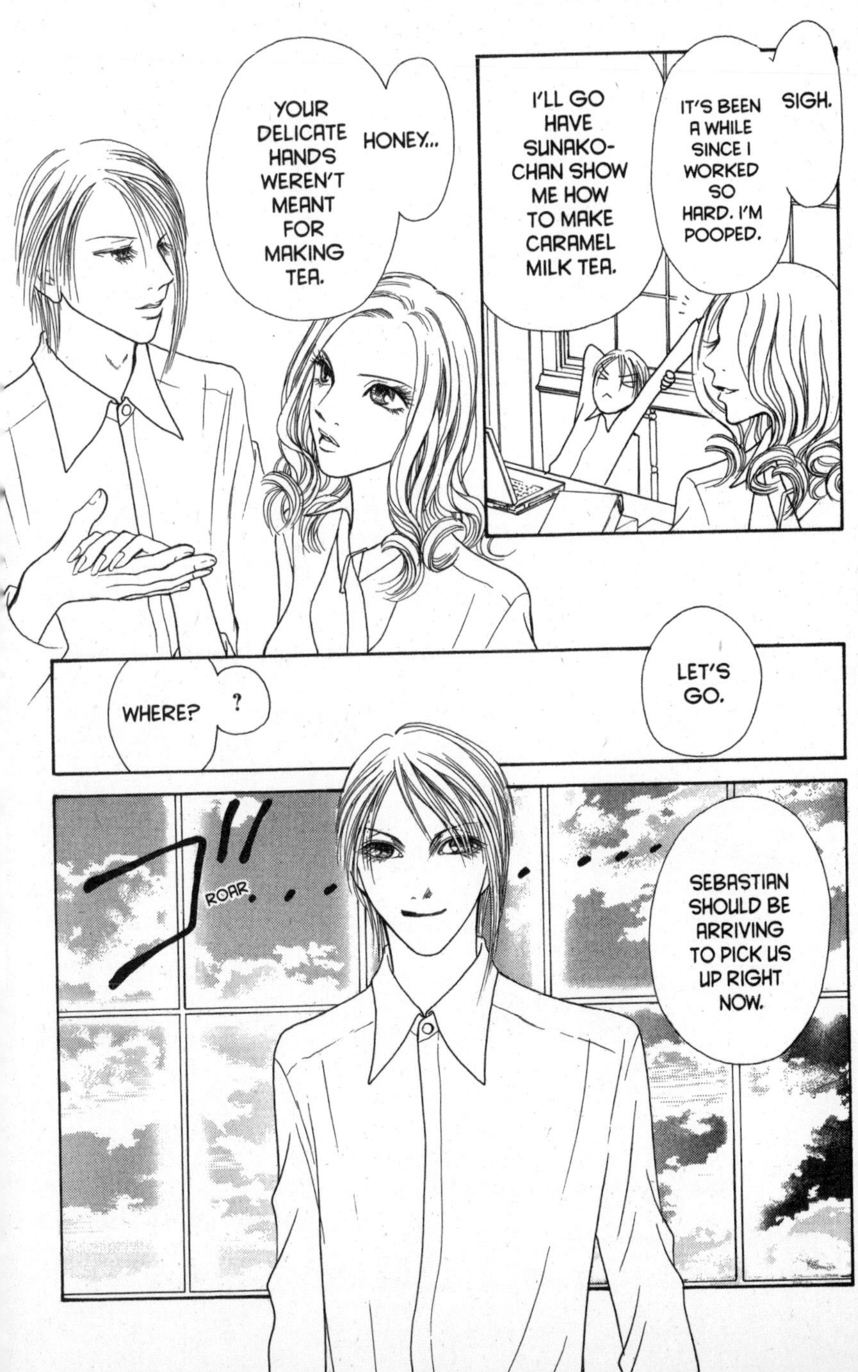
SIGH.
IT'S BEEN A WHILE SINCE I WORKED SO HARD. I'M POOPED.
I'LL GO HAVE SUNAKO-CHAN SHOW ME HOW TO MAKE CARAMEL MILK TEA.
HONEY...
YOUR DELICATE HANDS WEREN'T MEANT FOR MAKING TEA.
LET'S GO.
?
WHERE?
SEBASTIAN SHOULD BE ARRIVING TO PICK US UP RIGHT NOW.
ROAR
!!

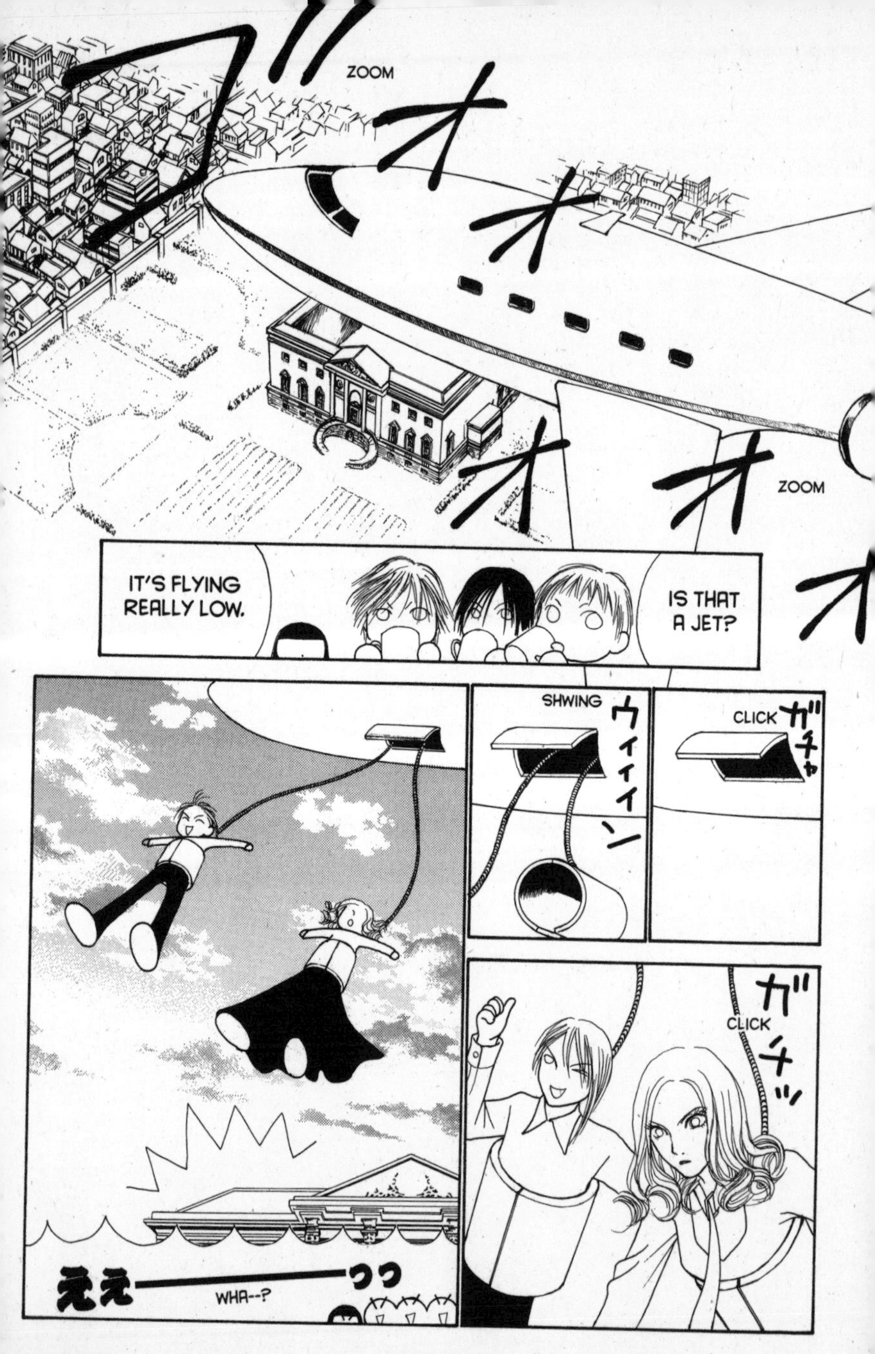
ゴオオオオオ
ZOOM
ZOOM
IS THAT A JET?
IT'S FLYING REALLY LOW.
ガチャ
CLICK
ウィイイン
SHWING
ガチッ
CLICK
ええ――っっ
WHA--?

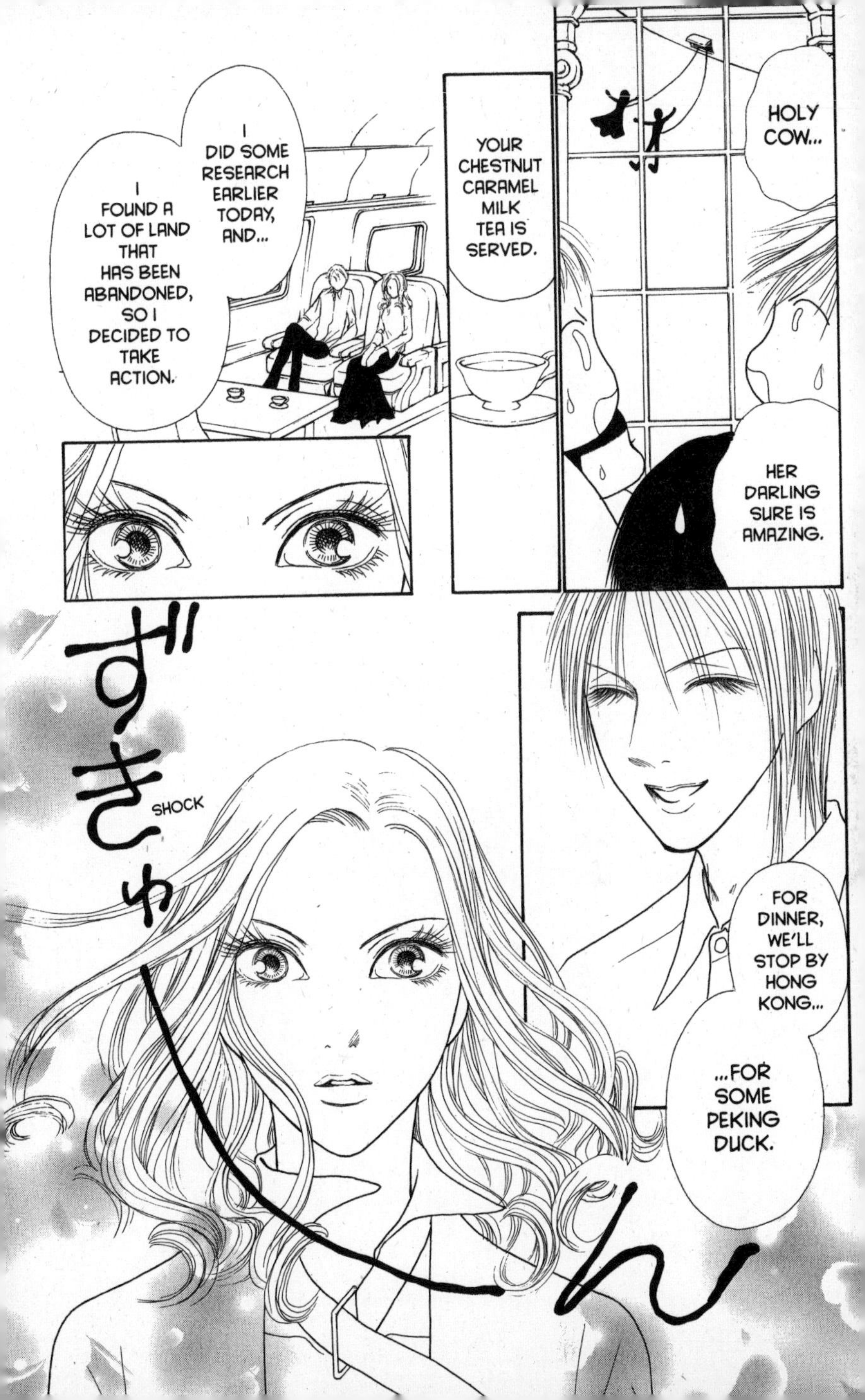
HOLY COW...
HER DARLING SURE IS AMAZING.
YOUR CHESTNUT CARAMEL MILK TEA IS SERVED.
I DID SOME RESEARCH EARLIER TODAY, AND...
I FOUND A LOT OF LAND THAT HAS BEEN ABANDONED, SO I DECIDED TO TAKE ACTION.
FOR DINNER, WE'LL STOP BY HONG KONG...
...FOR SOME PEKING DUCK.
ずきゅん
SHOCK

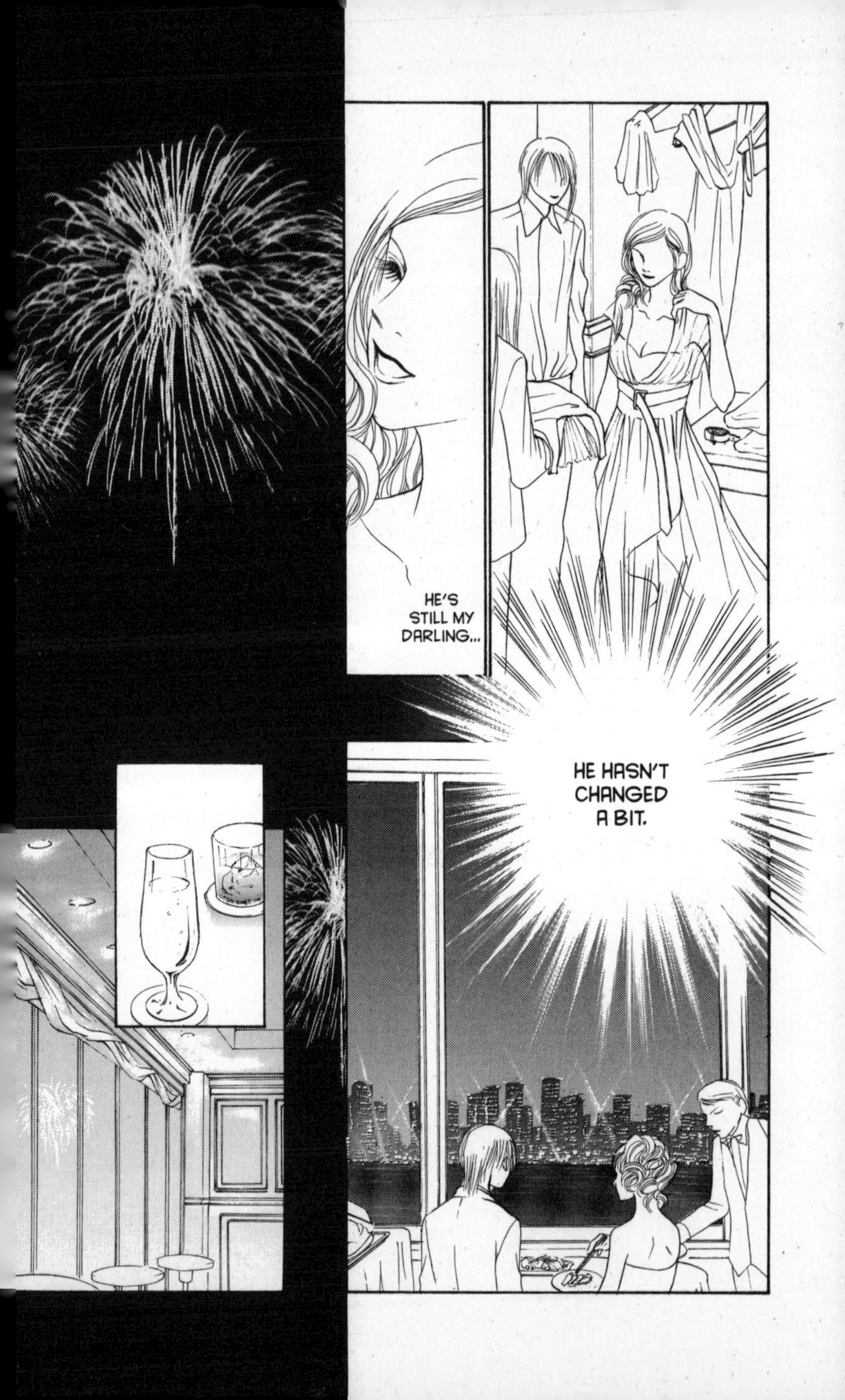
HE'S STILL MY DARLING...
HE HASN'T CHANGED A BIT.

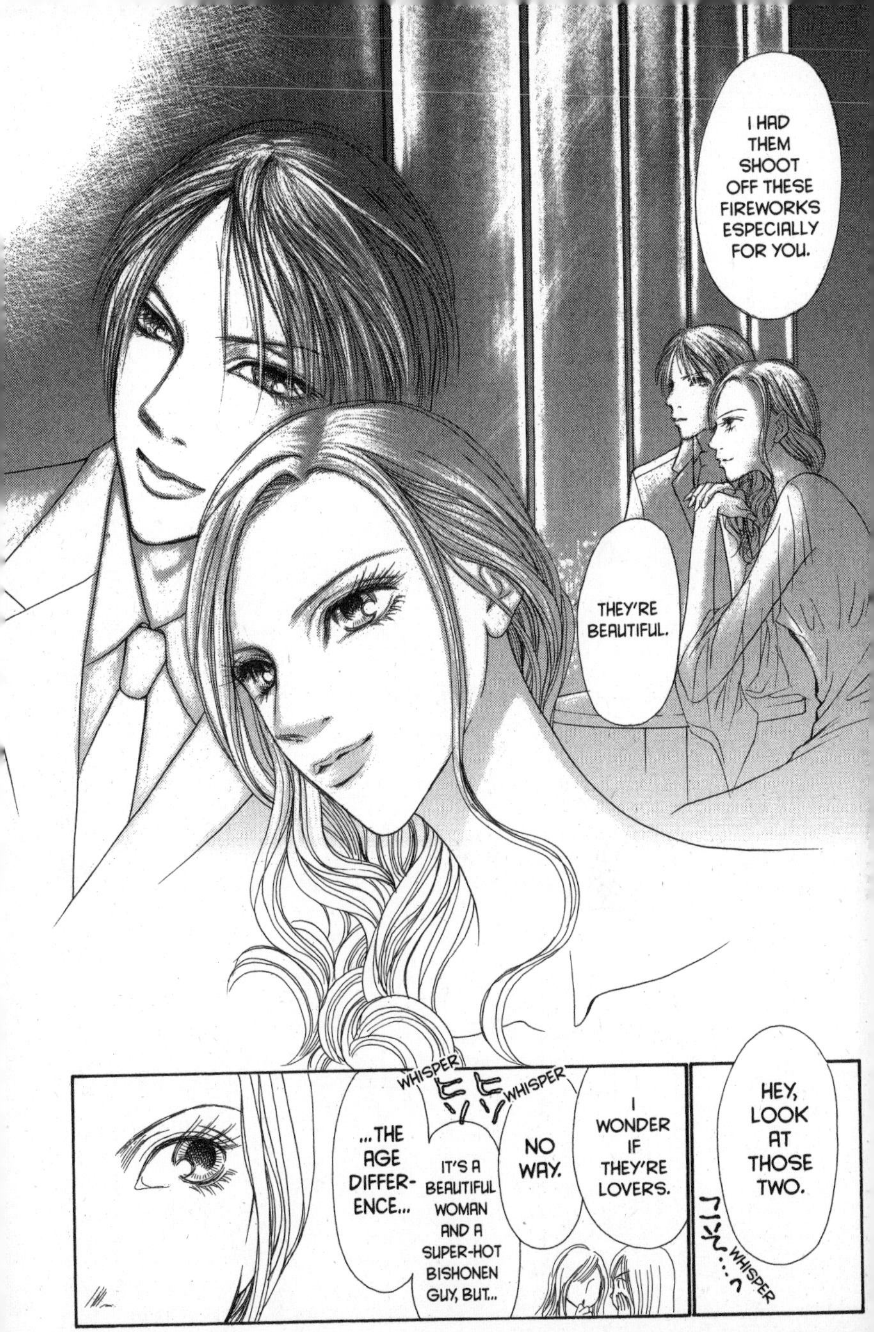
I HAD THEM SHOOT OFF THESE FIREWORKS ESPECIALLY FOR YOU.
THEY'RE BEAUTIFUL.
HEY, LOOK AT THOSE TWO.
WHISPER
I WONDER IF THEY'RE LOVERS.
NO WAY.
WHISPER
WHISPER
IT'S A BEAUTIFUL WOMAN AND A SUPER-HOT BISHONEN GUY, BUT...
...THE AGE DIFFER-ENCE...

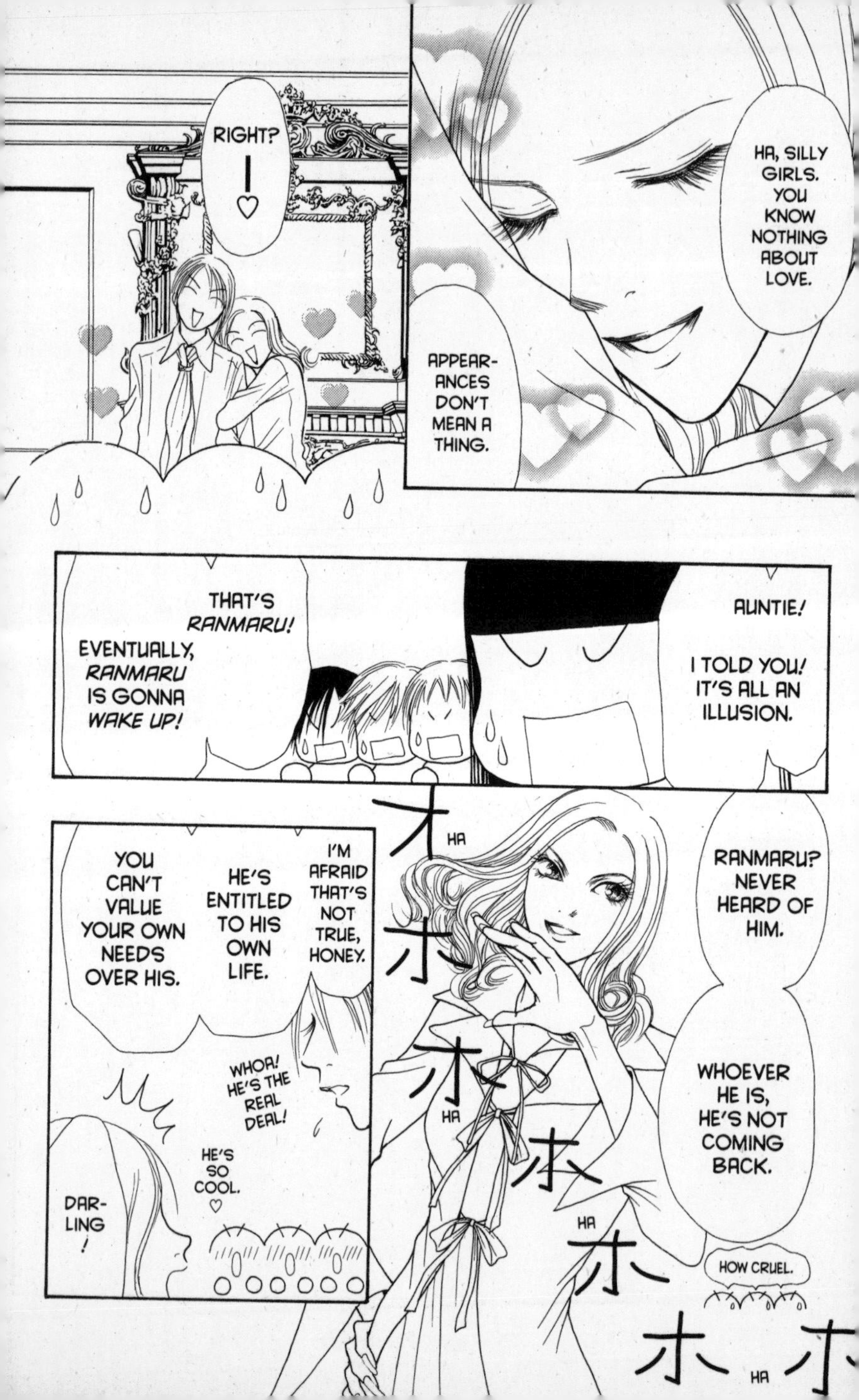
HA, SILLY GIRLS. YOU KNOW NOTHING ABOUT LOVE.
APPEARANCES DON'T MEAN A THING.
RIGHT? ♡
AUNTIE!
I TOLD YOU! IT'S ALL AN ILLUSION.
THAT'S RANMARU!
EVENTUALLY, RANMARU IS GONNA WAKE UP!
RANMARU? NEVER HEARD OF HIM.
WHOEVER HE IS, HE'S NOT COMING BACK.
オ HA
ホ
ホ HA
ホ HA
ホ
ホ HA
HOW CRUEL.
I'M AFRAID THAT'S NOT TRUE, HONEY.
HE'S ENTITLED TO HIS OWN LIFE.
YOU CAN'T VALUE YOUR OWN NEEDS OVER HIS.
WHOA! HE'S THE REAL DEAL!
HE'S SO COOL. ♡
DARLING!

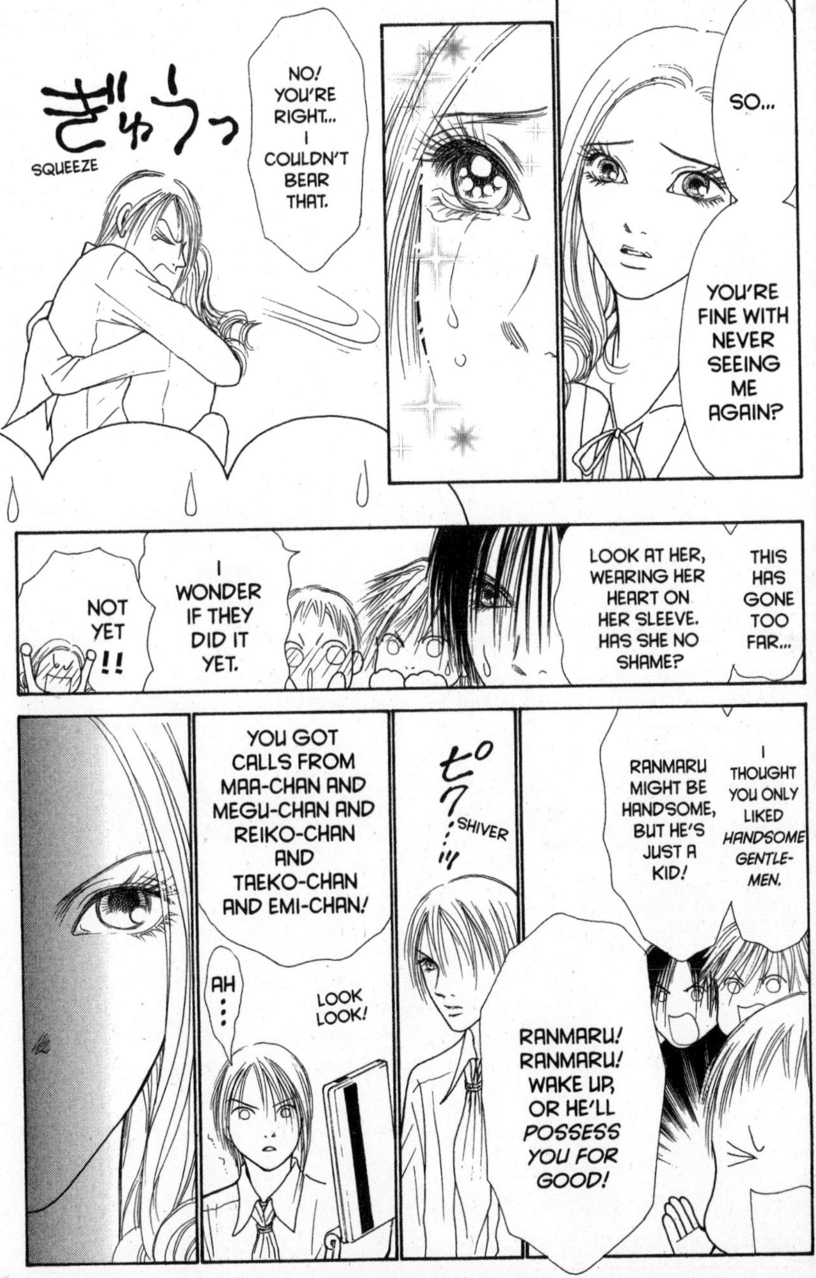
SO...
YOU'RE FINE WITH NEVER SEEING ME AGAIN?
NO! YOU'RE RIGHT... I COULDN'T BEAR THAT.
ぎゅうっ
SQUEEZE
THIS HAS GONE TOO FAR...
LOOK AT HER, WEARING HER HEART ON HER SLEEVE. HAS SHE NO SHAME?
I WONDER IF THEY DID IT YET.
NOT YET!!
I THOUGHT YOU ONLY LIKED *HANDSOME GENTLE-MEN.*
RANMARU MIGHT BE HANDSOME, BUT HE'S JUST A KID!
RANMARU! RANMARU! WAKE UP, OR HE'LL *POSSESS YOU FOR GOOD!*
ピク
SHIVER
YOU GOT CALLS FROM MAA-CHAN AND MEGU-CHAN AND REIKO-CHAN AND TAEKO-CHAN AND EMI-CHAN!
LOOK LOOK!
AH...

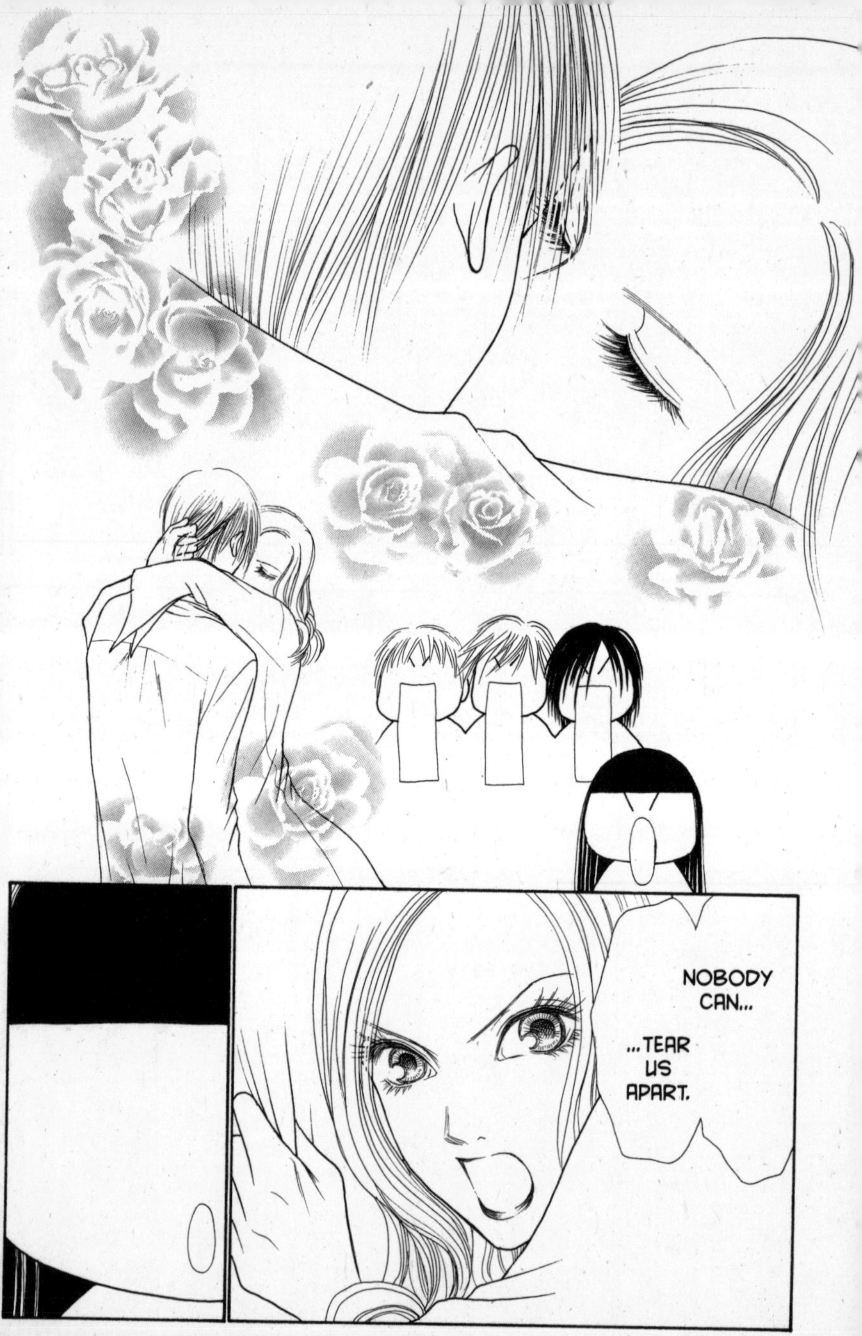
NOBODY CAN...
...TEAR US APART.

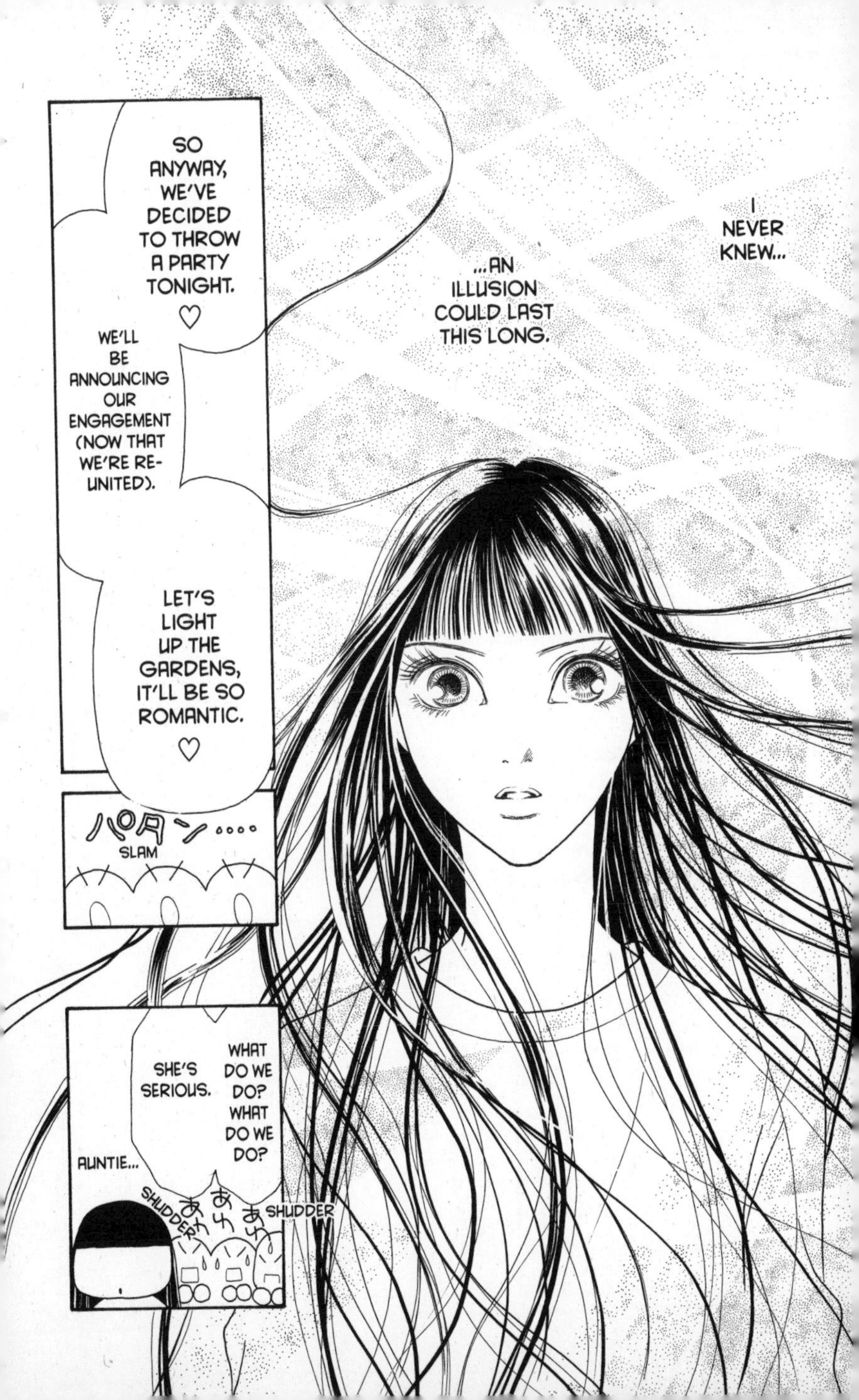
I NEVER KNEW...
...AN ILLUSION COULD LAST THIS LONG.
SO ANYWAY, WE'VE DECIDED TO THROW A PARTY TONIGHT. ♡
WE'LL BE ANNOUNCING OUR ENGAGEMENT (NOW THAT WE'RE RE-UNITED).
LET'S LIGHT UP THE GARDENS, IT'LL BE SO ROMANTIC. ♡
パタン
SLAM
WHAT DO WE DO? WHAT DO WE DO?
SHE'S SERIOUS.
AUNTIE...
あわ あわ あわ
SHUDDER
SHUDDER

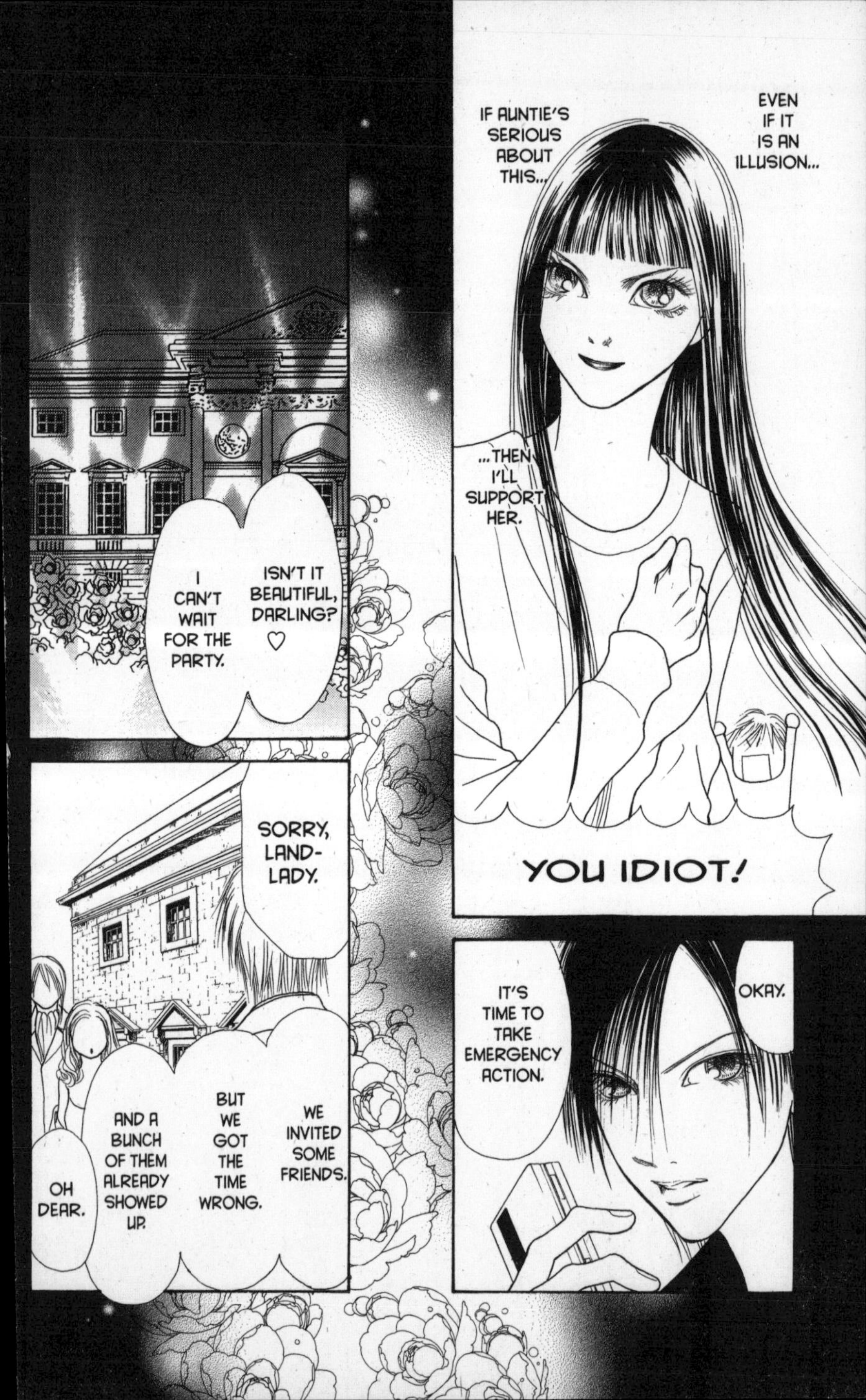
EVEN IF IT IS AN ILLUSION...
IF AUNTIE'S SERIOUS ABOUT THIS...
...THEN I'LL SUPPORT HER.
YOU IDIOT!
OKAY.
IT'S TIME TO TAKE EMERGENCY ACTION.
ISN'T IT BEAUTIFUL, DARLING? ♡
I CAN'T WAIT FOR THE PARTY.
SORRY, LANDLADY.
WE INVITED SOME FRIENDS.
BUT WE GOT THE TIME WRONG.
AND A BUNCH OF THEM ALREADY SHOWED UP.
OH DEAR.

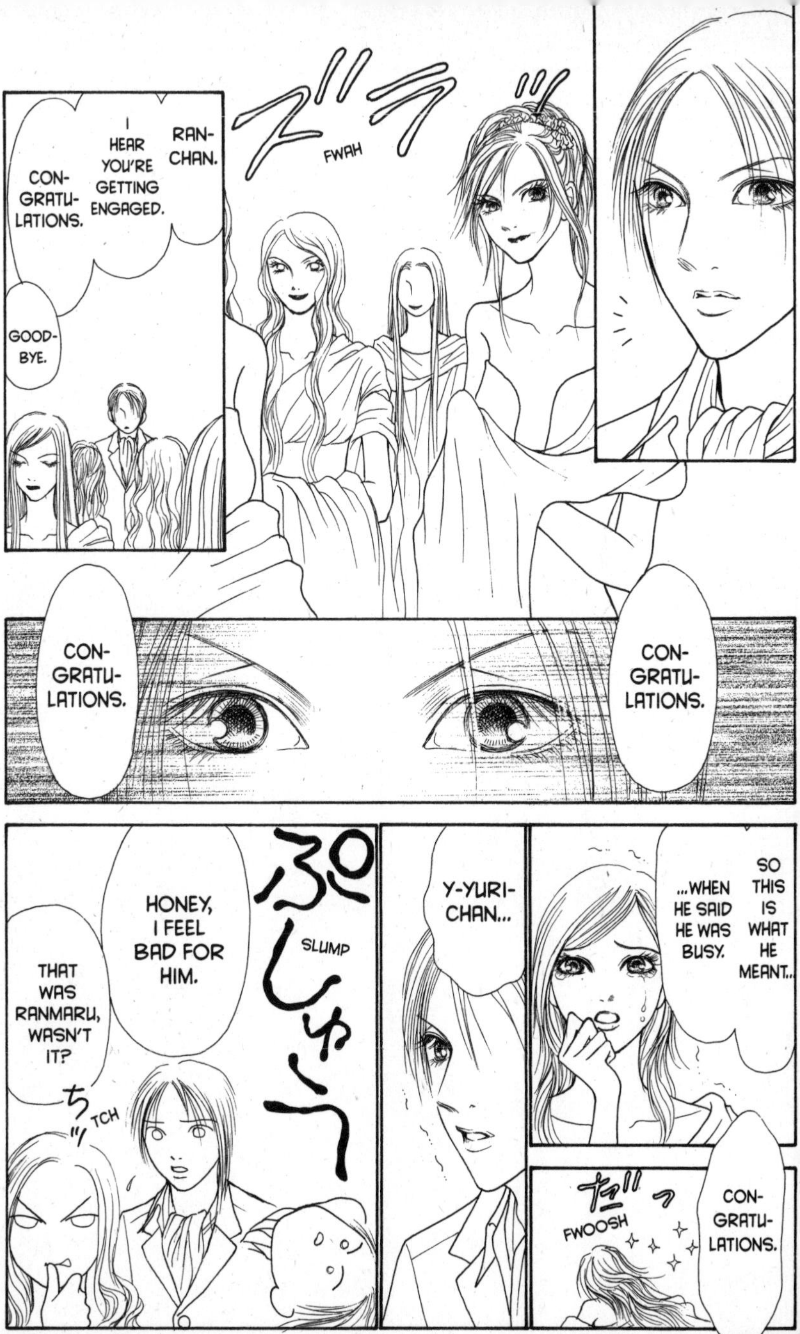
ズラ
FWAH
RAN-CHAN.
I HEAR YOU'RE GETTING ENGAGED.
CONGRATULATIONS.
GOODBYE.
CONGRATULATIONS.
CONGRATULATIONS.
SO THIS IS WHAT HE MEANT...
...WHEN HE SAID HE WAS BUSY.
CONGRATULATIONS.
FWOOSH
Y-YURI-CHAN...
ぷしゅう
SLUMP
HONEY, I FEEL BAD FOR HIM.
THAT WAS RANMARU, WASN'T IT?
ち
TCH

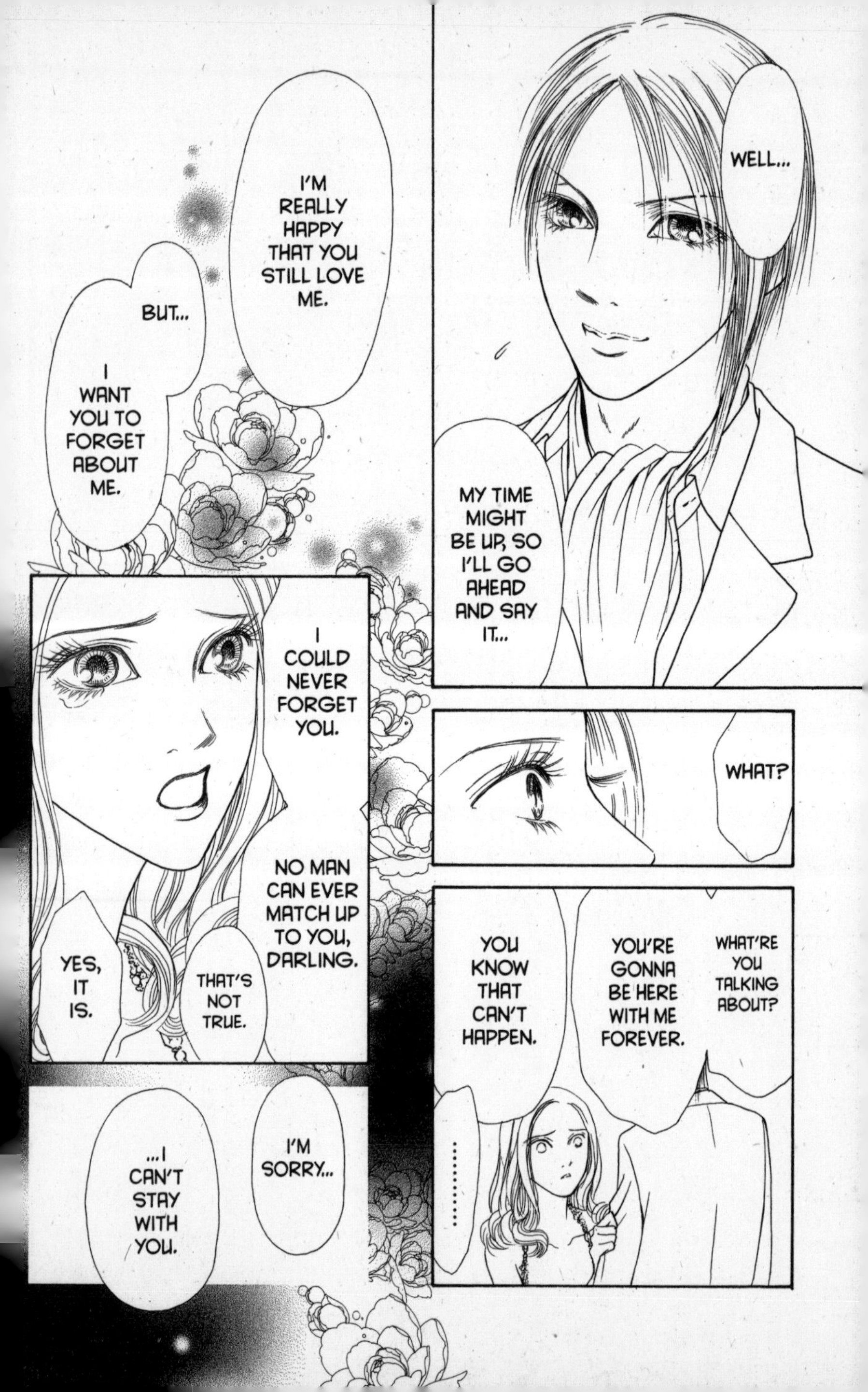
WELL...
MY TIME MIGHT BE UP, SO I'LL GO AHEAD AND SAY IT...
I'M REALLY HAPPY THAT YOU STILL LOVE ME.
BUT...
I WANT YOU TO FORGET ABOUT ME.
WHAT?
WHAT'RE YOU TALKING ABOUT?
YOU'RE GONNA BE HERE WITH ME FOREVER.
YOU KNOW THAT CAN'T HAPPEN.
......
I COULD NEVER FORGET YOU.
NO MAN CAN EVER MATCH UP TO YOU, DARLING.
THAT'S NOT TRUE.
YES, IT IS.
I'M SORRY...
...I CAN'T STAY WITH YOU.

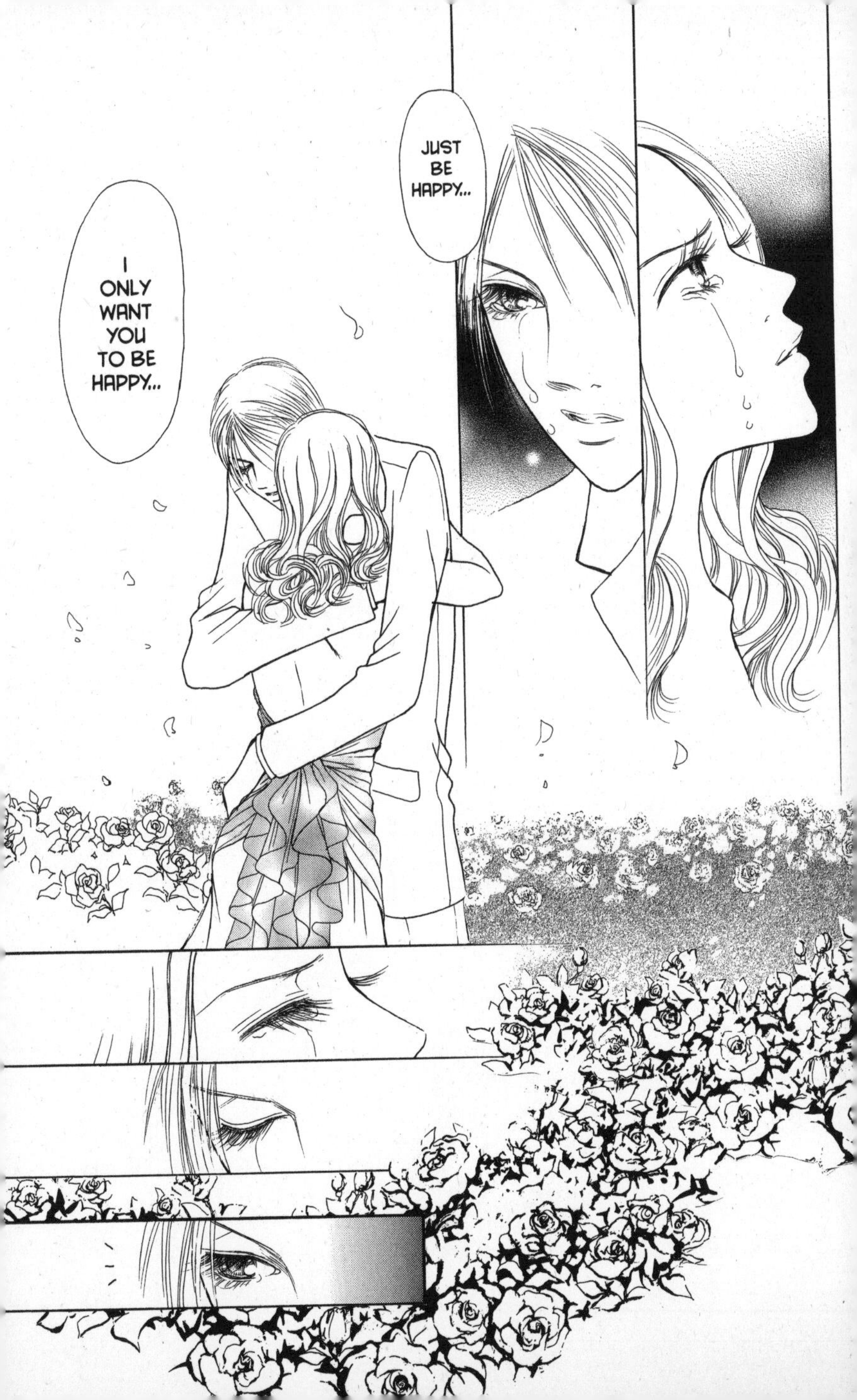
JUST BE HAPPY...
I ONLY WANT YOU TO BE HAPPY...

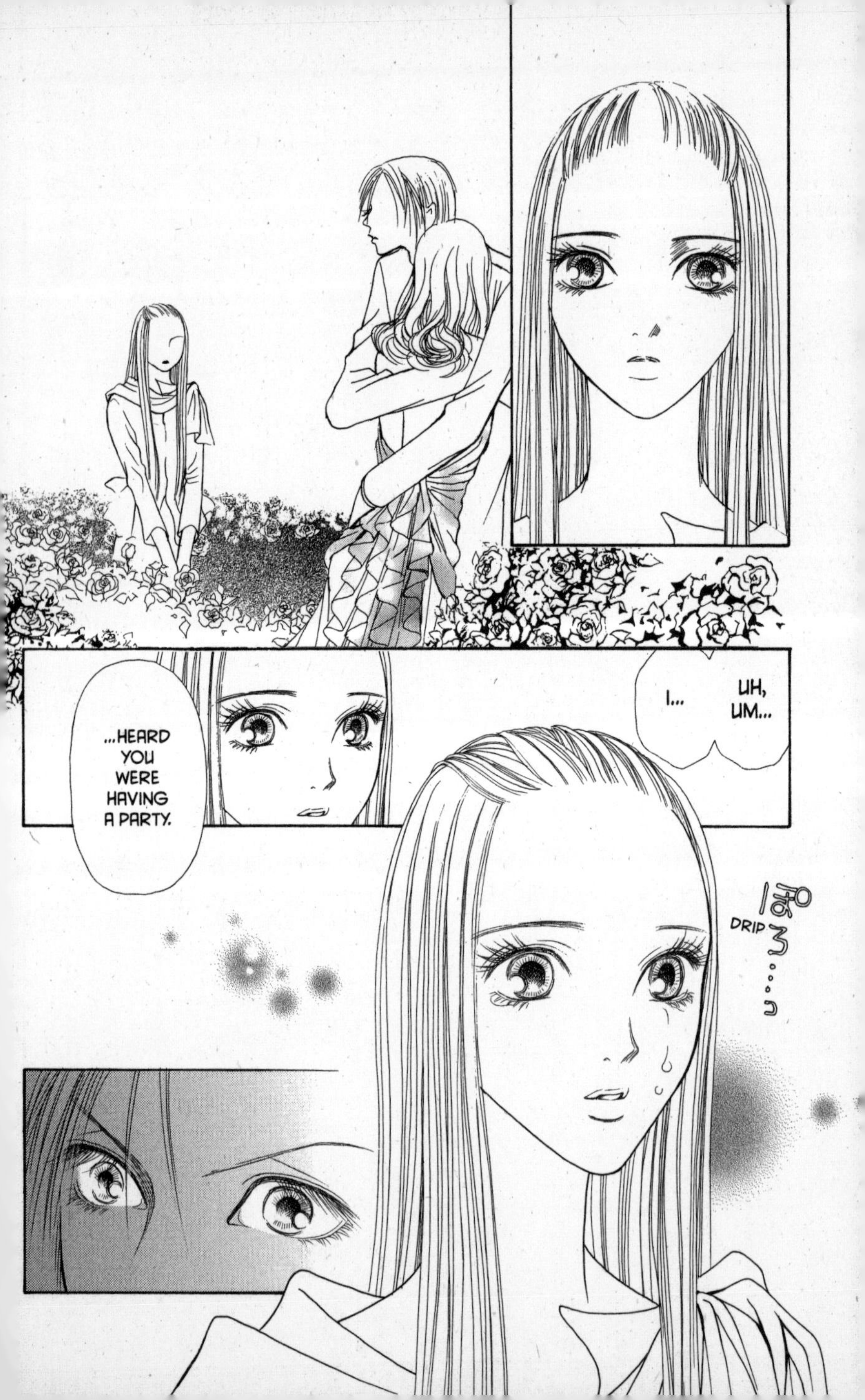

I... UH, UM...
...HEARD YOU WERE HAVING A PARTY.
DRIP

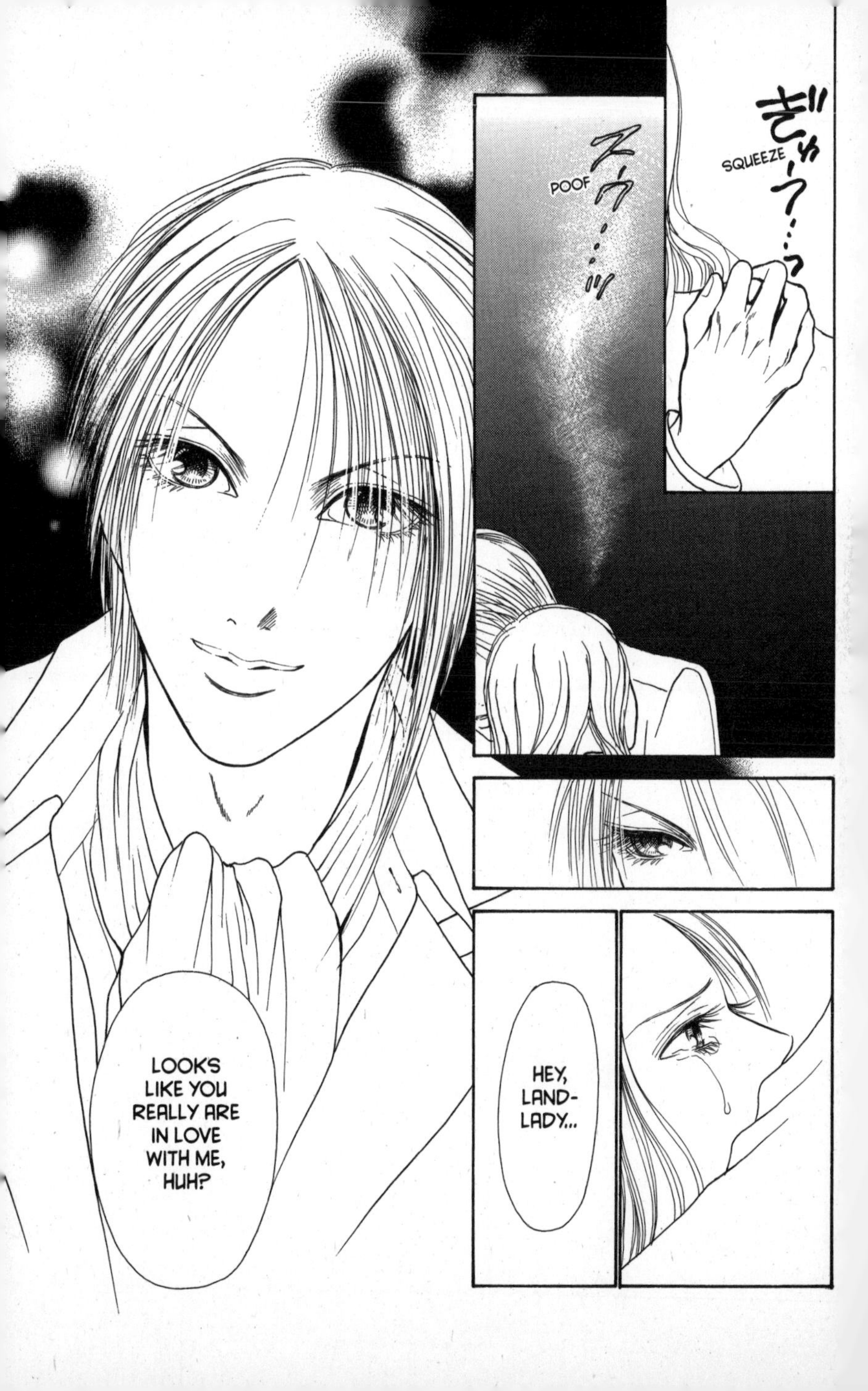
SQUEEZE
POOF
HEY, LAND-LADY...
LOOKS LIKE YOU REALLY ARE IN LOVE WITH ME, HUH?

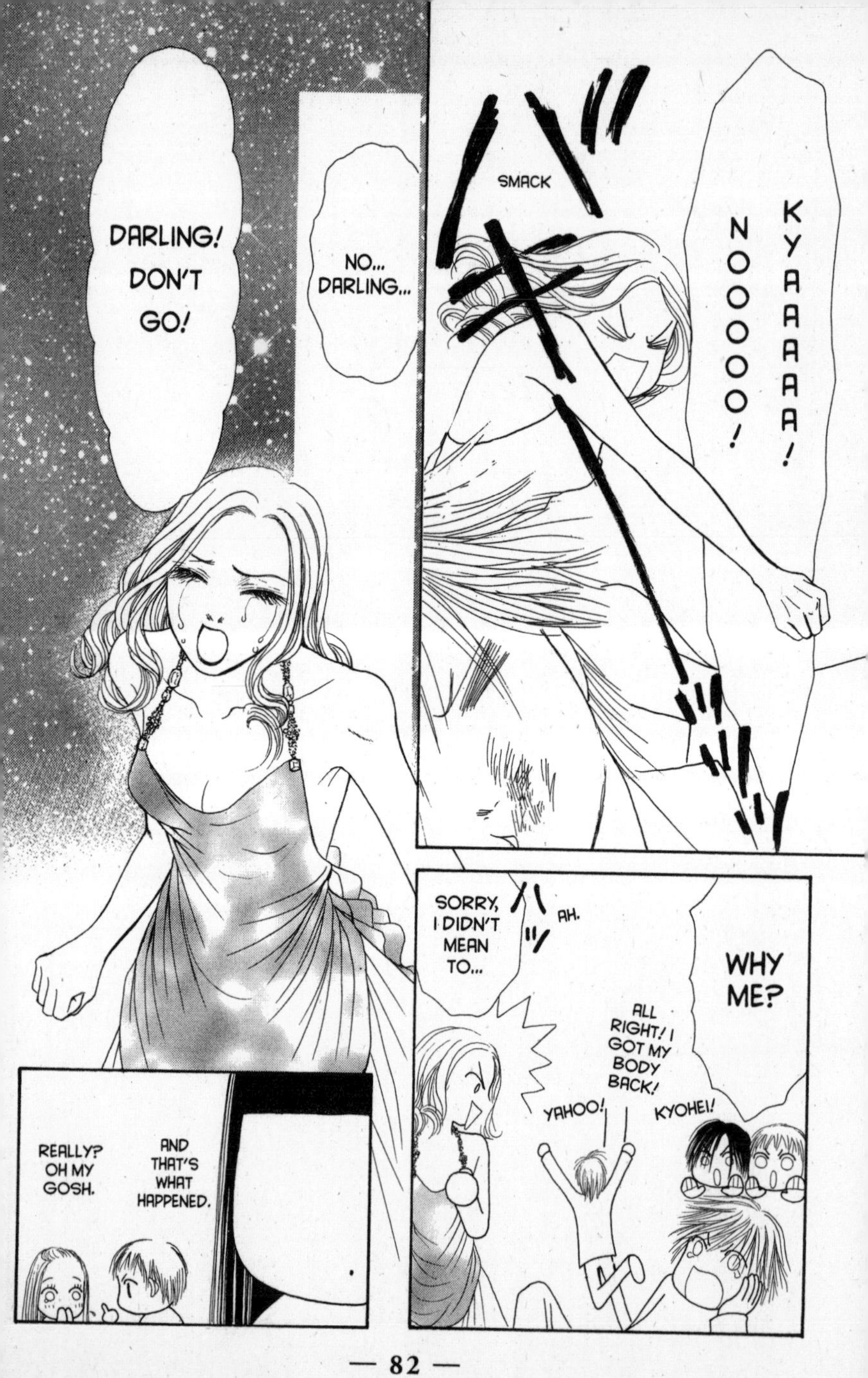
SMACK
KYAAAAA! NOOOOO!
NO... DARLING...
DARLING! DON'T GO!
WHY ME?
SORRY, I DIDN'T MEAN TO...
AH.
ALL RIGHT! I GOT MY BODY BACK!
KYOHEI!
YAHOO!
AND THAT'S WHAT HAPPENED.
REALLY? OH MY GOSH.

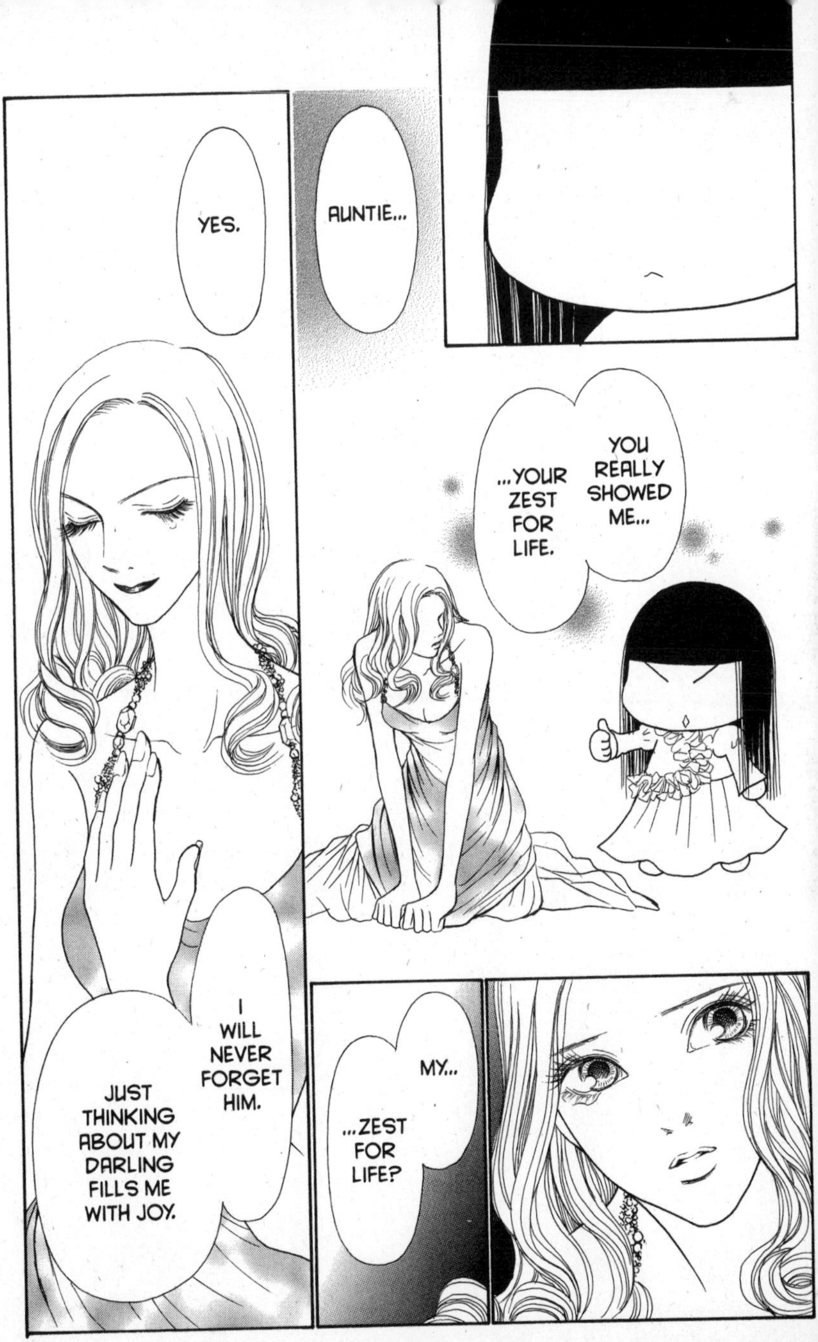
AUNTIE...
YOU REALLY SHOWED ME...
...YOUR ZEST FOR LIFE.
MY...
...ZEST FOR LIFE?
YES.
I WILL NEVER FORGET HIM.
JUST THINKING ABOUT MY DARLING FILLS ME WITH JOY.

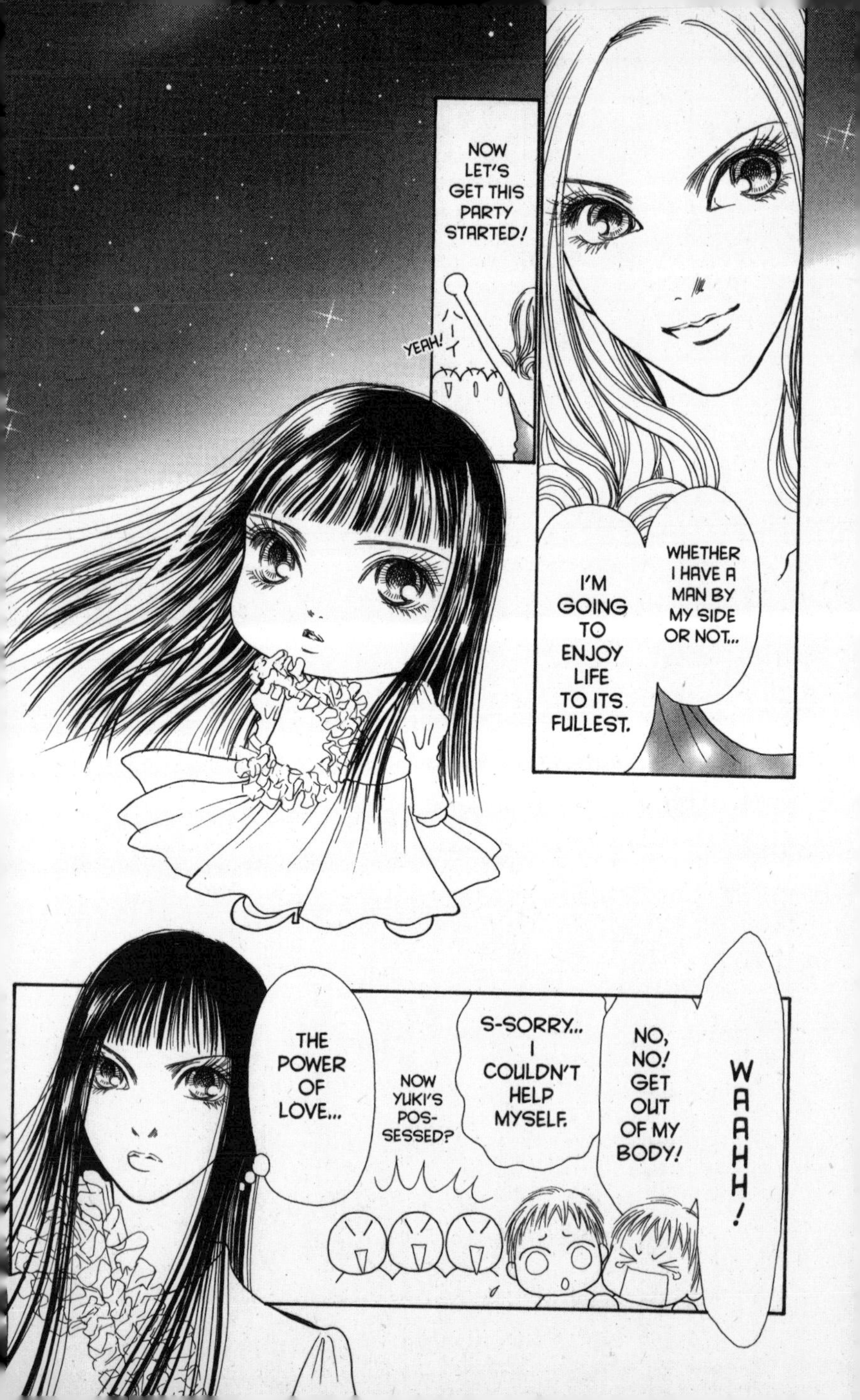
WHETHER I HAVE A MAN BY MY SIDE OR NOT...
I'M GOING TO ENJOY LIFE TO ITS FULLEST.
NOW LET'S GET THIS PARTY STARTED!
ハーイ
YEAH!
WAAHH!
NO, NO! GET OUT OF MY BODY!
S-SORRY... I COULDN'T HELP MYSELF.
NOW YUKI'S POS-SESSED?
THE POWER OF LOVE...

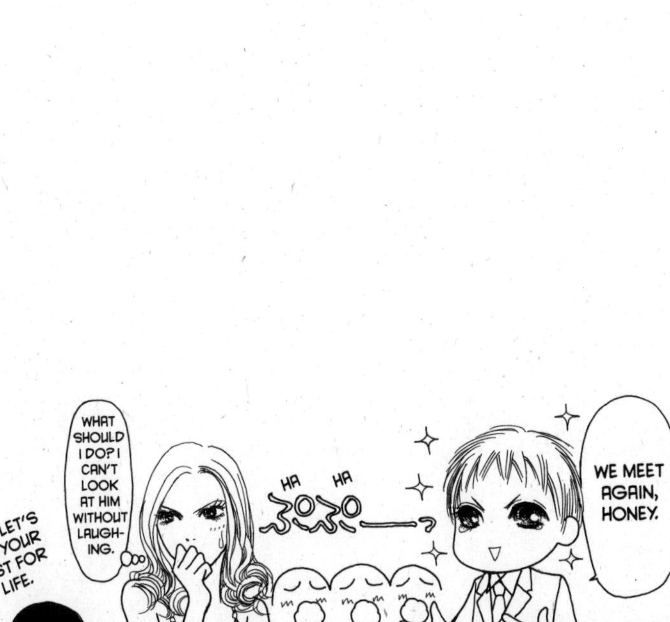
WE MEET AGAIN, HONEY.
HA HA
WHAT SHOULD I DO? I CAN'T LOOK AT HIM WITHOUT LAUGH-ING.
NOW LET'S SEE YOUR ZEST FOR LIFE.

[Ch]apter 77 HOW TO BE A [...]LE DOMESTIC

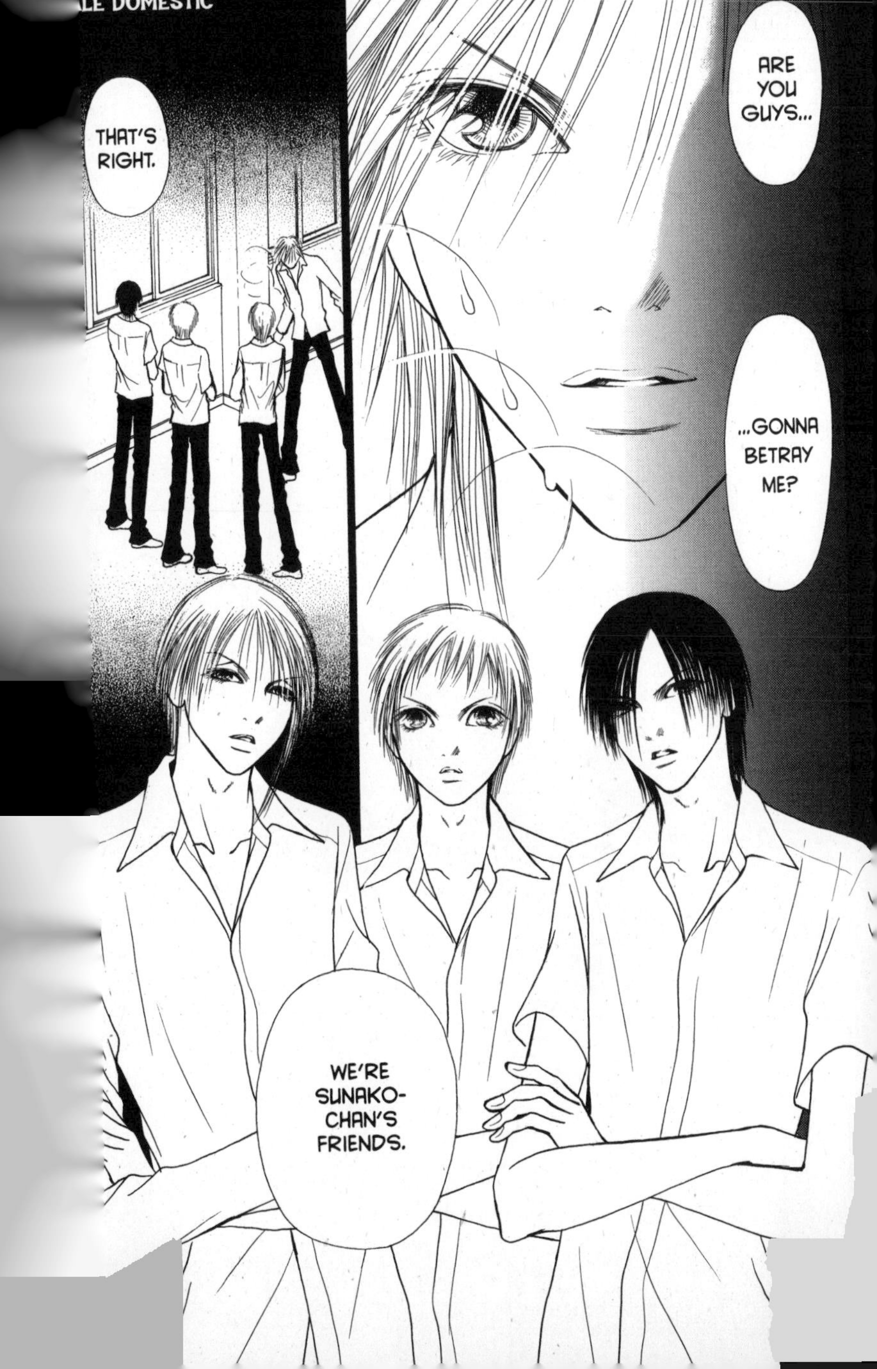
ARE YOU GUYS...
...GONNA BETRAY ME?
THAT'S RIGHT.
WE'RE SUNAKO-CHAN'S FRIENDS.

Chapter 77

HOW TO BE A MALE DOMESTIC

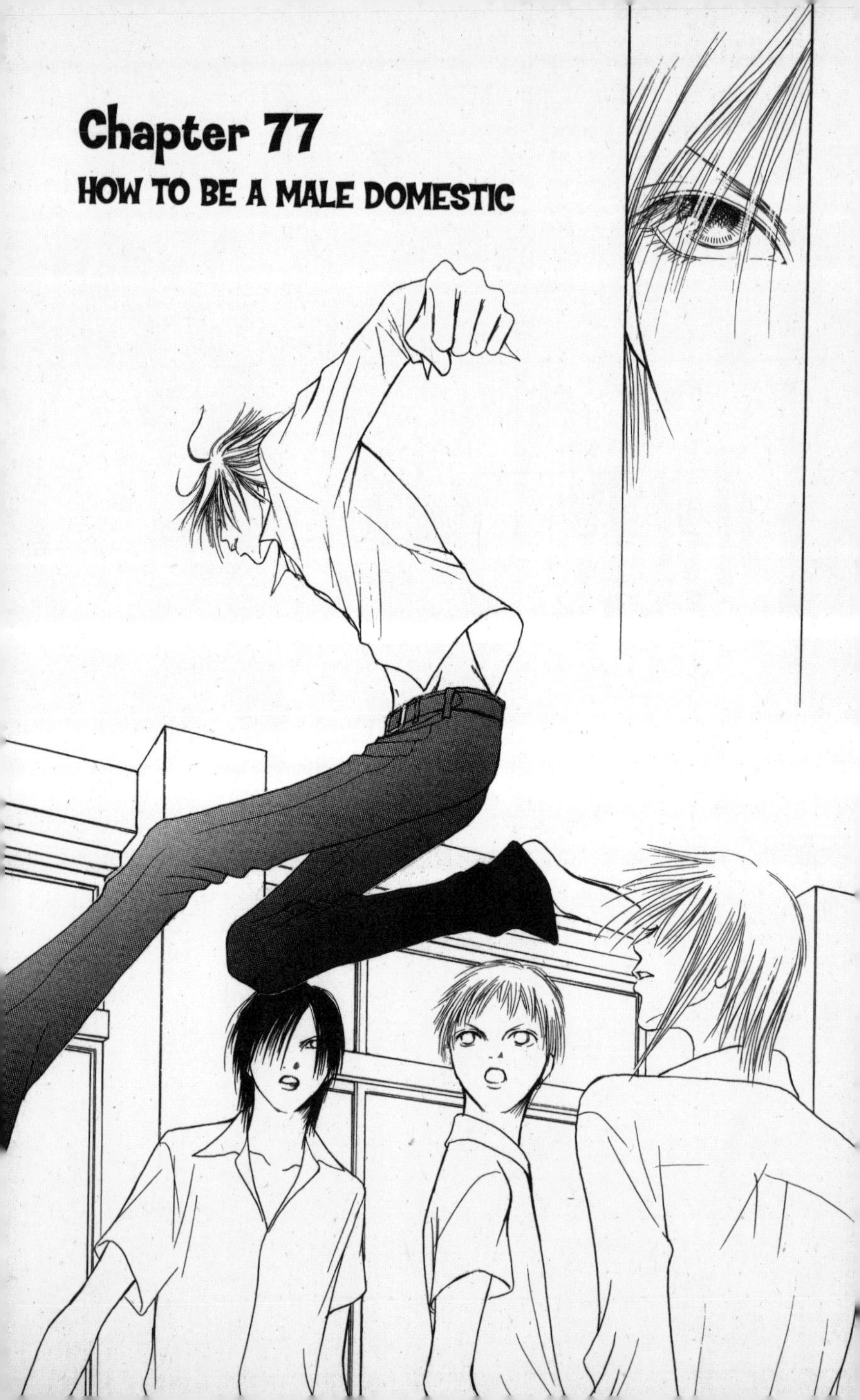

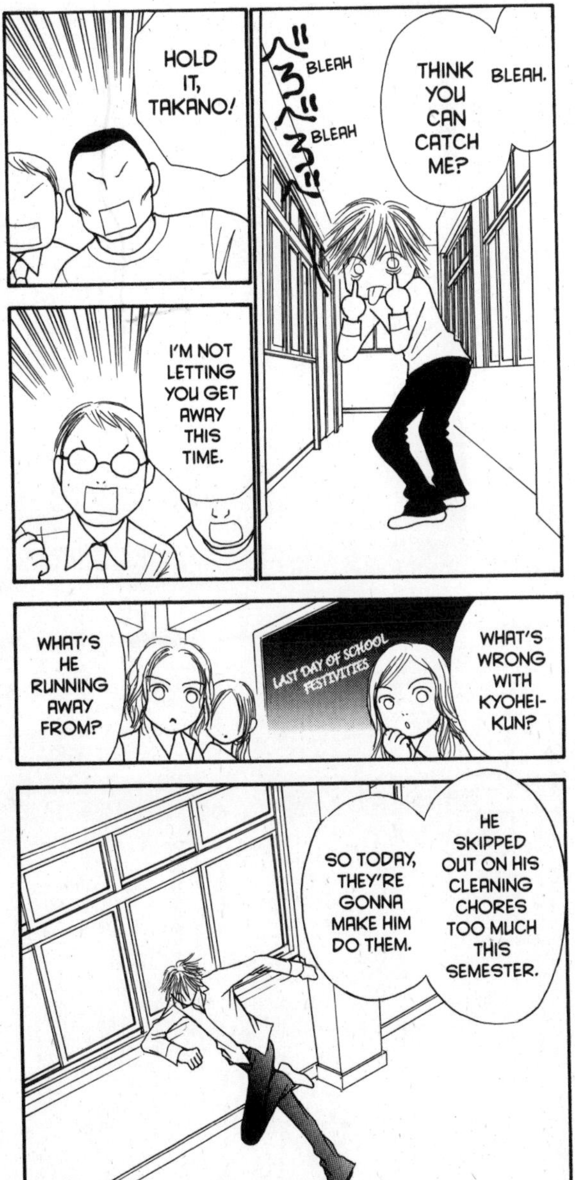

THINK YOU CAN CATCH ME?
BLEAH.
BLEAH
BLEAH
HOLD IT, TAKANO!
I'M NOT LETTING YOU GET AWAY THIS TIME.
WHAT'S WRONG WITH KYOHEI-KUN?
LAST DAY OF SCHOOL FESTIVITIES
WHAT'S HE RUNNING AWAY FROM?
HE SKIPPED OUT ON HIS CLEANING CHORES TOO MUCH THIS SEMESTER.
SO TODAY, THEY'RE GONNA MAKE HIM DO THEM.

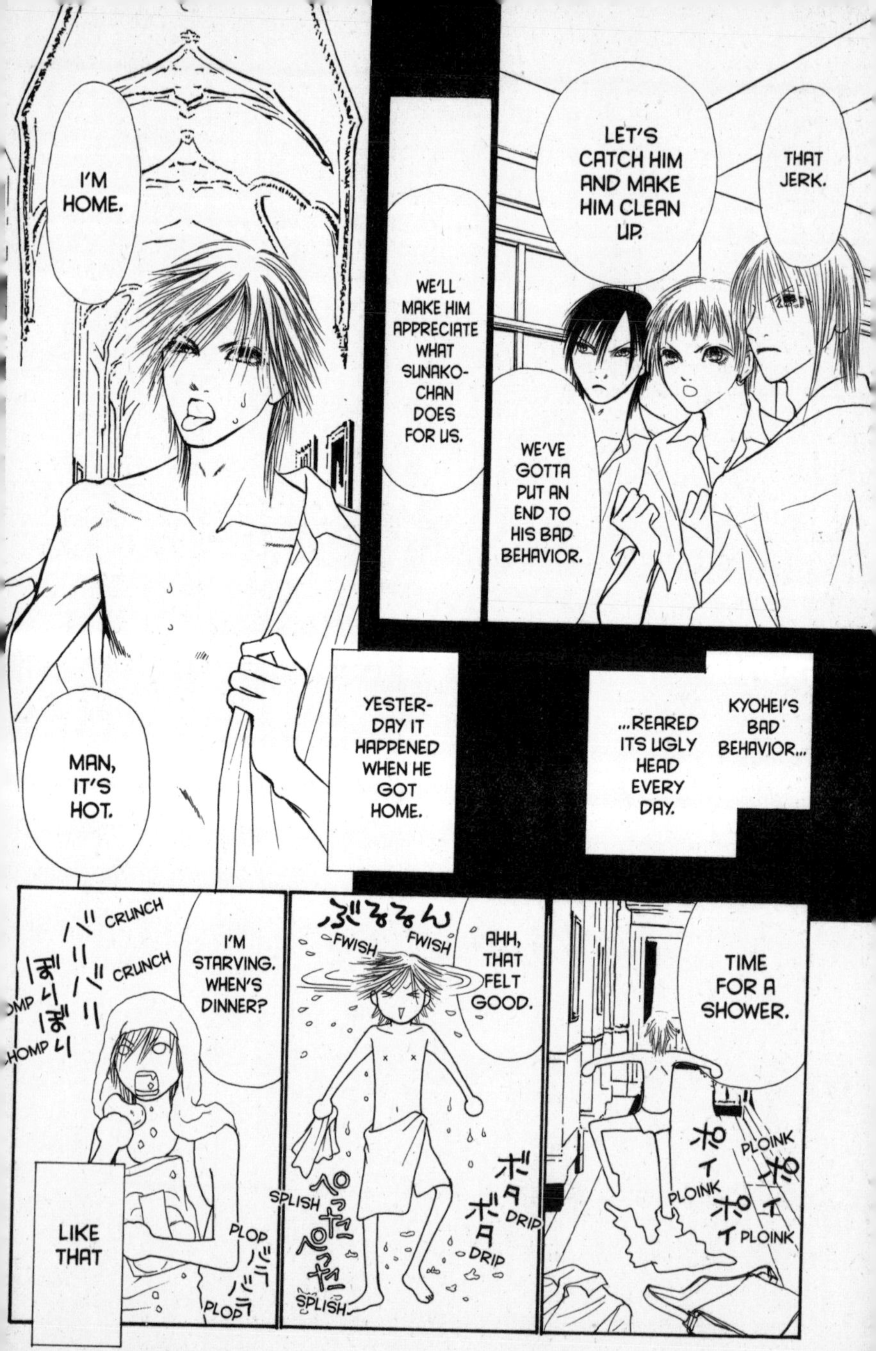
THAT JERK.
LET'S CATCH HIM AND MAKE HIM CLEAN UP.
WE'VE GOTTA PUT AN END TO HIS BAD BEHAVIOR.
WE'LL MAKE HIM APPRECIATE WHAT SUNAKO-CHAN DOES FOR US.
KYOHEI'S BAD BEHAVIOR...
...REARED ITS UGLY HEAD EVERY DAY.
YESTERDAY IT HAPPENED WHEN HE GOT HOME.
I'M HOME.
MAN, IT'S HOT.
TIME FOR A SHOWER.
ポイ PLOINK
ポイ PLOINK
ポイ PLOINK
AHH, THAT FELT GOOD.
ぶるるん
FWISH FWISH
ボタ DRIP
ボタ DRIP
ぺった SPLISH
ぺった SPLISH
I'M STARVING. WHEN'S DINNER?
バリ CRUNCH
バリ CRUNCH
ぼりぼり
バラバラ PLOP PLOP
LIKE THAT

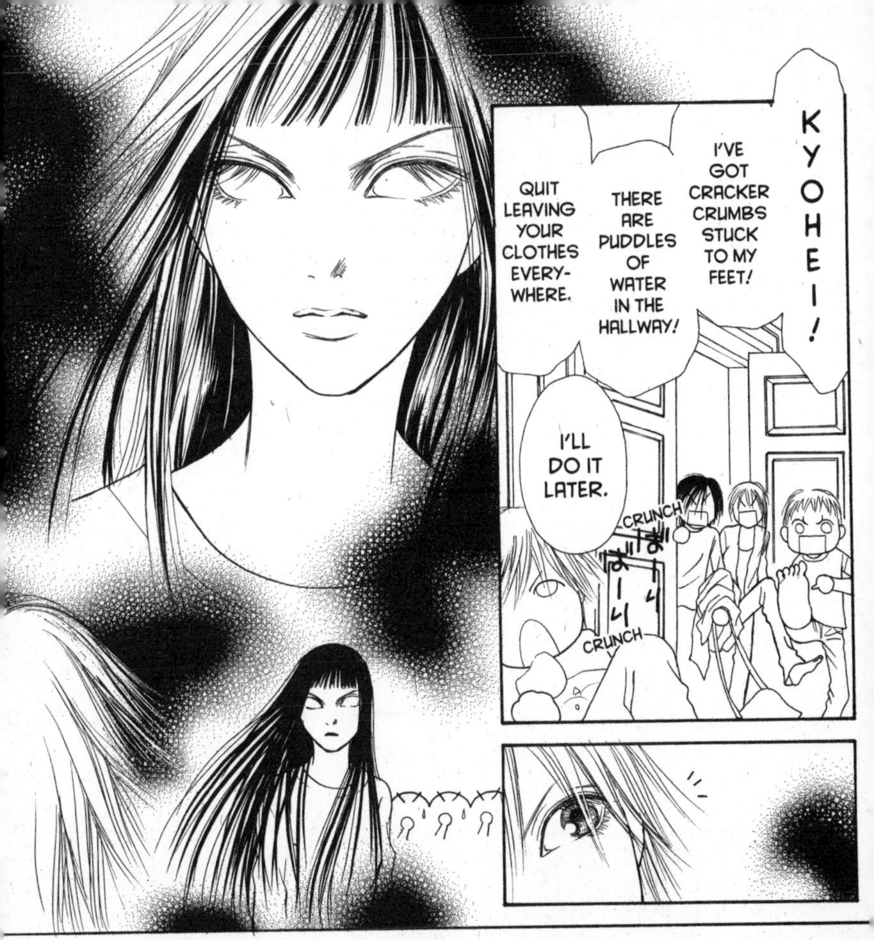
KYOHEI!
I'VE GOT CRACKER CRUMBS STUCK TO MY FEET!
THERE ARE PUDDLES OF WATER IN THE HALLWAY!
QUIT LEAVING YOUR CLOTHES EVERY-WHERE.
I'LL DO IT LATER.
CRUNCH
CRUNCH

BEHIND THE SCENES

CONTINUED FROM PAGE 48.

OF COURSE EVERYBODY ON THE STAFF WAS REALLY NICE TOO. ♡ NABESHIN-SAMA, THE DIRECTOR, AND HARUKA-SAN, THE WRITER, AND EVERYBODY ELSE WAS REALLY COOL. ♡ THERE WAS ONE PERSON THERE WHO WAS JUST MY TYPE. ♡ I'M FEELING REALLY LONELY BECAUSE I HAVEN'T SEEN THAT PERSON SINCE. ♡

I WONDER HOW I CAN LEARN TO SOCIALIZE IN PUBLIC BETTER. AS SOON AS I'M STANDING IN FRONT OF PEOPLE, MY MIND GOES BLANK. I'D LIKE TO GET OVER MY NERVES. I'M REALLY TERRIBLE. I EMBARRASS EVERYBODY. AT MY AGE, I SHOULD BE OVER THIS.

ANYWAY, IT WAS A FUN PARTY. I WAS SAD TO SEE THE SHOW END. I'D LIKE TO THANK EVERYONE INVOLVED FROM THE BOTTOM OF MY HEART!

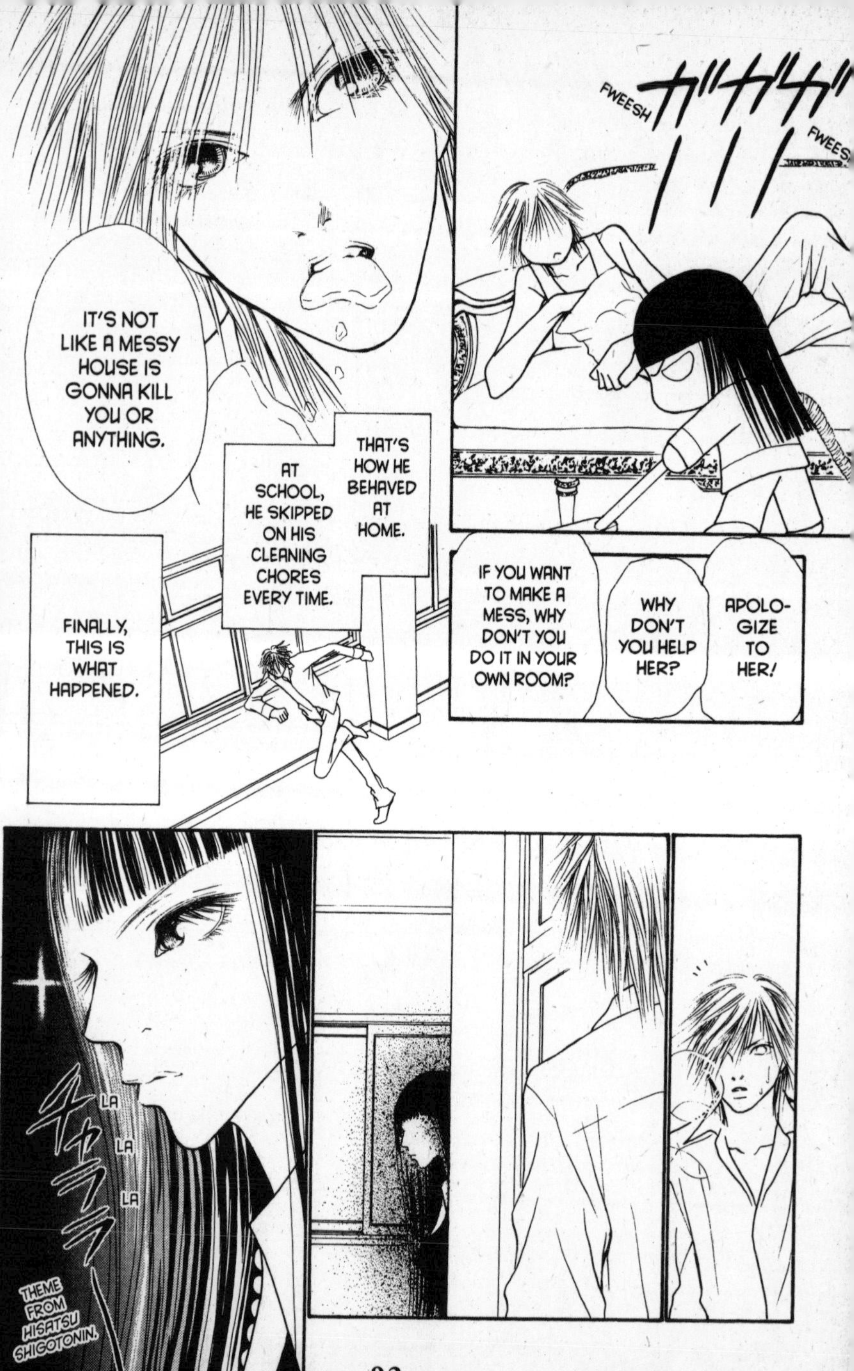
FWEESH
FWEES
APOLO-GIZE TO HER!
WHY DON'T YOU HELP HER?
IF YOU WANT TO MAKE A MESS, WHY DON'T YOU DO IT IN YOUR OWN ROOM?
IT'S NOT LIKE A MESSY HOUSE IS GONNA KILL YOU OR ANYTHING.
THAT'S HOW HE BEHAVED AT HOME.
AT SCHOOL, HE SKIPPED ON HIS CLEANING CHORES EVERY TIME.
FINALLY, THIS IS WHAT HAPPENED.
LA
LA
LA
THEME FROM HISATSU SHIGOTONIN.

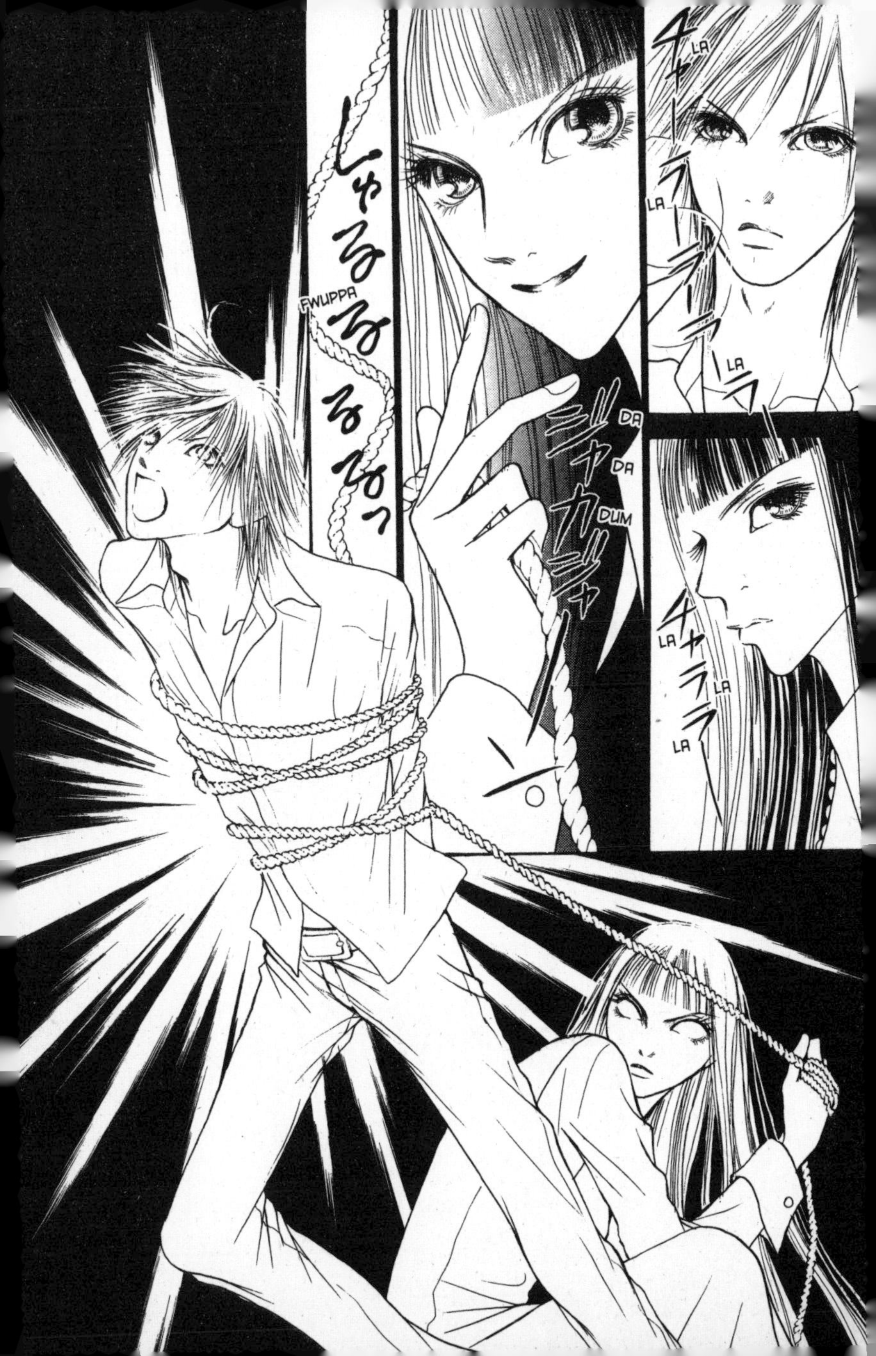

チャーラーラーラー
LA LA LA
チャララ
LA LA LA
ジャカジャーン
DA DA DUM
しゅるるるるっ
FWUPPA

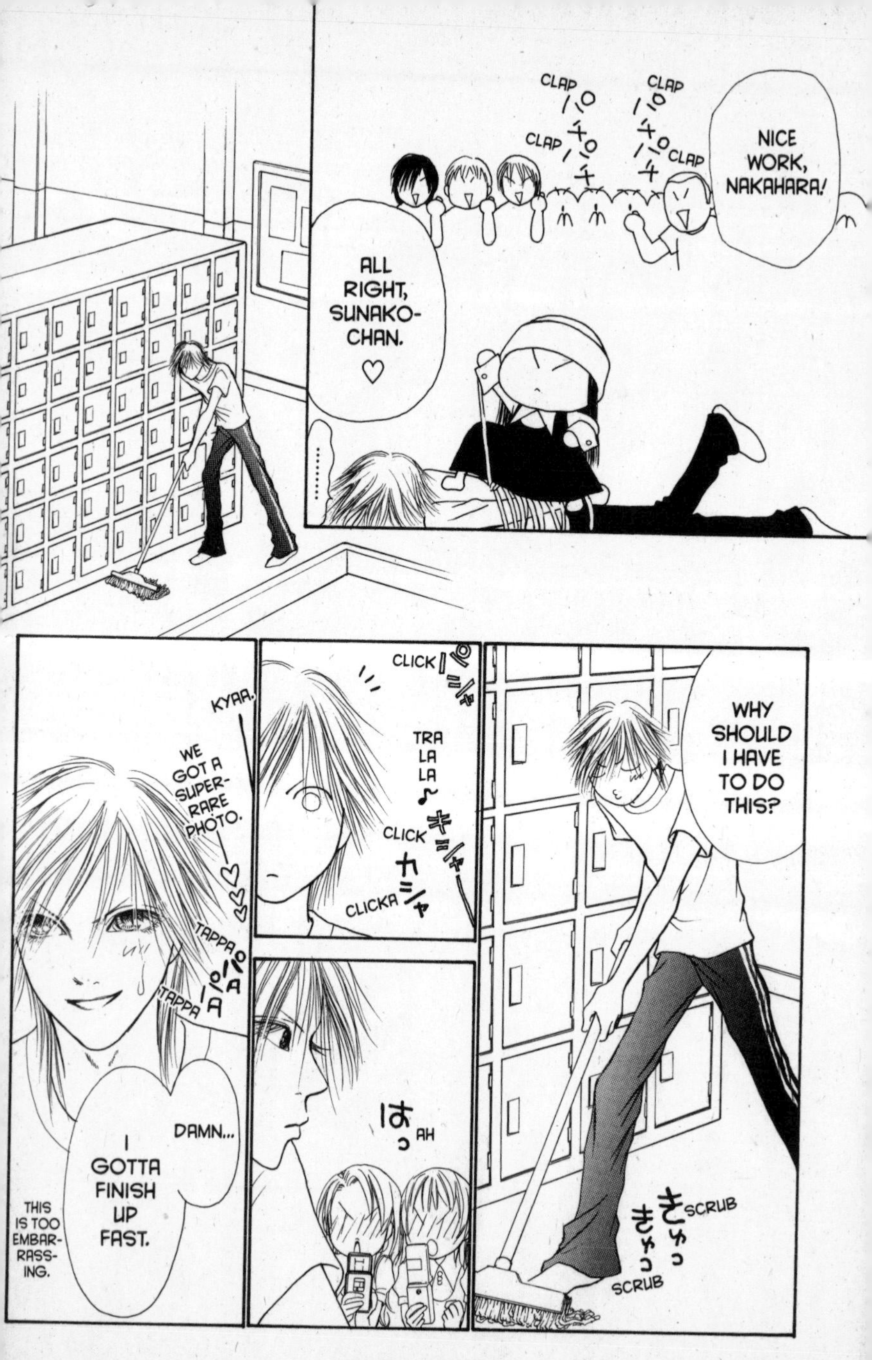

CLAP CLAP CLAP CLAP
NICE WORK, NAKAHARA!
ALL RIGHT, SUNAKO-CHAN. ♡
......
WHY SHOULD I HAVE TO DO THIS?
SCRUB SCRUB
CLICK
TRA LA LA ♪
CLICK
CLICKA
AH
KYAA.
WE GOT A SUPER-RARE PHOTO. ♡ ♡ ♡
TAPPA TAPPA
DAMN...
I GOTTA FINISH UP FAST.
THIS IS TOO EMBARRASSING.

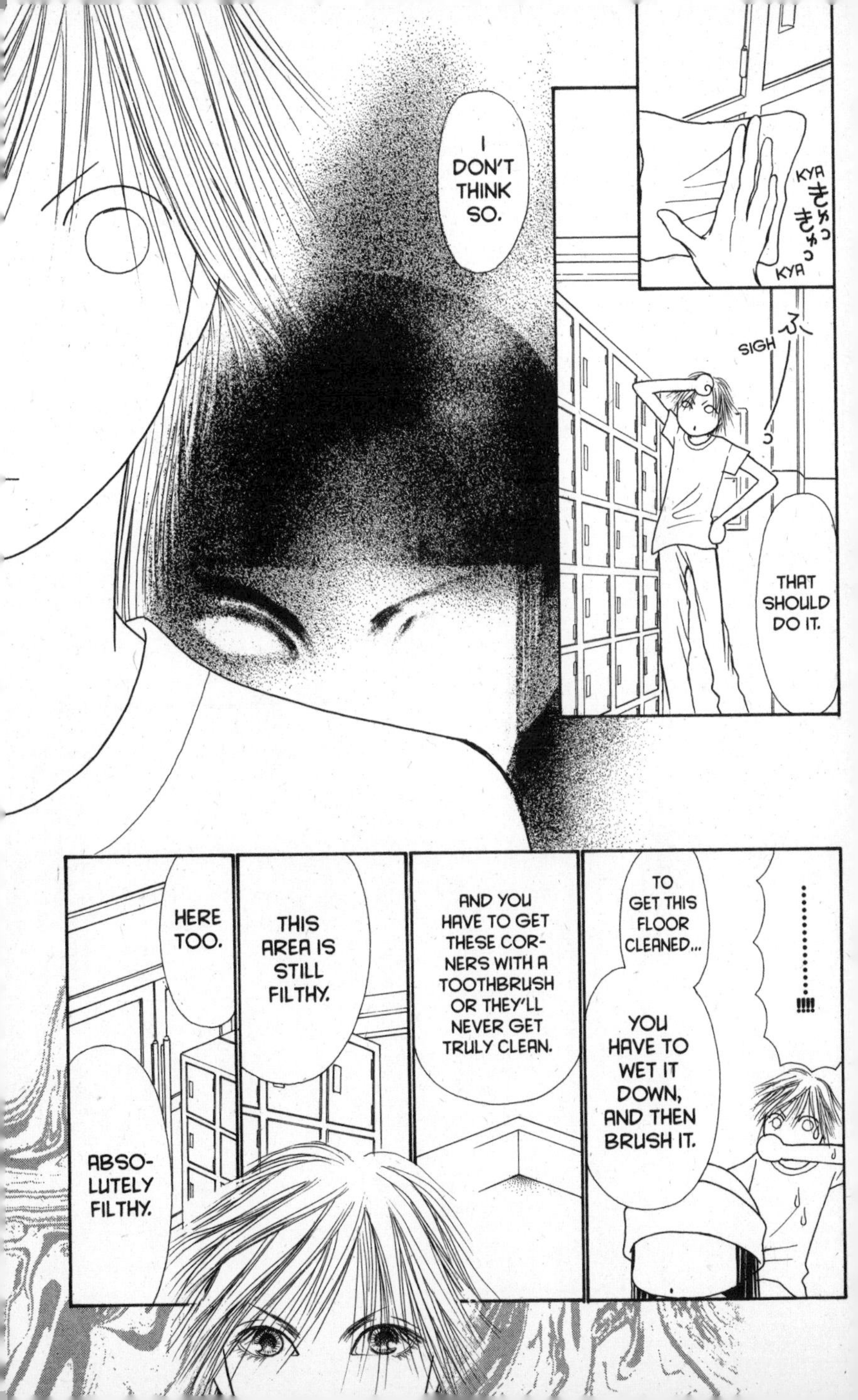

きゅっ きゅっ
KYA
KYA
ふ～っ
SIGH
THAT SHOULD DO IT.
I DON'T THINK SO.
..........!!!!
TO GET THIS FLOOR CLEANED...
YOU HAVE TO WET IT DOWN, AND THEN BRUSH IT.
AND YOU HAVE TO GET THESE CORNERS WITH A TOOTHBRUSH OR THEY'LL NEVER GET TRULY CLEAN.
THIS AREA IS STILL FILTHY.
HERE TOO.
ABSOLUTELY FILTHY.

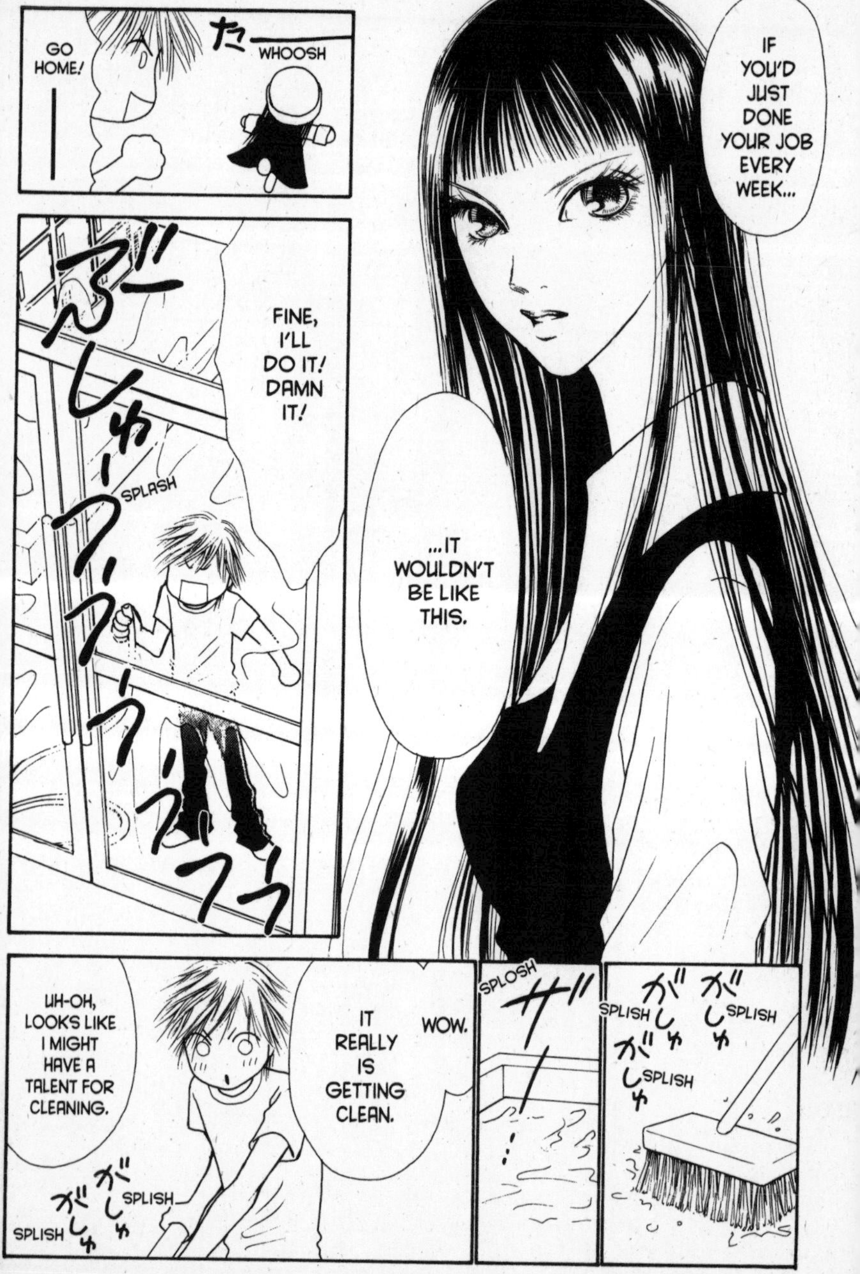
IF YOU'D JUST DONE YOUR JOB EVERY WEEK...
...IT WOULDN'T BE LIKE THIS.
たー
WHOOSH
GO HOME!
FINE, I'LL DO IT! DAMN IT!
SPLASH
がしゅ
SPLISH
がしゅ
SPLISH
SPLISH
ザー
SPLOSH
WOW.
IT REALLY IS GETTING CLEAN.
UH-OH, LOOKS LIKE I MIGHT HAVE A TALENT FOR CLEANING.
がしゅ
SPLISH
がしゅ
SPLISH

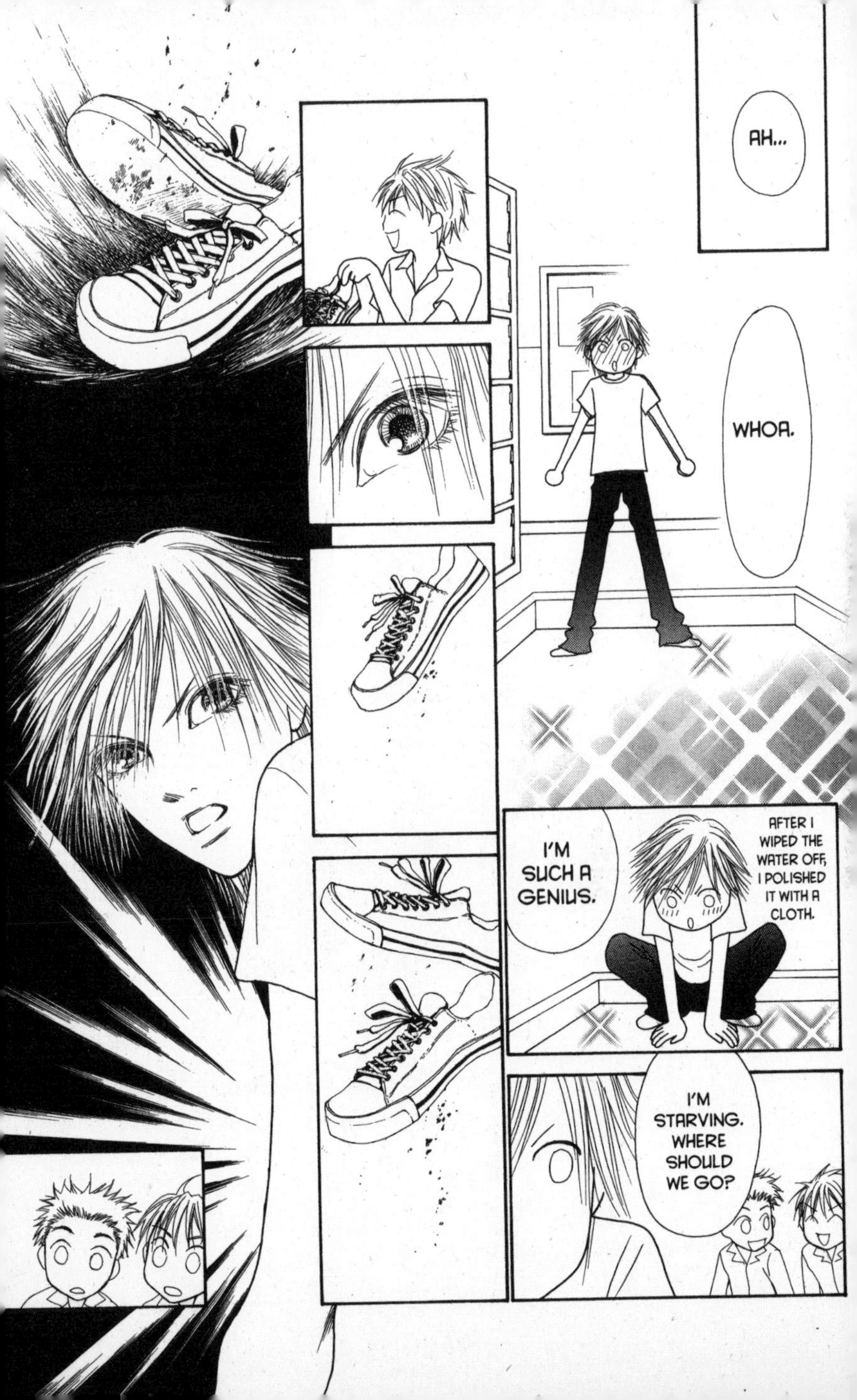
AH...
WHOA.
AFTER I WIPED THE WATER OFF, I POLISHED IT WITH A CLOTH.
I'M SUCH A GENIUS.
I'M STARVING. WHERE SHOULD WE GO?

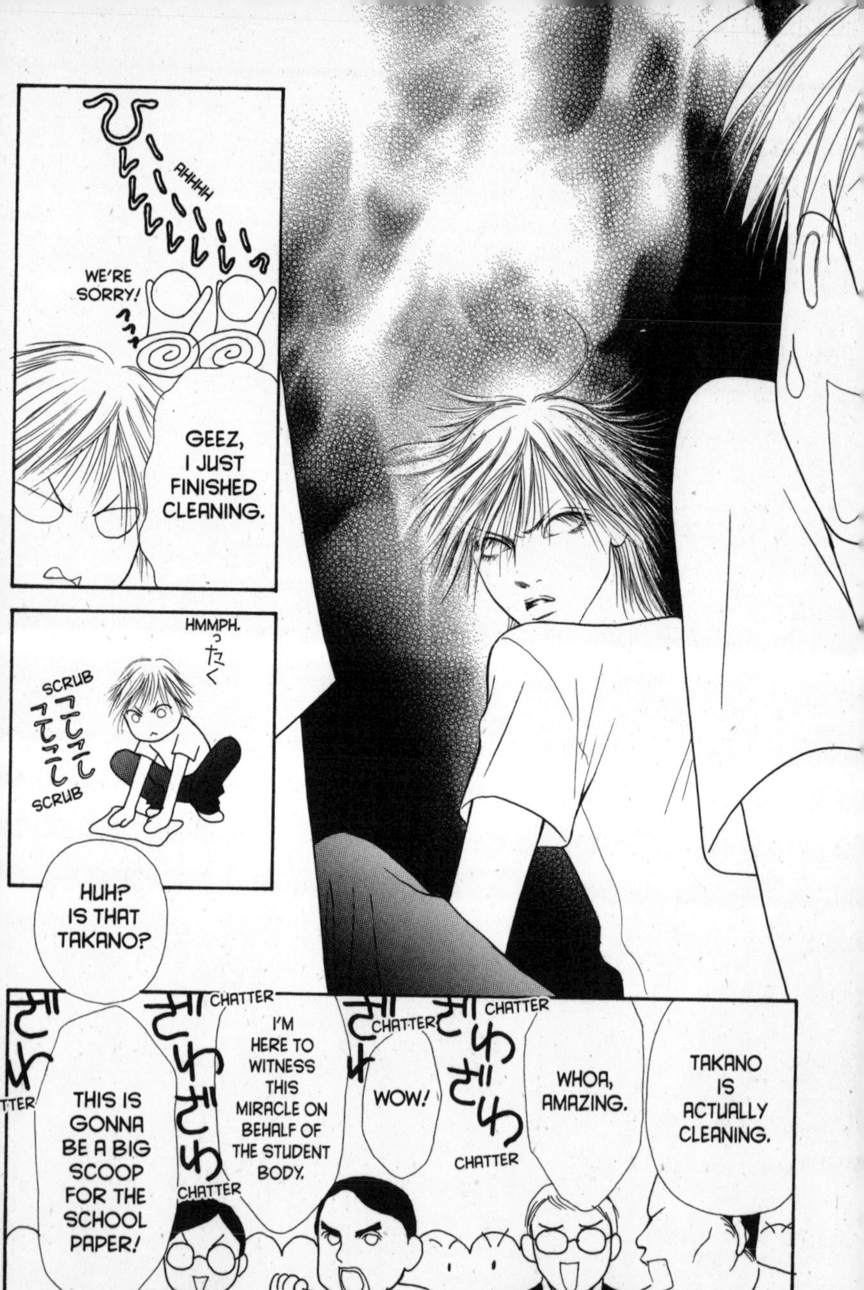
AHHHH
WE'RE SORRY!
GEEZ, I JUST FINISHED CLEANING.
HMMPH.
っ たく
SCRUB
SCRUB
HUH? IS THAT TAKANO?
TAKANO IS ACTUALLY CLEANING.
CHATTER
WHOA, AMAZING.
CHATTER
CHATTER
WOW!
CHATTER
I'M HERE TO WITNESS THIS MIRACLE ON BEHALF OF THE STUDENT BODY.
CHATTER
CHATTER
THIS IS GONNA BE A BIG SCOOP FOR THE SCHOOL PAPER!

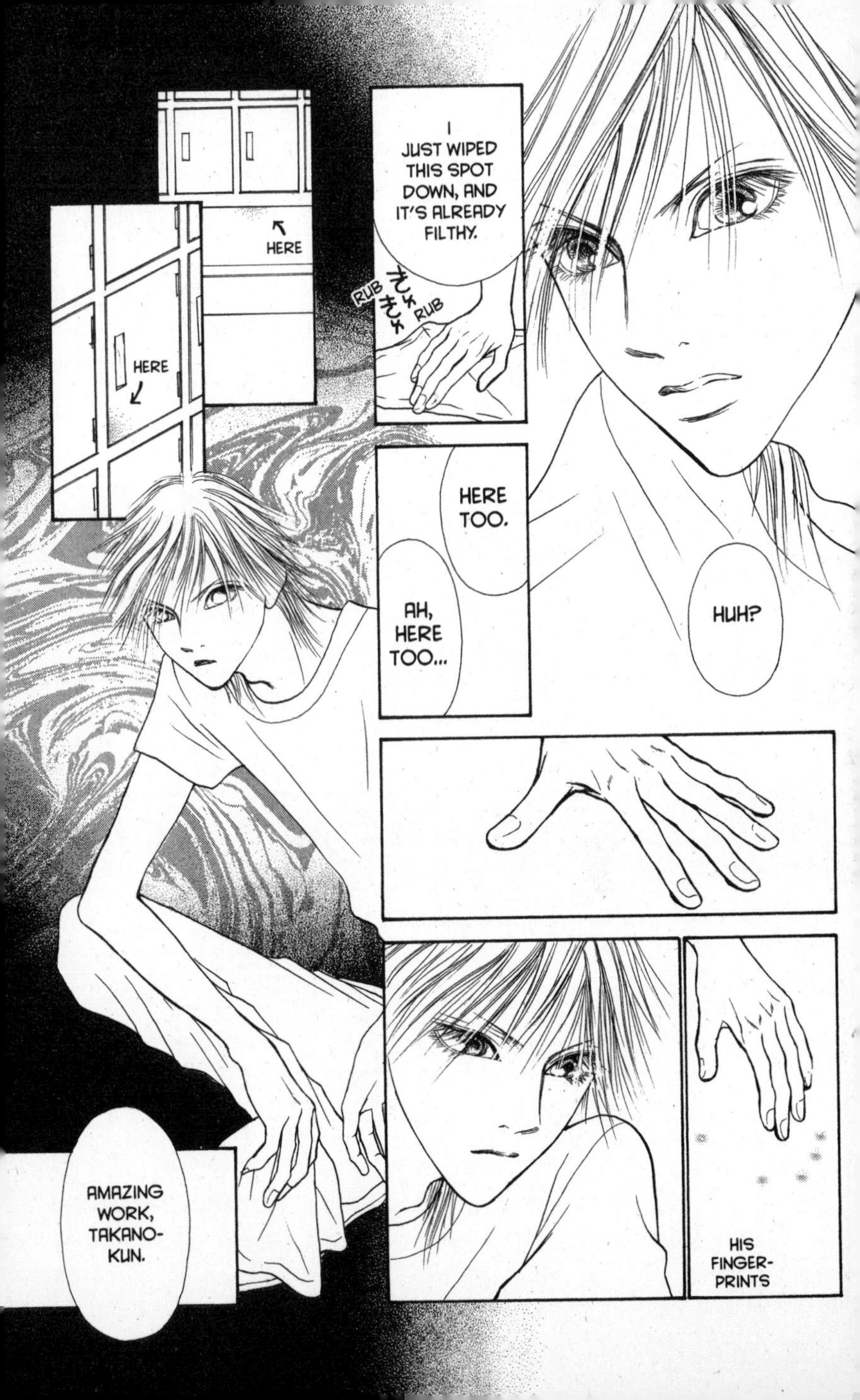
I JUST WIPED THIS SPOT DOWN, AND IT'S ALREADY FILTHY.
RUB RUB
HERE TOO.
AH, HERE TOO...
HUH?
HERE
HERE
HIS FINGER-PRINTS
AMAZING WORK, TAKANO-KUN.

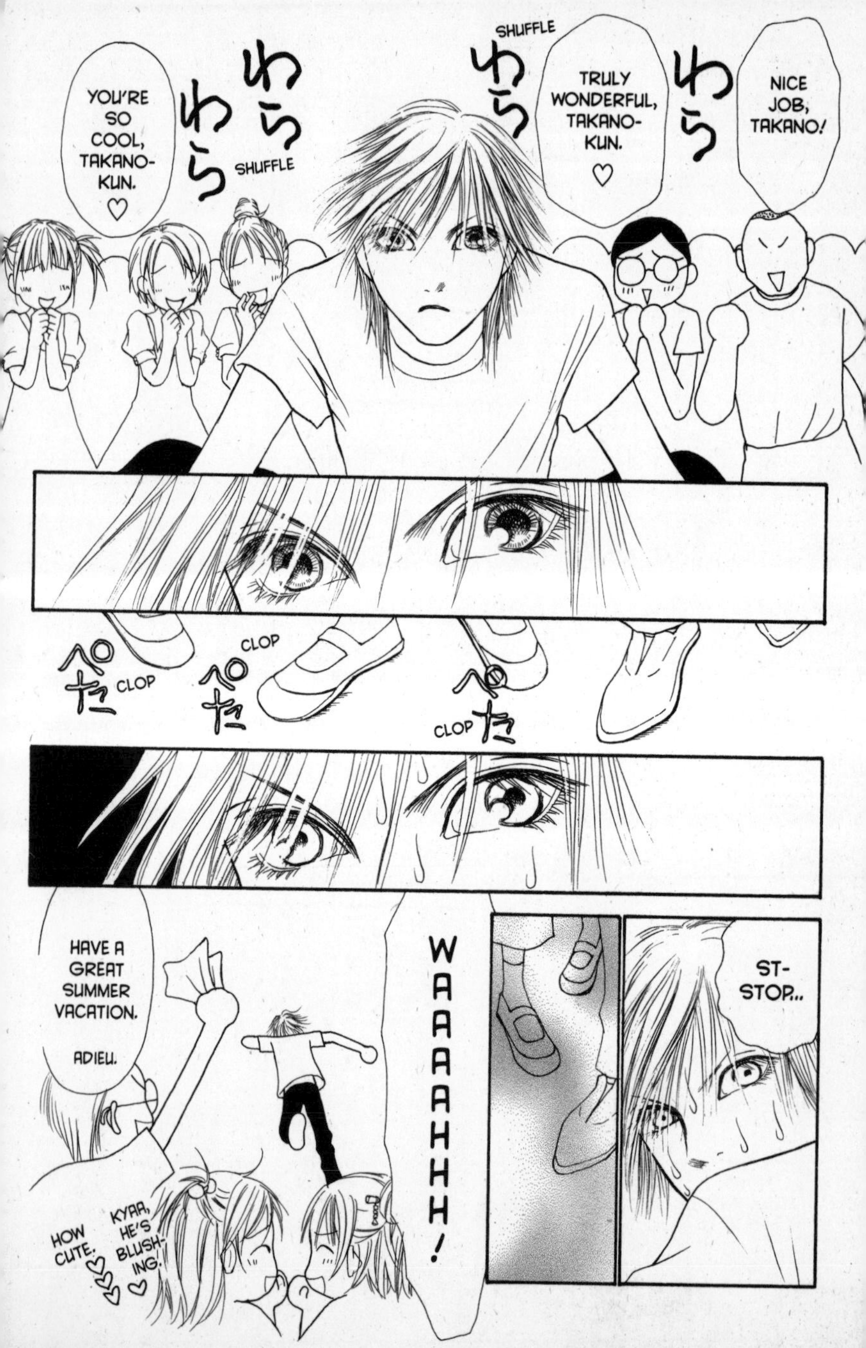

NICE JOB, TAKANO!
わら
TRULY WONDERFUL, TAKANO-KUN. ♡
SHUFFLE
わら
わら
わら
SHUFFLE
YOU'RE SO COOL, TAKANO-KUN. ♡
ぺた CLOP
ぺた CLOP
ぺた CLOP
ST-STOP...
WAAAAAHHHH!
HAVE A GREAT SUMMER VACATION.
ADIEU.
KYAA, HE'S BLUSHING! ♡
HOW CUTE. ♡♡♡

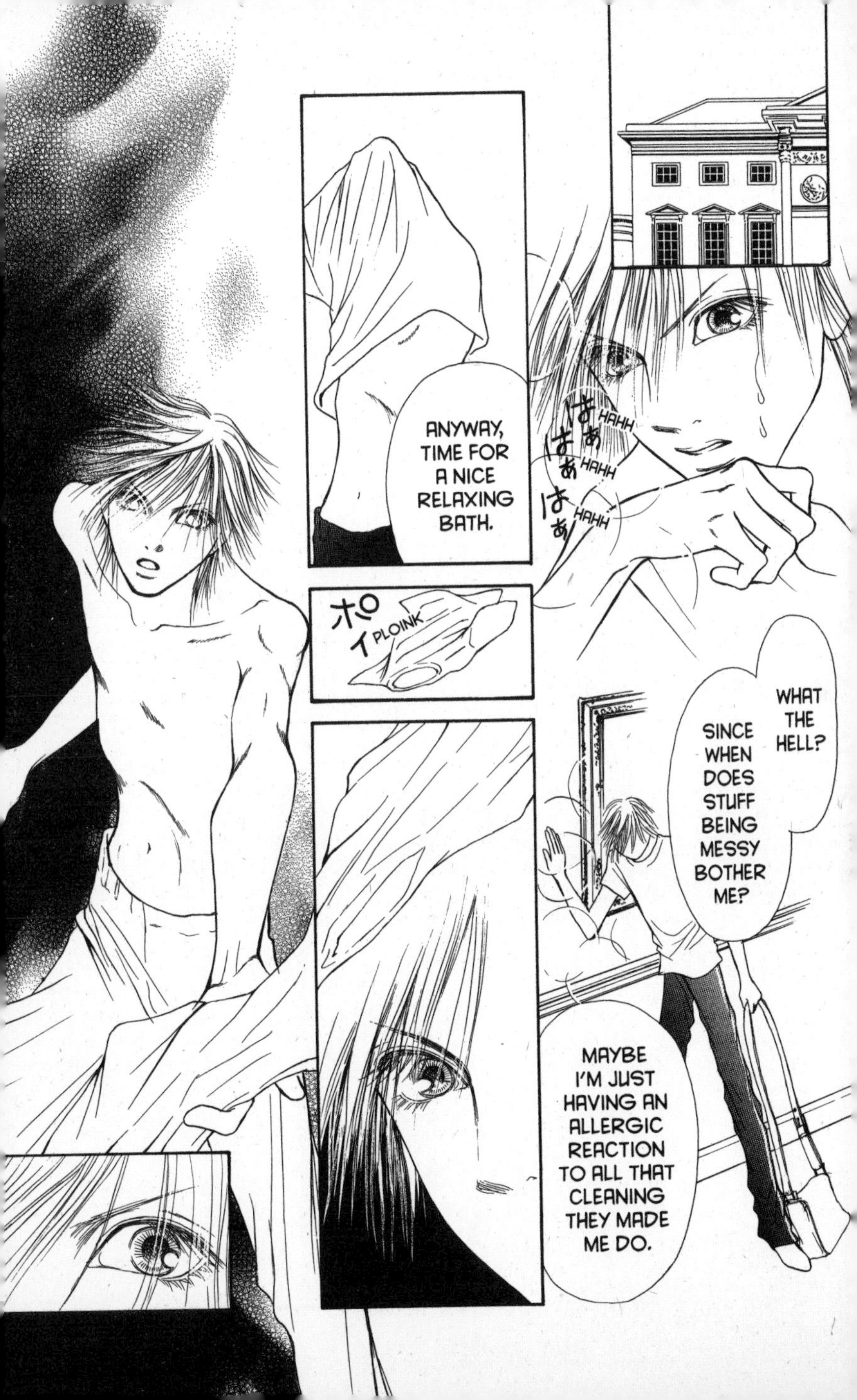
はあ HAHH
はあ HAHH
はあ HAHH
WHAT THE HELL?
SINCE WHEN DOES STUFF BEING MESSY BOTHER ME?
MAYBE I'M JUST HAVING AN ALLERGIC REACTION TO ALL THAT CLEANING THEY MADE ME DO.
ANYWAY, TIME FOR A NICE RELAXING BATH.
ポイ PLOINK

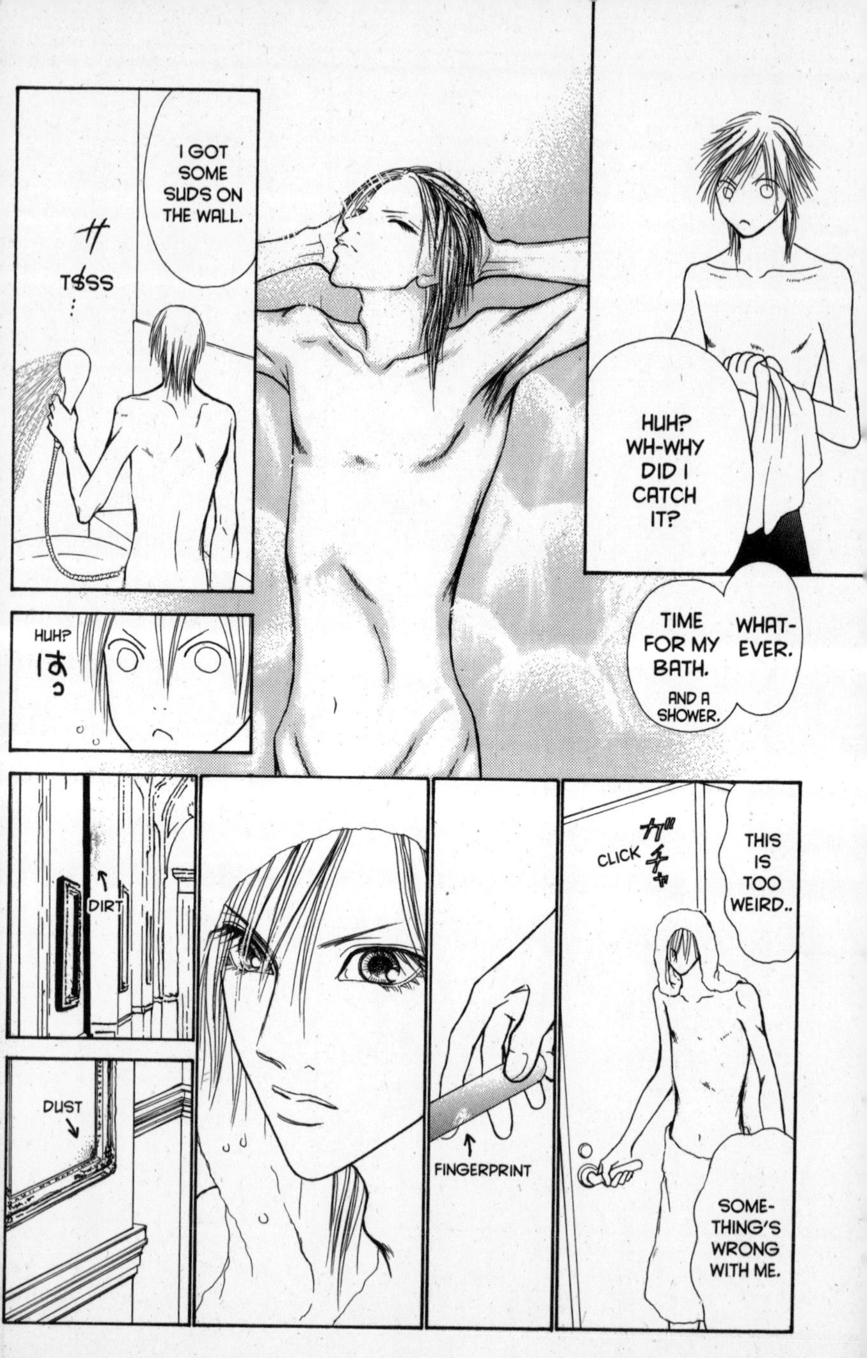
HUH? WH-WHY DID I CATCH IT?
WHAT-EVER.
TIME FOR MY BATH.
AND A SHOWER.
I GOT SOME SUDS ON THE WALL.
ザ
TSSS
HUH?
はっ
ガチャ
CLICK
THIS IS TOO WEIRD..
SOME-THING'S WRONG WITH ME.
FINGERPRINT
DIRT
DUST

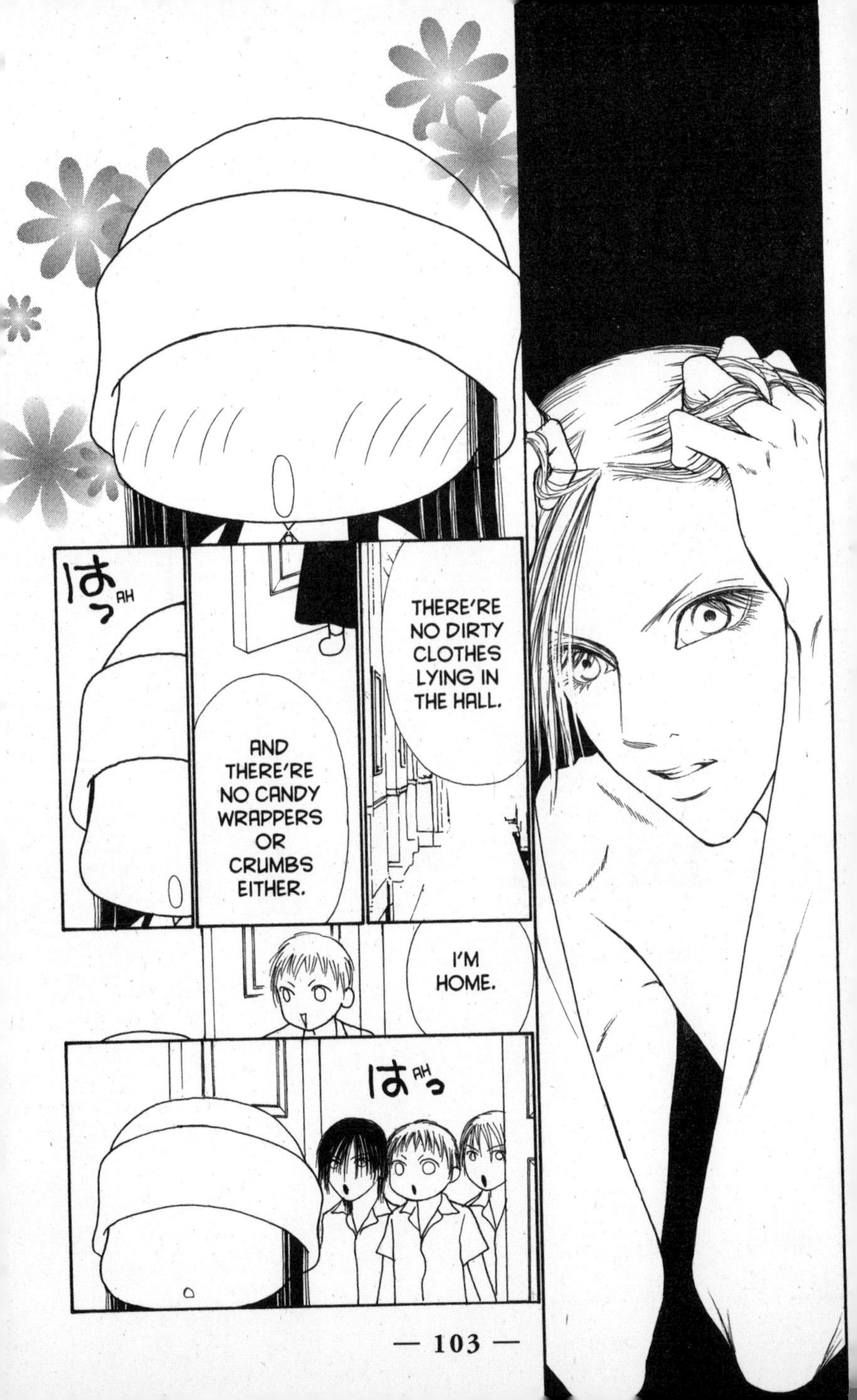
THERE'RE NO DIRTY CLOTHES LYING IN THE HALL.
AND THERE'RE NO CANDY WRAPPERS OR CRUMBS EITHER.
はっ AH
I'M HOME.
はっ AH

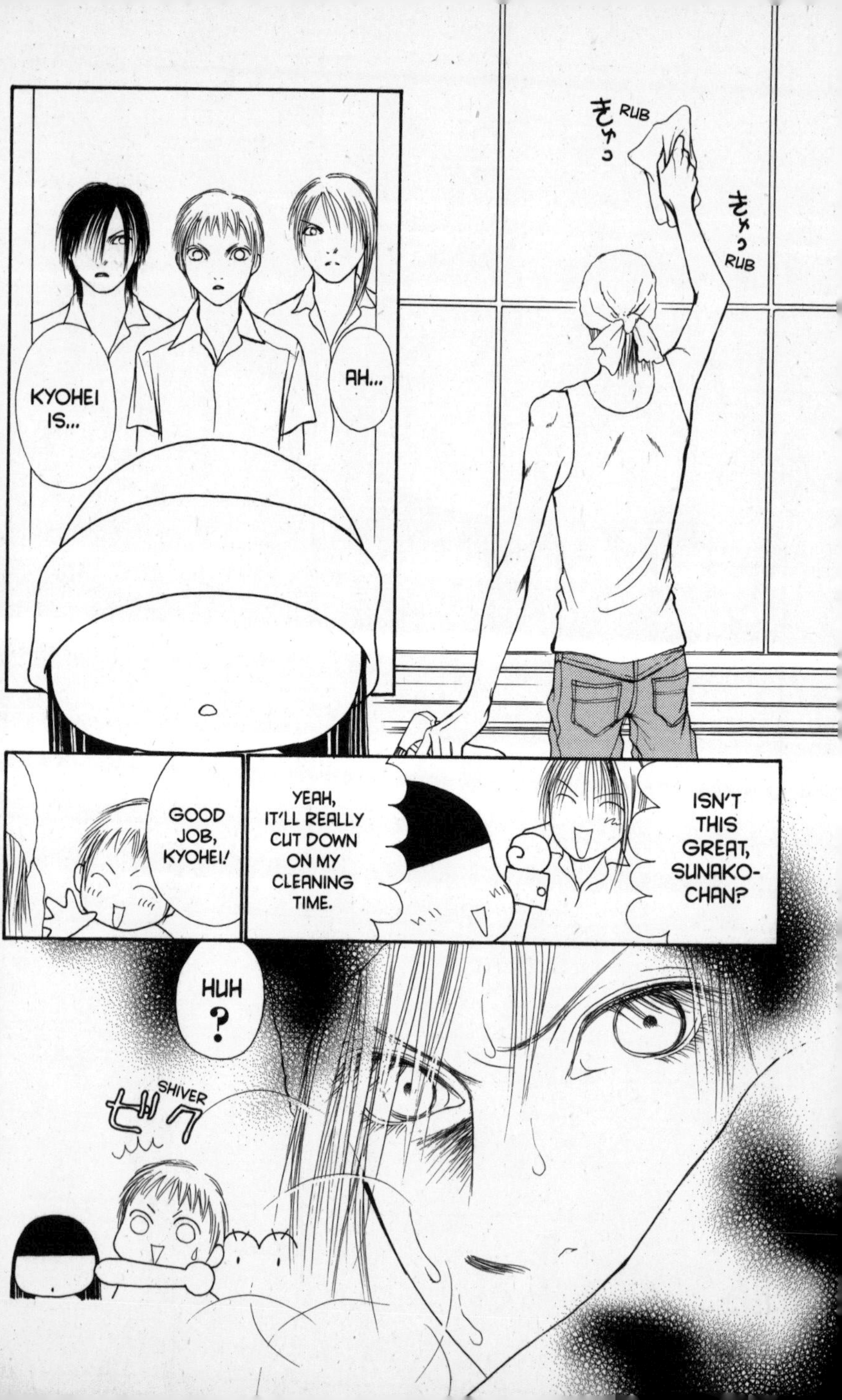
RUB
RUB
AH...
KYOHEI IS...
ISN'T THIS GREAT, SUNAKO-CHAN?
YEAH, IT'LL REALLY CUT DOWN ON MY CLEANING TIME.
GOOD JOB, KYOHEI!
HUH?
SHIVER

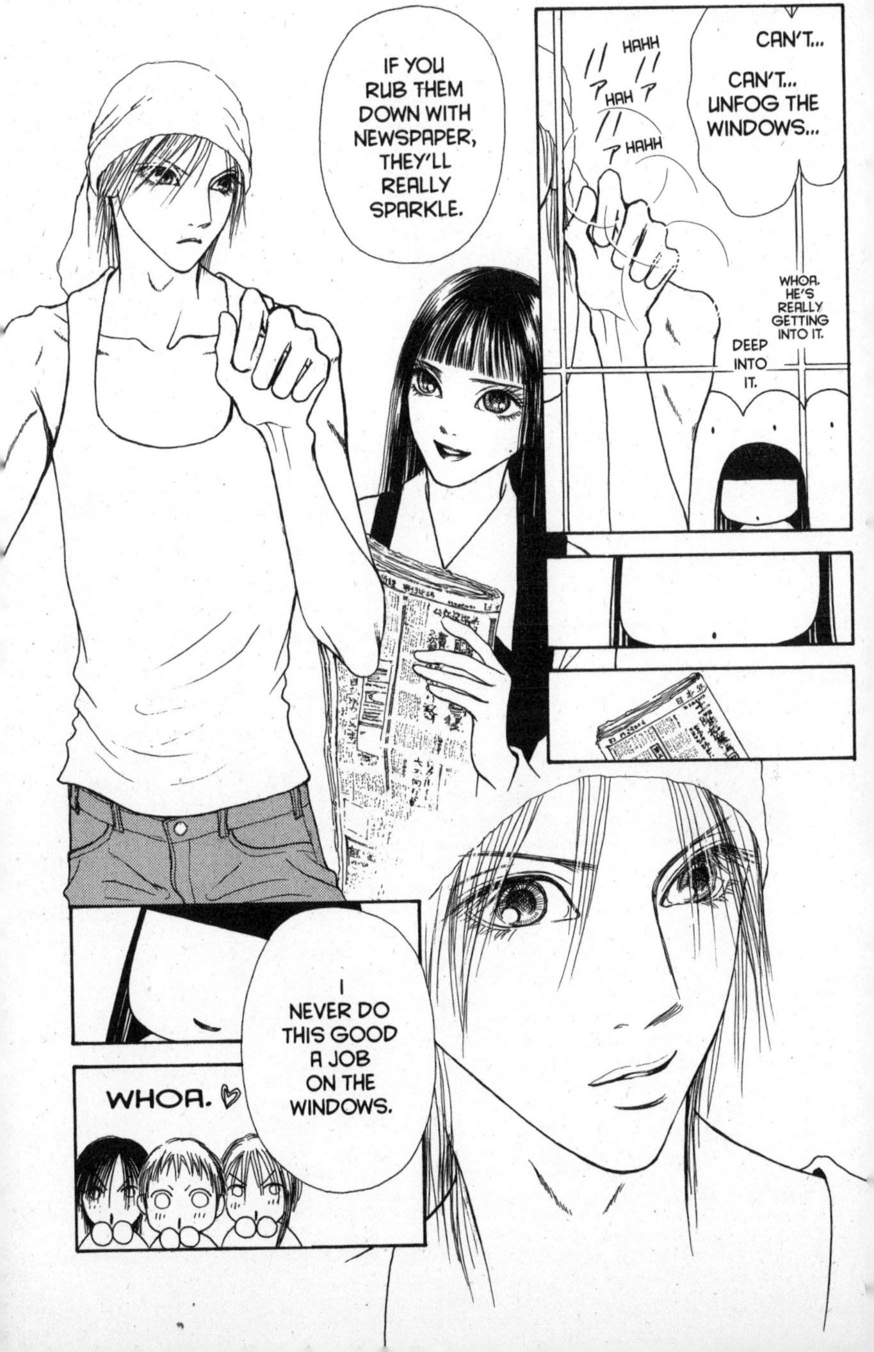

HAHH
HAH
HAHH
CAN'T...
CAN'T... UNFOG THE WINDOWS...
WHOA. HE'S REALLY GETTING INTO IT.
DEEP INTO IT.
IF YOU RUB THEM DOWN WITH NEWSPAPER, THEY'LL REALLY SPARKLE.
I NEVER DO THIS GOOD A JOB ON THE WINDOWS.
WHOA. ♡

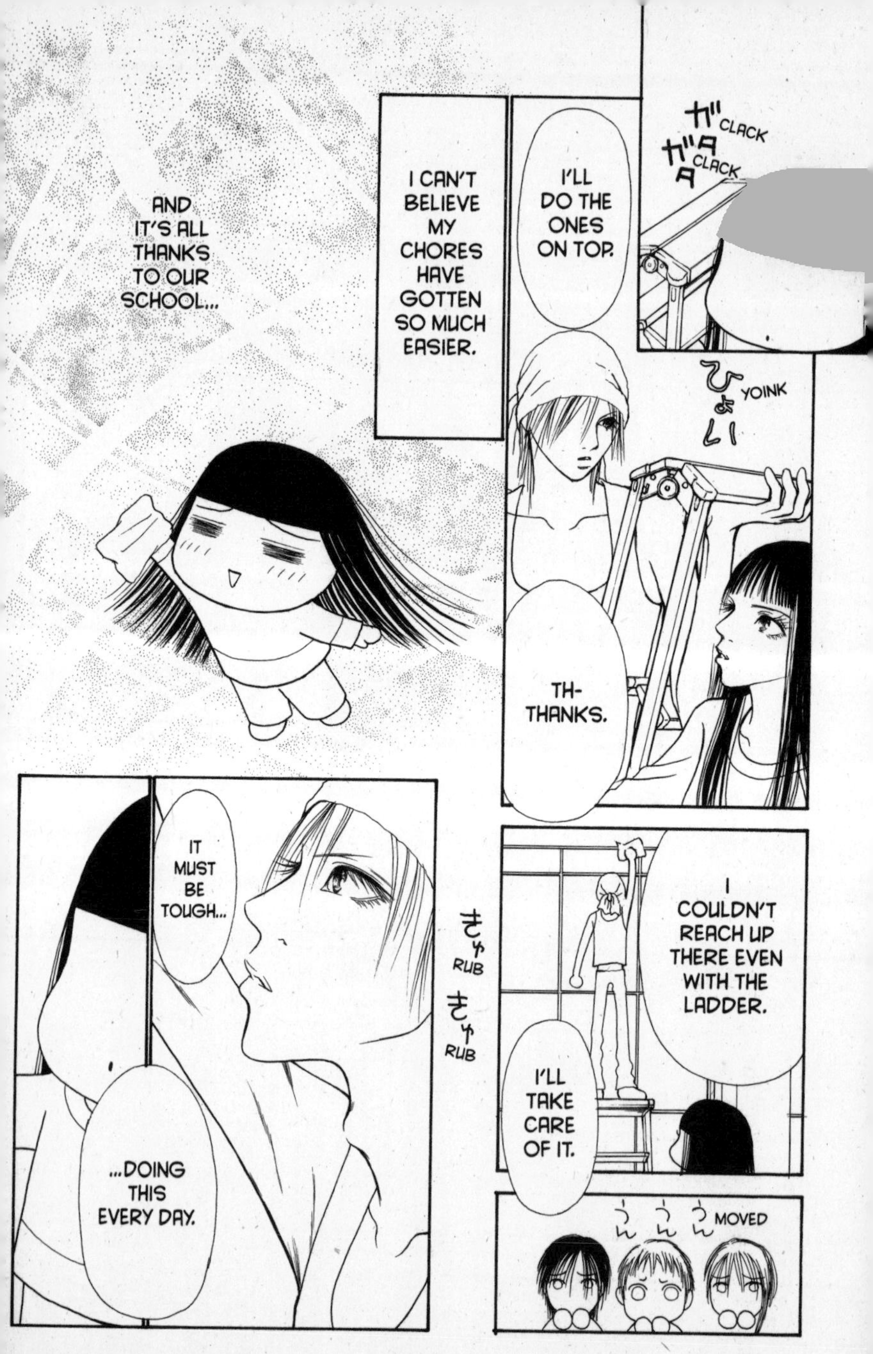
ガタ CLACK
ガタ CLACK
I'LL DO THE ONES ON TOP.
ひょい YOINK
TH-THANKS.
I CAN'T BELIEVE MY CHORES HAVE GOTTEN SO MUCH EASIER.
AND IT'S ALL THANKS TO OUR SCHOOL...
I COULDN'T REACH UP THERE EVEN WITH THE LADDER.
I'LL TAKE CARE OF IT.
うん うん うん MOVED
きゅ RUB
きゅ RUB
IT MUST BE TOUGH...
...DOING THIS EVERY DAY.

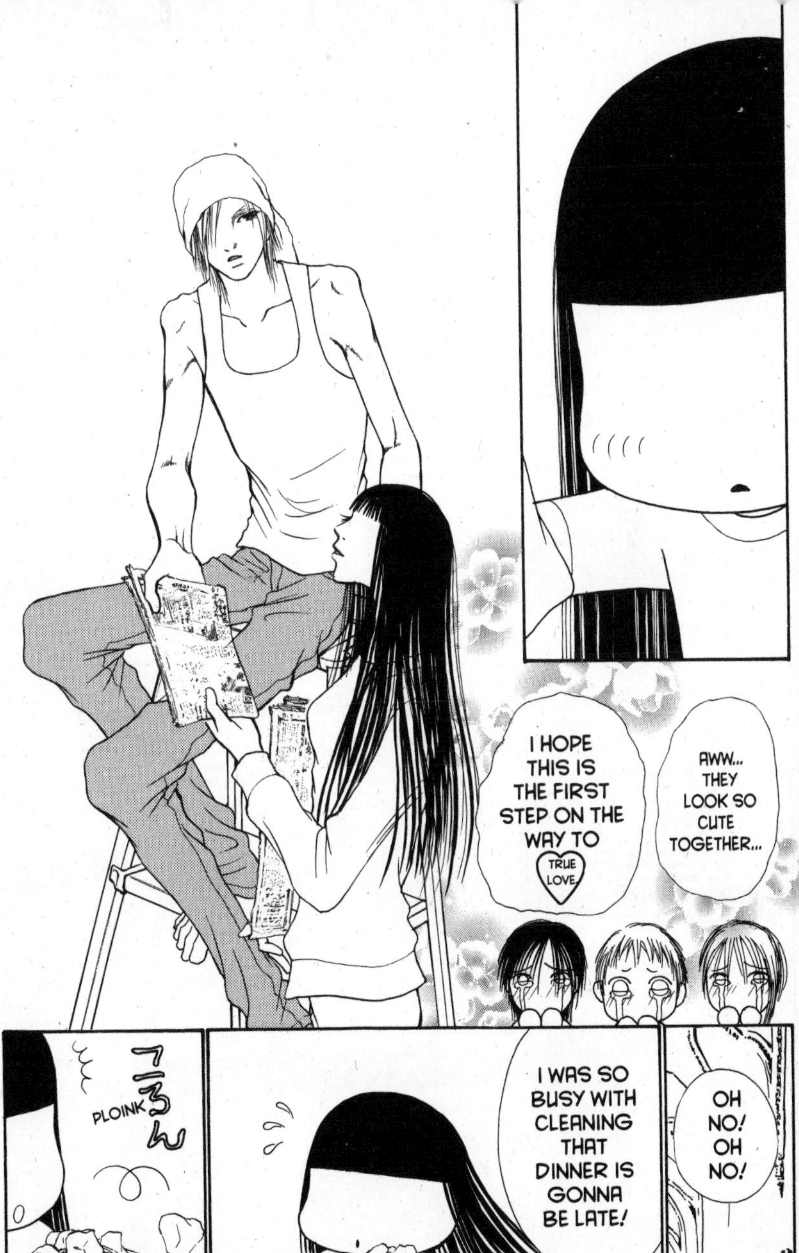
AWW... THEY LOOK SO CUTE TOGETHER...
I HOPE THIS IS THE FIRST STEP ON THE WAY TO TRUE LOVE
OH NO! OH NO!
I WAS SO BUSY WITH CLEANING THAT DINNER IS GONNA BE LATE!
ころん
PLOINK

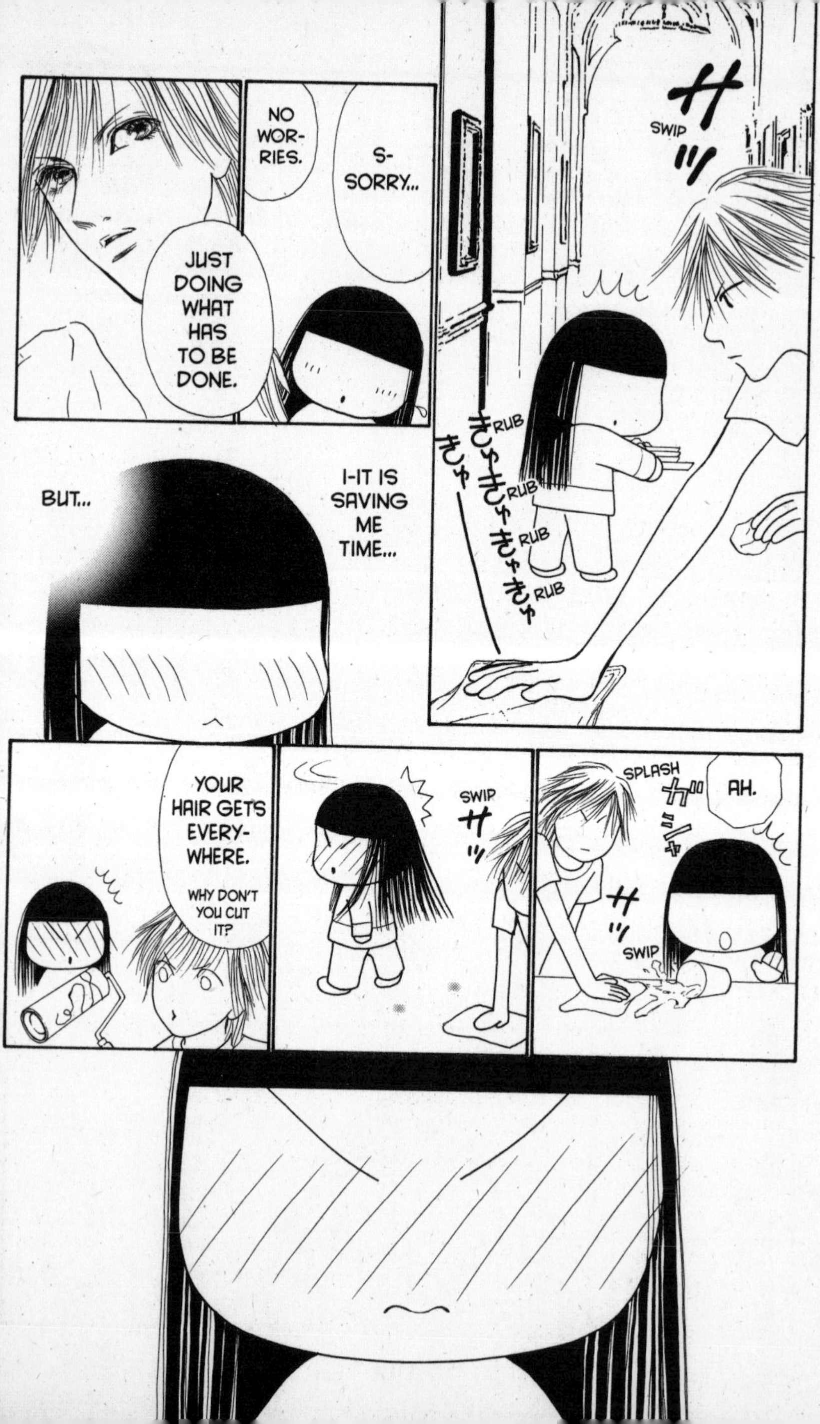
サッ
SWIP
きゅきゅきゅきゅきゅ
RUB
RUB
RUB
RUB
S-SORRY...
NO WORRIES.
JUST DOING WHAT HAS TO BE DONE.
I-IT IS SAVING ME TIME...
BUT...
AH.
SPLASH
ガシャ
サッ
SWIP
SWIP
サッ
YOUR HAIR GETS EVERYWHERE.
WHY DON'T YOU CUT IT?

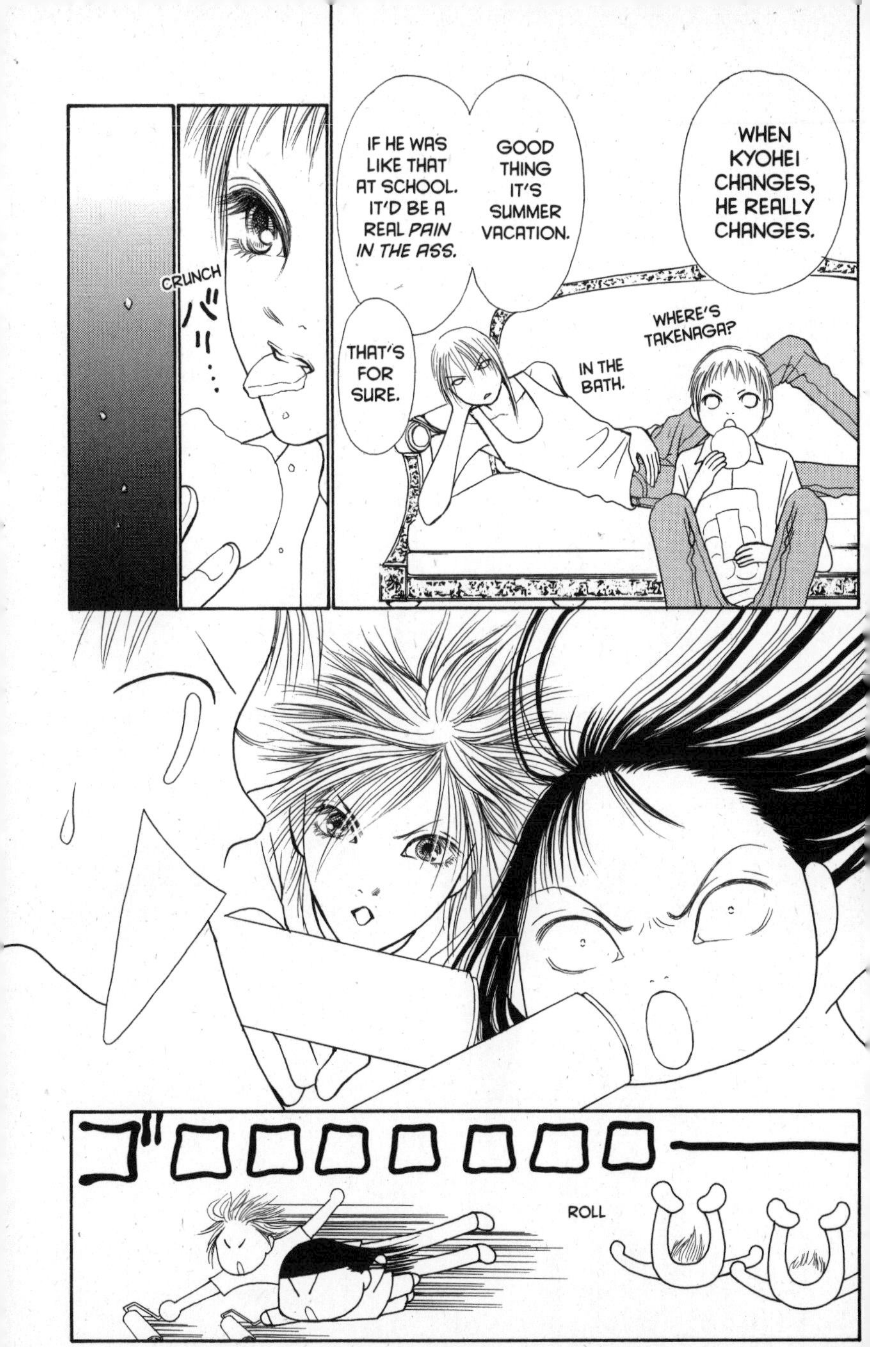
WHEN KYOHEI CHANGES, HE REALLY CHANGES.
GOOD THING IT'S SUMMER VACATION.
IF HE WAS LIKE THAT AT SCHOOL. IT'D BE A REAL *PAIN IN THE ASS.*
WHERE'S TAKENAGA?
IN THE BATH.
THAT'S FOR SURE.
CRUNCH
バリ…
ゴロロロロロロロ——
ROLL

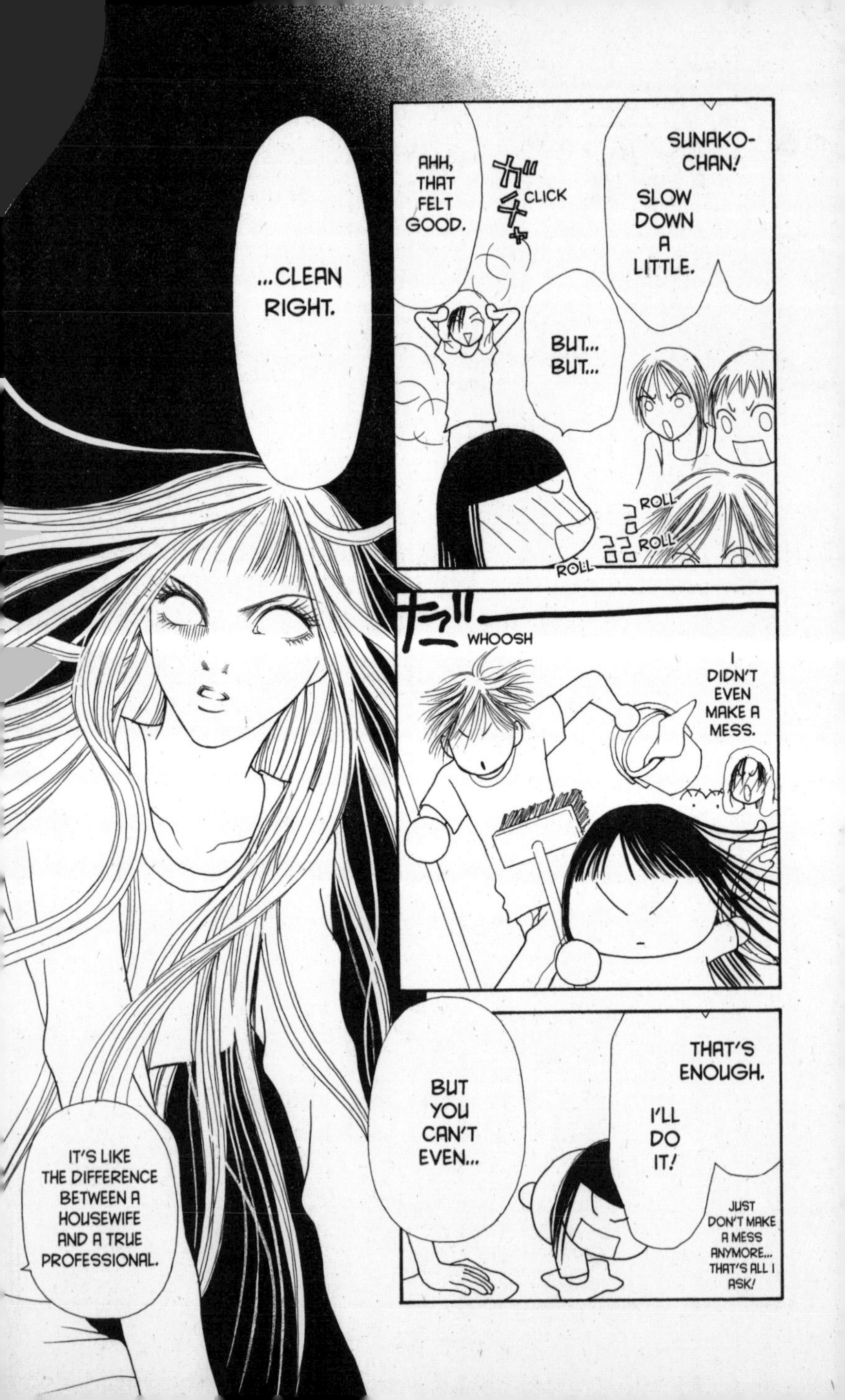
SUNAKO-CHAN!
SLOW DOWN A LITTLE.
BUT... BUT...
CLICK
AHH, THAT FELT GOOD.
ROLL
ROLL
ROLL
WHOOSH
I DIDN'T EVEN MAKE A MESS.
THAT'S ENOUGH.
I'LL DO IT!
BUT YOU CAN'T EVEN...
JUST DON'T MAKE A MESS ANYMORE... THAT'S ALL I ASK!
...CLEAN RIGHT.
IT'S LIKE THE DIFFERENCE BETWEEN A HOUSEWIFE AND A TRUE PROFESSIONAL.

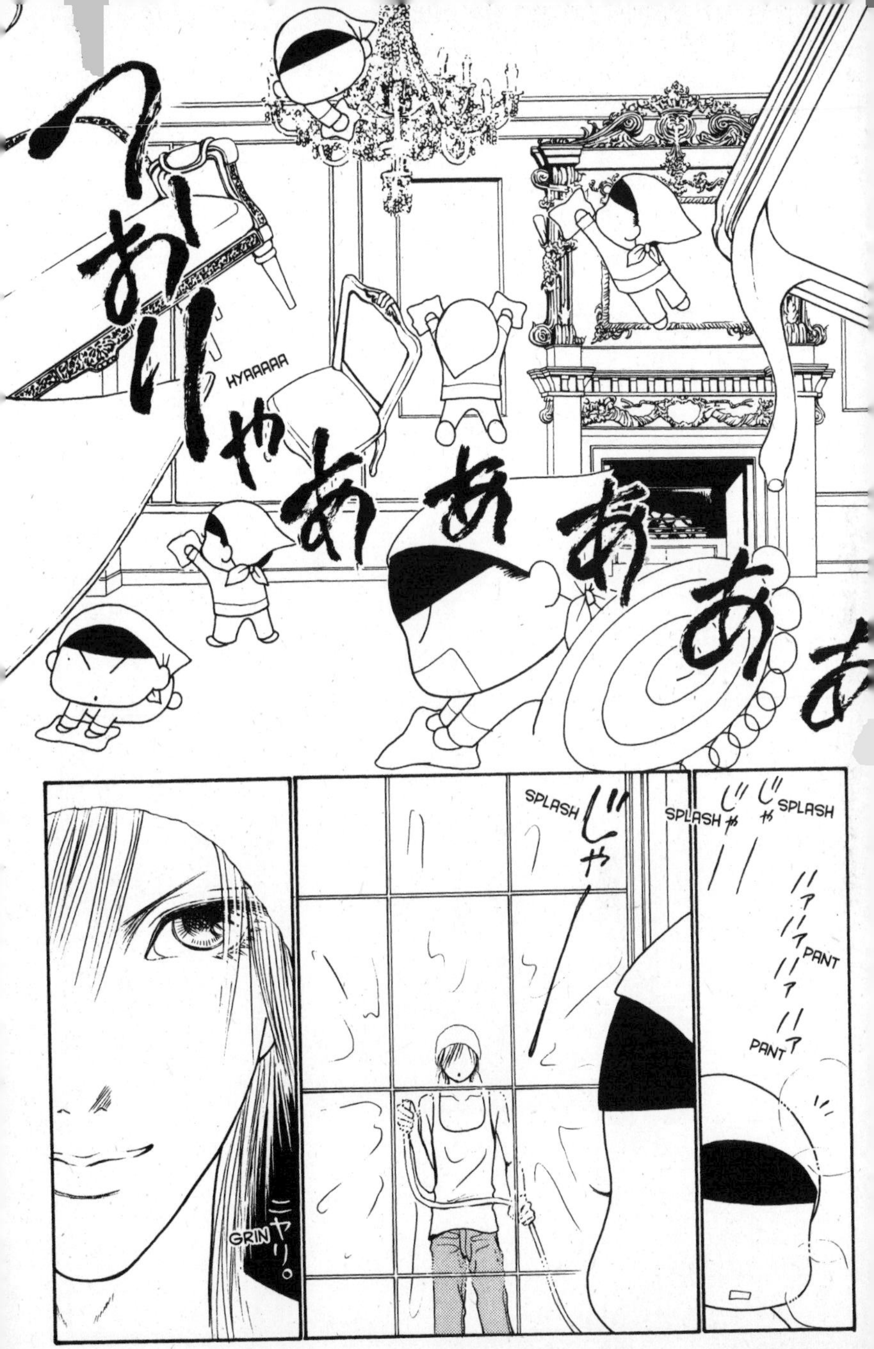
KYAAAAA
SPLASH
SPLASH
PANT
PANT
SPLASH
GRIN
ニヤリ。

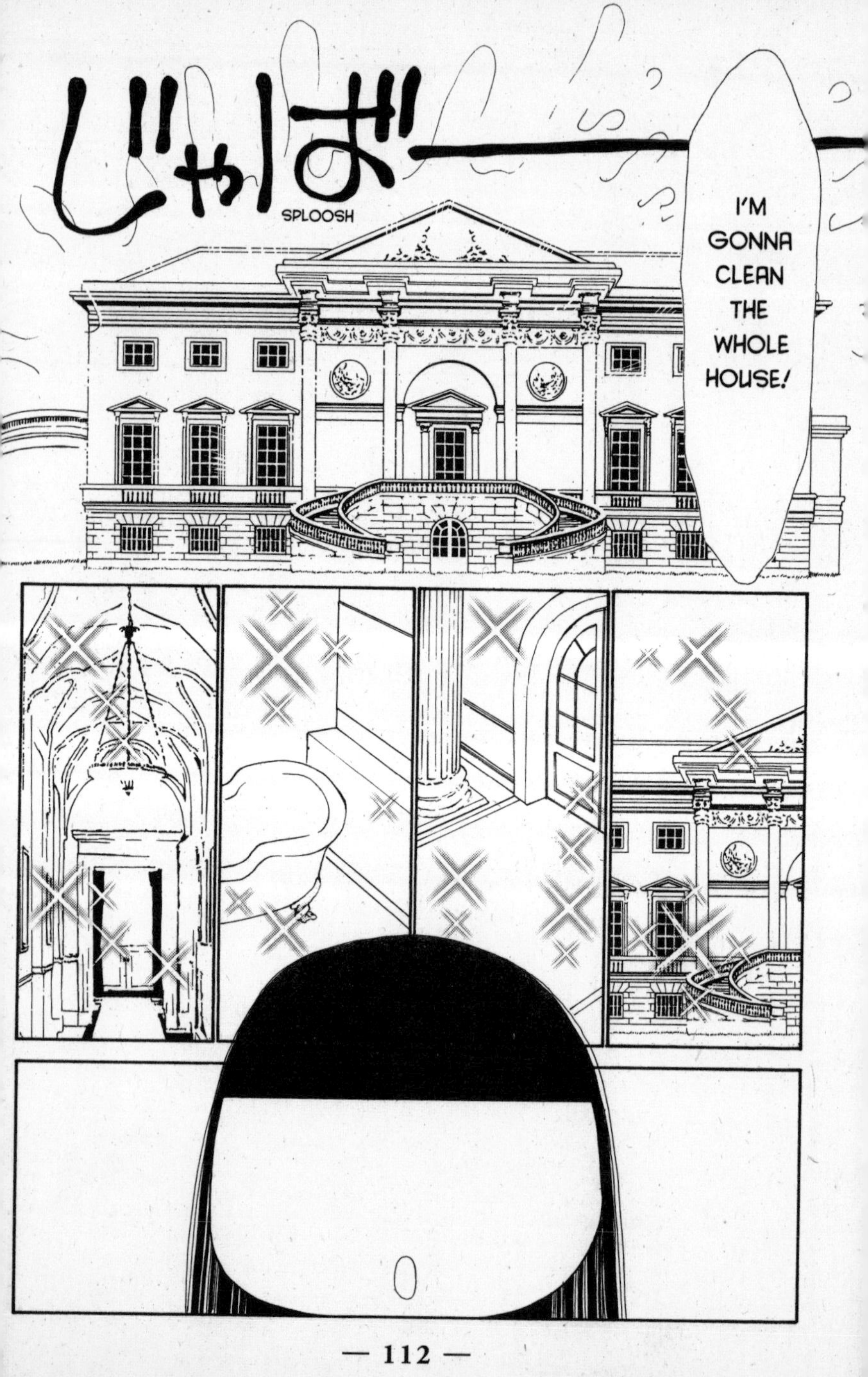
じゃばー
SPLOOSH
I'M GONNA CLEAN THE WHOLE HOUSE!

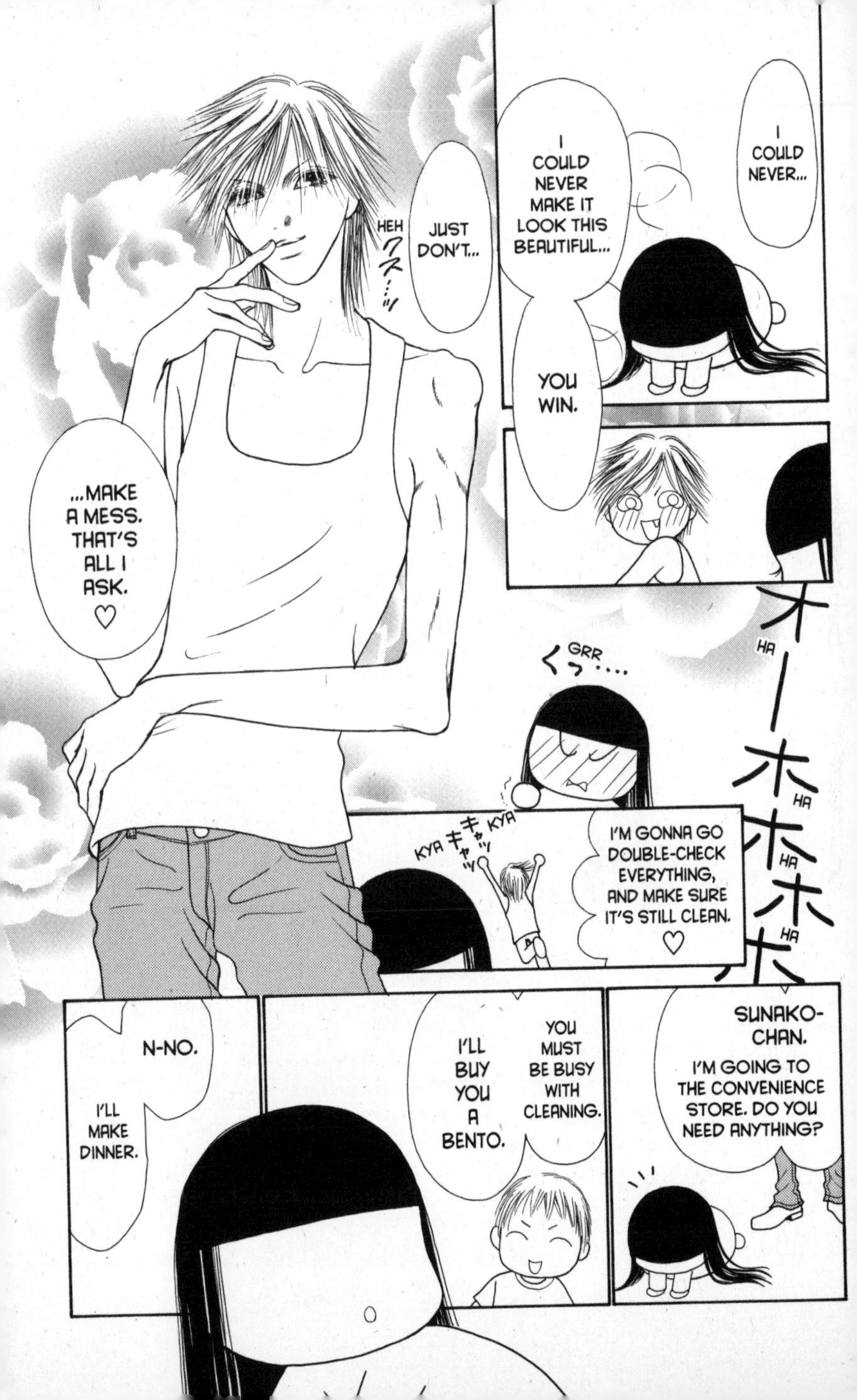
I COULD NEVER...
I COULD NEVER MAKE IT LOOK THIS BEAUTIFUL...
YOU WIN.
オーホホホホ
HA HA HA HA
くっ GRR....
I'M GONNA GO DOUBLE-CHECK EVERYTHING, AND MAKE SURE IT'S STILL CLEAN. ♡
キャッ KYA キャッ KYA
クスーッ HEH
JUST DON'T...
...MAKE A MESS. THAT'S ALL I ASK. ♡
SUNAKO-CHAN.
I'M GOING TO THE CONVENIENCE STORE. DO YOU NEED ANYTHING?
YOU MUST BE BUSY WITH CLEANING.
I'LL BUY YOU A BENTO.
N-NO.
I'LL MAKE DINNER.

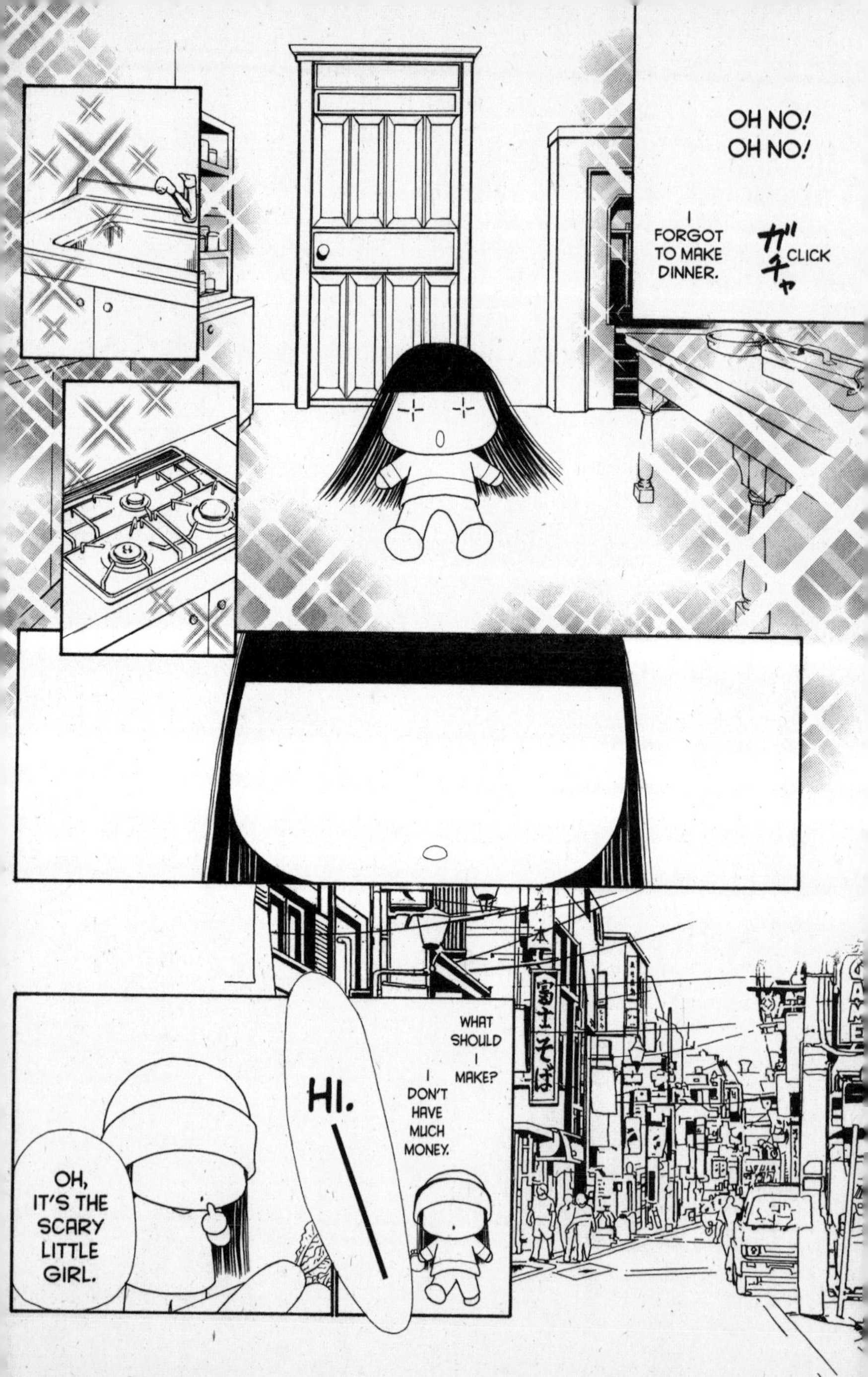
OH NO! OH NO!
ガチャ CLICK
I FORGOT TO MAKE DINNER.
富士そば
WHAT SHOULD I MAKE?
I DON'T HAVE MUCH MONEY.
HI.
OH, IT'S THE SCARY LITTLE GIRL.

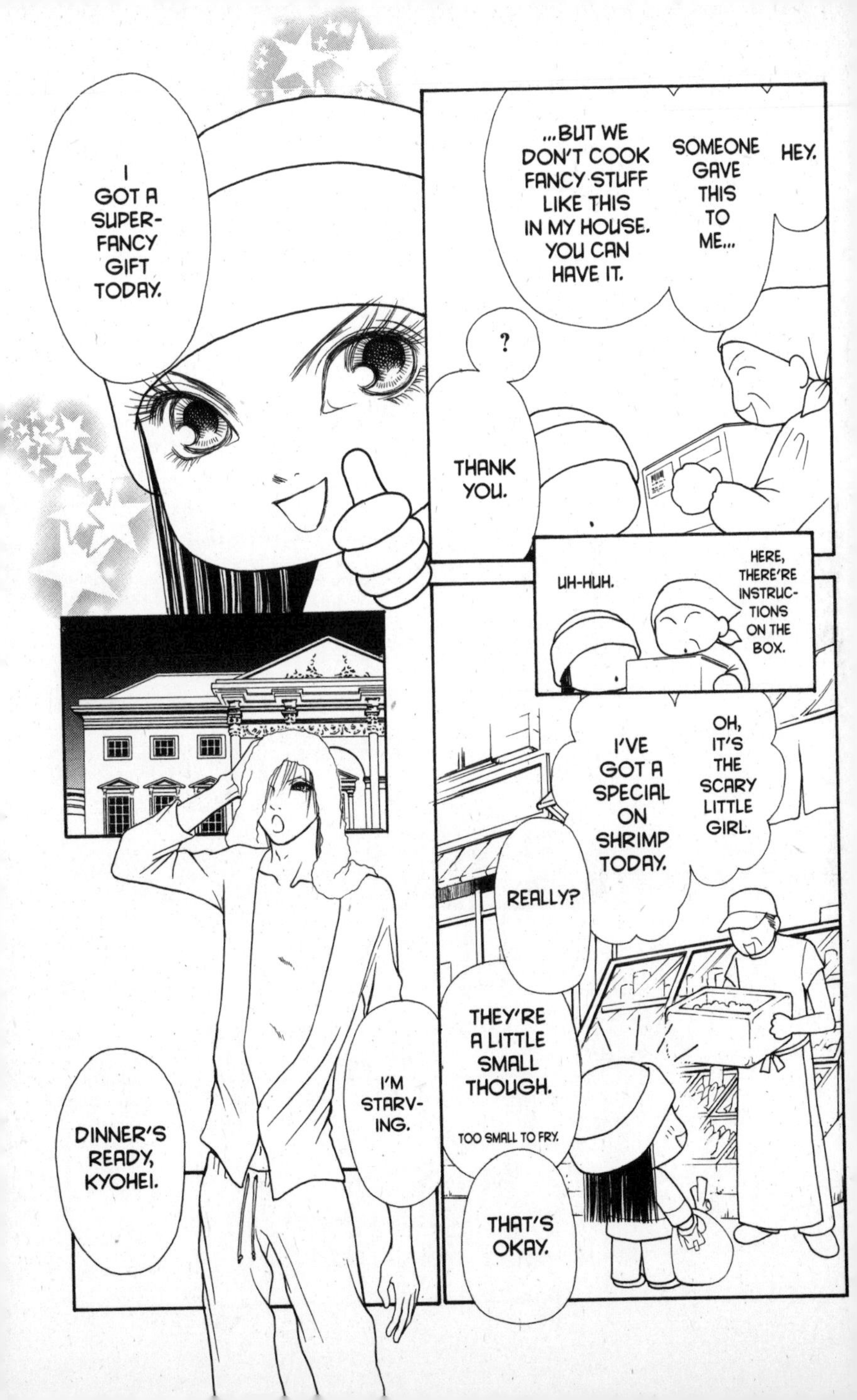

HEY.
SOMEONE GAVE THIS TO ME...
...BUT WE DON'T COOK FANCY STUFF LIKE THIS IN MY HOUSE. YOU CAN HAVE IT.
?
THANK YOU.
I GOT A SUPER-FANCY GIFT TODAY.
HERE, THERE'RE INSTRUCTIONS ON THE BOX.
UH-HUH.
OH, IT'S THE SCARY LITTLE GIRL.
I'VE GOT A SPECIAL ON SHRIMP TODAY.
REALLY?
THEY'RE A LITTLE SMALL THOUGH.
TOO SMALL TO FRY.
THAT'S OKAY.
I'M STARVING.
DINNER'S READY, KYOHEI.

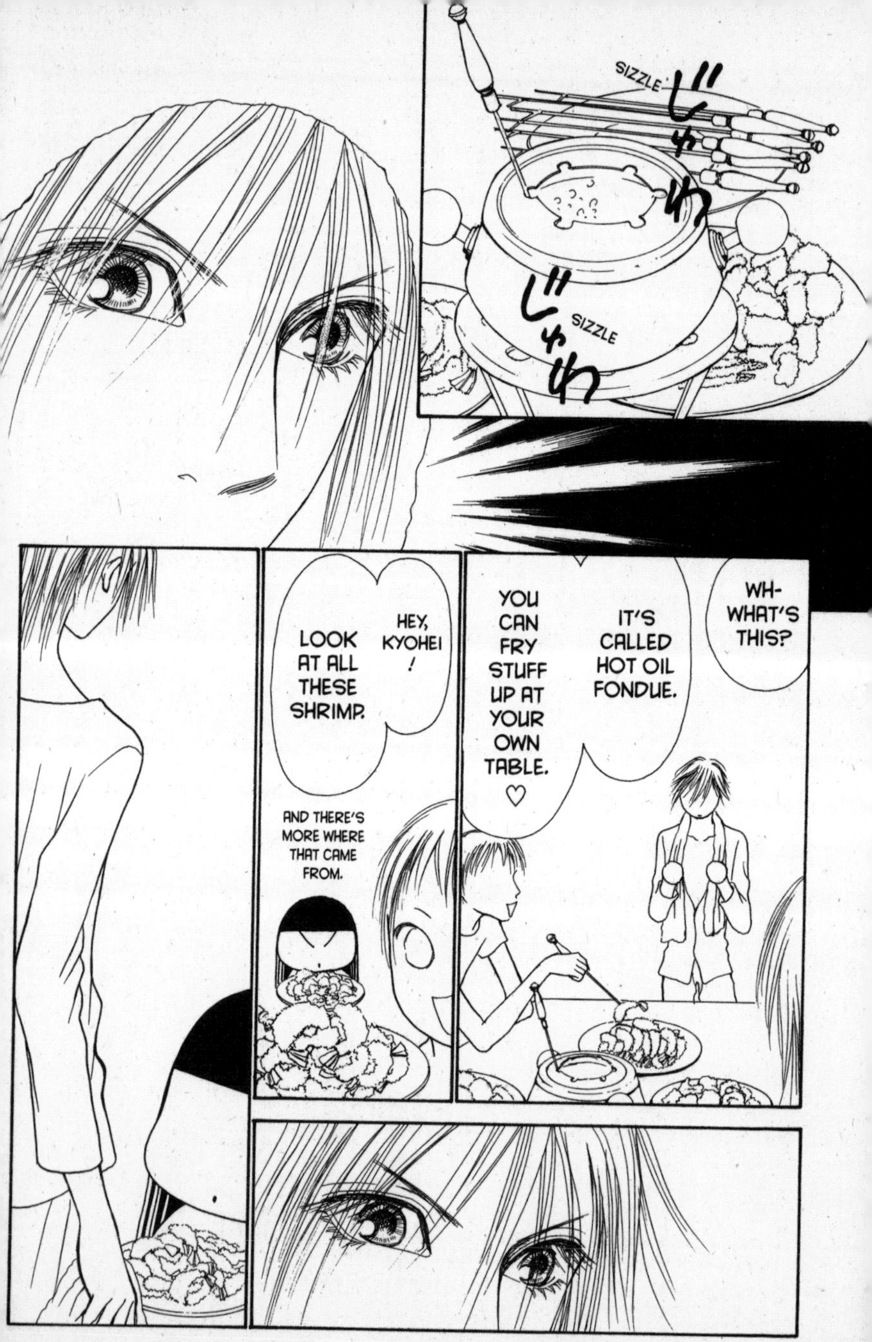

じゅわ
SIZZLE
じゅわ
SIZZLE
WH-WHAT'S THIS?
IT'S CALLED HOT OIL FONDUE.
YOU CAN FRY STUFF UP AT YOUR OWN TABLE. ♡
HEY, KYOHEI!
LOOK AT ALL THESE SHRIMP.
AND THERE'S MORE WHERE THAT CAME FROM.

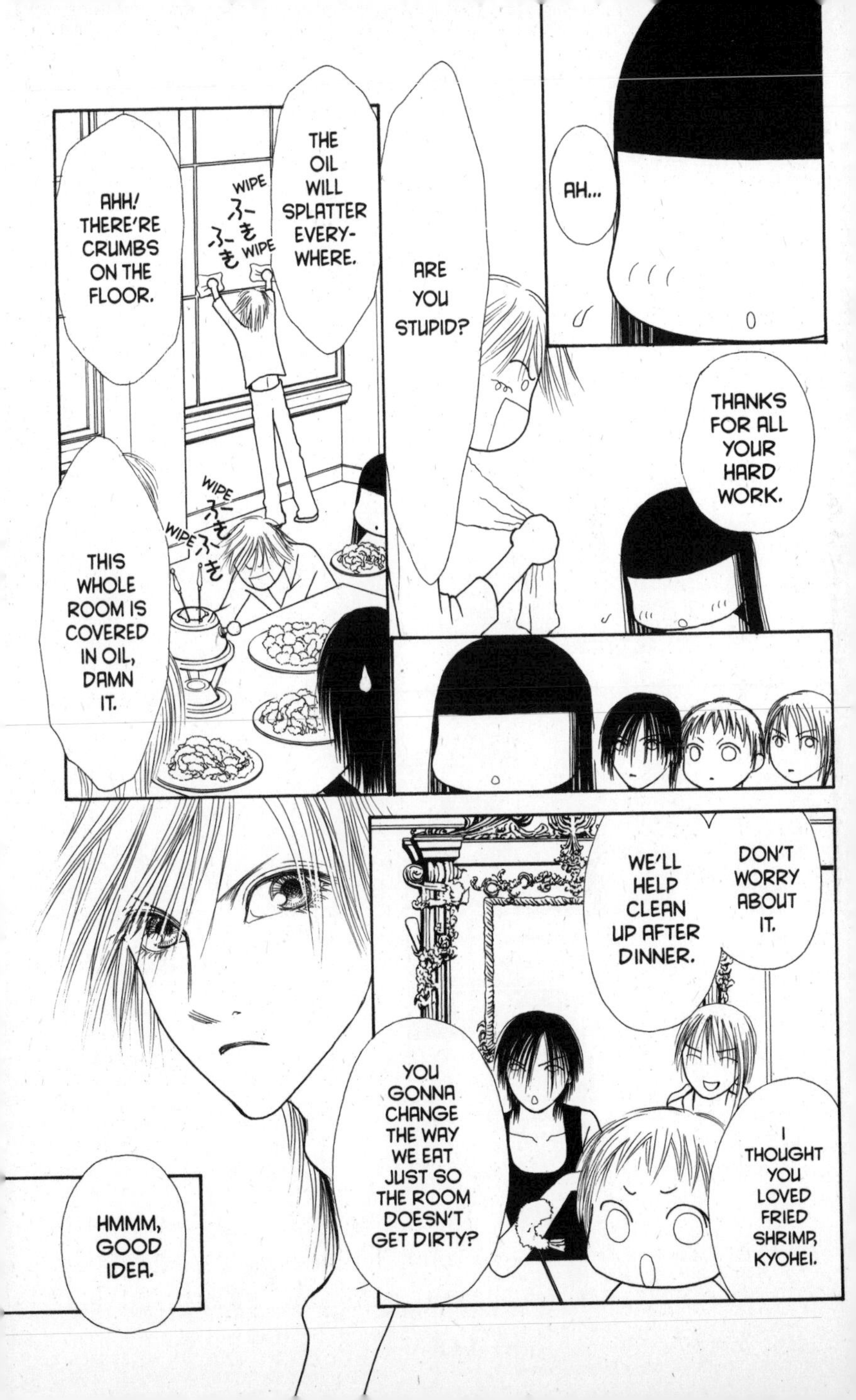
AH...
THANKS FOR ALL YOUR HARD WORK.
ARE YOU STUPID?
THE OIL WILL SPLATTER EVERY-WHERE.
WIPE ふき WIPE ふき
AHH! THERE'RE CRUMBS ON THE FLOOR.
WIPE ふき WIPE ふき
THIS WHOLE ROOM IS COVERED IN OIL, DAMN IT.
DON'T WORRY ABOUT IT.
WE'LL HELP CLEAN UP AFTER DINNER.
I THOUGHT YOU LOVED FRIED SHRIMP, KYOHEI.
YOU GONNA CHANGE THE WAY WE EAT JUST SO THE ROOM DOESN'T GET DIRTY?
HMMM, GOOD IDEA.

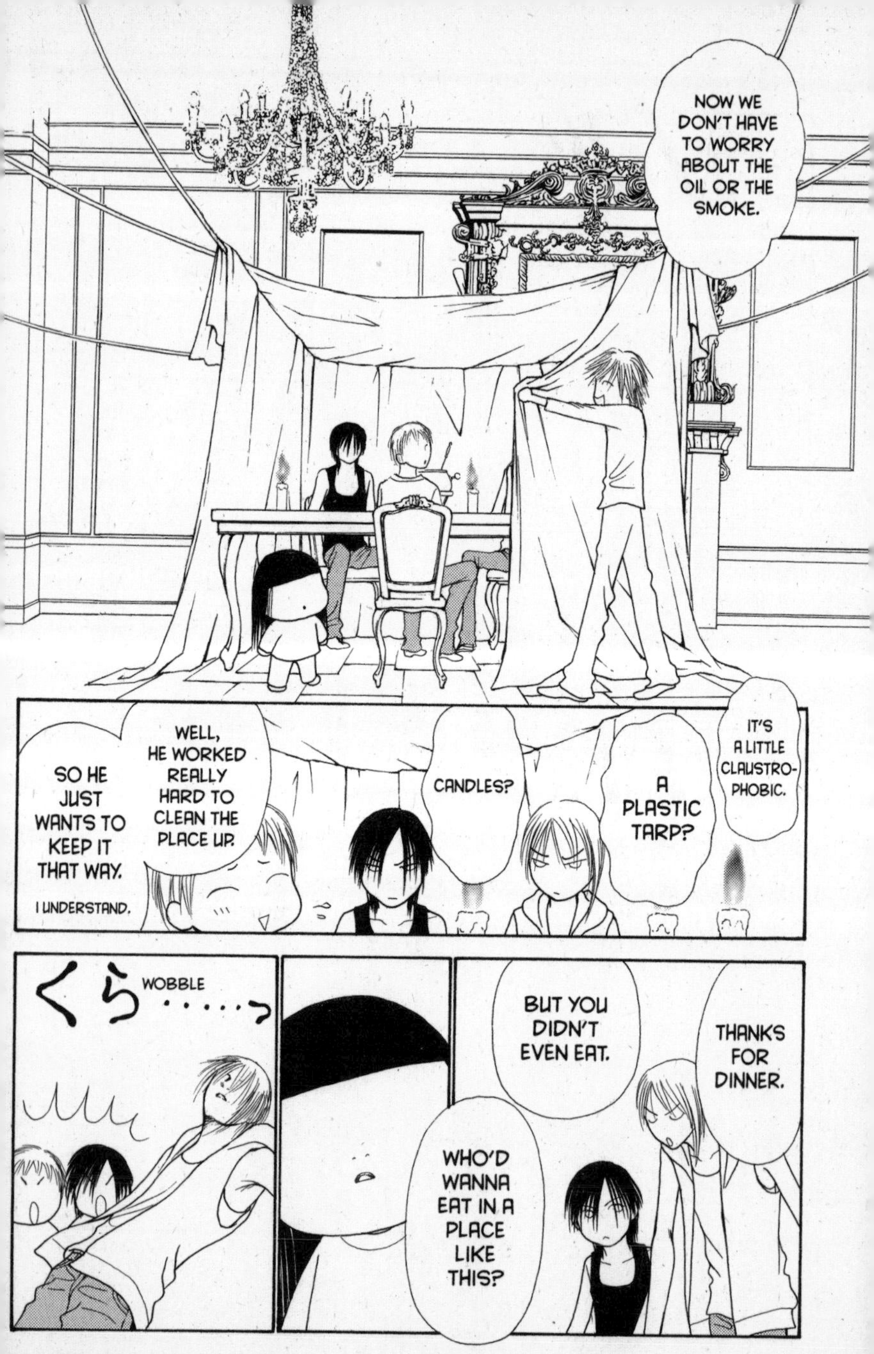
NOW WE DON'T HAVE TO WORRY ABOUT THE OIL OR THE SMOKE.
IT'S A LITTLE CLAUSTRO-PHOBIC.
A PLASTIC TARP?
CANDLES?
WELL, HE WORKED REALLY HARD TO CLEAN THE PLACE UP.
SO HE JUST WANTS TO KEEP IT THAT WAY.
I UNDERSTAND.
THANKS FOR DINNER.
BUT YOU DIDN'T EVEN EAT.
WHO'D WANNA EAT IN A PLACE LIKE THIS?
くら
WOBBLE

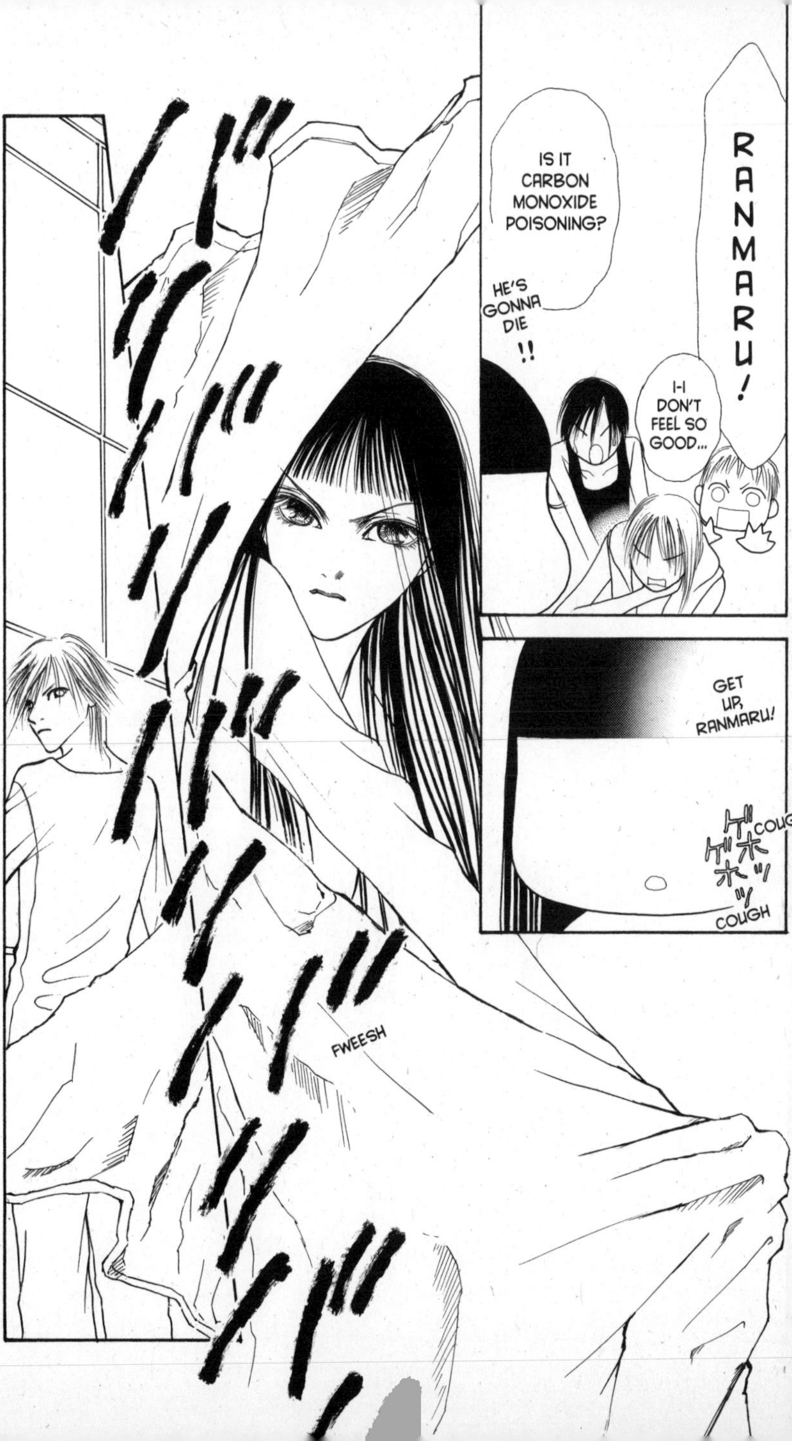
RANMARU!
IS IT CARBON MONOXIDE POISONING?
HE'S GONNA DIE !!
I-I DON'T FEEL SO GOOD...
GET UP, RANMARU!
COUGH
COUGH
FWEESH

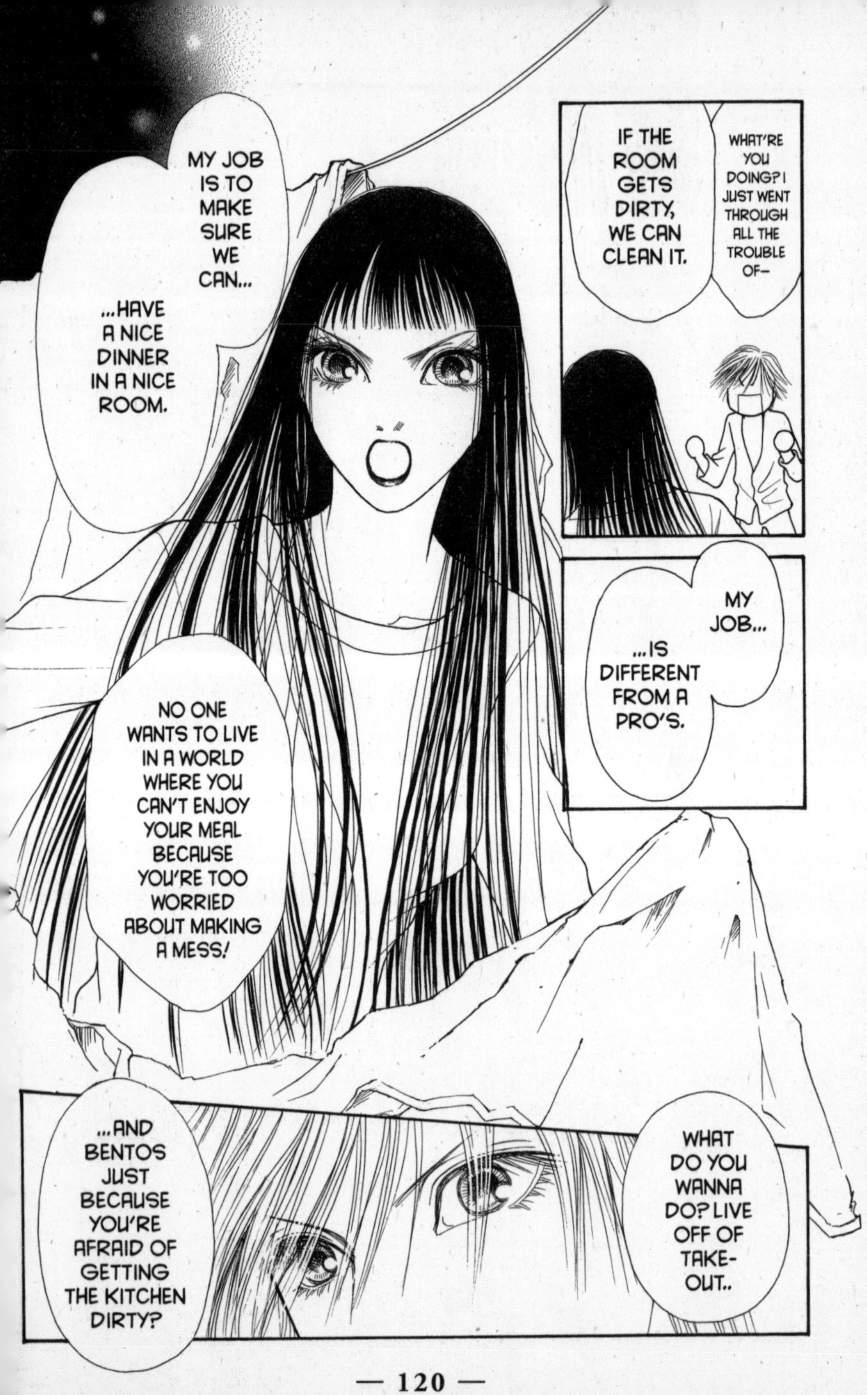
WHAT'RE YOU DOING? I JUST WENT THROUGH ALL THE TROUBLE OF—
IF THE ROOM GETS DIRTY, WE CAN CLEAN IT.
MY JOB...
...IS DIFFERENT FROM A PRO'S.
MY JOB IS TO MAKE SURE WE CAN...
...HAVE A NICE DINNER IN A NICE ROOM.
NO ONE WANTS TO LIVE IN A WORLD WHERE YOU CAN'T ENJOY YOUR MEAL BECAUSE YOU'RE TOO WORRIED ABOUT MAKING A MESS!
WHAT DO YOU WANNA DO? LIVE OFF OF TAKE-OUT..
...AND BENTOS JUST BECAUSE YOU'RE AFRAID OF GETTING THE KITCHEN DIRTY?

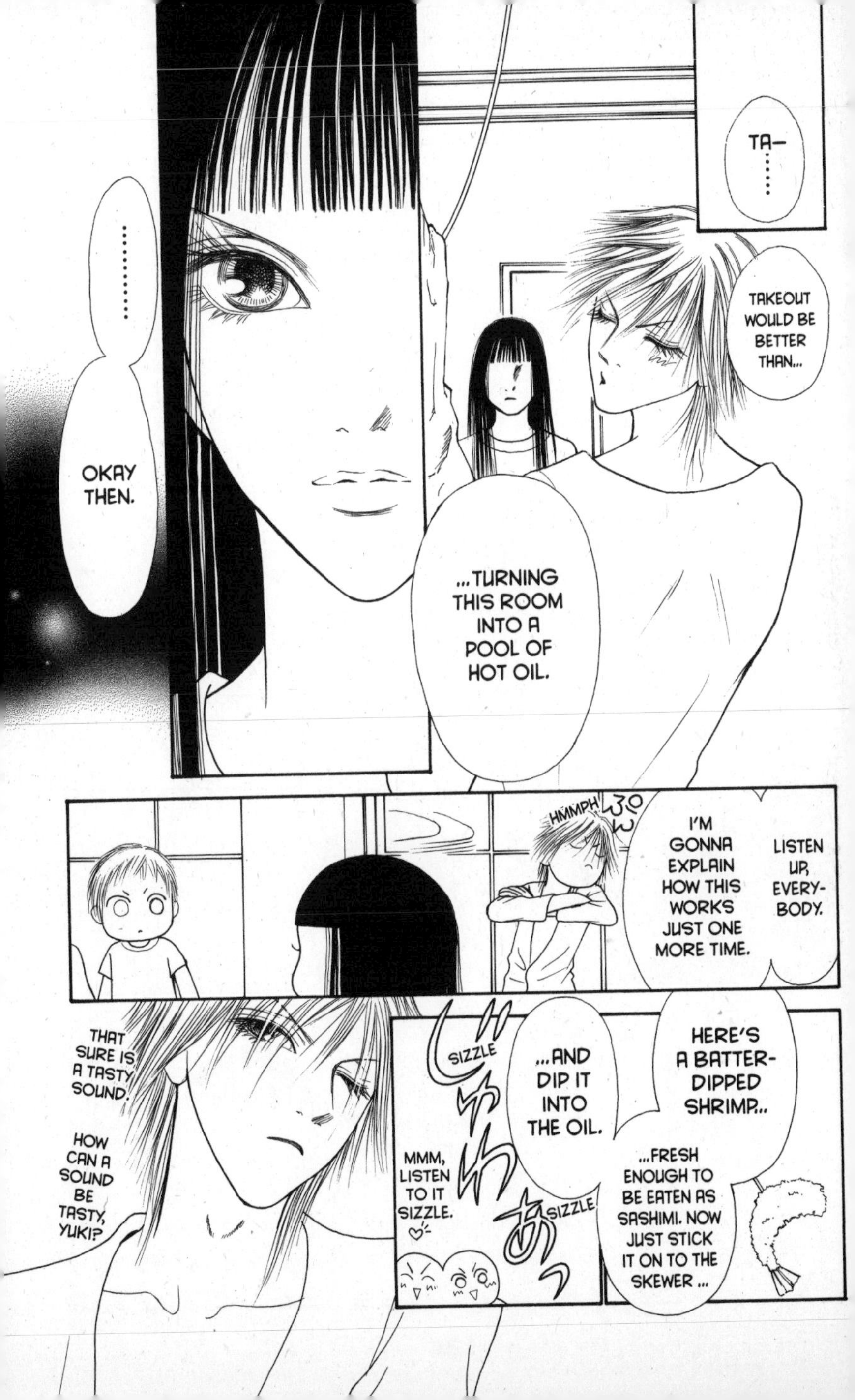
TA— ......
TAKEOUT WOULD BE BETTER THAN...
...TURNING THIS ROOM INTO A POOL OF HOT OIL.
......
OKAY THEN.
LISTEN UP, EVERYBODY.
I'M GONNA EXPLAIN HOW THIS WORKS JUST ONE MORE TIME.
HMMPH
HERE'S A BATTER-DIPPED SHRIMP...
...FRESH ENOUGH TO BE EATEN AS SASHIMI. NOW JUST STICK IT ON TO THE SKEWER ...
...AND DIP IT INTO THE OIL.
SIZZLE
SIZZLE
MMM, LISTEN TO IT SIZZLE.
THAT SURE IS A TASTY SOUND.
HOW CAN A SOUND BE TASTY, YUKI?

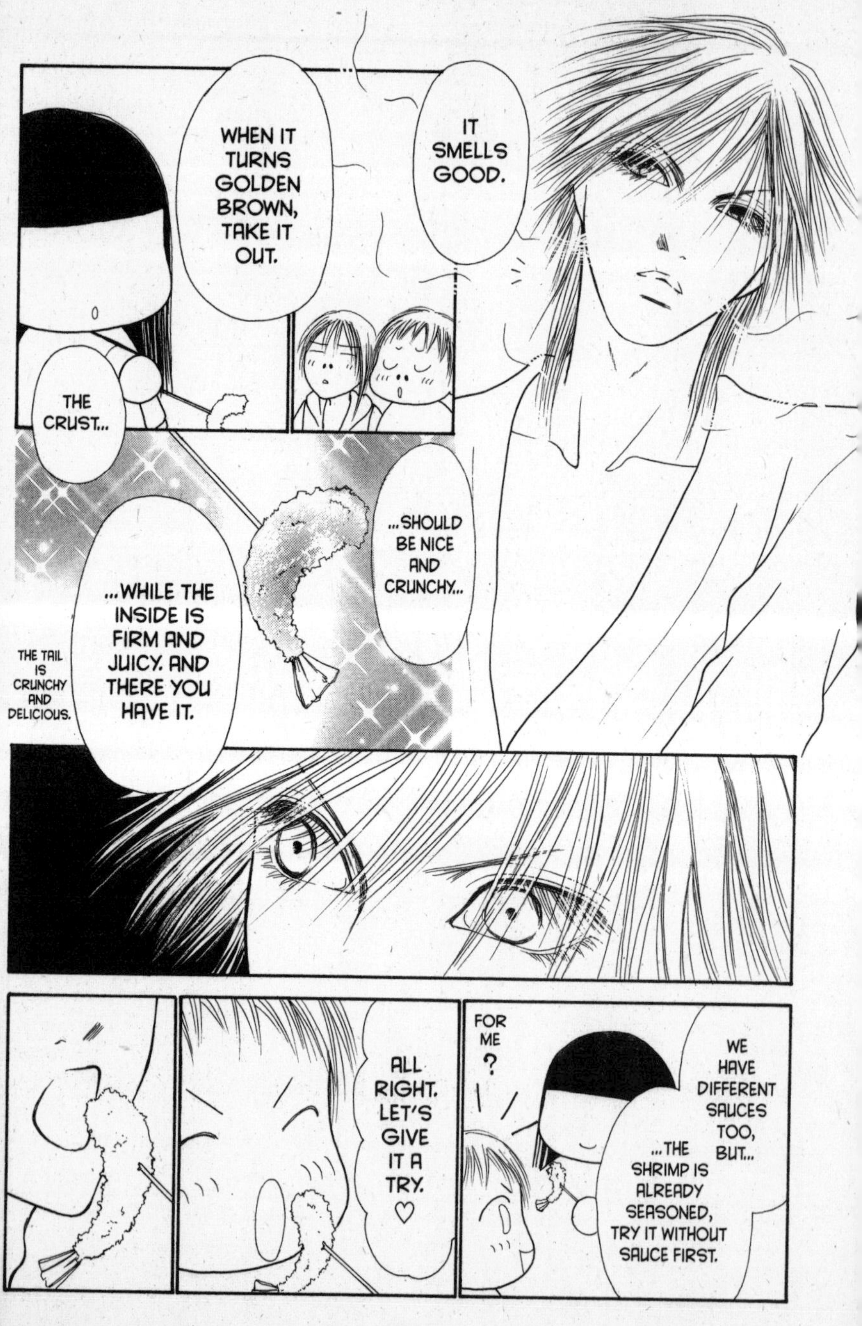
IT SMELLS GOOD.
WHEN IT TURNS GOLDEN BROWN, TAKE IT OUT.
THE CRUST...
...SHOULD BE NICE AND CRUNCHY...
...WHILE THE INSIDE IS FIRM AND JUICY. AND THERE YOU HAVE IT.
THE TAIL IS CRUNCHY AND DELICIOUS.
WE HAVE DIFFERENT SAUCES TOO, BUT...
...THE SHRIMP IS ALREADY SEASONED, TRY IT WITHOUT SAUCE FIRST.
FOR ME ?
ALL RIGHT. LET'S GIVE IT A TRY. ♡

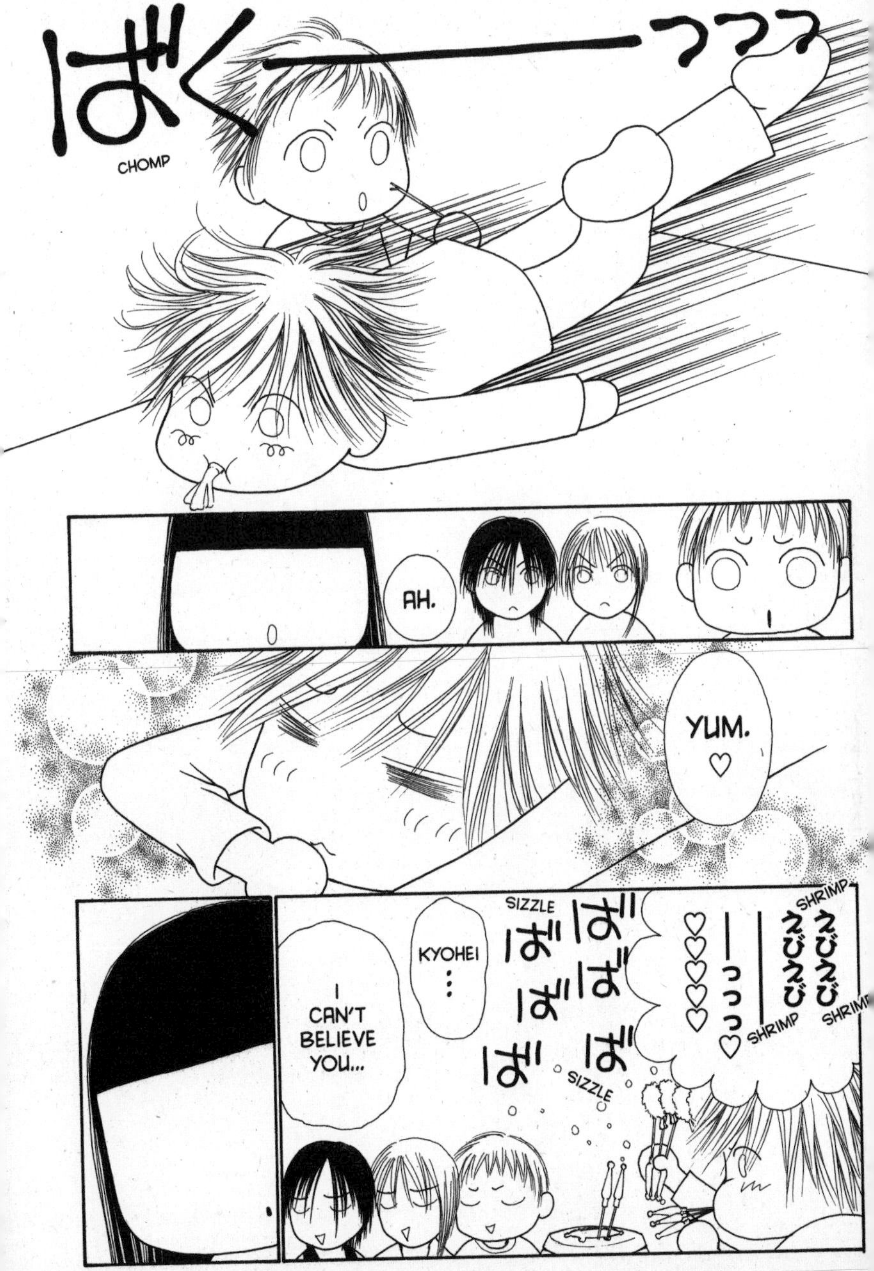
ぱく———っっっ
CHOMP
AH.
YUM. ♡
えびえび
SHRIMP
えびえび
SHRIMP
———っっっっ♡
♡♡♡♡♡
ばばば
SIZZLE
ばばば
SIZZLE
KYOHEI...
I CAN'T BELIEVE YOU...

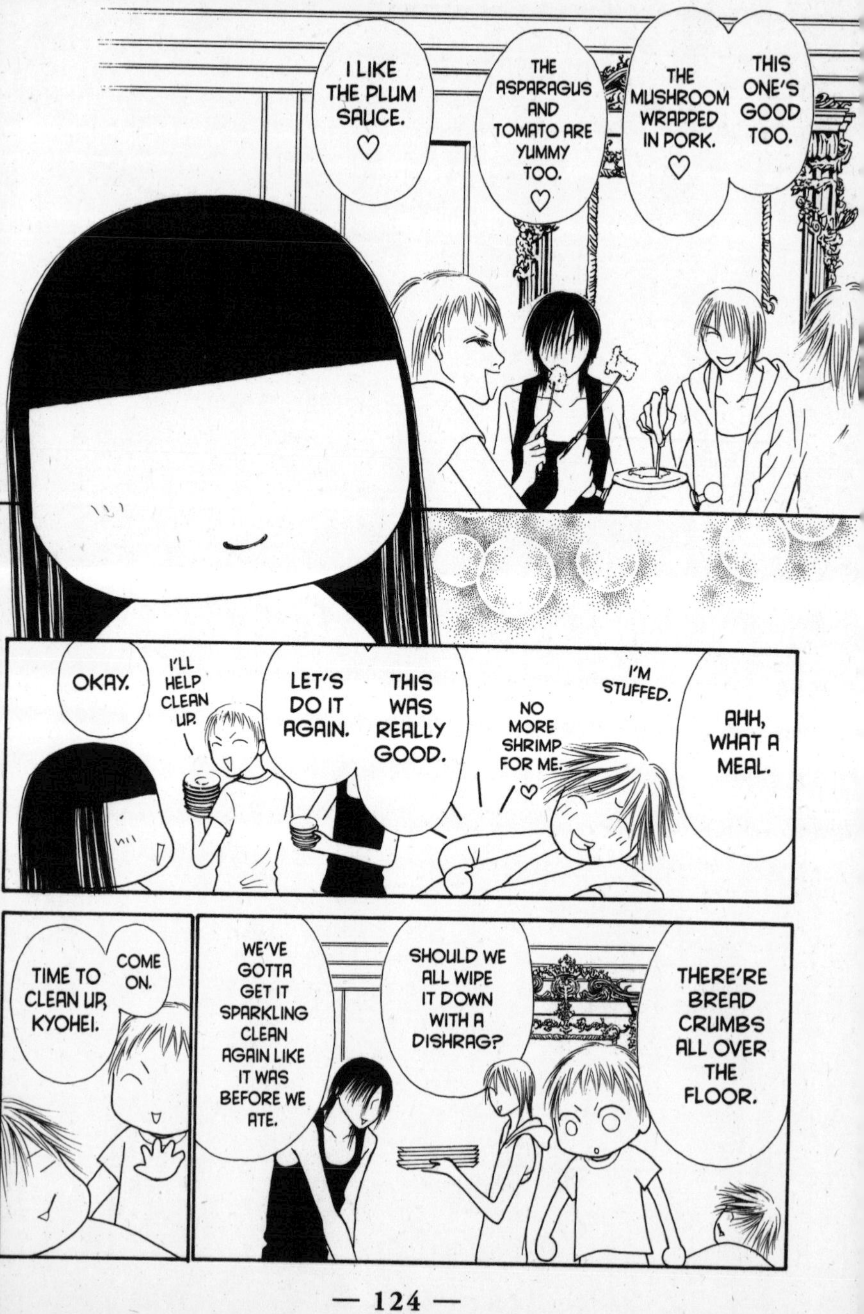
THIS ONE'S GOOD TOO.
THE MUSHROOM WRAPPED IN PORK. ♡
THE ASPARAGUS AND TOMATO ARE YUMMY TOO. ♡
I LIKE THE PLUM SAUCE. ♡
AHH, WHAT A MEAL.
I'M STUFFED.
NO MORE SHRIMP FOR ME. ♡
THIS WAS REALLY GOOD.
LET'S DO IT AGAIN.
I'LL HELP CLEAN UP.
OKAY.
THERE'RE BREAD CRUMBS ALL OVER THE FLOOR.
SHOULD WE ALL WIPE IT DOWN WITH A DISHRAG?
WE'VE GOTTA GET IT SPARKLING CLEAN AGAIN LIKE IT WAS BEFORE WE ATE.
COME ON.
TIME TO CLEAN UP, KYOHEI.

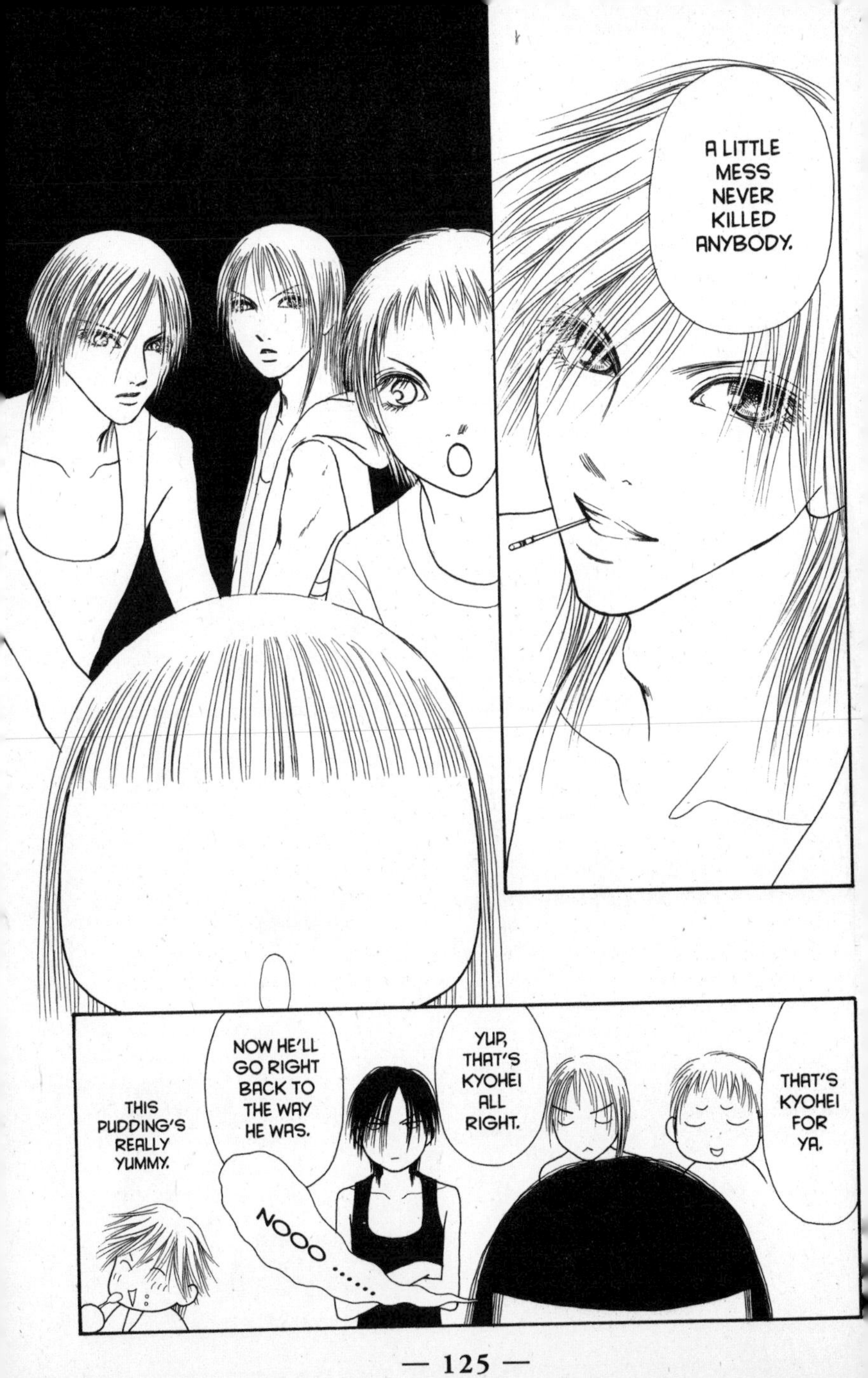
A LITTLE MESS NEVER KILLED ANYBODY.
THAT'S KYOHEI FOR YA.
YUP, THAT'S KYOHEI ALL RIGHT.
NOW HE'LL GO RIGHT BACK TO THE WAY HE WAS.
NOOO......
THIS PUDDING'S REALLY YUMMY.

YUP, RIGHT
BACK TO THE
WAY HE WAS.

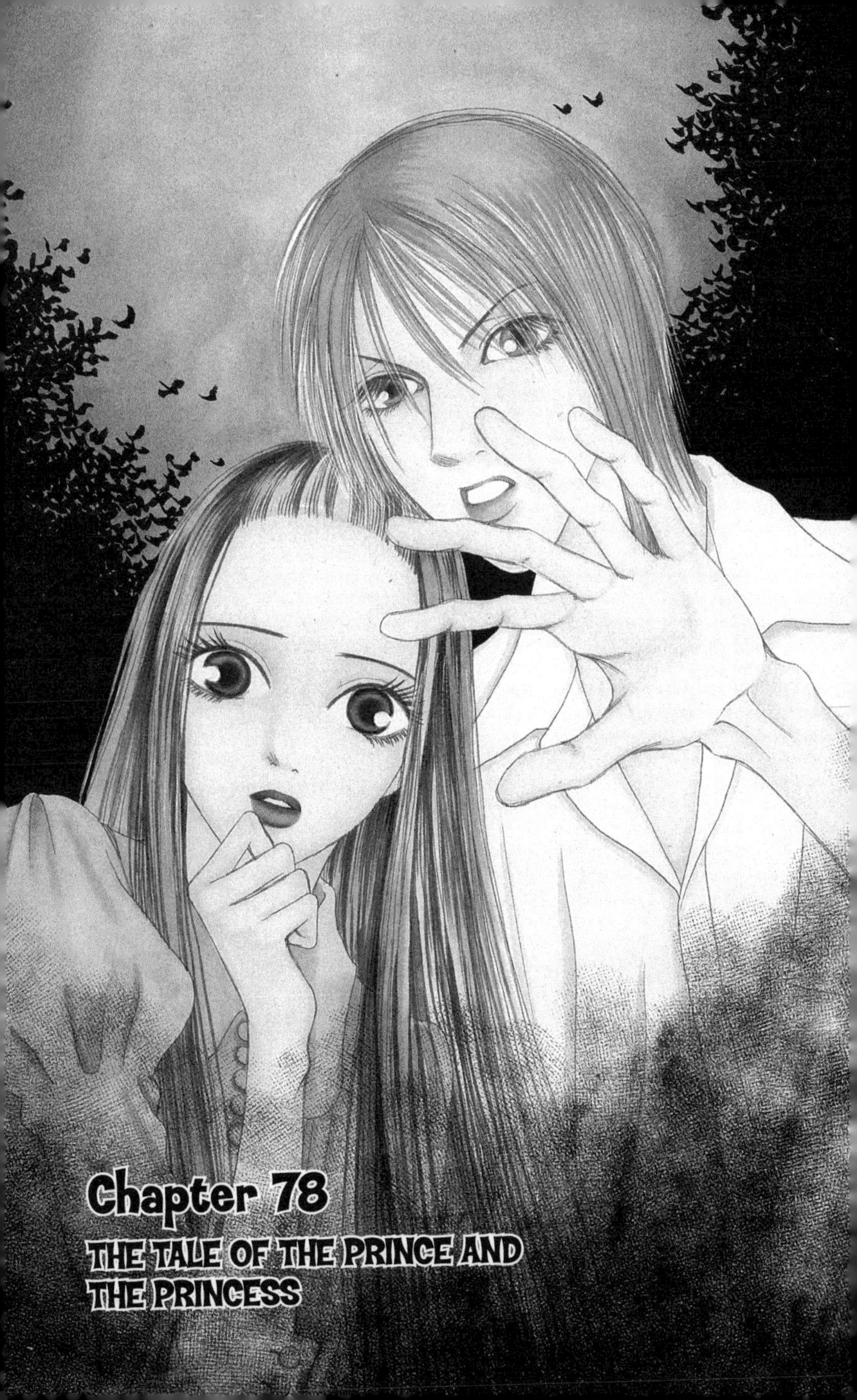

Chapter 78

THE TALE OF THE PRINCE AND THE PRINCESS

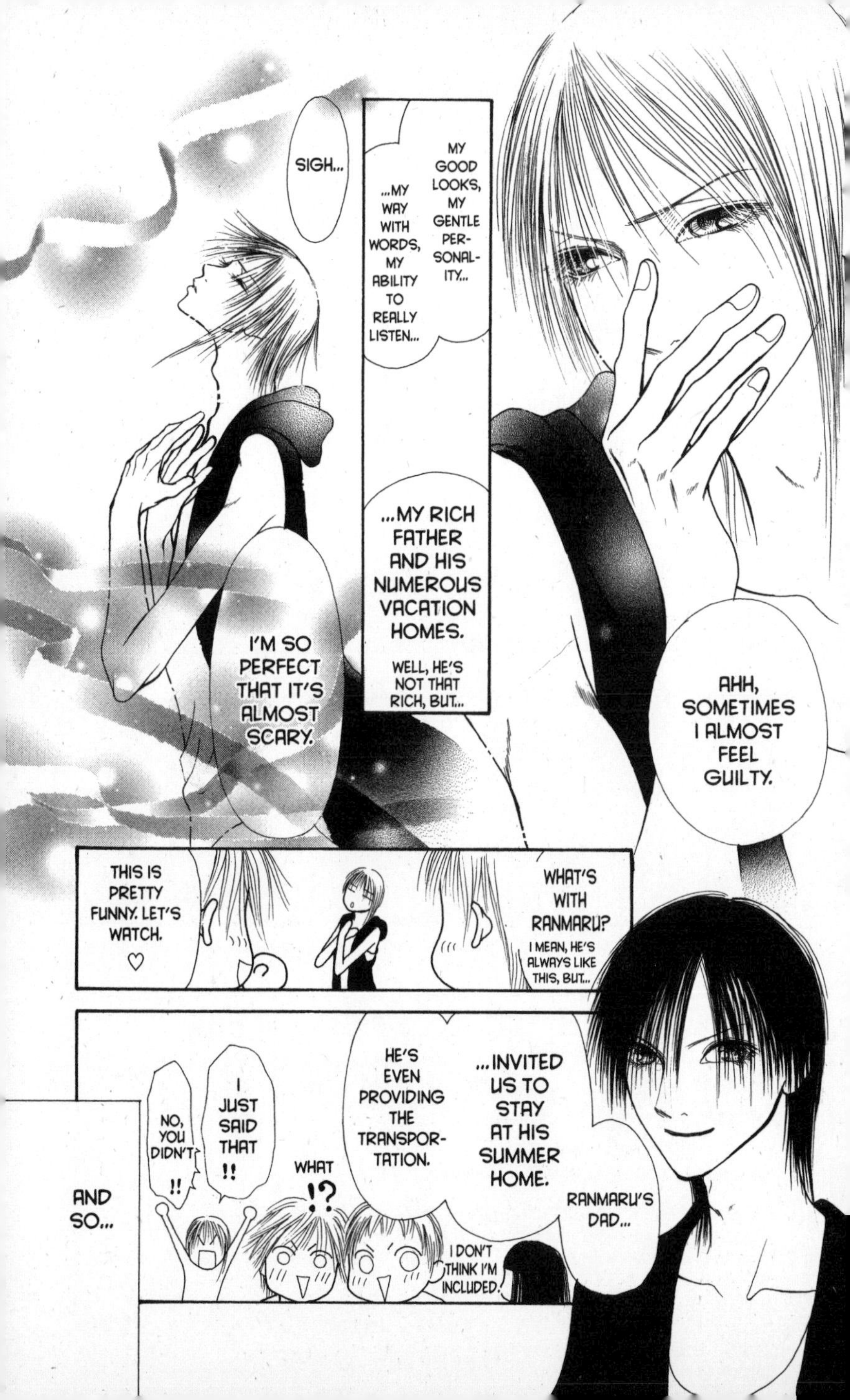
MY GOOD LOOKS, MY GENTLE PERSONALITY...
...MY WAY WITH WORDS, MY ABILITY TO REALLY LISTEN...
...MY RICH FATHER AND HIS NUMEROUS VACATION HOMES.
WELL, HE'S NOT THAT RICH, BUT...
AHH, SOMETIMES I ALMOST FEEL GUILTY.
I'M SO PERFECT THAT IT'S ALMOST SCARY.
SIGH...
WHAT'S WITH RANMARU?
I MEAN, HE'S ALWAYS LIKE THIS, BUT...
THIS IS PRETTY FUNNY. LET'S WATCH. ♡
RANMARU'S DAD...
...INVITED US TO STAY AT HIS SUMMER HOME.
HE'S EVEN PROVIDING THE TRANSPORTATION.
I DON'T THINK I'M INCLUDED.
WHAT !?
I JUST SAID THAT !!
NO, YOU DIDN'T !!
AND SO...

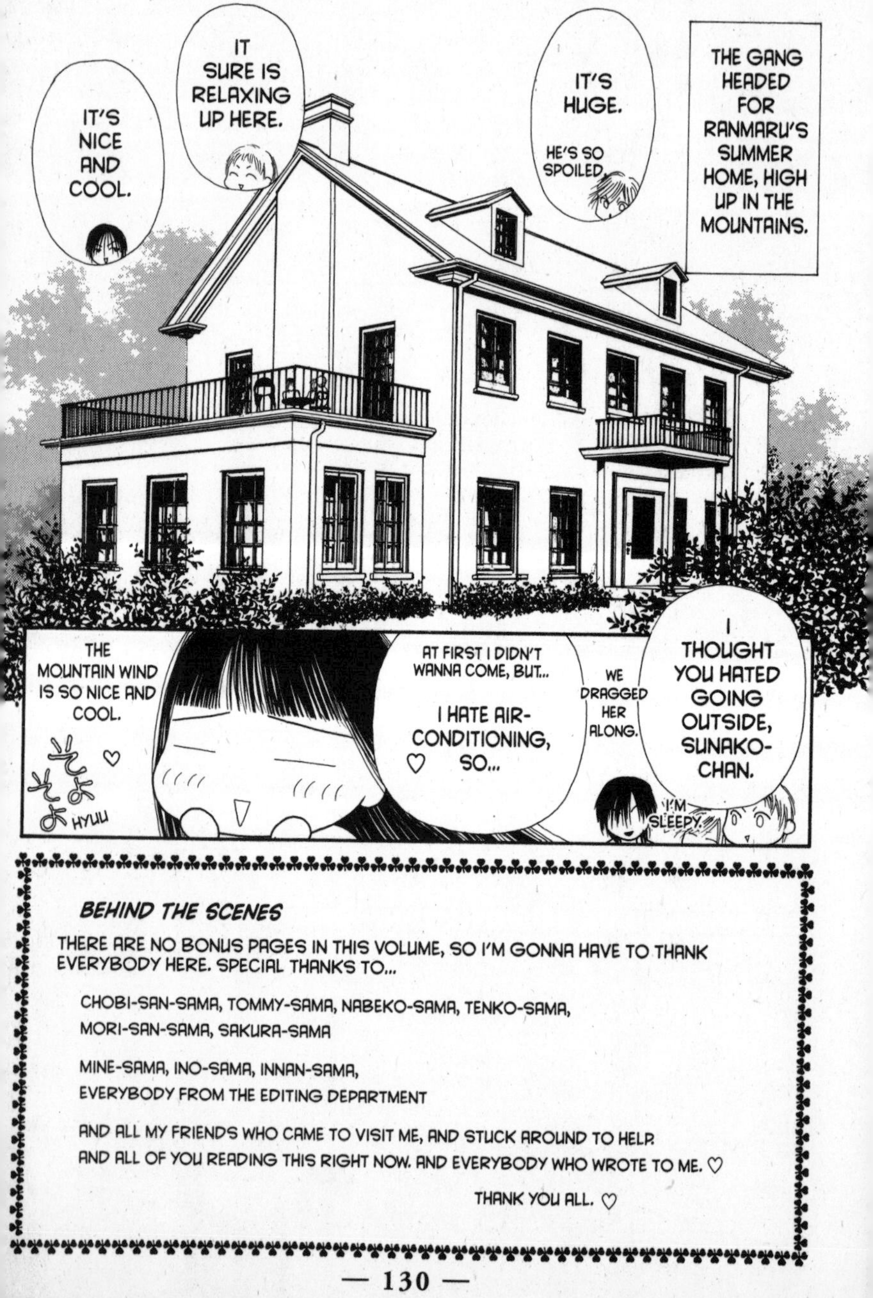
THE GANG HEADED FOR RANMARU'S SUMMER HOME, HIGH UP IN THE MOUNTAINS.
IT'S HUGE.
HE'S SO SPOILED.
IT SURE IS RELAXING UP HERE.
IT'S NICE AND COOL.
I THOUGHT YOU HATED GOING OUTSIDE, SUNAKO-CHAN.
I'M SLEEPY.
WE DRAGGED HER ALONG.
AT FIRST I DIDN'T WANNA COME, BUT...
I HATE AIR-CONDITIONING, SO... ♡
THE MOUNTAIN WIND IS SO NICE AND COOL.
そよそよ ♡
HYUU

BEHIND THE SCENES

THERE ARE NO BONUS PAGES IN THIS VOLUME, SO I'M GONNA HAVE TO THANK EVERYBODY HERE. SPECIAL THANKS TO...

CHOBI-SAN-SAMA, TOMMY-SAMA, NABEKO-SAMA, TENKO-SAMA,
MORI-SAN-SAMA, SAKURA-SAMA

MINE-SAMA, INO-SAMA, INNAN-SAMA,
EVERYBODY FROM THE EDITING DEPARTMENT

AND ALL MY FRIENDS WHO CAME TO VISIT ME, AND STUCK AROUND TO HELP.
AND ALL OF YOU READING THIS RIGHT NOW. AND EVERYBODY WHO WROTE TO ME. ♡

THANK YOU ALL. ♡

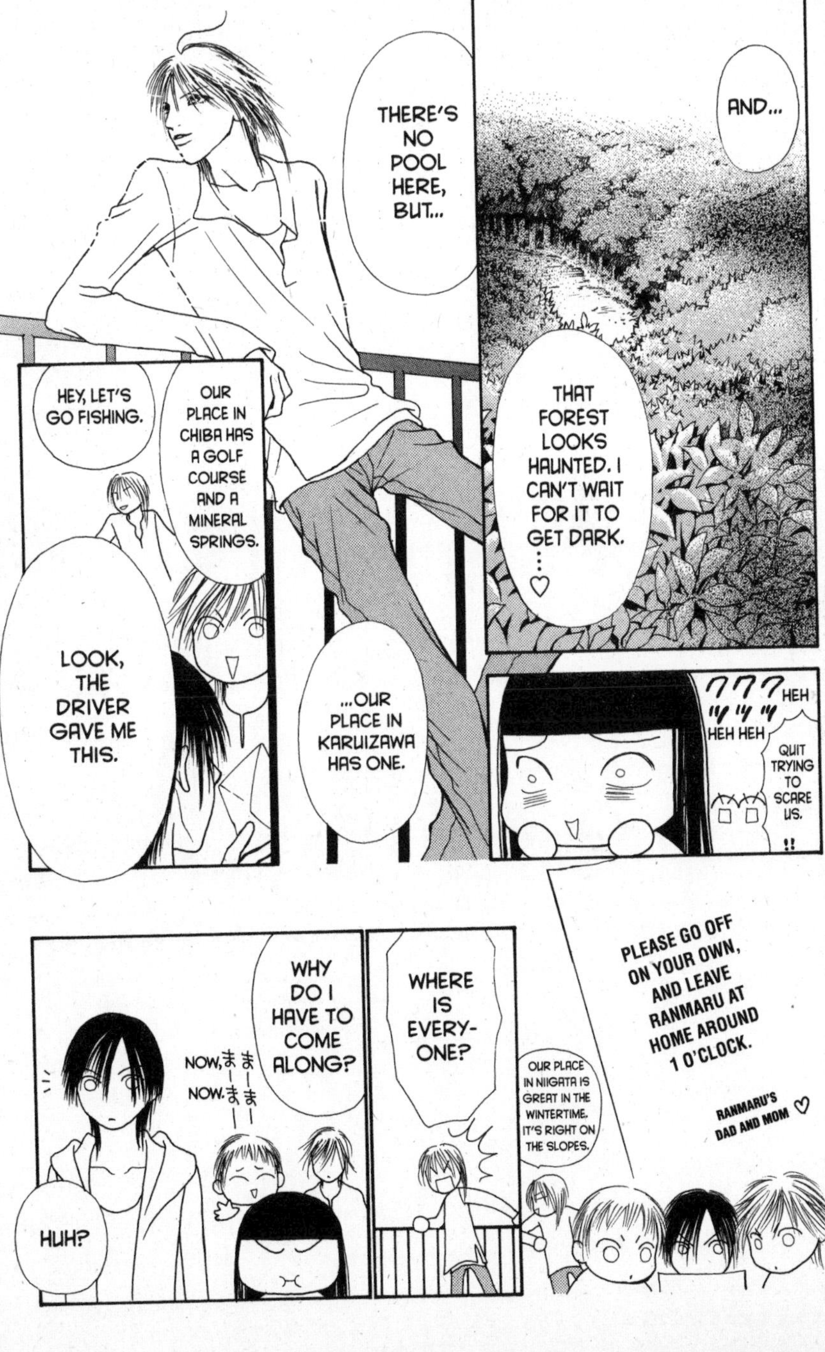
AND...
THAT FOREST LOOKS HAUNTED. I CAN'T WAIT FOR IT TO GET DARK. ...♡
クッ クッ クッ HEH HEH HEH
QUIT TRYING TO SCARE US. !!
THERE'S NO POOL HERE, BUT...
...OUR PLACE IN KARUIZAWA HAS ONE.
OUR PLACE IN CHIBA HAS A GOLF COURSE AND A MINERAL SPRINGS.
HEY, LET'S GO FISHING.
LOOK, THE DRIVER GAVE ME THIS.
PLEASE GO OFF ON YOUR OWN, AND LEAVE RANMARU AT HOME AROUND 1 O'CLOCK.
RANMARU'S DAD AND MOM ♡
OUR PLACE IN NIIGATA IS GREAT IN THE WINTERTIME. IT'S RIGHT ON THE SLOPES.
WHERE IS EVERYONE?
WHY DO I HAVE TO COME ALONG?
NOW, まーまー NOW. まーまー
HUH?

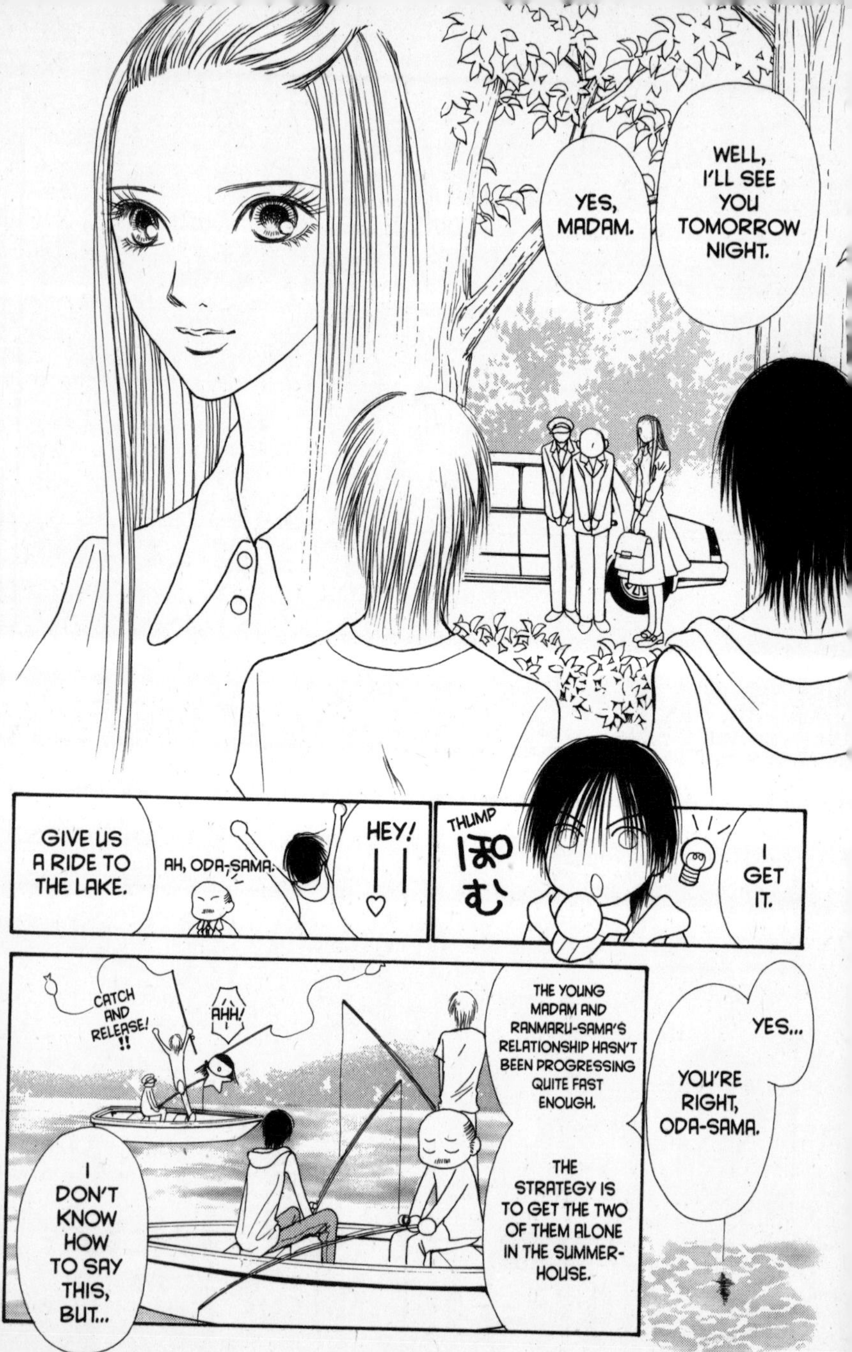

WELL, I'LL SEE YOU TOMORROW NIGHT.
YES, MADAM.
I GET IT.
THUMP
ぽむ
HEY!
AH, ODA-SAMA.
GIVE US A RIDE TO THE LAKE.
YES...
YOU'RE RIGHT, ODA-SAMA.
THE YOUNG MADAM AND RANMARU-SAMA'S RELATIONSHIP HASN'T BEEN PROGRESSING QUITE FAST ENOUGH.
THE STRATEGY IS TO GET THE TWO OF THEM ALONE IN THE SUMMER-HOUSE.
AHH!
CATCH AND RELEASE!!!
I DON'T KNOW HOW TO SAY THIS, BUT...

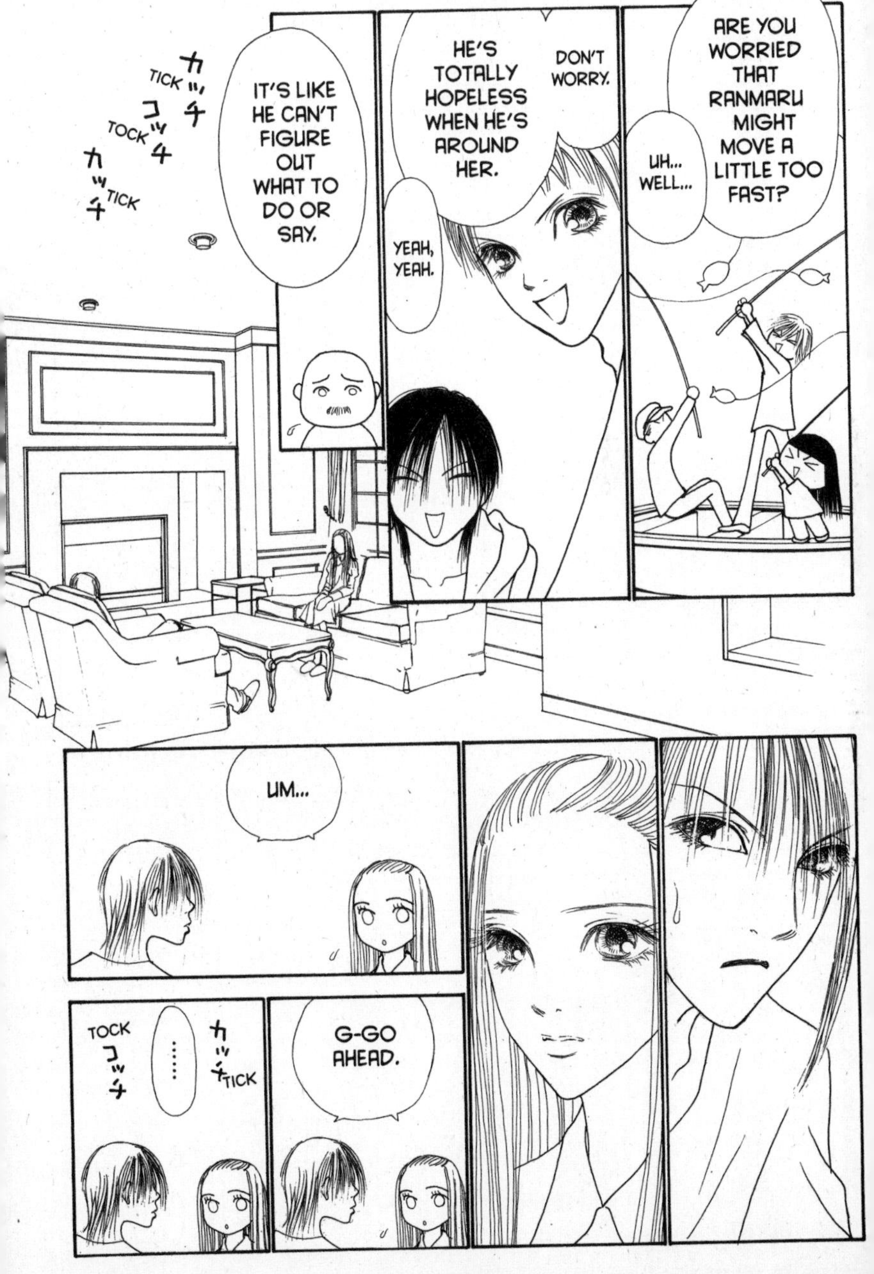
ARE YOU WORRIED THAT RANMARU MIGHT MOVE A LITTLE TOO FAST?
UH... WELL...
DON'T WORRY.
HE'S TOTALLY HOPELESS WHEN HE'S AROUND HER.
YEAH, YEAH.
IT'S LIKE HE CAN'T FIGURE OUT WHAT TO DO OR SAY.
カッチ TICK
コッチ TOCK
カッチ TICK
UM...
G-GO AHEAD.
カッチ TICK
......
コッチ TOCK

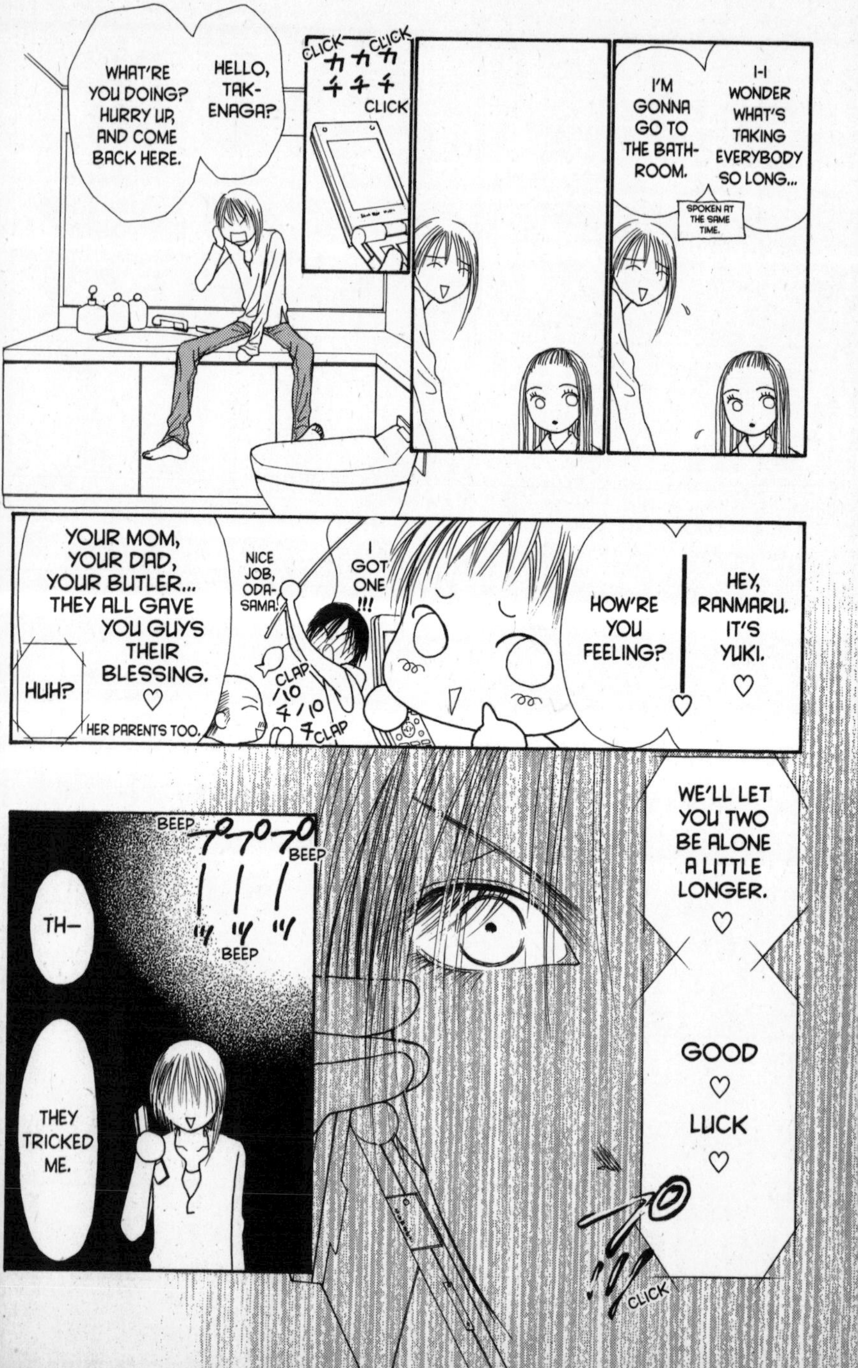
I-I WONDER WHAT'S TAKING EVERYBODY SO LONG...
I'M GONNA GO TO THE BATHROOM.
SPOKEN AT THE SAME TIME.
CLICK
CLICK
CLICK
HELLO, TAK-ENAGA?
WHAT'RE YOU DOING? HURRY UP, AND COME BACK HERE.
HEY, RANMARU. IT'S YUKI. ♡
HOW'RE YOU FEELING? ♡
I GOT ONE !!!
NICE JOB, ODA-SAMA!
CLAP
CLAP
YOUR MOM, YOUR DAD, YOUR BUTLER... THEY ALL GAVE YOU GUYS THEIR BLESSING. ♡
HER PARENTS TOO.
HUH?
WE'LL LET YOU TWO BE ALONE A LITTLE LONGER. ♡
GOOD ♡ LUCK ♡
CLICK
BEEP
BEEP
BEEP
TH—
THEY TRICKED ME.

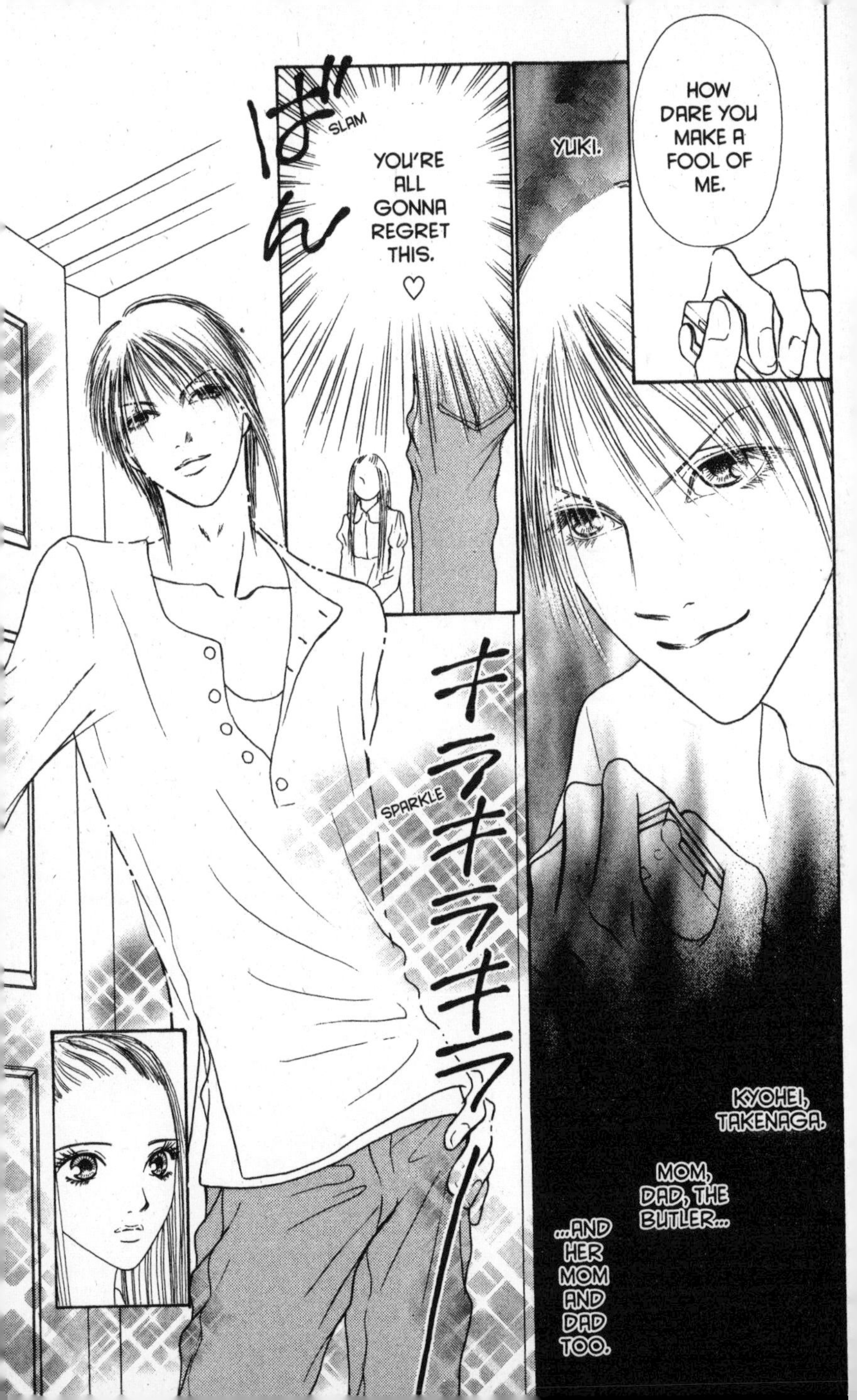
HOW DARE YOU MAKE A FOOL OF ME.
YUKI.
KYOHEI, TAKENAGA.
MOM, DAD, THE BUTLER...
...AND HER MOM AND DAD TOO.
ばん
SLAM
YOU'RE ALL GONNA REGRET THIS. ♡
キラキラ
SPARKLE

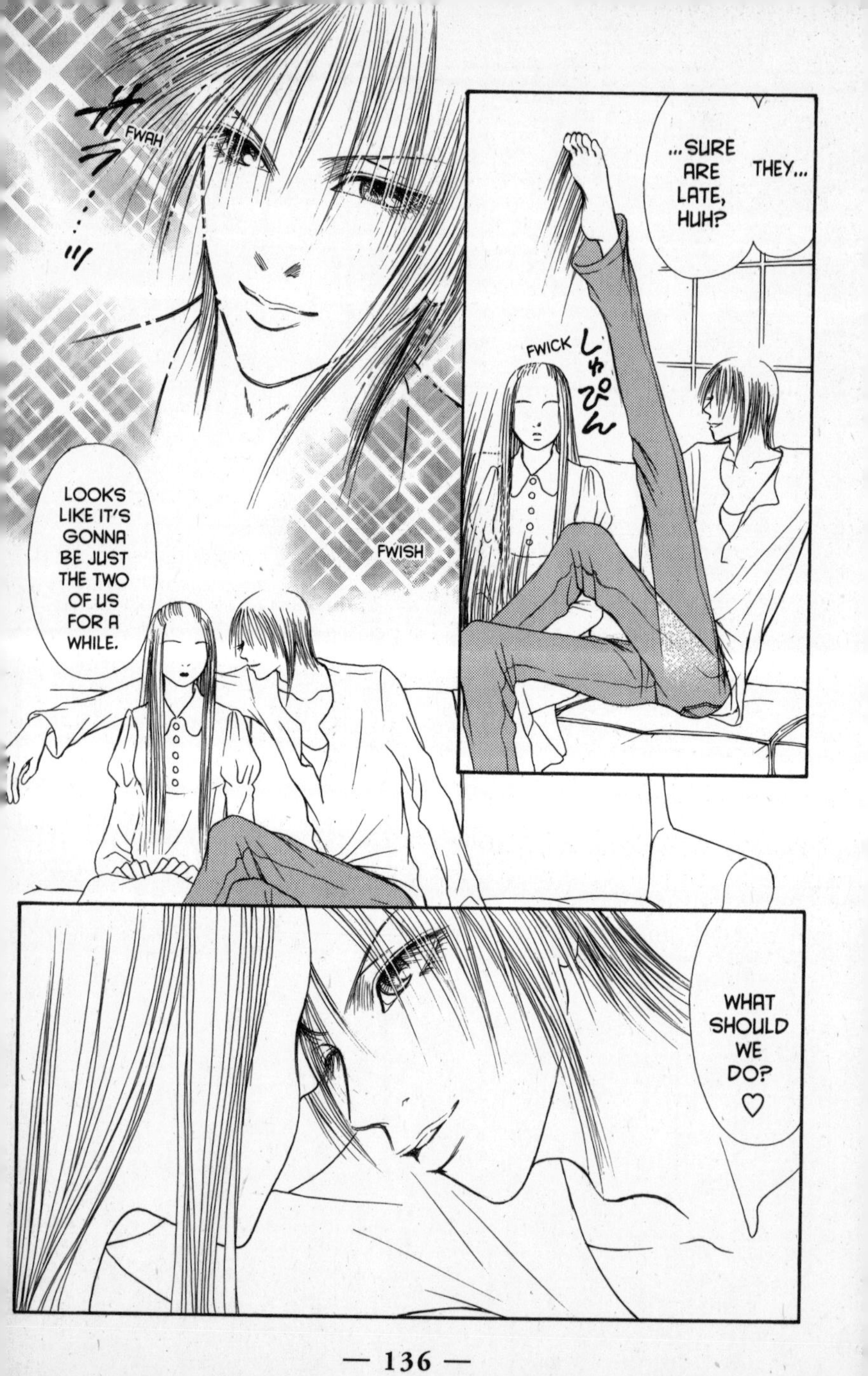
THEY...
...SURE ARE LATE, HUH?
FWICK
しゅぽん
ガラ…ッ
FWAH
FWISH
LOOKS LIKE IT'S GONNA BE JUST THE TWO OF US FOR A WHILE.
WHAT SHOULD WE DO? ♡

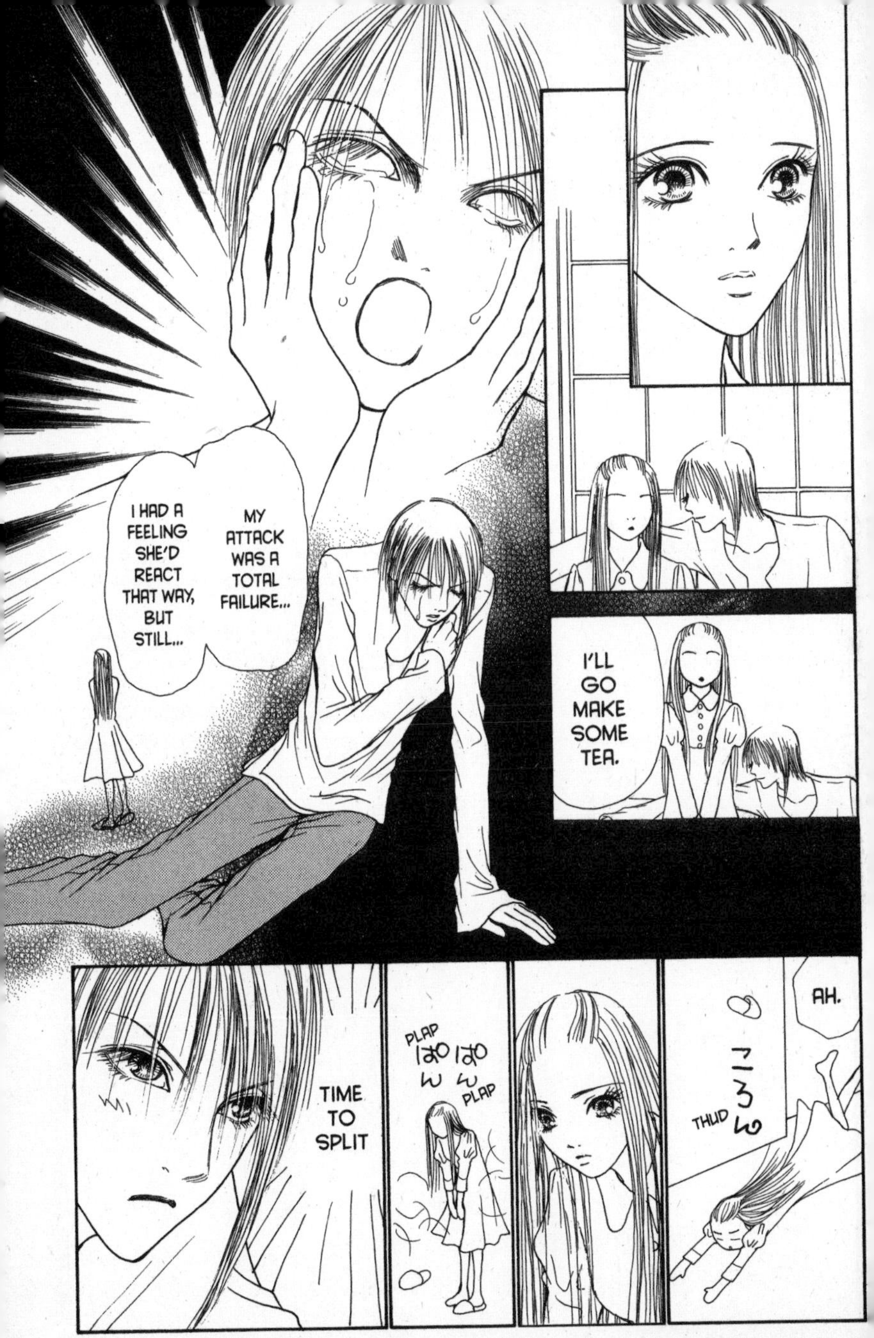
I'LL GO MAKE SOME TEA.
MY ATTACK WAS A TOTAL FAILURE...
I HAD A FEELING SHE'D REACT THAT WAY, BUT STILL...
AH.
ころん
THUD
ぱんぱん
PLAP PLAP
TIME TO SPLIT

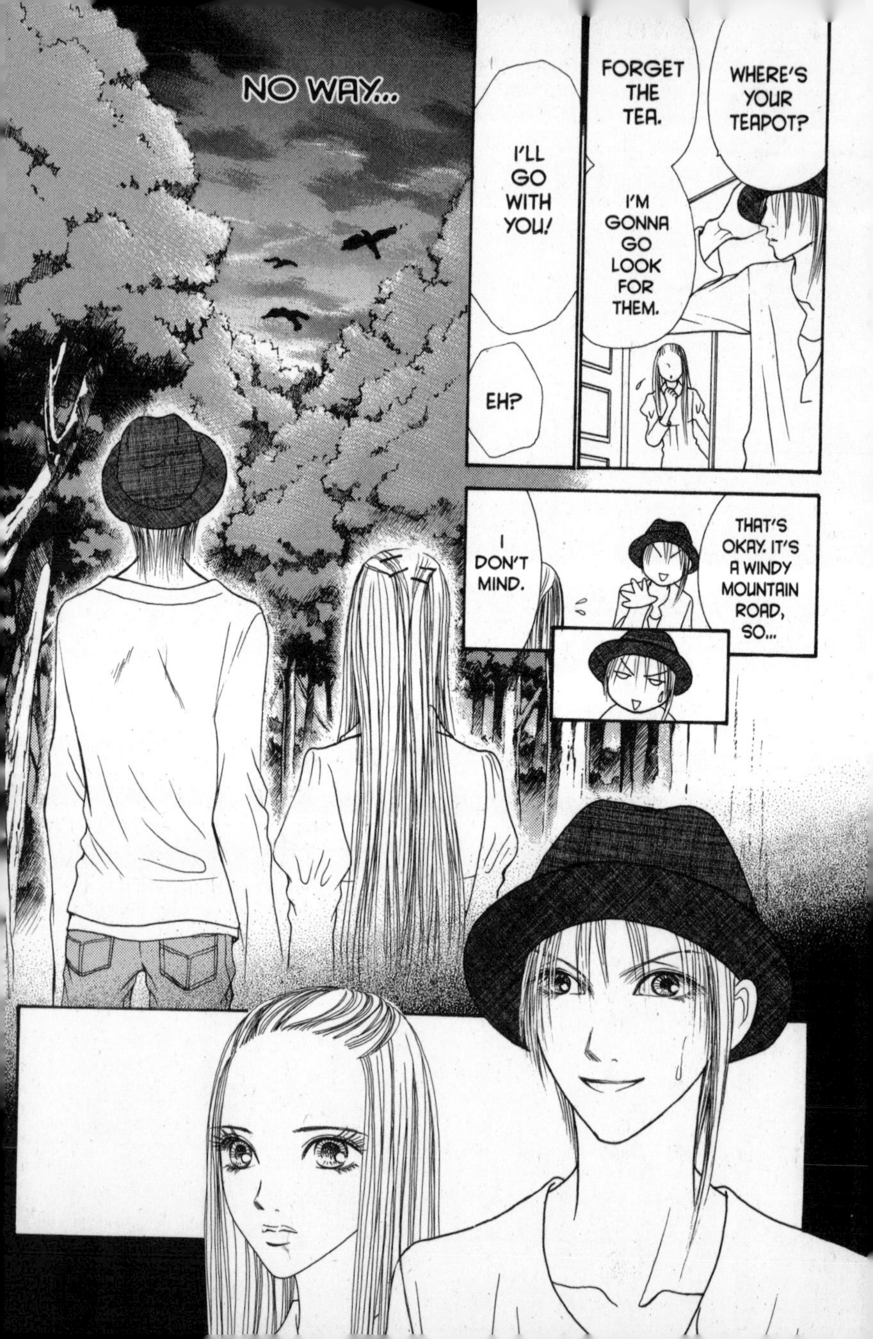
WHERE'S YOUR TEAPOT?
FORGET THE TEA.
I'M GONNA GO LOOK FOR THEM.
I'LL GO WITH YOU!
EH?
THAT'S OKAY. IT'S A WINDY MOUNTAIN ROAD, SO...
I DON'T MIND.
NO WAY...

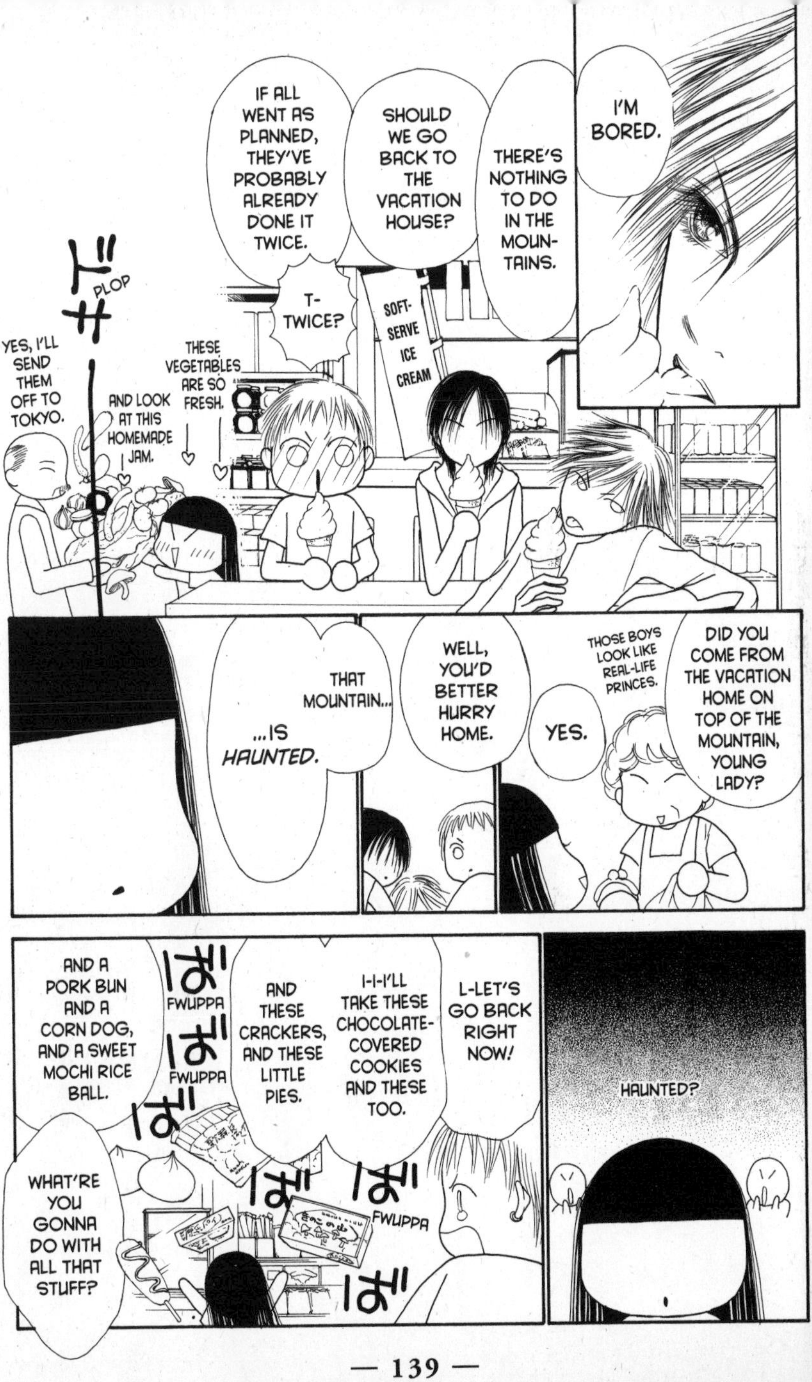
I'M BORED.
THERE'S NOTHING TO DO IN THE MOUNTAINS.
SHOULD WE GO BACK TO THE VACATION HOUSE?
IF ALL WENT AS PLANNED, THEY'VE PROBABLY ALREADY DONE IT TWICE.
T-TWICE?
SOFT-SERVE ICE CREAM
THESE VEGETABLES ARE SO FRESH.
AND LOOK AT THIS HOMEMADE JAM.
YES, I'LL SEND THEM OFF TO TOKYO.
ドサ
PLOP
DID YOU COME FROM THE VACATION HOME ON TOP OF THE MOUNTAIN, YOUNG LADY?
THOSE BOYS LOOK LIKE REAL-LIFE PRINCES.
YES.
WELL, YOU'D BETTER HURRY HOME.
THAT MOUNTAIN...
...IS *HAUNTED.*
HAUNTED?
L-LET'S GO BACK RIGHT NOW!
I-I-I'LL TAKE THESE CHOCOLATE-COVERED COOKIES AND THESE TOO.
AND THESE CRACKERS, AND THESE LITTLE PIES.
AND A PORK BUN AND A CORN DOG, AND A SWEET MOCHI RICE BALL.
ぼ FWUPPA
ぼ FWUPPA
ぼ FWUPPA
WHAT'RE YOU GONNA DO WITH ALL THAT STUFF?

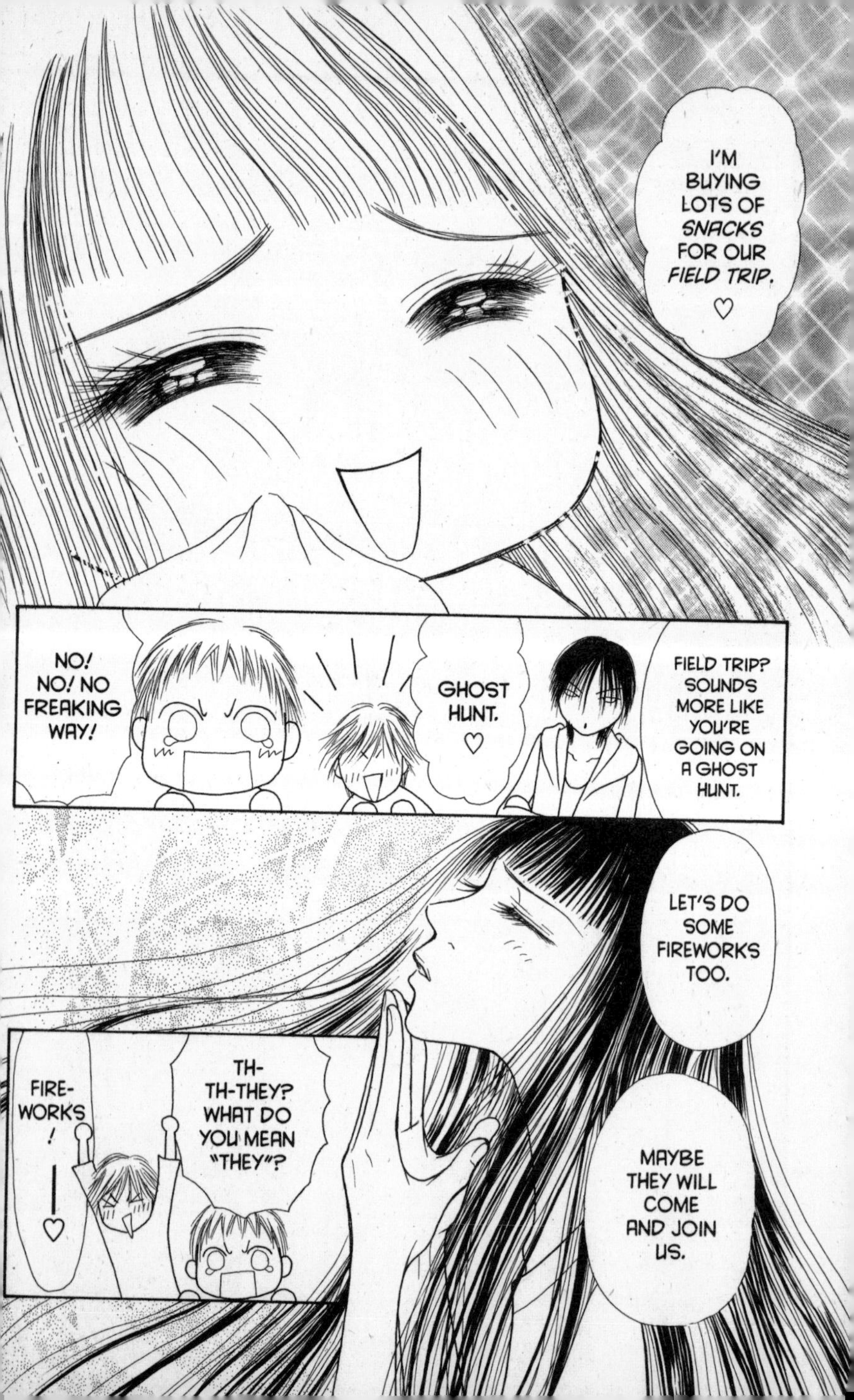
I'M BUYING LOTS OF *SNACKS* FOR OUR *FIELD TRIP.* ♡
FIELD TRIP? SOUNDS MORE LIKE YOU'RE GOING ON A GHOST HUNT.
GHOST HUNT. ♡
NO! NO! NO FREAKING WAY!
LET'S DO SOME FIREWORKS TOO.
MAYBE THEY WILL COME AND JOIN US.
TH-TH-THEY? WHAT DO YOU MEAN "THEY"?
FIRE-WORKS! —♡

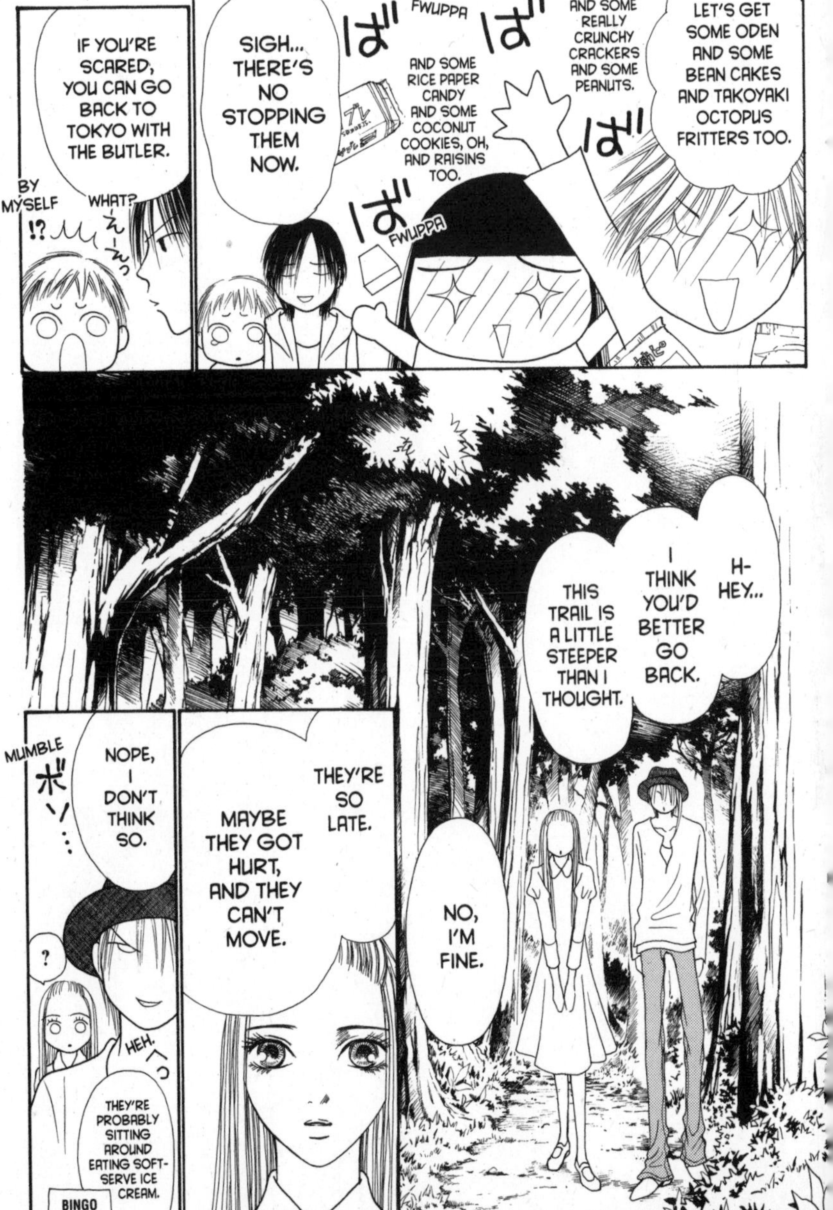
LET'S GET SOME ODEN AND SOME BEAN CAKES AND TAKOYAKI OCTOPUS FRITTERS TOO.
AND SOME REALLY CRUNCHY CRACKERS AND SOME PEANUTS.
FWUPPA
AND SOME RICE PAPER CANDY AND SOME COCONUT COOKIES, OH, AND RAISINS TOO.
SIGH... THERE'S NO STOPPING THEM NOW.
FWUPPA
IF YOU'RE SCARED, YOU CAN GO BACK TO TOKYO WITH THE BUTLER.
WHAT?
BY MYSELF !?
H-HEY...
I THINK YOU'D BETTER GO BACK.
THIS TRAIL IS A LITTLE STEEPER THAN I THOUGHT.
NO, I'M FINE.
THEY'RE SO LATE.
MAYBE THEY GOT HURT, AND THEY CAN'T MOVE.
NOPE, I DON'T THINK SO.
MUMBLE
?
HEH.
THEY'RE PROBABLY SITTING AROUND EATING SOFT-SERVE ICE CREAM.
BINGO

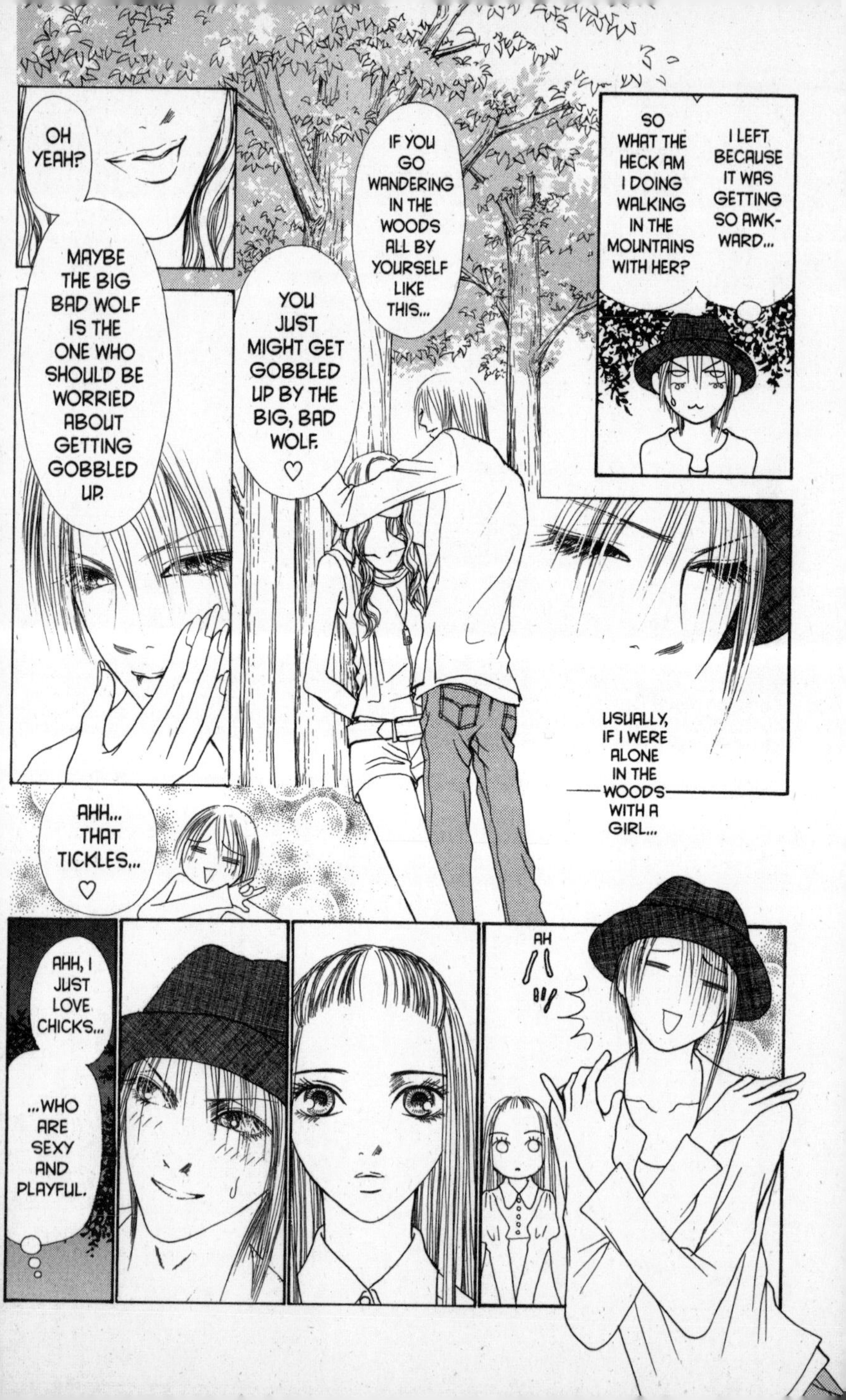
I LEFT BECAUSE IT WAS GETTING SO AWKWARD...
SO WHAT THE HECK AM I DOING WALKING IN THE MOUNTAINS WITH HER?
IF YOU GO WANDERING IN THE WOODS ALL BY YOURSELF LIKE THIS...
YOU JUST MIGHT GET GOBBLED UP BY THE BIG, BAD WOLF. ♡
OH YEAH?
MAYBE THE BIG BAD WOLF IS THE ONE WHO SHOULD BE WORRIED ABOUT GETTING GOBBLED UP.
USUALLY, IF I WERE ALONE IN THE WOODS WITH A GIRL...
AHH... THAT TICKLES... ♡
AH !!
AHH, I JUST LOVE CHICKS...
...WHO ARE SEXY AND PLAYFUL.

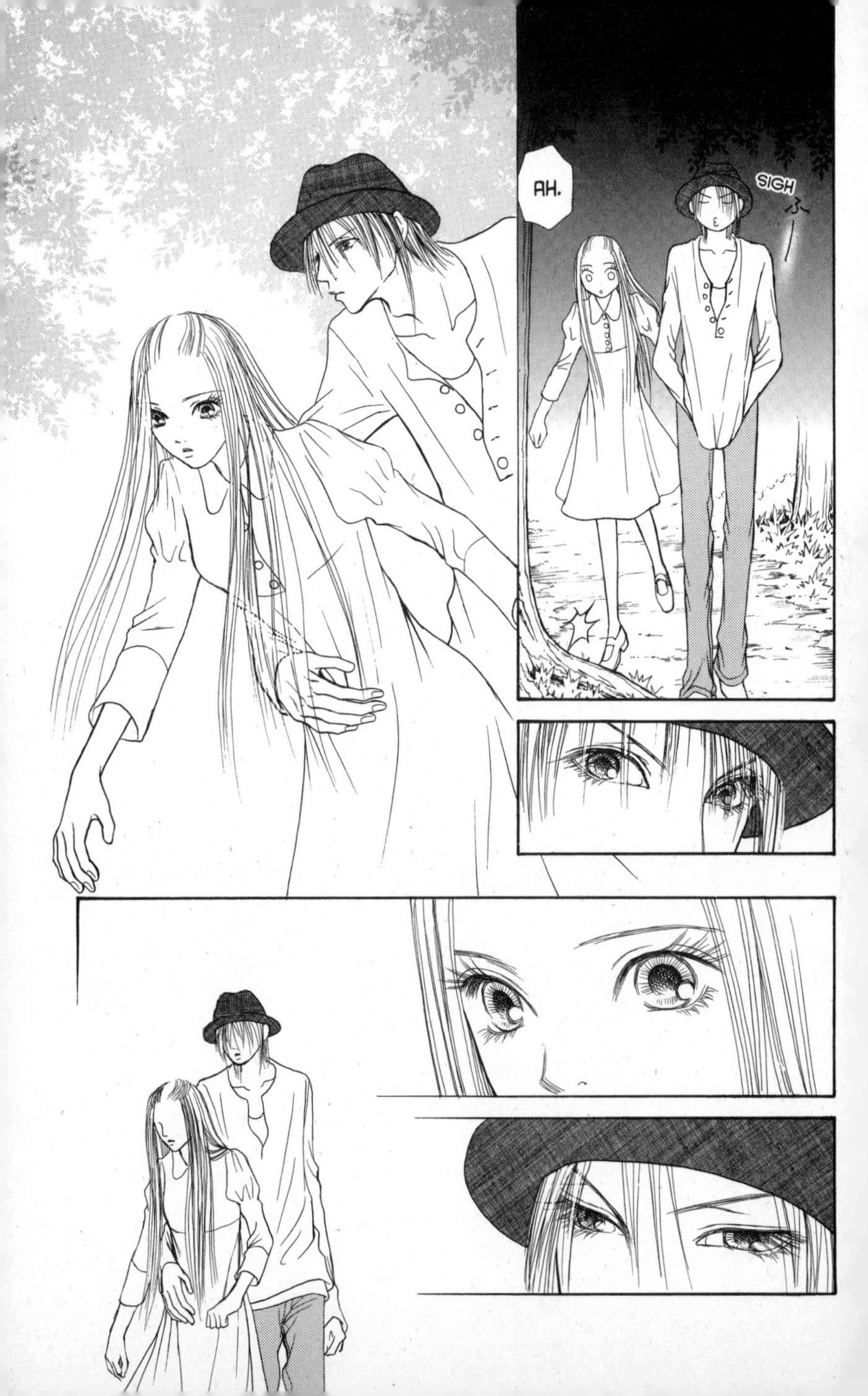
AH.
SIGH
ふ~

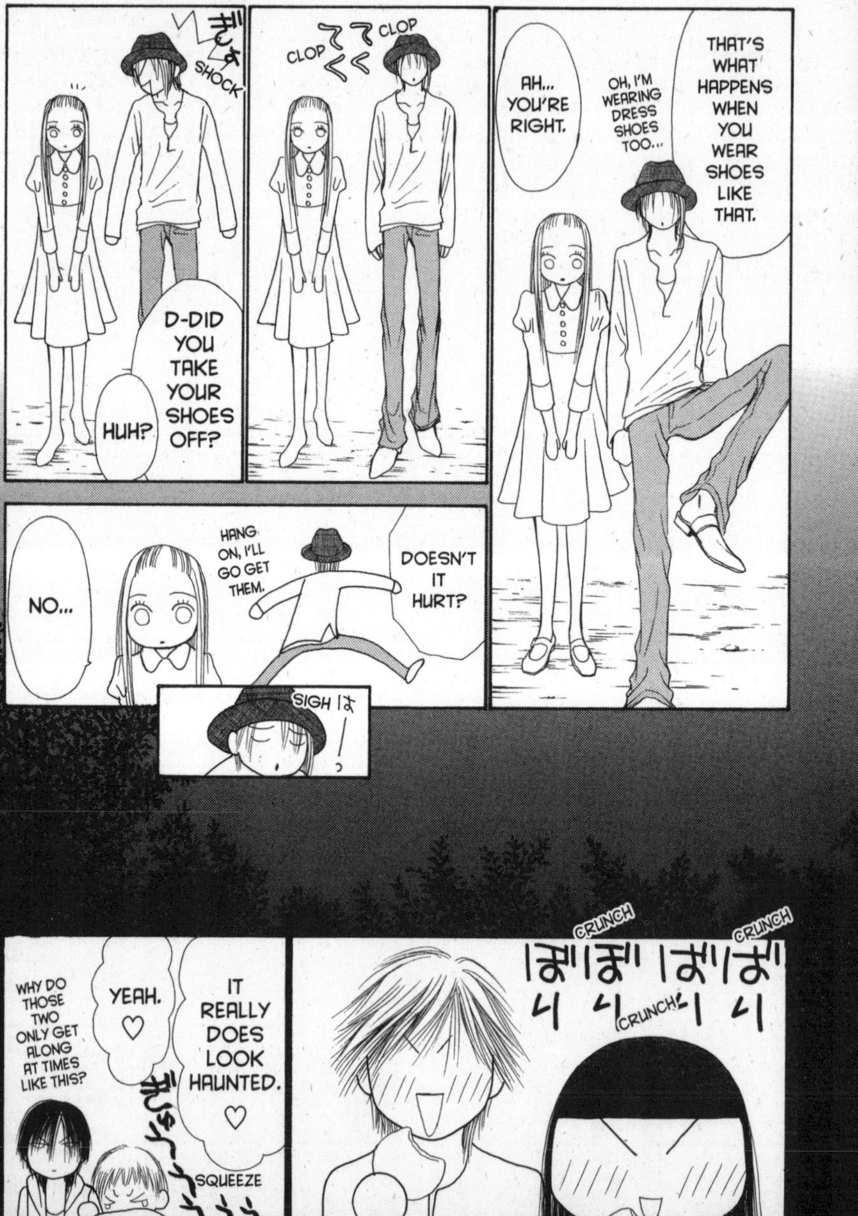
THAT'S WHAT HAPPENS WHEN YOU WEAR SHOES LIKE THAT.
OH, I'M WEARING DRESS SHOES TOO...
AH... YOU'RE RIGHT.
CLOP てくてく CLOP
SHOCK
D-DID YOU TAKE YOUR SHOES OFF?
HUH?
DOESN'T IT HURT?
HANG ON, I'LL GO GET THEM.
NO...
SIGH は—っ
CRUNCH ぽりぽり CRUNCH ぱりぱり CRUNCH
IT REALLY DOES LOOK HAUNTED. ♡
YEAH. ♡
SQUEEZE
WHY DO THOSE TWO ONLY GET ALONG AT TIMES LIKE THIS?

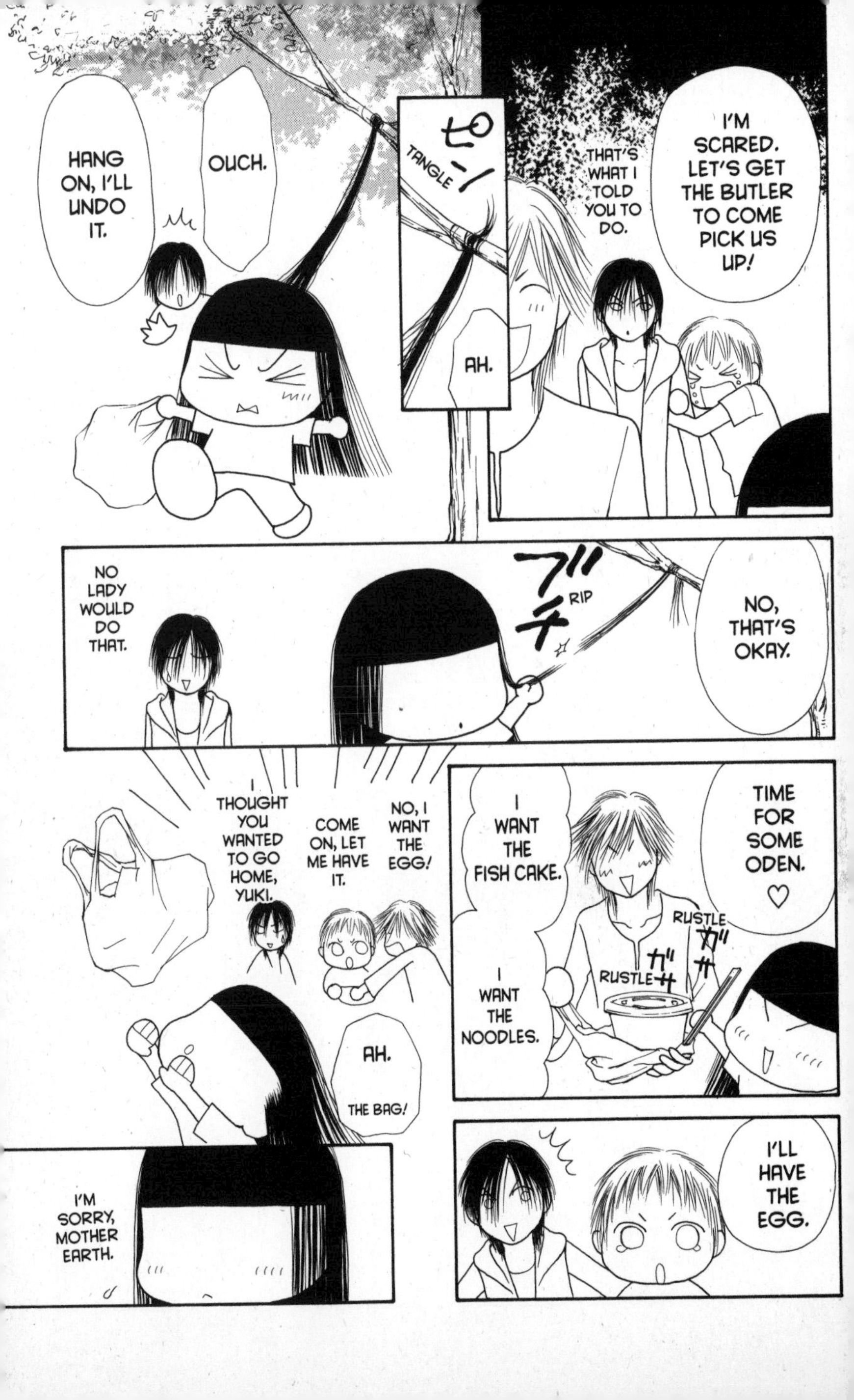
I'M SCARED. LET'S GET THE BUTLER TO COME PICK US UP!
THAT'S WHAT I TOLD YOU TO DO.
TANGLE
AH.
OUCH.
HANG ON, I'LL UNDO IT.
NO, THAT'S OKAY.
RIP
NO LADY WOULD DO THAT.
TIME FOR SOME ODEN. ♡
RUSTLE
RUSTLE
I WANT THE FISH CAKE.
I WANT THE NOODLES.
NO, I WANT THE EGG!
COME ON, LET ME HAVE IT.
I THOUGHT YOU WANTED TO GO HOME, YUKI.
AH.
THE BAG!
I'LL HAVE THE EGG.
I'M SORRY, MOTHER EARTH.

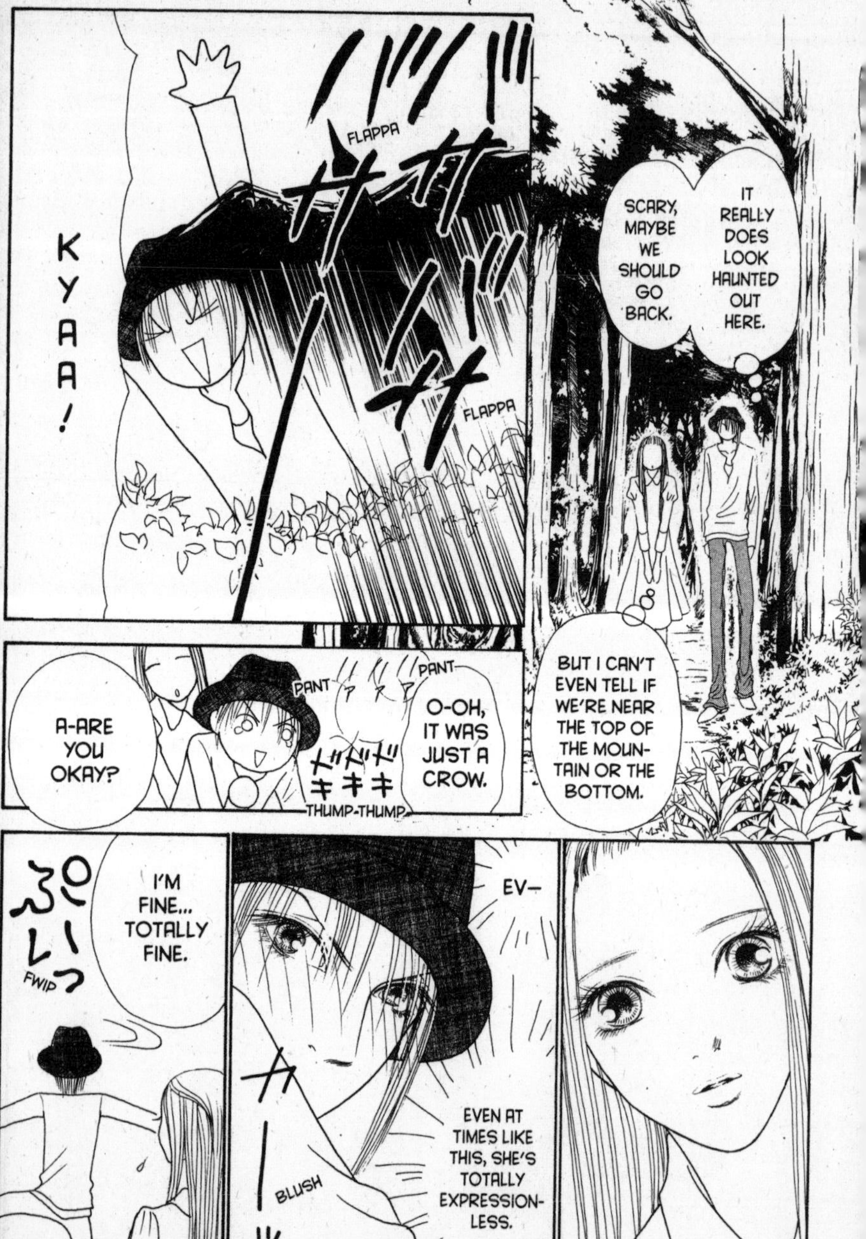
IT REALLY DOES LOOK HAUNTED OUT HERE.
SCARY, MAYBE WE SHOULD GO BACK.
BUT I CAN'T EVEN TELL IF WE'RE NEAR THE TOP OF THE MOUN-TAIN OR THE BOTTOM.
FLAPPA
FLAPPA
KYAAA!
PANT
PANT
O-OH, IT WAS JUST A CROW.
THUMP-THUMP
A-ARE YOU OKAY?
EV—
EVEN AT TIMES LIKE THIS, SHE'S TOTALLY EXPRESSION-LESS.
BLUSH
I'M FINE... TOTALLY FINE.
FWIP

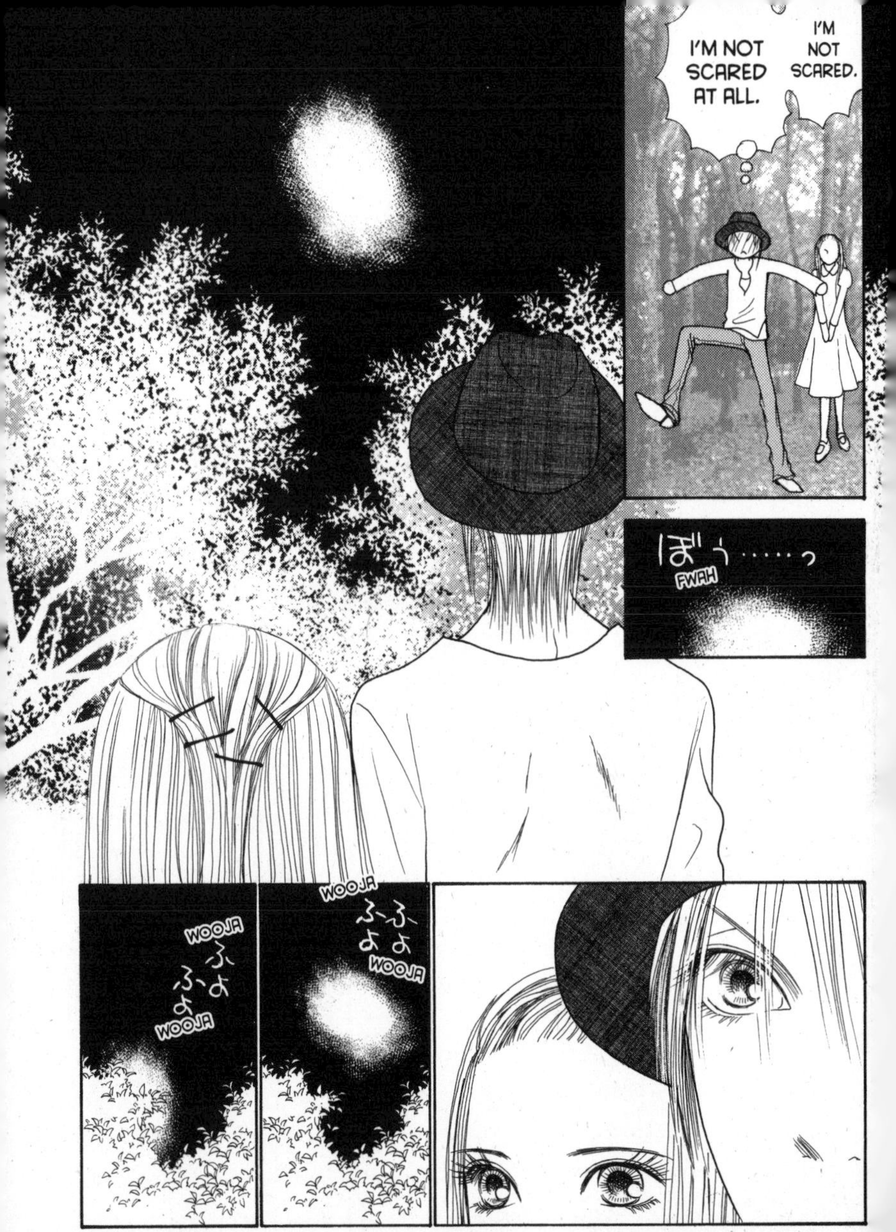
I'M NOT SCARED.
I'M NOT SCARED AT ALL.
ぼぅ……っ
FWAH
WOOJA
ふよふよ
WOOJA
WOOJA
ふよふよ
WOOJA

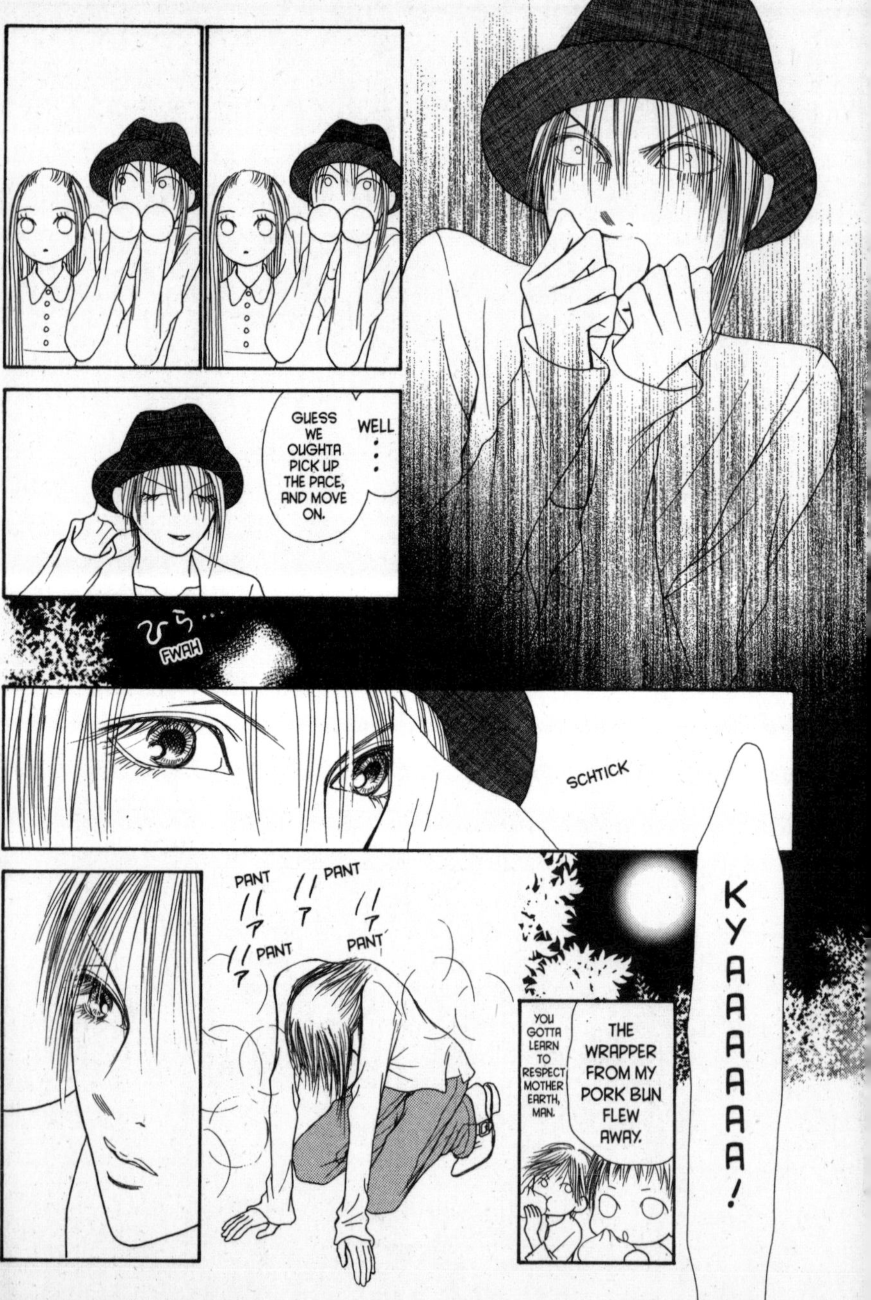
WELL . . .
GUESS WE OUGHTA PICK UP THE PACE, AND MOVE ON.
ひら…
FWAH
SCHTICK
KYAAAAAAA!
THE WRAPPER FROM MY PORK BUN FLEW AWAY.
YOU GOTTA LEARN TO RESPECT MOTHER EARTH, MAN.
PANT
PANT
PANT
PANT

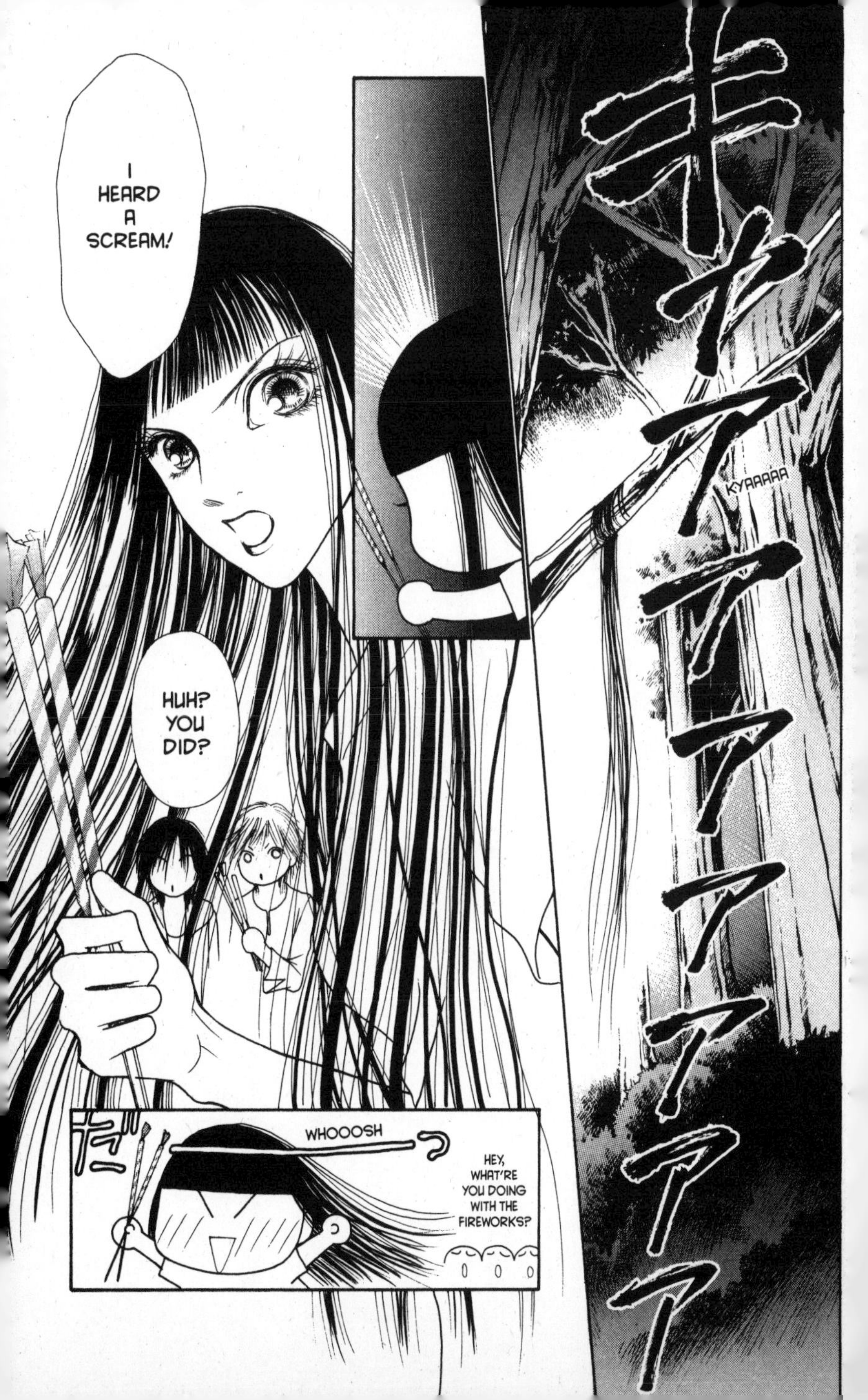
キャアアアアアアア
KYAAAAA
I HEARD A SCREAM!
HUH? YOU DID?
WHOOOSH
HEY, WHAT'RE YOU DOING WITH THE FIREWORKS?

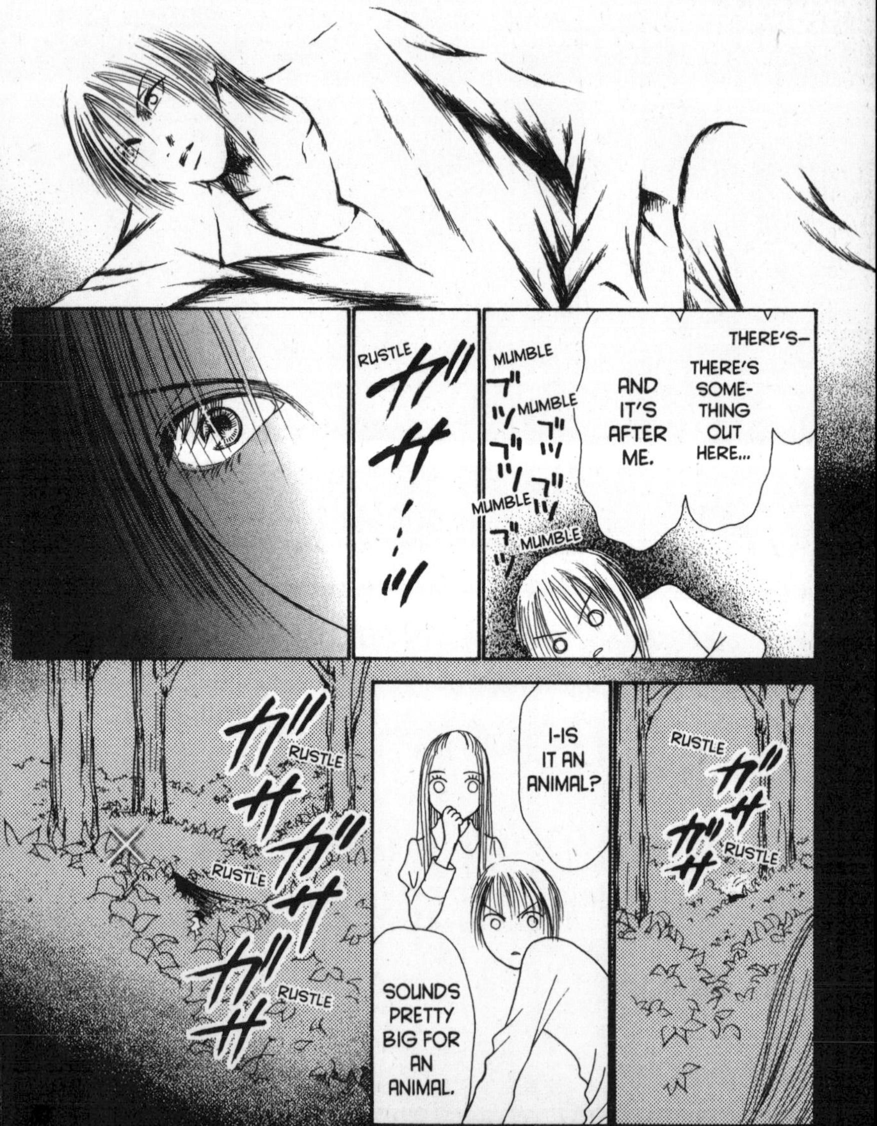
THERE'S—
THERE'S SOMETHING OUT HERE...
AND IT'S AFTER ME.
MUMBLE
ブツブツ
MUMBLE
ブツブツ
MUMBLE
ブツ
MUMBLE
RUSTLE
ガサ…ッ
RUSTLE
ガサ
RUSTLE
ガサ
I-IS IT AN ANIMAL?
SOUNDS PRETTY BIG FOR AN ANIMAL.
ガサ
RUSTLE
ガサ
RUSTLE
ガサ
RUSTLE
ガサ

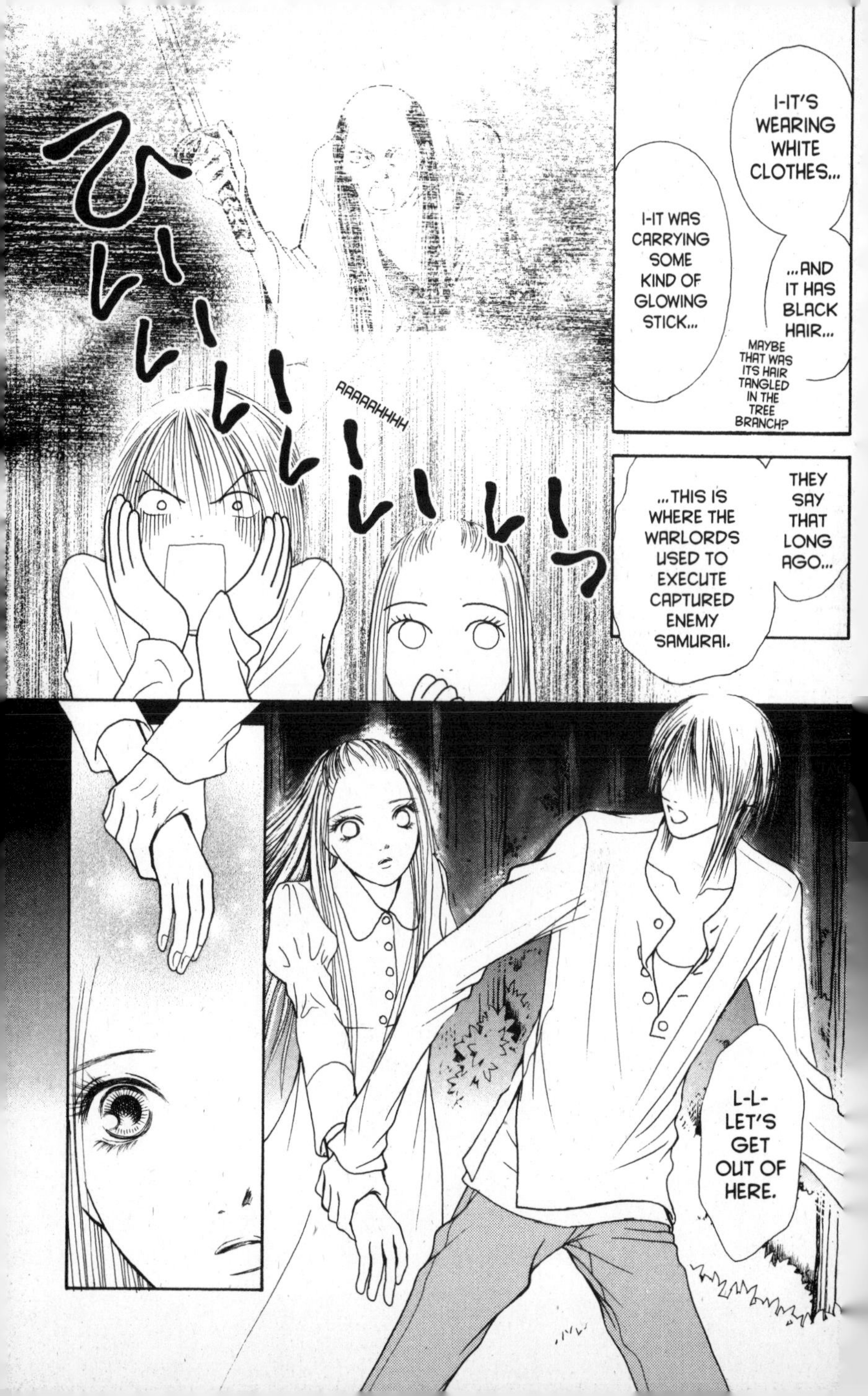

I-IT'S WEARING WHITE CLOTHES...
...AND IT HAS BLACK HAIR...
I-IT WAS CARRYING SOME KIND OF GLOWING STICK...
MAYBE THAT WAS ITS HAIR TANGLED IN THE TREE BRANCH?
THEY SAY THAT LONG AGO...
...THIS IS WHERE THE WARLORDS USED TO EXECUTE CAPTURED ENEMY SAMURAI.
ひいいいいいいっ
AAAAAHHHH
L-L-LET'S GET OUT OF HERE.

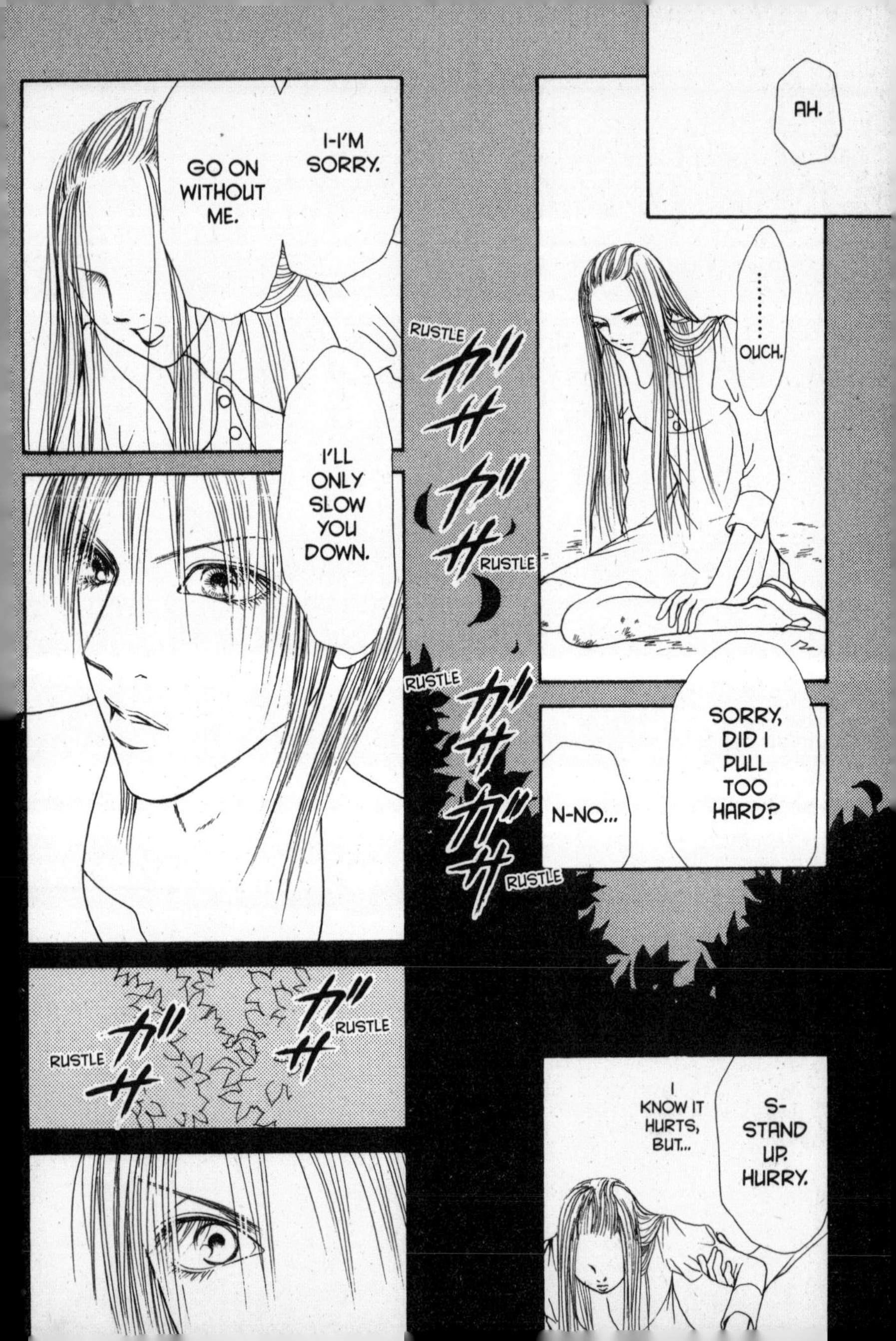
AH.
......OUCH.
SORRY, DID I PULL TOO HARD?
N-NO...
I-I'M SORRY.
GO ON WITHOUT ME.
I'LL ONLY SLOW YOU DOWN.
RUSTLE
RUSTLE
RUSTLE
RUSTLE
RUSTLE
RUSTLE
S-STAND UP. HURRY.
I KNOW IT HURTS, BUT...

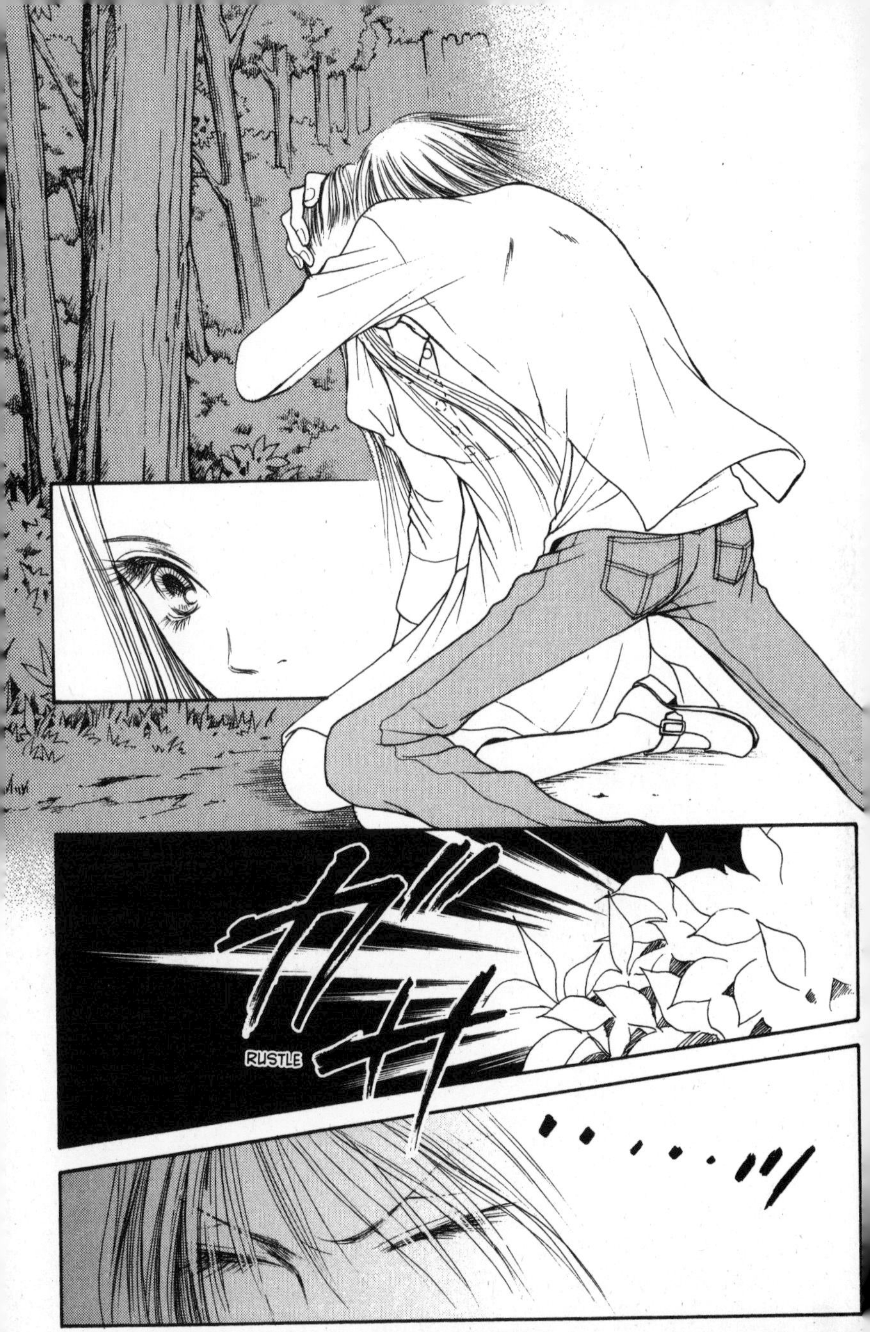
RUSTLE
......!!

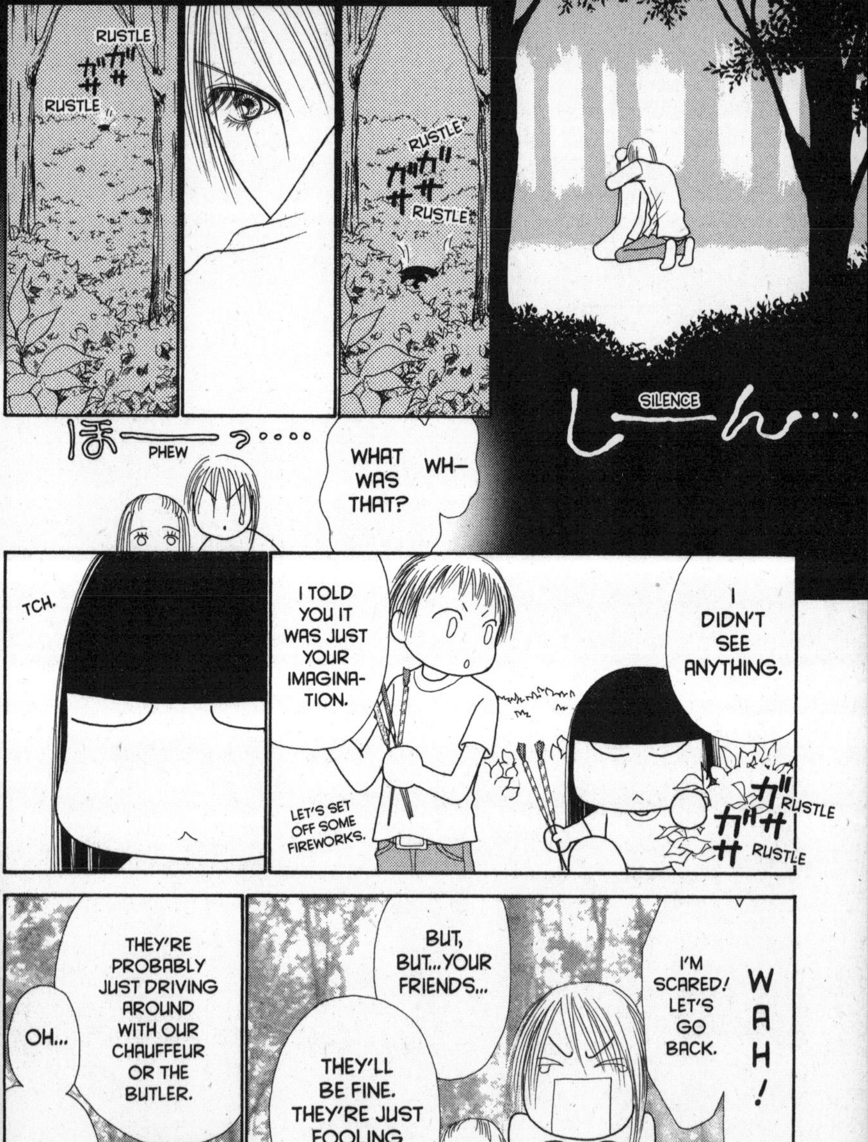
SILENCE
しーん…
RUSTLE
ガガサ
RUSTLE
RUSTLE
ガガサ
RUSTLE
WH—
WHAT WAS THAT?
ほーっ….
PHEW
I DIDN'T SEE ANYTHING.
RUSTLE
ガガサ
RUSTLE
I TOLD YOU IT WAS JUST YOUR IMAGINATION.
LET'S SET OFF SOME FIREWORKS.
TCH.
WAH!
I'M SCARED! LET'S GO BACK.
BUT, BUT...YOUR FRIENDS...
THEY'LL BE FINE. THEY'RE JUST FOOLING AROUND ANYWAY.
EH?
THEY'RE PROBABLY JUST DRIVING AROUND WITH OUR CHAUFFEUR OR THE BUTLER.
OH...
OKAY.

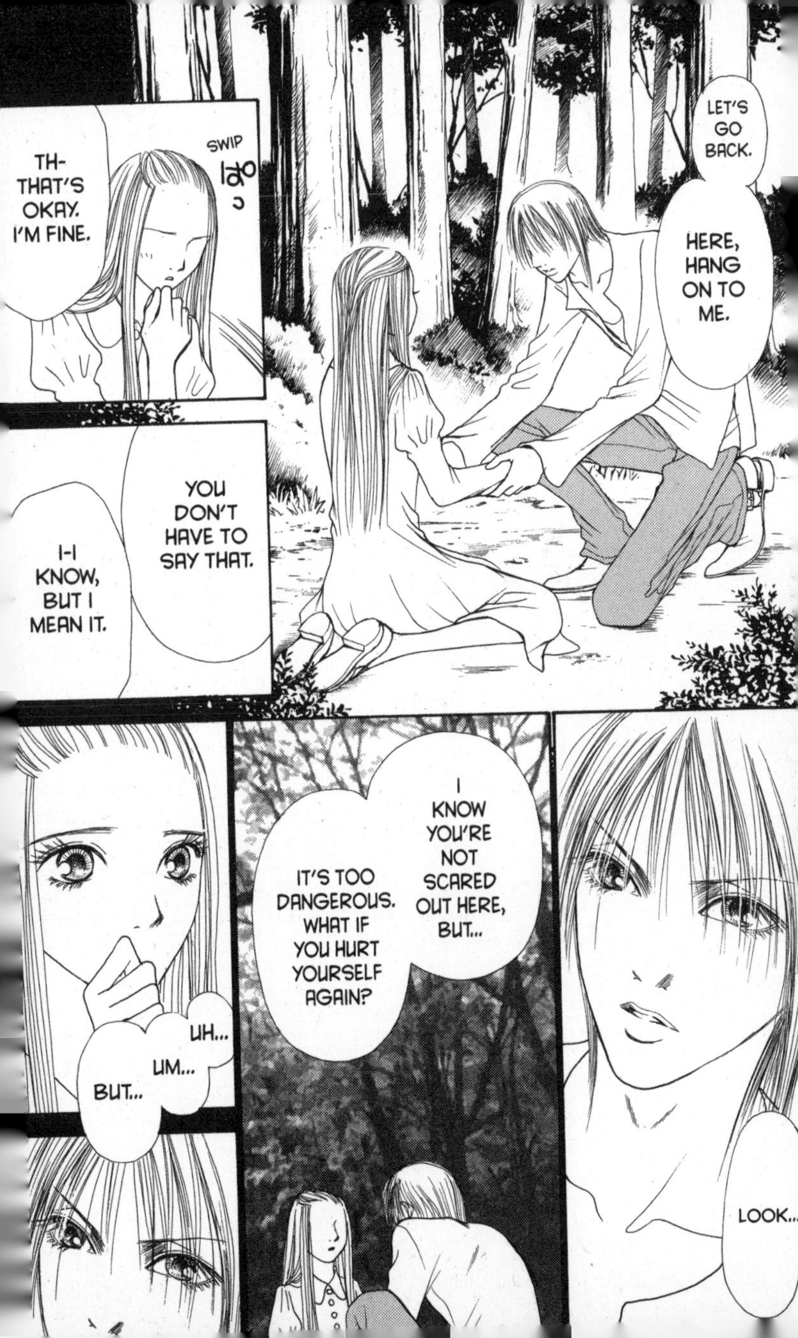
LET'S GO BACK.
HERE, HANG ON TO ME.
SWIP
はっ
TH-THAT'S OKAY. I'M FINE.
YOU DON'T HAVE TO SAY THAT.
I-I KNOW, BUT I MEAN IT.
LOOK...
I KNOW YOU'RE NOT SCARED OUT HERE, BUT...
IT'S TOO DANGEROUS. WHAT IF YOU HURT YOURSELF AGAIN?
UH...
UM...
BUT...

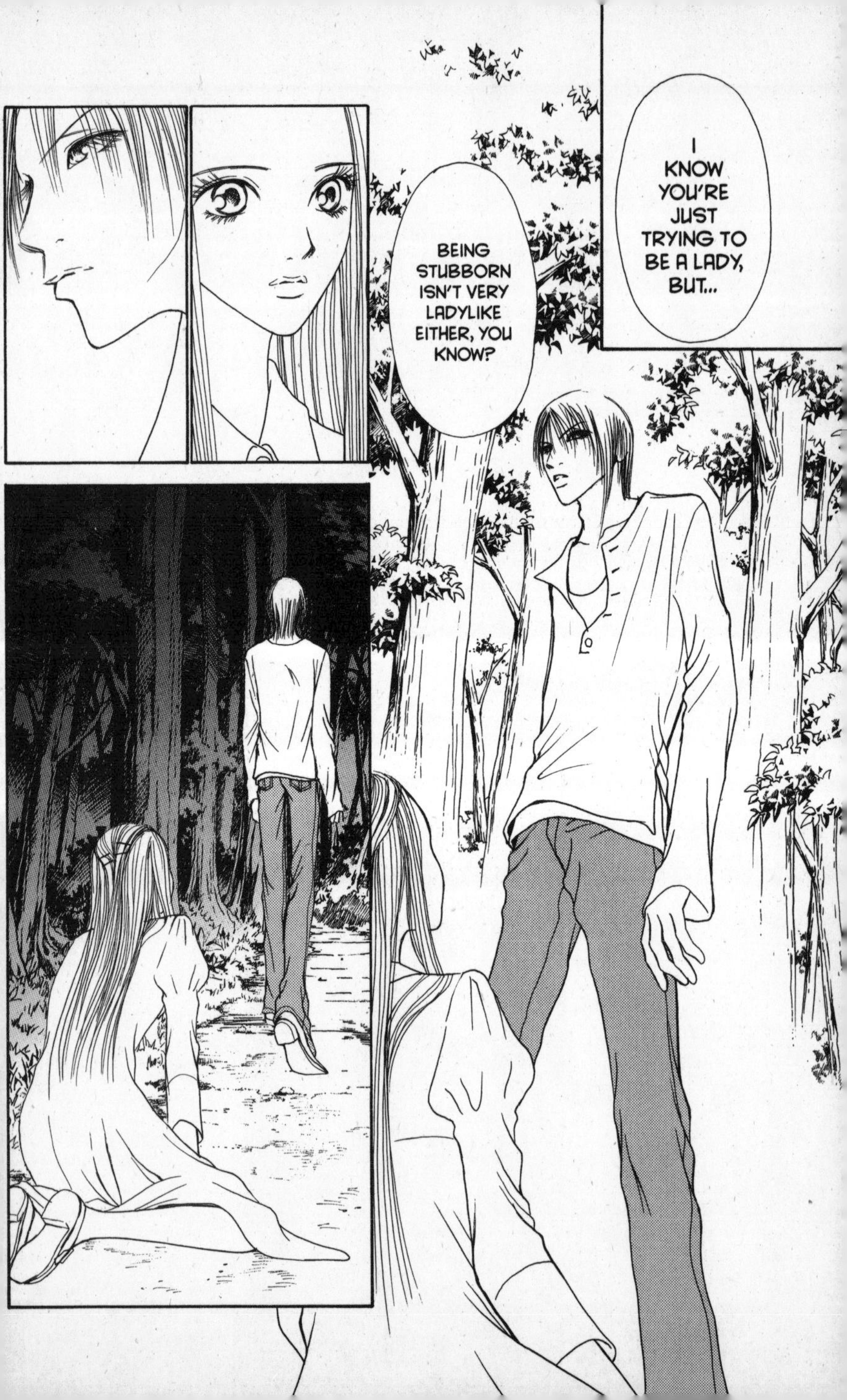
I KNOW YOU'RE JUST TRYING TO BE A LADY, BUT...
BEING STUBBORN ISN'T VERY LADYLIKE EITHER, YOU KNOW?

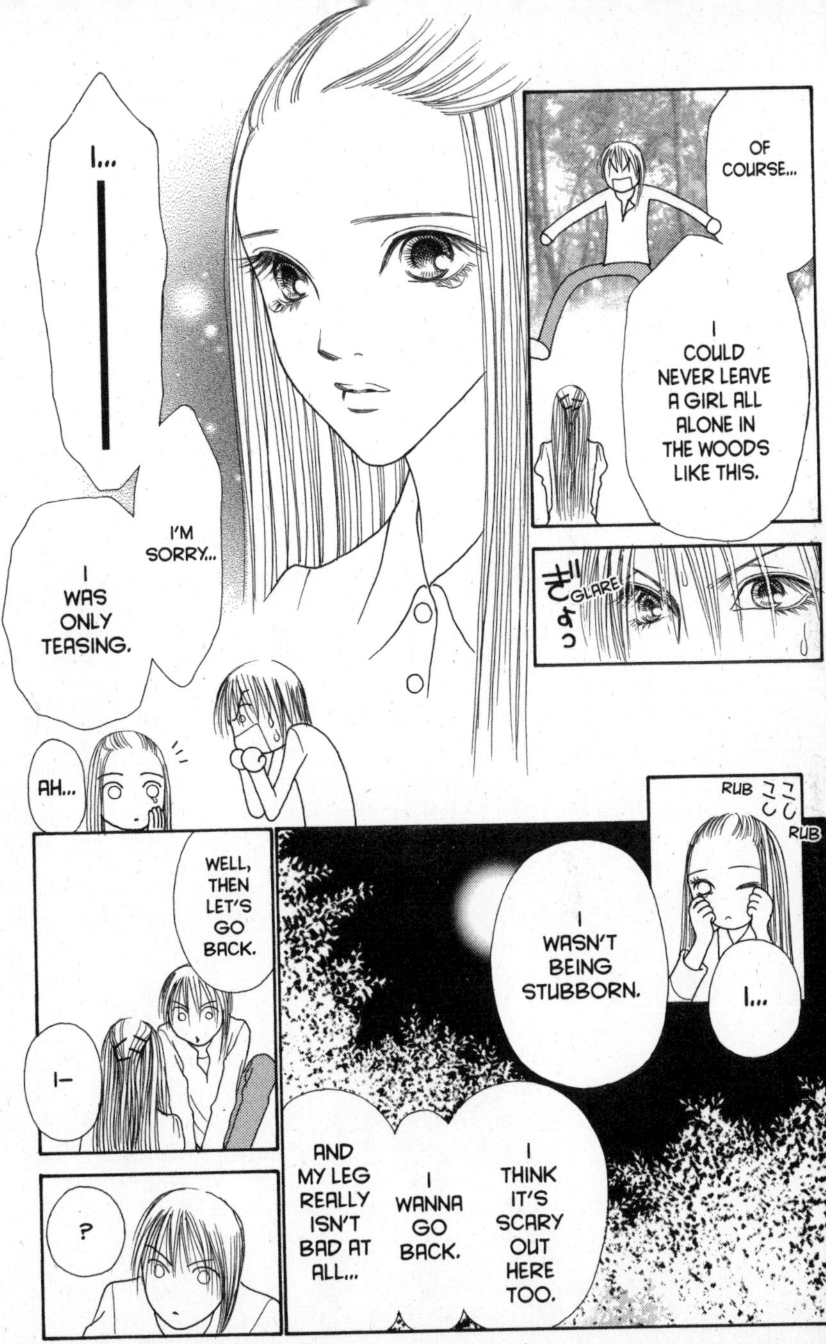

OF COURSE...
I COULD NEVER LEAVE A GIRL ALL ALONE IN THE WOODS LIKE THIS.
GLARE
I...
I'M SORRY...
I WAS ONLY TEASING.
AH...
RUB RUB
I...
I WASN'T BEING STUBBORN.
I THINK IT'S SCARY OUT HERE TOO.
I WANNA GO BACK.
AND MY LEG REALLY ISN'T BAD AT ALL...
WELL, THEN LET'S GO BACK.
I—
?

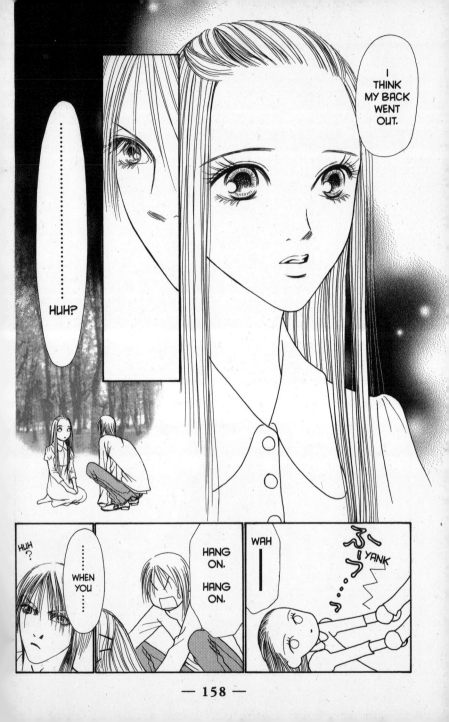

I THINK MY BACK WENT OUT.

•••••••••••

HUH?

HUH?

•••••• WHEN YOU

HANG ON. HANG ON.

WAH

•••••• YANK

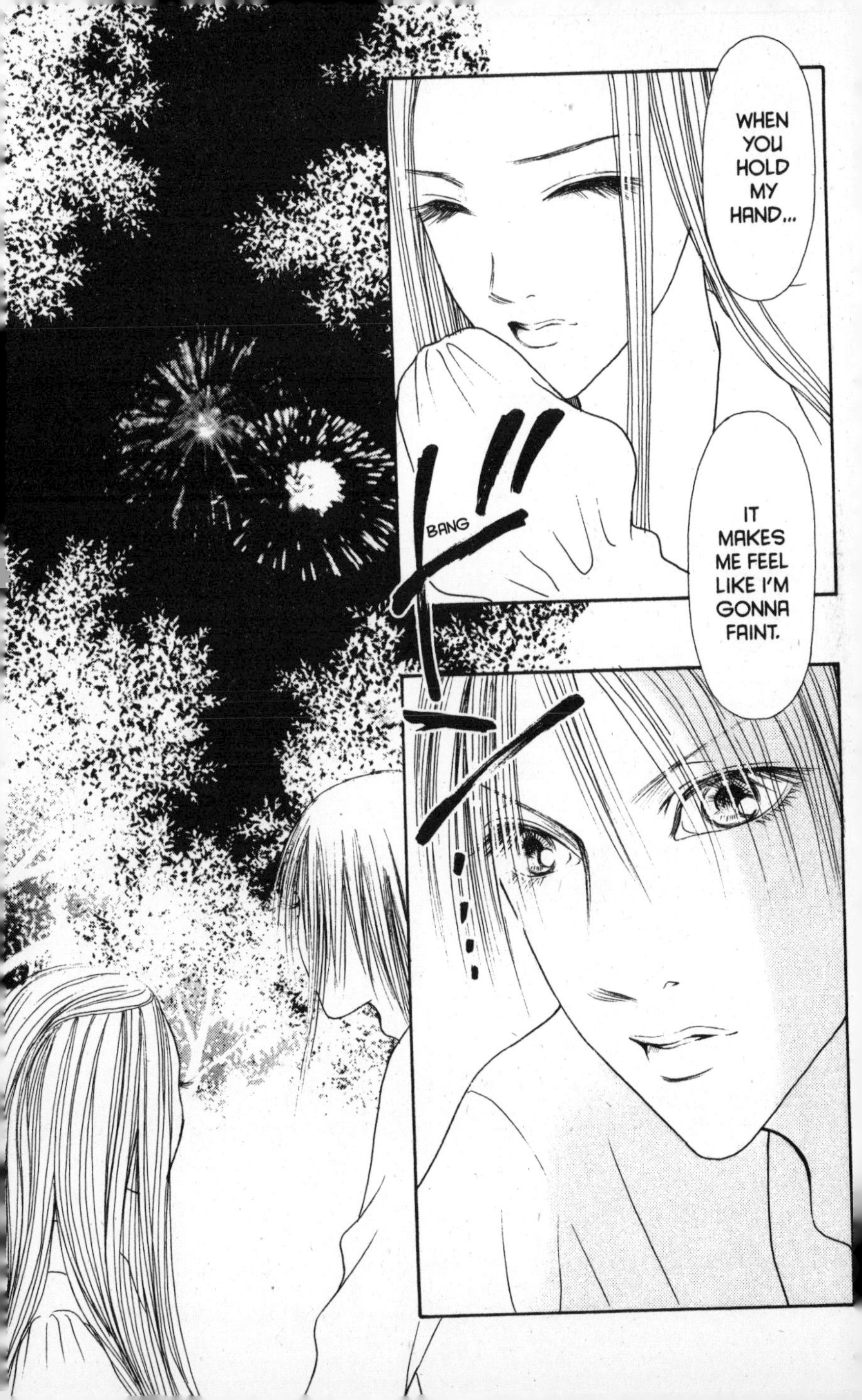
WHEN YOU HOLD MY HAND...
IT MAKES ME FEEL LIKE I'M GONNA FAINT.
BANG

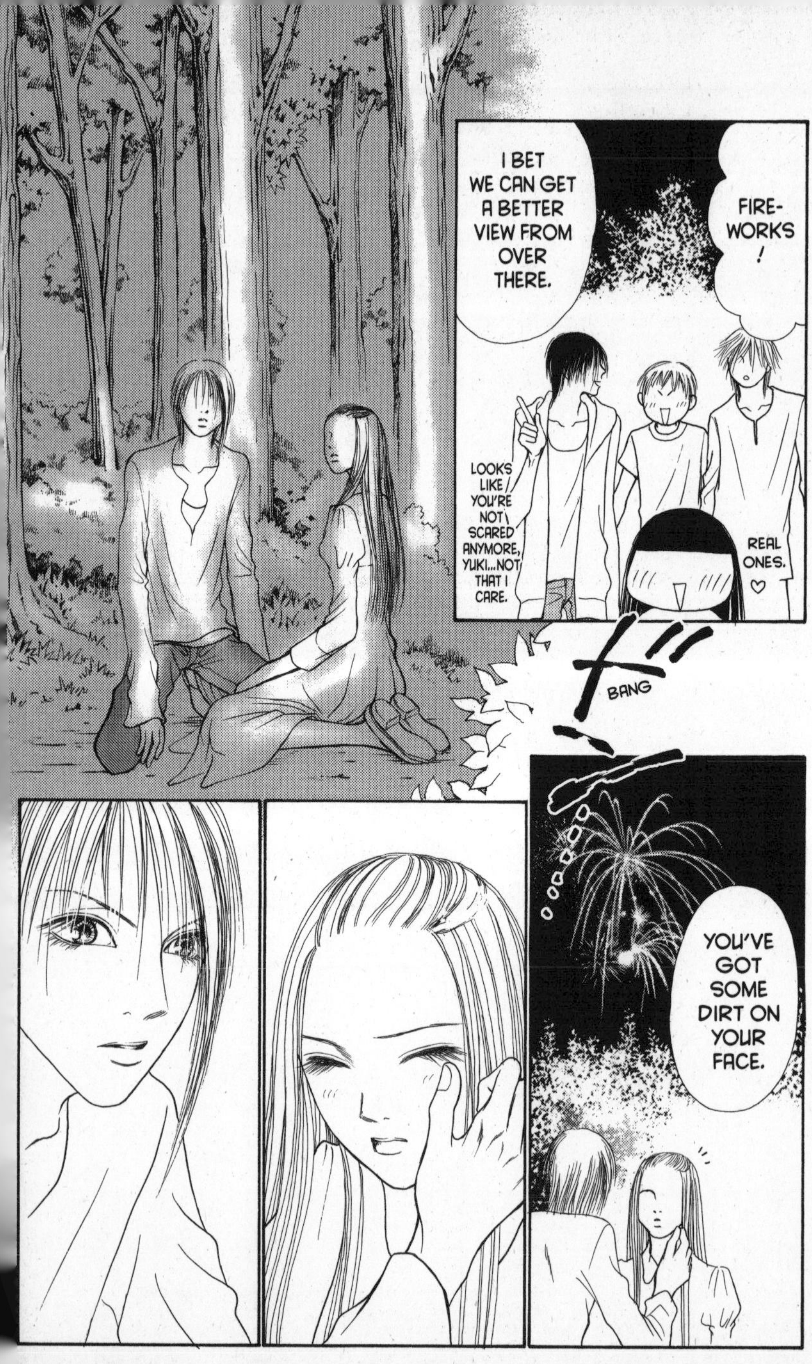
FIRE-WORKS!
I BET WE CAN GET A BETTER VIEW FROM OVER THERE.
REAL ONES. ♡
LOOKS LIKE YOU'RE NOT SCARED ANYMORE, YUKI...NOT THAT I CARE.
BANG
YOU'VE GOT SOME DIRT ON YOUR FACE.

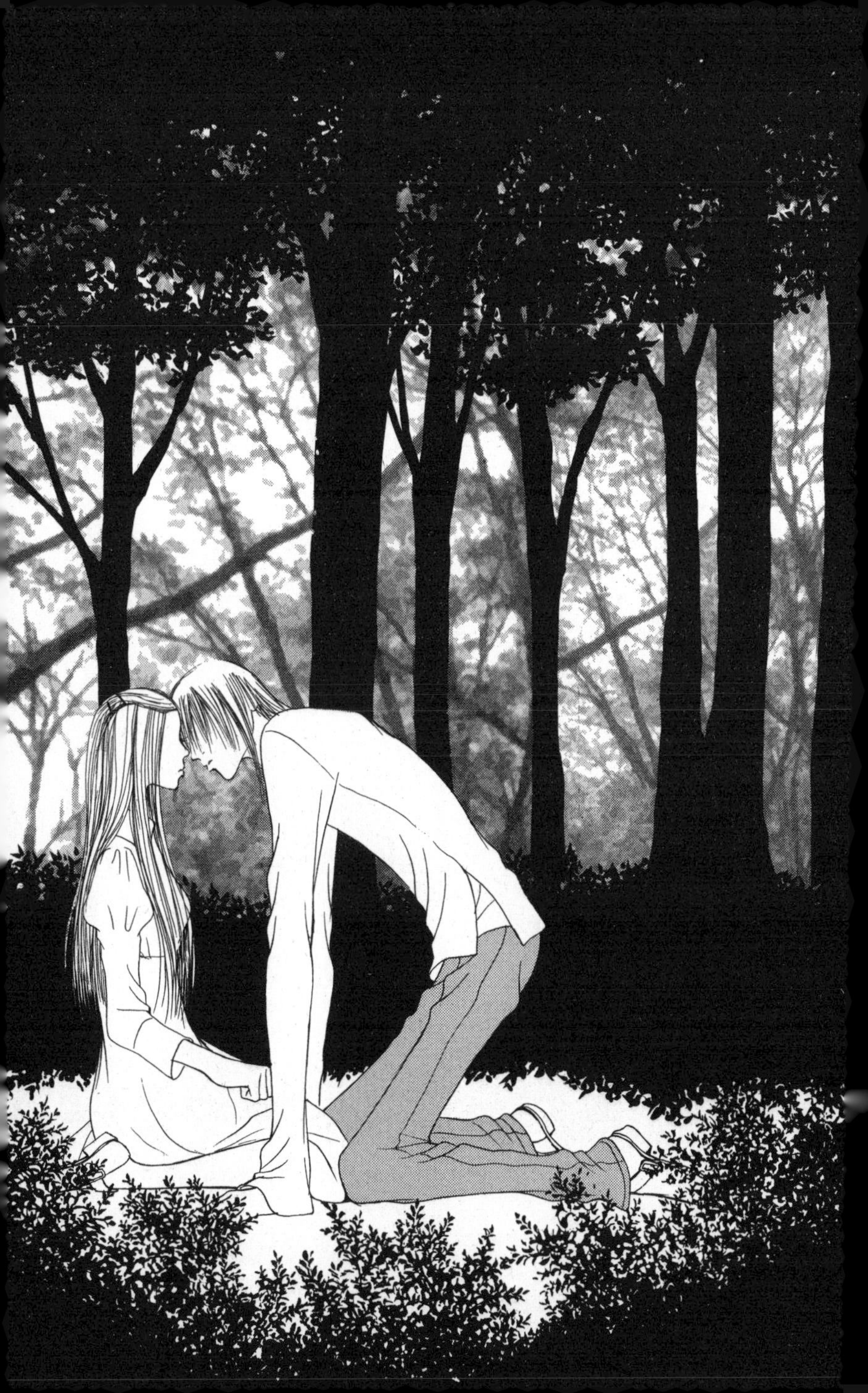

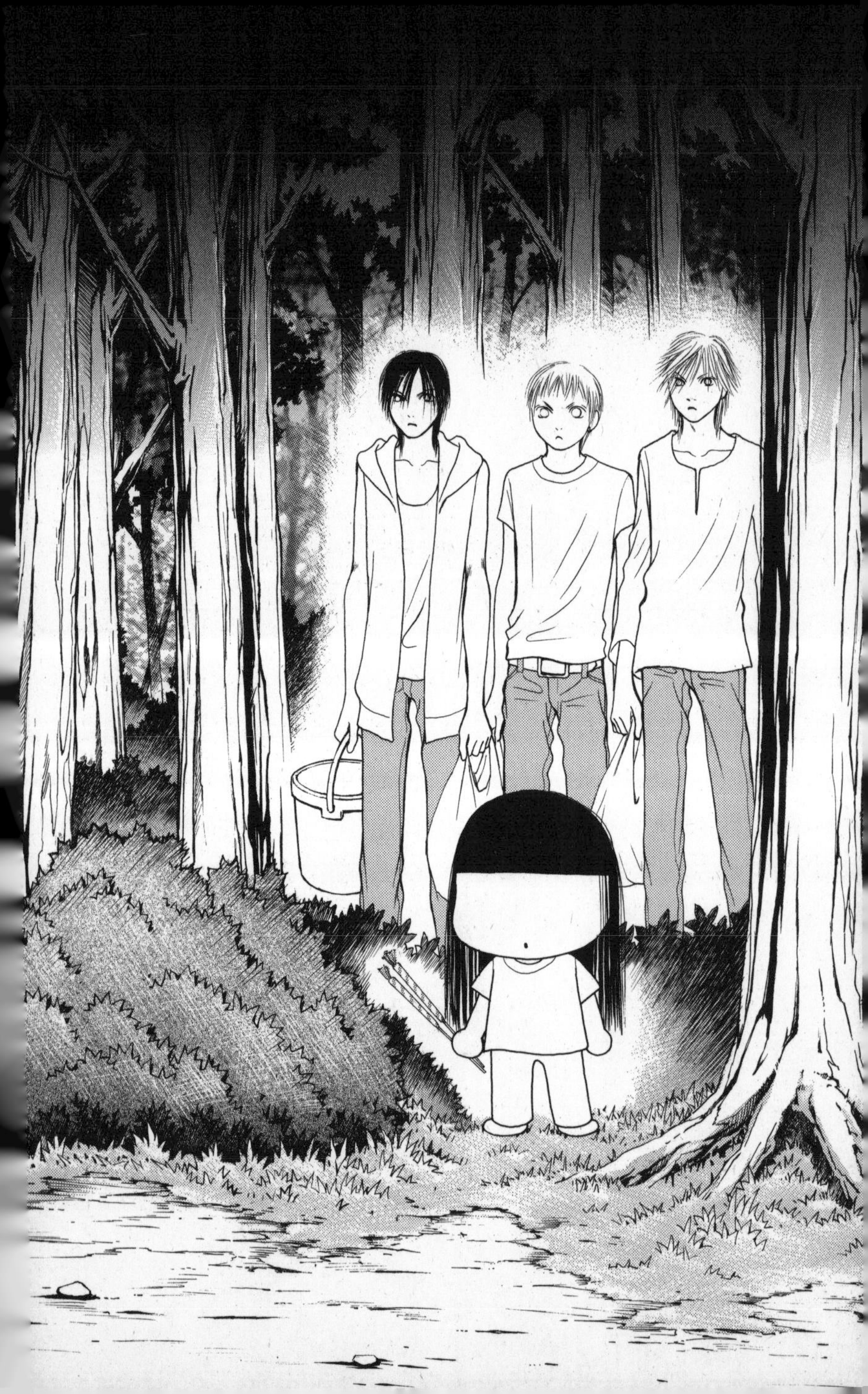

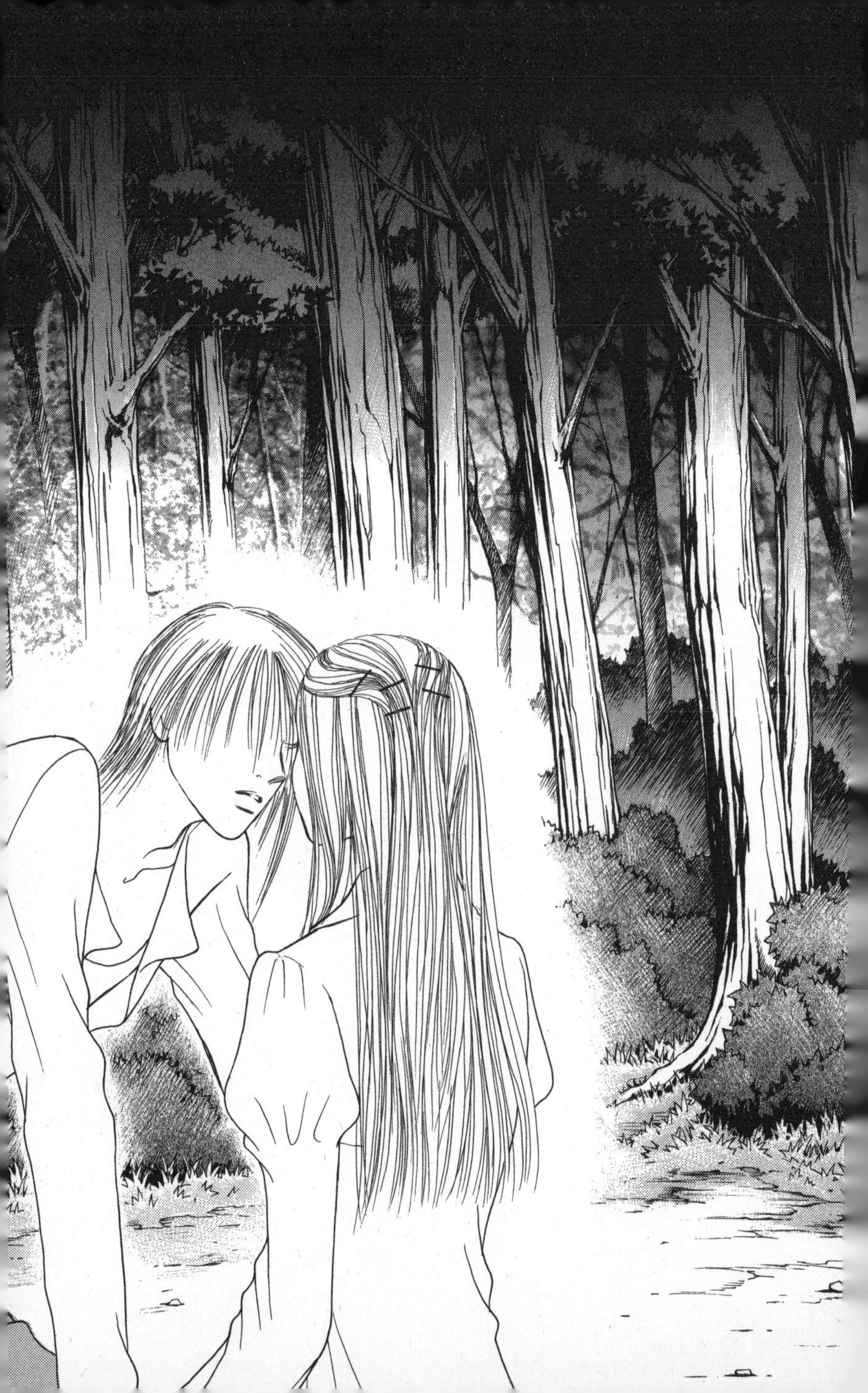

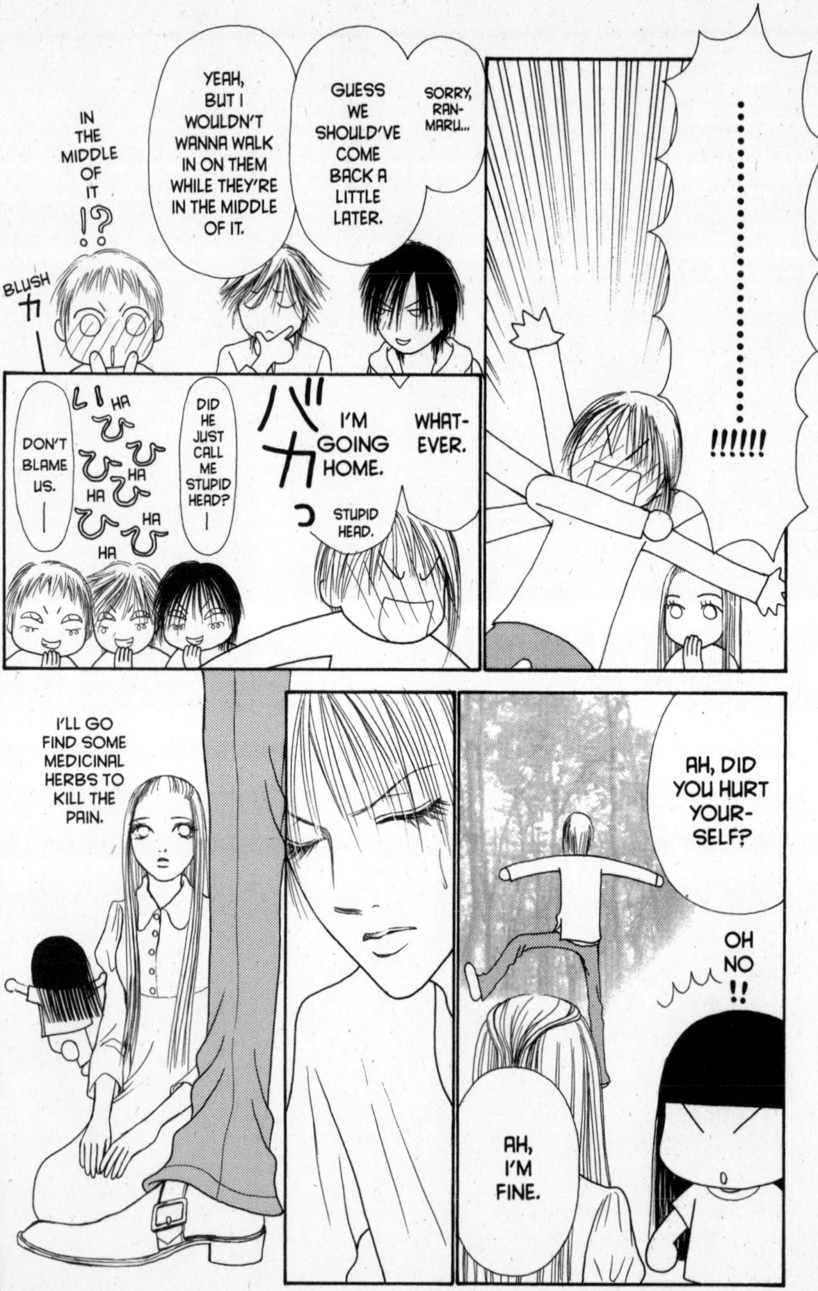
......
!!!!!!
SORRY, RANMARU...
GUESS WE SHOULD'VE COME BACK A LITTLE LATER.
YEAH, BUT I WOULDN'T WANNA WALK IN ON THEM WHILE THEY'RE IN THE MIDDLE OF IT.
IN THE MIDDLE OF IT !?
BLUSH
カ
WHAT-EVER.
I'M GOING HOME.
STUPID HEAD.
バカっ
DID HE JUST CALL ME STUPID HEAD? —
ひひひひひひ HA HA HA HA HA
DON'T BLAME US. —
AH, DID YOU HURT YOURSELF?
OH NO !!
AH, I'M FINE.
I'LL GO FIND SOME MEDICINAL HERBS TO KILL THE PAIN.

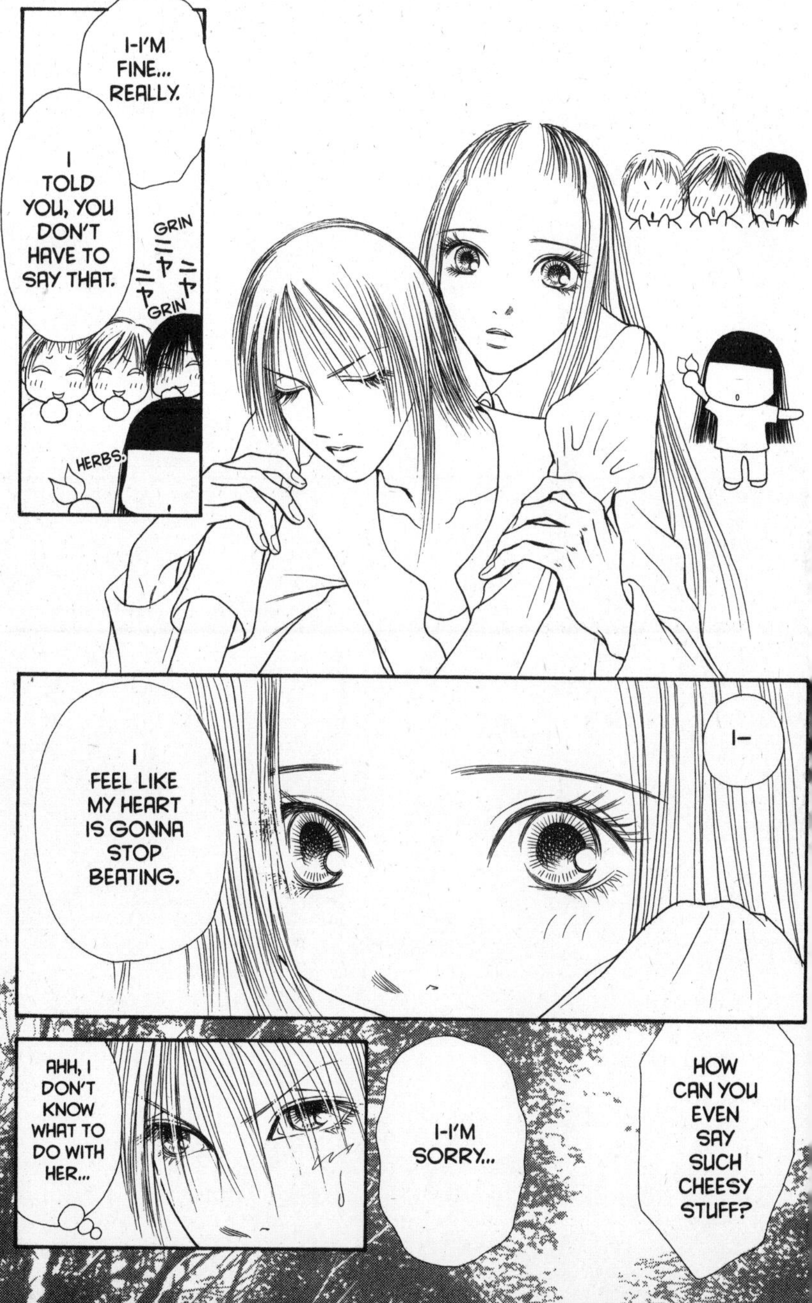
I-I'M FINE... REALLY.
I TOLD YOU, YOU DON'T HAVE TO SAY THAT.
GRIN ニヤ
ニヤ GRIN
HERBS.
I–
I FEEL LIKE MY HEART IS GONNA STOP BEATING.
HOW CAN YOU EVEN SAY SUCH CHEESY STUFF?
I-I'M SORRY...
AHH, I DON'T KNOW WHAT TO DO WITH HER...

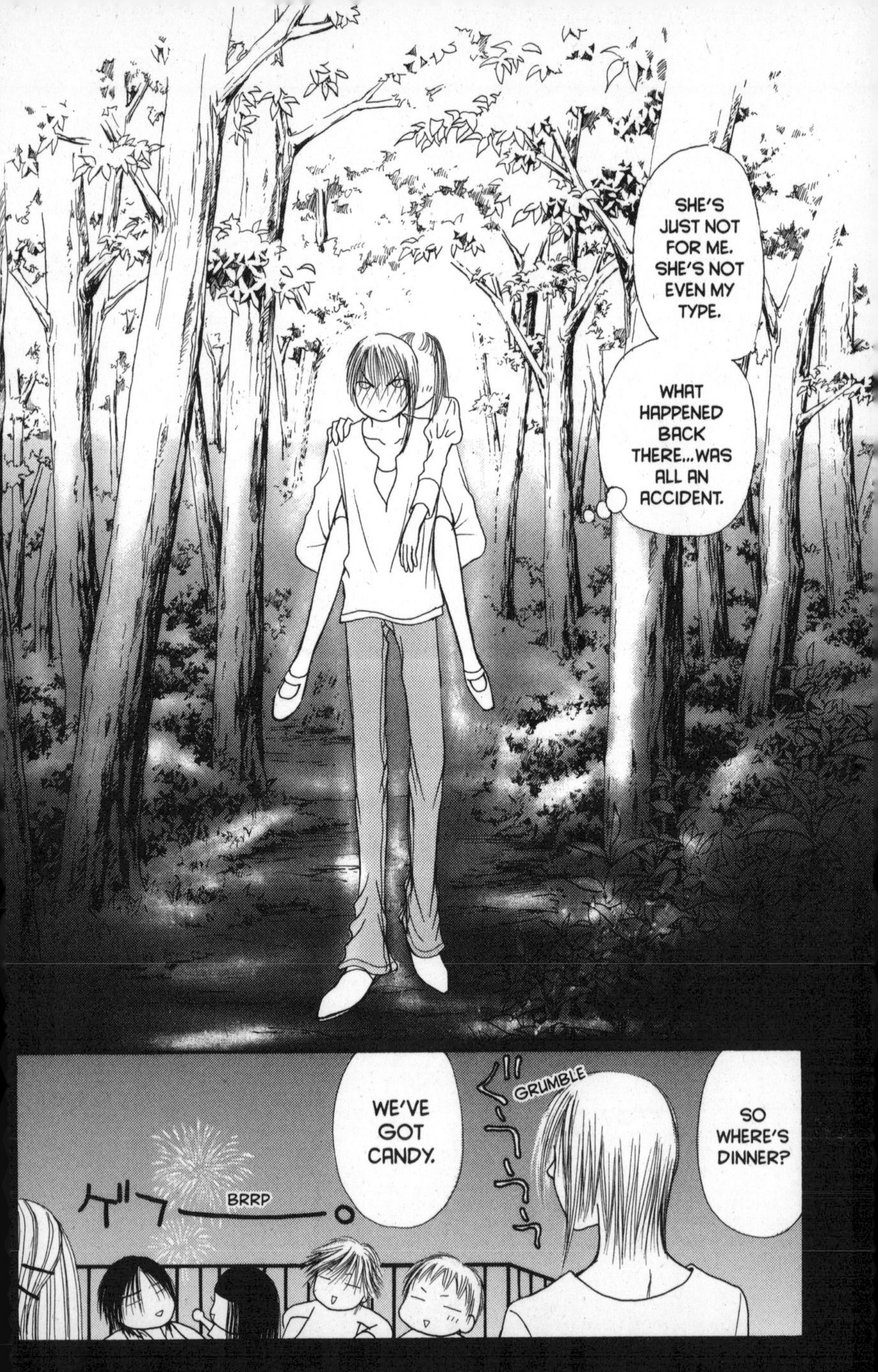
SHE'S JUST NOT FOR ME. SHE'S NOT EVEN MY TYPE.
WHAT HAPPENED BACK THERE...WAS ALL AN ACCIDENT.
SO WHERE'S DINNER?
GRUMBLE
WE'VE GOT CANDY.
BRRP

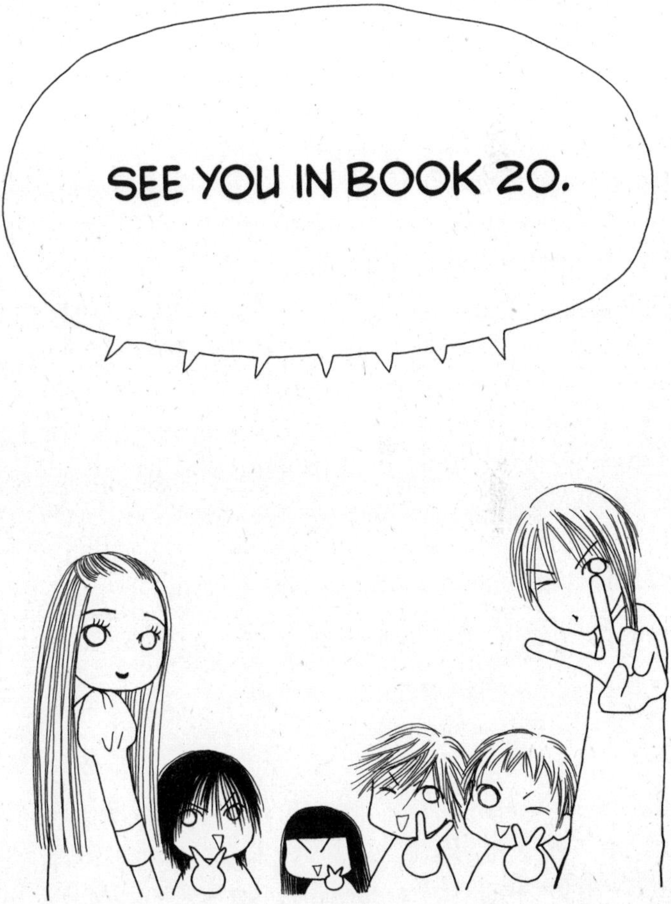
SEE YOU IN BOOK 20.

About the Creator

Tomoko Hayakawa was born on March 4.

Since her debut as a manga creator, Tomoko Hayakawa has worked on many shojo titles with the theme of romantic love—only to realize that she could write about other subjects as well. She decided to pack her newest story with the things she likes most, which led to her current, enormously popular series, *The Wallflower*.

Her favorite things are: Tim Burton's *The Nightmare Before Christmas*, Jean-Paul Gaultier, and samurai dramas on TV. Her hobbies are collecting items with skull designs and watching bishonen (beautiful boys). Her dream is to build a mansion like the one the Addams family lives in. Her favorite pastime is to lie around at home with her cat, Ten (whose full name is Tennosuke).

Her zodiac sign is Pisces, and her blood group is AB.

Translation Notes

Japanese is a tricky language for most Westerners, and translation is often more art than science. For your edification and reading pleasure, here are notes on some of the places where we could have gone in a different direction in our translation of the work, or where a Japanese cultural reference is used.

Strawberry Pocky, page 15

Pocky are a brand of thin, stick-shaped cookies covered with chocolate, strawberry, or other flavors.

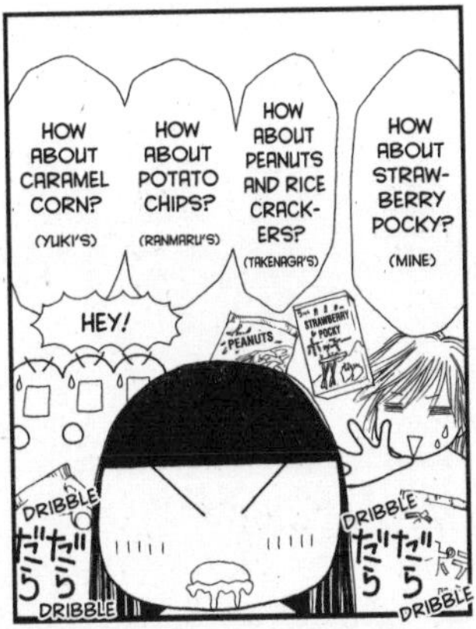
HOW ABOUT STRAW-BERRY POCKY?
(MINE)
HOW ABOUT PEANUTS AND RICE CRACK-ERS?
(TAKENAGA'S)
HOW ABOUT POTATO CHIPS?
(RANMARU'S)
HOW ABOUT CARAMEL CORN?
(YUKI'S)
HEY!
STRAWBERRY POCKY
PEANUTS
DRIBBLE
DRIBBLE
だらだら
DRIBBLE
DRIBBLE
だらだら

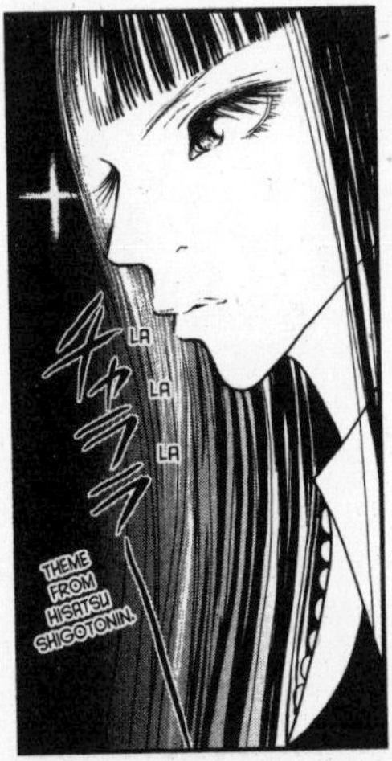
LA
LA
LA
THEME FROM HISATSU SHIGOTONIN.

***Hisatsu Shigotonin*, page 92**

Hisastsu Shigotonin is a popular Japanese TV crime drama.

Karuizawa, page 131
Karuizawa is a famous hot springs resort area located in the mountains of Nagano Prefecture, a few hours outside of Tokyo.

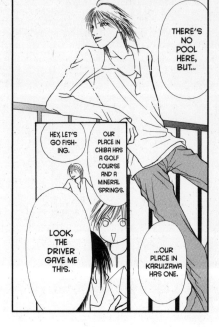

THERE'S NO POOL HERE, BUT...
OUR PLACE IN CHIBA HAS A GOLF COURSE AND A MINERAL SPRINGS.
HEY, LET'S GO FISH-ING.
LOOK, THE DRIVER GAVE ME THIS.
...OUR PLACE IN KARUIZAWA HAS ONE.

Niigata, page 131
Niigata is a coastal prefecture famous for its ski resorts and hot springs and frequent earthquakes.

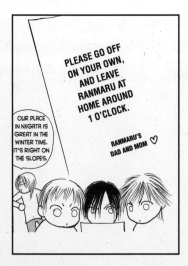

PLEASE GO OFF ON YOUR OWN, AND LEAVE RANMARU AT HOME AROUND 1 O'CLOCK.
RANMARU'S DAD AND MOM ♡
OUR PLACE IN NIIGATA IS GREAT IN THE WINTER TIME. IT'S RIGHT ON THE SLOPES.

Oden, page 141

Oden is a tasty dish made up of various ingredients boiled in soup stock. Common ingredients include daikon radish, hard-boiled eggs, konyaku (yam cake), and fish cakes.

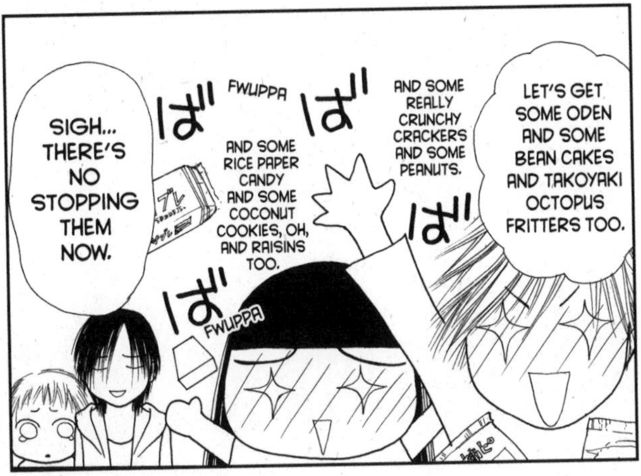
LET'S GET SOME ODEN AND SOME BEAN CAKES AND TAKOYAKI OCTOPUS FRITTERS TOO.
AND SOME REALLY CRUNCHY CRACKERS AND SOME PEANUTS.
ば
ば
FWUPPA
AND SOME RICE PAPER CANDY AND SOME COCONUT COOKIES, OH, AND RAISINS TOO.
ば
SIGH... THERE'S NO STOPPING THEM NOW.
ば
FWUPPA

Preview of volume 20

We're pleased to present you a preview from volume 20. Please check our website (www.delreymanga.com) to see when this volume will be available.

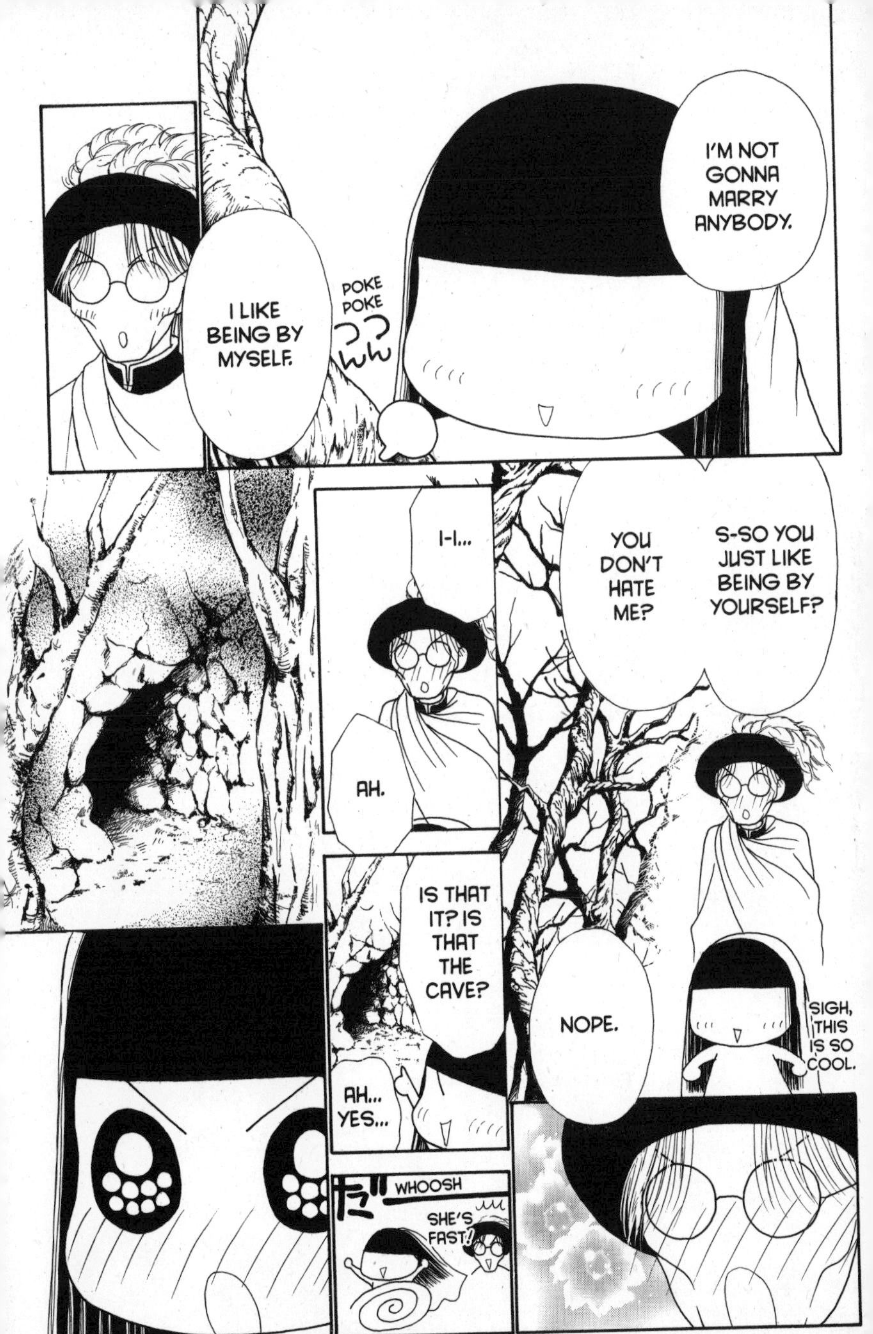
I'M NOT GONNA MARRY ANYBODY.
POKE POKE
I LIKE BEING BY MYSELF.
S-SO YOU JUST LIKE BEING BY YOURSELF?
YOU DON'T HATE ME?
I-I...
AH.
NOPE.
SIGH, THIS IS SO COOL.
IS THAT IT? IS THAT THE CAVE?
AH... YES...
WHOOSH
SHE'S FAST!

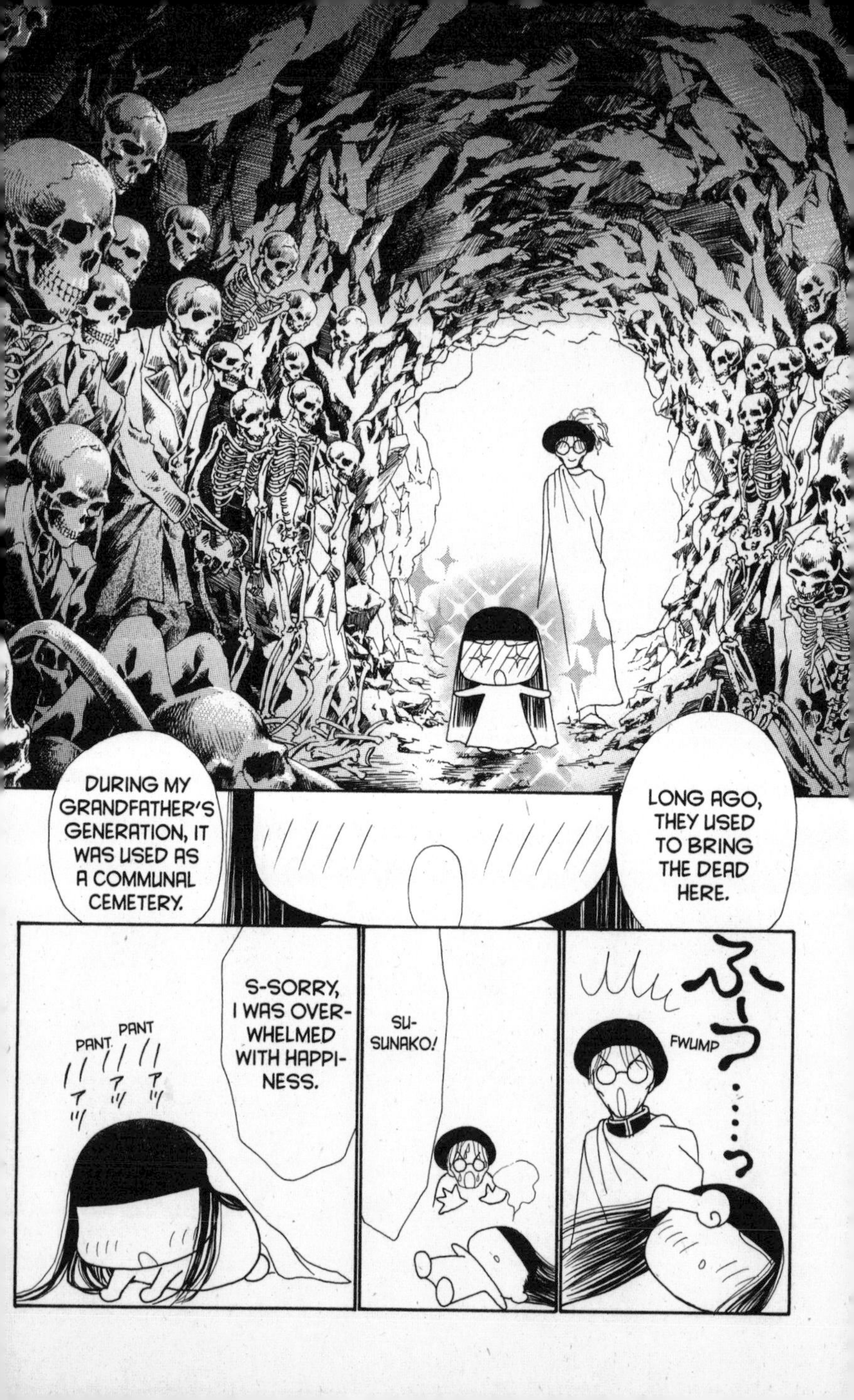
LONG AGO, THEY USED TO BRING THE DEAD HERE.
DURING MY GRANDFATHER'S GENERATION, IT WAS USED AS A COMMUNAL CEMETERY.
FWUMP
SU-SUNAKO!
S-SORRY, I WAS OVER-WHELMED WITH HAPPI-NESS.
PANT. PANT

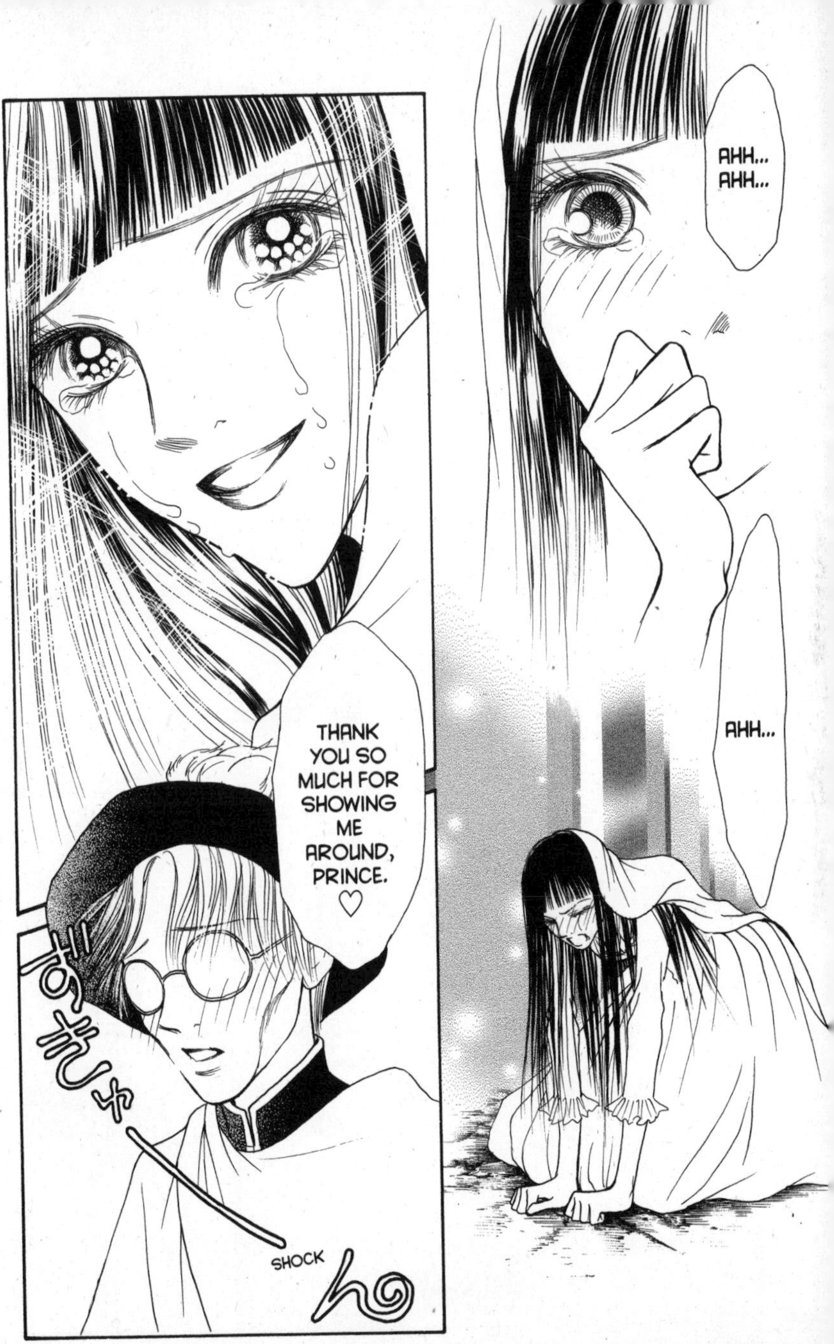
AHH... AHH...
AHH...
THANK YOU SO MUCH FOR SHOWING ME AROUND, PRINCE. ♡
SHOCK

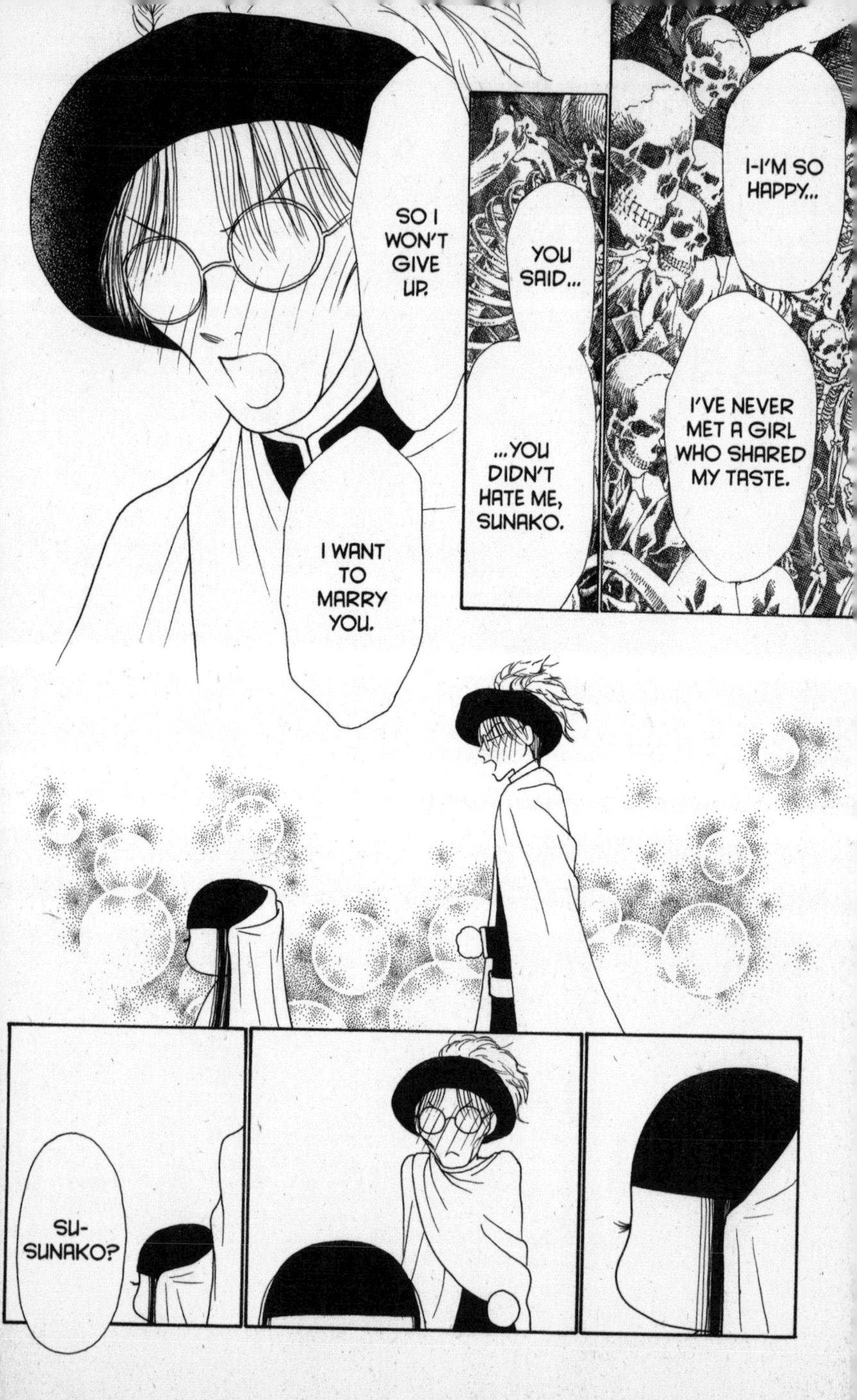
I-I'M SO HAPPY...
I'VE NEVER MET A GIRL WHO SHARED MY TASTE.
YOU SAID...
...YOU DIDN'T HATE ME, SUNAKO.
SO I WON'T GIVE UP.
I WANT TO MARRY YOU.
SU-SUNAKO?

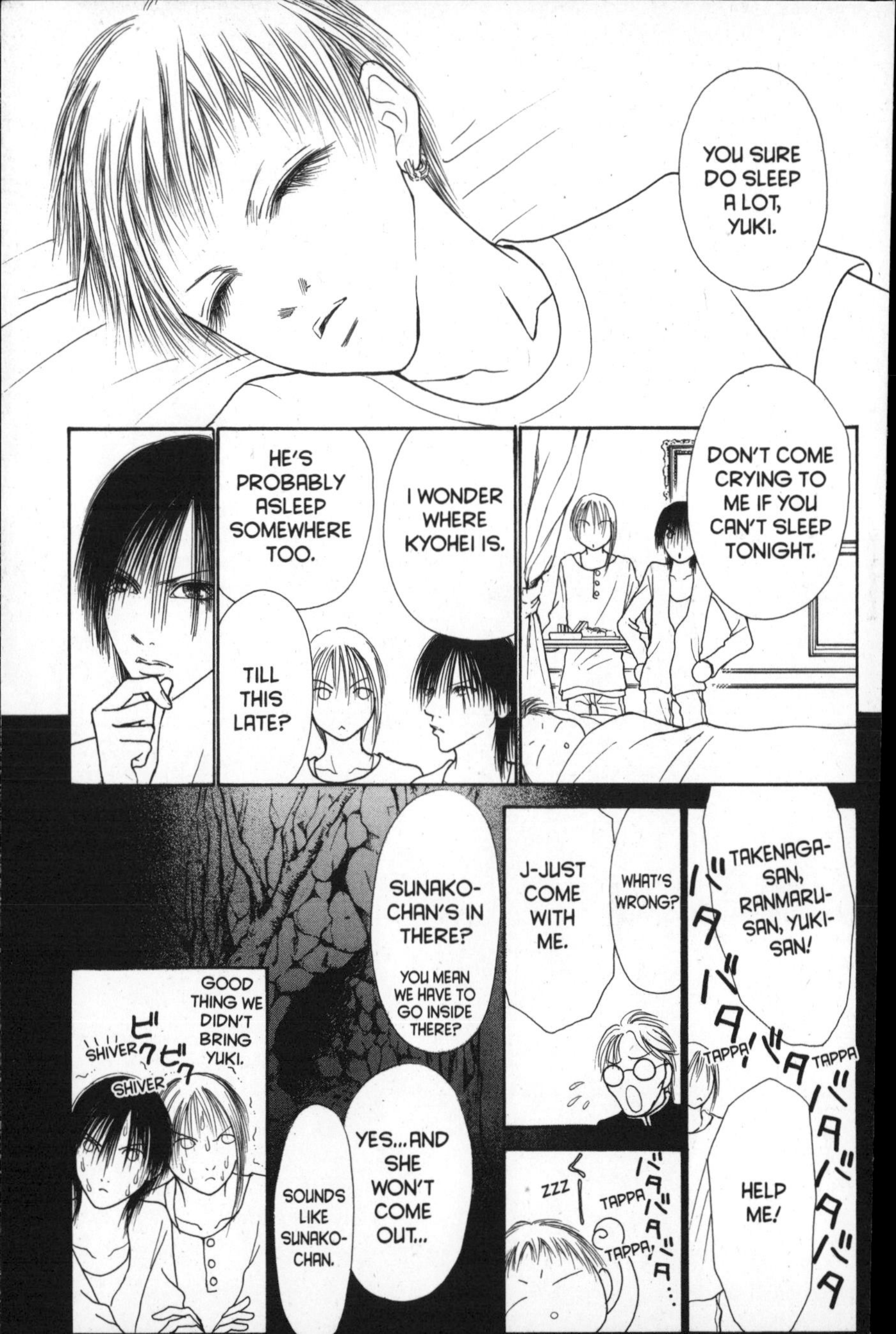
YOU SURE DO SLEEP A LOT, YUKI.
DON'T COME CRYING TO ME IF YOU CAN'T SLEEP TONIGHT.
I WONDER WHERE KYOHEI IS.
HE'S PROBABLY ASLEEP SOMEWHERE TOO.
TILL THIS LATE?
TAKENAGA-SAN, RANMARU-SAN, YUKI-SAN!
バタバタ
TAPPA
TAPPA
HELP ME!
WHAT'S WRONG?
J-JUST COME WITH ME.
ZZZ
バタバタ
TAPPA
TAPPA...
SUNAKO-CHAN'S IN THERE?
YOU MEAN WE HAVE TO GO INSIDE THERE?
YES...AND SHE WON'T COME OUT...
SOUNDS LIKE SUNAKO-CHAN.
GOOD THING WE DIDN'T BRING YUKI.
ビクビク
SHIVER
SHIVER

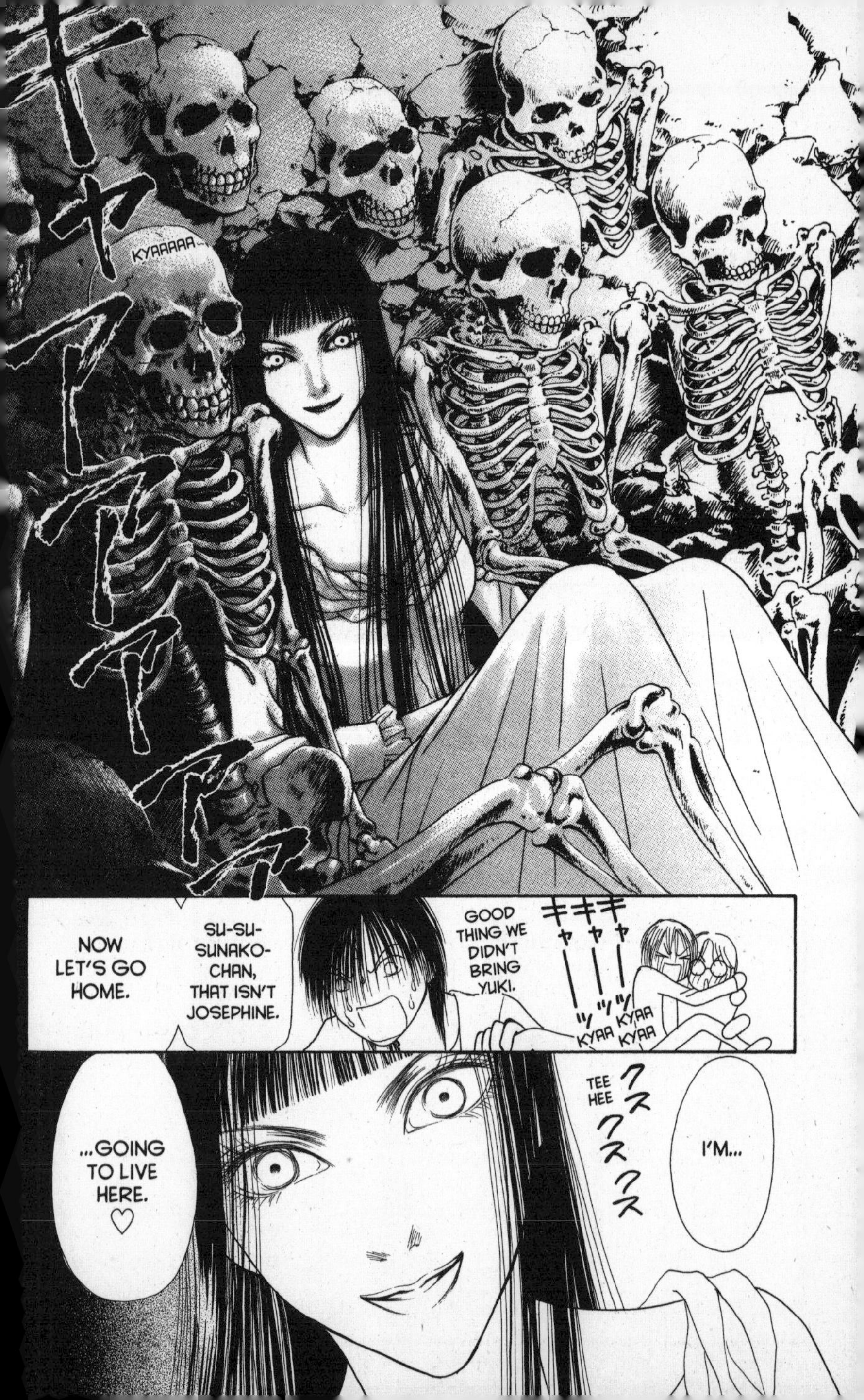
KYAAAAA...
キャアアアア
キャーッ
キャーッ
キャーッ
KYAA KYAA
KYAA
GOOD THING WE DIDN'T BRING YUKI.
SU-SU-SUNAKO-CHAN, THAT ISN'T JOSEPHINE.
NOW LET'S GO HOME.
TEE HEE
クスクスクスクス
I'M...
...GOING TO LIVE HERE. ♡

MY HEAVENLY HOCKEY CLUB

BY AI MORINAGA

WHERE THE BOYS ARE!

Hana Suzuki loves only two things in life: eating and sleeping. So when handsome classmate Izumi Oda asks Hana—his major crush—to join the school hockey club, convincing her proves to be a difficult task. True, the Grand Hockey Club is full of boys—and all the boys are super-cute—but, given a choice, Hana prefers a sizzling steak to a hot date. Then Izumi mentions the field trips to fancy resorts. Now Hana can't wait for the first away game, with its promise of delicious food and luxurious linens. Of course there's the getting up early, working hard, and playing well with others. How will Hana survive?

Special extras in each volume! Read them all!

STORY BY SURT LIM
ART BY HIROFUMI SUGIMOTO

A DEL REY MANGA ORIGINAL

Exploring the woods, young Kasumi encounters an ancient tree god, who bestows upon her the power of invisibility. Together with classmates who have had similar experiences, Kasumi forms the Magic Play Club, dedicated to using their powers for good while avoiding sinister forces that would exploit them.

Special extras in each volume! Read them all!

VISIT WWW.DELREYMANGA.COM TO:
- Read sample pages
- View release date calendars for upcoming volumes
- Sign up for Del Rey's free manga e-newsletter
- Find out the latest about new Del Rey Manga series

RATING   T AGES 13+

KITCHEN PRINCESS

STORY BY MIYUKI KOBAYASHI
MANGA BY NATSUMI ANDO
CREATOR OF ZODIAC P.I.

HUNGRY HEART

Najika is a great cook and likes to make meals for the people she loves. But something is missing from her life. When she was a child, she met a boy who touched her heart— and now Najika is determined to find him. The only clue she has is a silver spoon that leads her to the prestigious Seika Academy.

Attending Seika will be a challenge. Every kid at the school has a special talent, and the girls in Najika's class think she doesn't deserve to be there. But Sora and Daichi, two popular brothers who barely speak to each other, recognize Najika's cooking for what it is—magical. Could one of the boys be Najika's mysterious prince?

Special extras in each volume! Read them all!

BY MACHIKO SAKURAI

A LITTLE LIVING DOLL!

What would you do if your favorite toy came to life and became your best friend? Well, that's just what happens to Ame Oikawa, a shy schoolgirl. Nicori is a super-cute doll with a mind of its own—and a plan to make Ame's dreams come true!

Special extras in each volume! Read them all!

VISIT WWW.DELREYMANGA.COM TO:
• Read sample pages
• View release date calendars for upcoming volumes
• Sign up for Del Rey's free manga e-newsletter
• Find out the latest about new Del Rey Manga series

RATING   T AGES 13+

DEL REY MANGA

The Otaku's Choice.™

BY SUZUHITO YASUDA

A DIFFERENT SET OF SUPERTEENS!

Hime is a superheroine. Ao can read minds. Kotoha can conjure up anything with the right word. And Akina . . . well, he's just a regular guy, surrounded by three girls with superpowers! Together, they are the Hizumi Everyday Life Consultation Office, dedicated to protect the town of Sakurashin. And with demon dogs and supernatural threats around every corner, there's plenty to keep them busy!

Special extras in each volume! Read them all!

VISIT WWW.DELREYMANGA.COM TO:
- Read sample pages
- View release date calendars for upcoming volumes
- Sign up for Del Rey's free manga e-newsletter
- Find out the latest about new Del Rey Manga series

RATING   T AGES 13+

DEL REY MANGA デルレイ

The Otaku's Choice.™

TOMARE!

止まれ

[STOP!]

You're going the wrong way!

Manga is a completely different
type of reading experience.

To start at the *beginning,*
go to the *end!*

That's right! Authentic manga is read the traditional Japanese way—
from right to left. Exactly the *opposite* of how American books are
read. It's easy to follow: Just go to the other end of the book, and read
each page—and each panel—from right side to left side, starting at
the top right. Now you're experiencing manga as it was meant to be!